Low Poly 3D Modeling in Blender

Kickstart your career as a 3D artist by learning how to create low poly assets and scenes from scratch

Samuel Sullins

<packt>

BIRMINGHAM—MUMBAI

Low Poly 3D Modeling in Blender

Group Product Manager: Rohit Rajkumar

Publishing Product Manager: Vaideeshwari Muralikrishnan

Book Project Manager: Sonam Pandey

Senior Editor: Anuradha Joglekar

Technical Editor: Reenish Kulshrestha

Copy Editor: Safis Editing

Proofreader: Safis Editing

Indexer: Subalakshmi Govindhan

Production Designer: Prashant Ghare

DevRel Marketing Coordinators: Namita Velgekar and Nivedita Pandey

Publication date: January 2024

Production reference: 1050124

Published by Packt Publishing Ltd.

Grosvenor House

11 St Paul's Square

Birmingham

B3 1RB, UK

ISBN 978-1-80324-547-8

`www.packtpub.com`

Contributors

About the author

Samuel Sullins is an American writer and 3D artist. Ever since he discovered Blender, he's been fascinated by 3D art. He messes around in Blender far too often for his own good. He runs a weekly email newsletter on Blender called *The Blend* (which you should definitely subscribe to). He also makes helpful Blender videos on YouTube at `@samuelsullins`.

Special thanks to my family for helping me work on this project and keeping me moving forward—even when I really didn't want to.

About the reviewers

Ajay Suthar, an Indian, Mumbai-based 3D artist, excels at pushing creative boundaries in modeling, texturing, rigging, lighting, rendering, animation, and film production. With a career in mechanical engineering, freelancing, and 3D animation, for the past 18 years, he has supervised diverse commercial visualization 3D projects. Ajay expanded his skills by contributing as a 3D interior visualizer on various projects. Committed to education, he became a filmmaking, animation, and VFX lecturer, enhancing students' knowledge of industry trends. As a UI-UX design head and 3D visual artist in the IT field, Ajay showcased his expertise by creating a design system for enhanced consistency. Ajay is a versatile 3D artist and mentor.

Jane Suteerawanit is a 3D character artist at Gameloft Brisbane. Originally from Perth, her entry into the realm of 3D art was prompted by the realization that pursuing a career in animation and games was a viable option. This revelation, coupled with her lifelong passion for gaming, culminated in the successful completion of a bachelor's degree in animation and game design from Curtin University in 2020.

Her professional journey commenced with an internship offered by Curtin University at Landshark Games in 2019. This small indie game studio, based in Singapore, provided her with the opportunity to focus on crafting low-poly styled characters, creatures, environments, and props. Subsequently, in 2021, Jane transitioned to the realm of film, joining Flying Bark Production. There, she played a pivotal role in creating 3D characters for the children's show *100% Wolf: The Book of Hath*, which found its broadcast on ABC ME, a widely recognized Australian kids' channel. Notable among her most recent achievements are contributions to released titles such as *My Little Pony: Mane Merge* (2022) and *The Oregon Trail* (2021).

Table of Contents

Part 3: Creating Your Own Assets

7

8

9

Part 4: Building a Complete Low Poly Scene

12

13

14

Preface

Blender is a free app for working in 3D. This book helps you get started with using Blender to create art in 3D.

3D art is a wide, varied, and complex topic, but this book brings it down to the basics for you. Before you move forward with 3D art, you need to learn how to work with 3D software and learn the basic principles of 3D art.

Once you grasp the fundamentals, you can start learning more and learning faster, too. This book aims to teach you the fundamentals of working in Blender and creating 3D art. You're also going to learn the basic principles of low poly, a simplistic 3D art style.

This book helps you gain a fundamental understanding of 3D, followed by the basics of working in 3D in Blender. 3D art is a vast and rapidly evolving field, and this book will make a great starting point for you. We'll cover common tools, shortcuts, and techniques.

By the time you're done, you'll understand the basics of 3D, and you'll know how to use Blender to create simple 3D art. You'll be ready to move on and learn more.

Who this book is for

This book is for absolute beginners to 3D. However, it does assume you have basic knowledge of how to work a computer, manage files, and so on.

What this book covers

Chapter 1, Getting Familiar with Blender, shows you how to download Blender. You will get a walk-through of the interface, learn what the different panels are called, and learn the basic controls for 3D navigation.

Chapter 2, Understanding Low Poly Modeling, teaches you the basics of working in 3D. You will learn about concepts such as polygons and meshes and understand high - versus low poly objects.

Chapter 3, Creating a Low Poly Tree, teaches you basic operations in 3D. You will learn how to move, rotate, and scale objects. You will also learn about Edit Mode and several basic Edit Mode tools for editing your mesh.

Chapter 4, Exploring Modifiers, provides an introduction to modifiers in Blender. You will learn what modifiers are, what they do, and how to use them. You will be introduced to several basic and useful modifiers.

Chapter 5, Creating Low Poly Mushrooms, walks you through a project in which you will model a low poly stylized mushroom in 3D. You'll also learn about some new modeling tools and techniques.

Chapter 6, Understanding Materials and Shading, teaches you how to add color to your models using materials. You will learn what materials are and will be introduced to a new workspace for working with materials. You will learn how to use material slots to add different materials to different parts of an object.

Chapter 7, Creating a Low Poly Tractor, walks you through the creation of a basic low poly tractor model. You will start from scratch and model every part of the tractor, and wrap up by adding materials.

Chapter 8, Low Poly Environment Modeling, walks you through creating different elements for low poly environments. You will learn how to make simple cartoony grass, trees, and rocks.

Chapter 9, Modeling a Kangaroo, walks you through a slightly more advanced project. You will start from scratch and model an entire low poly animal, learning new techniques and tools along the way.

Chapter 10, Creating Low Poly Houses and Buildings, is an easy chapter. You will get some quick lessons on using simple shapes to create simple houses and buildings.

Chapter 11, Using the Asset Browser, teaches you how to store all the models you've created in a central location called an asset library, accessible from any Blender project.

Chapter 12, Blocking Out the Scene, explains why blocking out a scene is important. You will learn a few simple techniques for working out how your scene will look ahead of time. You will also learn how to set up your scene camera.

Chapter 13, Building the Scene, shows you how to use your models to build a complete scene, following the simple block out you created in the preceding chapter.

Chapter 14, The Big Render, teaches you what rendering is, and explains how it works. Then, you will learn how to create a final rendered image of the scene you've built.

Appendix, describes a tip for fixing your render if the color looks wrong.

To get the most out of this book

You'll need to know how to operate your computer and understand basics such as how to save files.

The only software you'll need is Blender.

Software/hardware covered in the book	**Operating system requirements**
Blender	Windows, macOS, or Linux

Download the example files

You can download the example files for this book from GitHub at `https://github.com/PacktPublishing/Low-Poly-3D-Modeling-in-Blender`.

Conventions used

There are a number of text conventions used throughout this book.

Bold: Indicates a new term, an important word, or words that you see onscreen. For instance, words in menus or dialog boxes appear in **bold**. Here is an example: "Open the **Modifier** tab in the **Properties** panel."

> **Tips or important notes**
> Appear like this.

Get in touch

Feedback from our readers is always welcome.

General feedback: If you have questions about any aspect of this book, email us at `customercare@packtpub.com` and mention the book title in the subject of your message.

Errata: Although we have taken every care to ensure the accuracy of our content, mistakes do happen. If you have found a mistake in this book, we would be grateful if you would report this to us. Please visit `www.packtpub.com/support/errata` and fill in the form.

Piracy: If you come across any illegal copies of our works in any form on the internet, we would be grateful if you would provide us with the location address or website name. Please contact us at `copyright@packtpub.com` with a link to the material.

If you are interested in becoming an author: If there is a topic that you have expertise in and you are interested in either writing or contributing to a book, please visit `authors.packtpub.com`.

Share Your Thoughts

Once you've read Low Poly 3D Modeling in Blender, we'd love to hear your thoughts! Scan the QR code below to go straight to the Amazon review page for this book and share your feedback.

`https://packt.link/r/1803245476`

Your review is important to us and the tech community and will help us make sure we're delivering excellent quality content.

Download a free PDF copy of this book

Thanks for purchasing this book!

Do you like to read on the go but are unable to carry your print books everywhere?

Is your eBook purchase not compatible with the device of your choice?

Don't worry, now with every Packt book you get a DRM-free PDF version of that book at no cost.

Read anywhere, any place, on any device. Search, copy, and paste code from your favorite technical books directly into your application.

The perks don't stop there, you can get exclusive access to discounts, newsletters, and great free content in your inbox daily

Follow these simple steps to get the benefits:

1. Scan the QR code or visit the link below

   https://packt.link/free-ebook/978-1-80324-547-8

2. Submit your proof of purchase
3. That's it! We'll send your free PDF and other benefits to your email directly

Part 1: Getting Started with Low Poly Modeling

This part introduces you to Blender and 3D. You'll learn how to navigate Blender and how to perform basic operations. You'll also learn the fundamentals of how 3D works.

This part has the following chapters:

- *Chapter 1, Getting Familiar with Blender*
- *Chapter 2, Understanding Low Poly Modeling*
- *Chapter 3, Creating a Low Poly Tree*

1

Getting Familiar with Blender

Once upon a time, 3D software was outrageously expensive. 3D artists had to choose between buying a house or buying a 3D app—and, well, you can't blame them for choosing the house.

Then came Blender. Blender was special because it cost less than a thumbtack (it was open source, and the price tag was $0). It was new, free, and exciting—but it didn't work so well. It had the potential to be great in 20 years or so—but who wants to wait that long?

That was 20 years ago. Now, Blender has reached incredible heights. For the last two decades, Blender has made 3D accessible to anyone with a laptop.

Ready to join the party?

In this chapter, we'll dive right in and start learning Blender. You'll download Blender and get it set up. You'll learn how the UI works, how to navigate 3D space, and how 3D space works in Blender. Then, you'll learn how simple it is to tweak the UI to fit your needs.

Here are the main topics we'll be covering in this chapter:

- Installing Blender
- Anatomy of the UI
- Navigating the 3D Viewport
- Getting to know the UI shortcuts
- Understanding Workspaces
- Saving your own Startup file

Installing Blender

In this chapter, you'll start by installing Blender. Then you'll learn about the different areas of Blender's interface. You'll learn what each section of the interface is for, and to wrap it up, you'll learn how it can be customized to fit your needs.

OK, let's get started. Time to download Blender and set it all up:

1. In a web browser, go to `www.blender.org`, the home of the Blender Foundation.
2. Click the **Download** tab to see the latest release. You can download the latest release and everything in this book should work just fine.
3. But if you want to work in the exact same Blender version as I am working in, click the **Long-term Support** tab at the top, between **Release Notes** and **Requirements**.

   Long-term support (**LTS**) versions of Blender will be supported for a few years, so they're very stable. Also, they still get bug fixes so they should be pretty bug-free.
4. Scroll down to **LTS Releases Currently Maintained** to see a list of the currently supported LTS versions of Blender. I'm using **Blender 3.3 LTS**, so click that one (it's a big aerial picture of a castle/city). You'll end up on a new page.
5. Scroll down to **Versions** and in the **Download** section, pick your operating system:

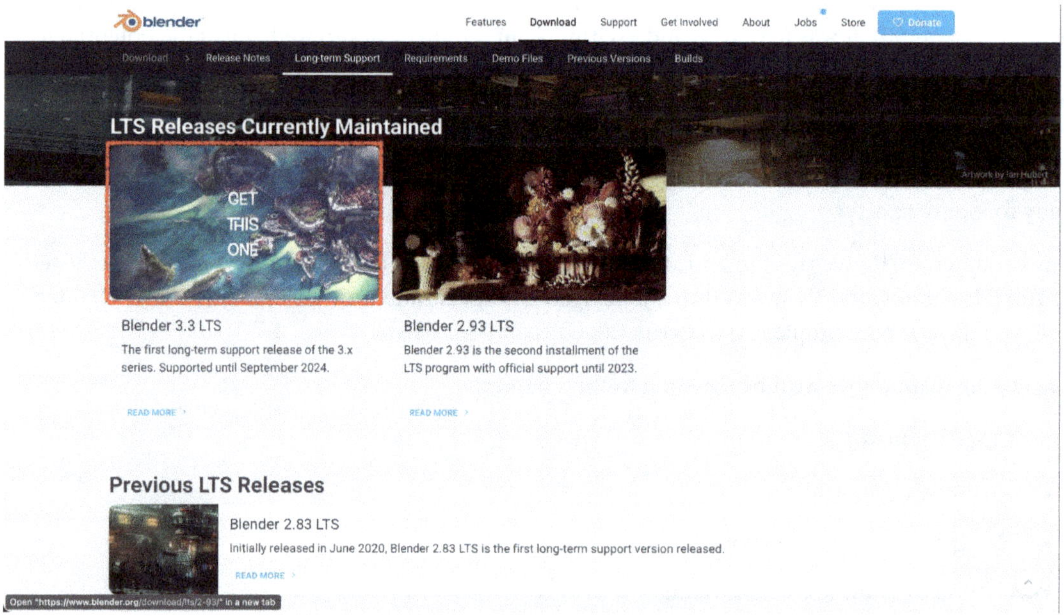

Figure 1.1 – The download page

Now, wait for Blender to download (this is the hardest part of the process). Once the download is complete, you'll have an installer of some kind in your `Downloads` folder.

It'll be slightly different depending on your operating system, but the installer should guide you through the installation process.

And that's it! You're done, great job. You've successfully installed Blender. In the next section, you'll learn about the different parts of Blender's user interface.

Anatomy of the UI

Now you'll learn what's what in Blender's UI. There's a lot to see when you first open Blender, but it's simpler than it looks. Launch Blender and you'll be greeted by a splash screen. Admire the cool artwork for a minute and then click anywhere to get rid of it. You're in a new, empty Blender file.

Files in Blender are called **Scenes**. It'll look extremely complex at first—but don't worry. You get to ignore most of that for now.

Blender's UI is broken down into simple sections. I'll cover the basics, but don't worry—I won't go into agonizing detail. The thing about the UI is that you'll pick up most of it on your own the more you use Blender.

I'm just here to get you started.

The 3D Viewport

The open area in the middle is called the **3D Viewport**. In this book, I'll eventually get tired of typing *the 3D Viewport* so I'll just be calling it the *viewport*.

The 3D Viewport is where all the 3D work happens. It's where you create, edit, and manipulate 3D models. *Figure 1.2* shows how the 3D Viewport looks:

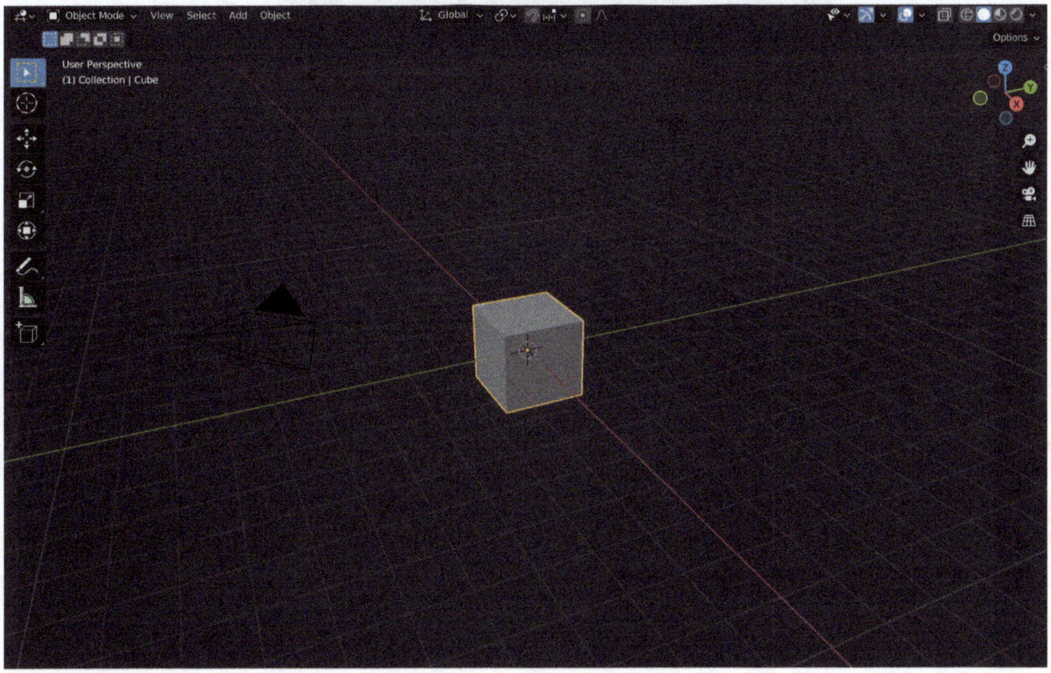

Figure 1.2 – The 3D Viewport

In the next section, let's learn about the top bar.

The top bar

At the top of the window is the top bar.

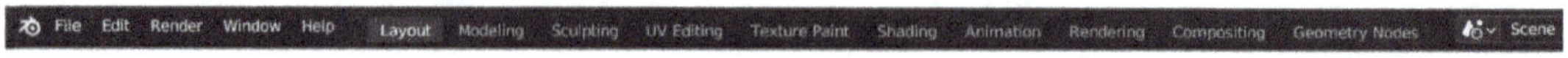

Figure 1.3 – The top bar

The top bar allows you to switch between different configurations of views (called **Workspaces**) with a single click.

The Outliner

In the top right is the **Outliner**. This is a bit like a computer's filesystem. It shows you a simple list of all the 3D objects in your Blender file, organized into folders called **Collections**:

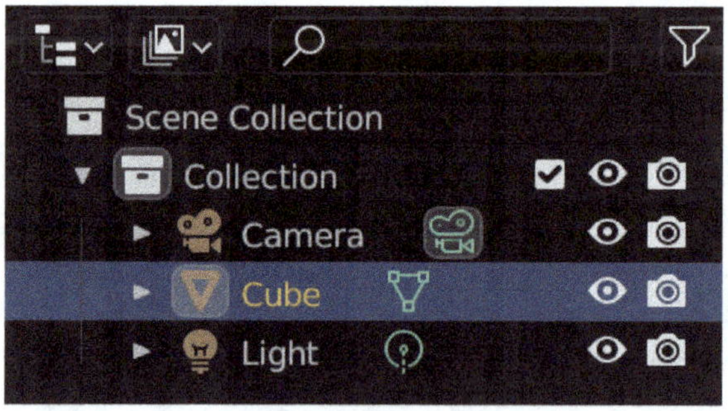

Figure 1.4 – The Outliner

You'll see **Camera**, **Light**, and **Cube** in the default **Collection**. These make up the simple default setup that comes in with every new Blender file. (You'll find yourself having to delete them a lot.)

The Properties panel

Below the Outliner is the **Properties** panel. Many of the most important settings you'll use, such as render settings, modifiers, and output options, are located in the **Properties** panel. The **Properties** panel is divided into its own set of tabs, as shown in *Figure 1.5*:

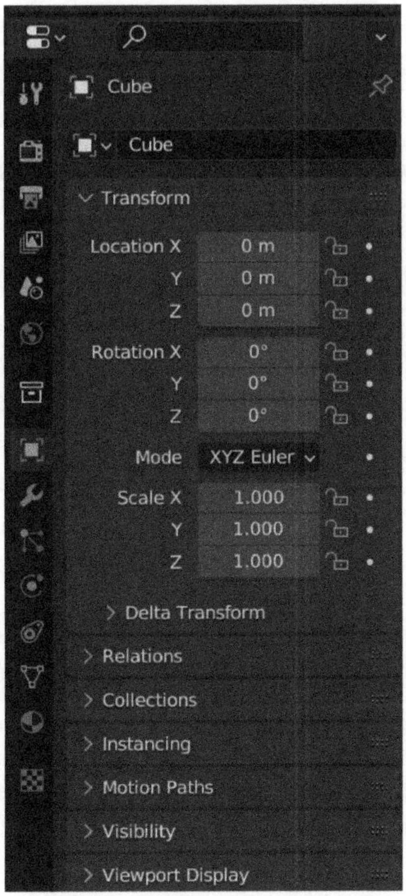

Figure 1.5 – The Properties panel

Next, let's see what the timeline is.

The Timeline

At the bottom of the window is the **Timeline**. This gives you play/pause controls that you would use if you were creating an animation. We won't be covering that in this book, though.

Below the Timeline is the Status bar. This is where you'll see information on processes (such as how close a render is to completion) and tools (such as extra keyboard shortcuts):

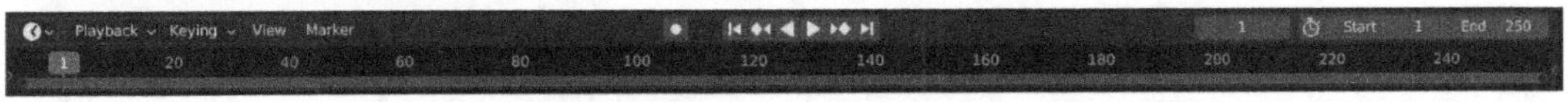

Figure 1.6 – The Timeline

Finally, let's see what customizing areas means.

Customizing areas

All the different panels we've just covered are called **areas**. Areas are extremely customizable, and it's not hard to do. It's super-useful to be able to reconfigure the view (for example, if you wanted two viewports side-by-side, or if you wanted to get rid of the Outliner).

All of your changes are file-specific: they'll be saved when you save your file, but you won't see them in other Blender files. In the corner of every area is the Editor Type menu. It looks slightly different depending on the area type, as shown in the following figure:

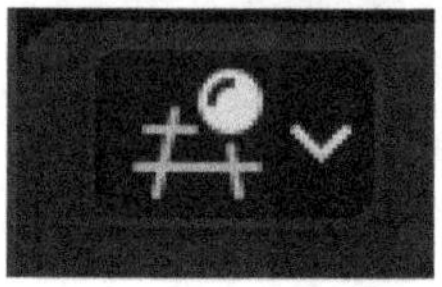

Figure 1.7 – The Editor Type menu

You can open this menu to change any type of area into any other type of area. For example, you could easily switch the 3D Viewport into a big Outliner by switching **Editor Type** to **Outliner**.

You can also adjust each area's size. Simply hover your mouse over the border between two areas until the cursor turns into an arrow, then left-click and drag to resize the area. Adding new areas is even easier. Hover your cursor over the corner of an area until it becomes a cross, then click and drag inward toward the center of the area. This will create a new area.

To get rid of areas, you can join two areas together. Hover over the corner of an area until it turns into a cross again, but this time, drag outward toward another area (and don't let go). Your cursor will turn into a little arrow, pointing outward. The areas will darken to show you how they will be joined.

Knowing how to manage areas is very important—so practice! Join and create some areas right now. It's fine if you mess up your Blender window—it'll all be fixed when you restart it.

In the next section, you'll learn how to look around in the 3D Viewport.

Navigating the 3D Viewport

The 3D Viewport is where you interact with 3D. You'll need to see your 3D models from all sides as you work, so it's important to learn how to navigate in 3D. You'll learn how to pan, orbit, and zoom your way around.

This basic navigation is easy to master, and won't take you very long. You'll become very good at this the more you use Blender, since you have to navigate in 3D to accomplish *anything* in 3D.

Moving around

Navigating in the 3D Viewport is extremely intuitive. It's a bit different depending on whether you're using a mouse or a trackpad.

With a trackpad, you simply scroll with two fingers (in any direction) to orbit in the 3D Viewport, and to pan, move two fingers around while holding down the *Shift* key.

That's orbiting and panning. To zoom in and out, you have two options: spread two fingers closer together or further apart on your trackpad (like zooming in and out on a smartphone), or hold down the *Ctrl* key and scroll up and down with two fingers.

Simple, right?

Now, if you're using a real mouse (fun fact: I'm not), you can click and drag with the middle mouse button to orbit, scroll to zoom, and press *Shift* + middle mouse button to pan.

These controls will seem difficult at first, but as you do more Blender work, they'll become natural.

Numpad controls

Sometimes, you'll want to view a 3D model exactly from the side, the top, or the front. In Blender, there are two ways to do this.

Do you see the little 3D cross in the upper-right corner of the viewport, as shown in *Figure 1.8*? That's called the **Gizmo**, which is like a little 3D compass:

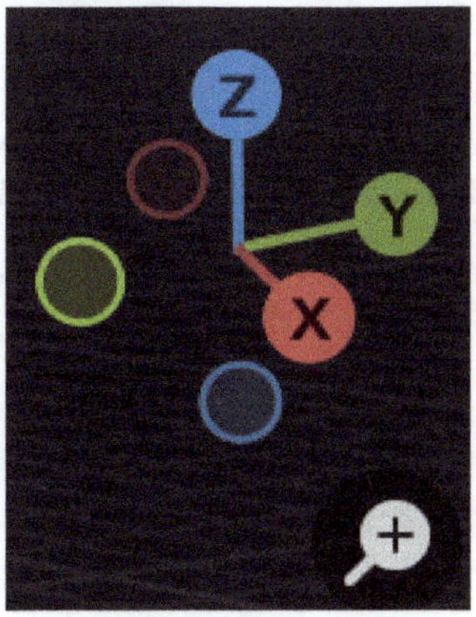

Figure 1.8 – The Gizmo

It's labeled with letters: **X** (red), **Y** (green), and **Z** (blue). In 3D, just like in reality, there are three spatial dimensions (think about the width, depth, and height of a cube). In Blender, these are called **X**, **Y**, and **Z**:

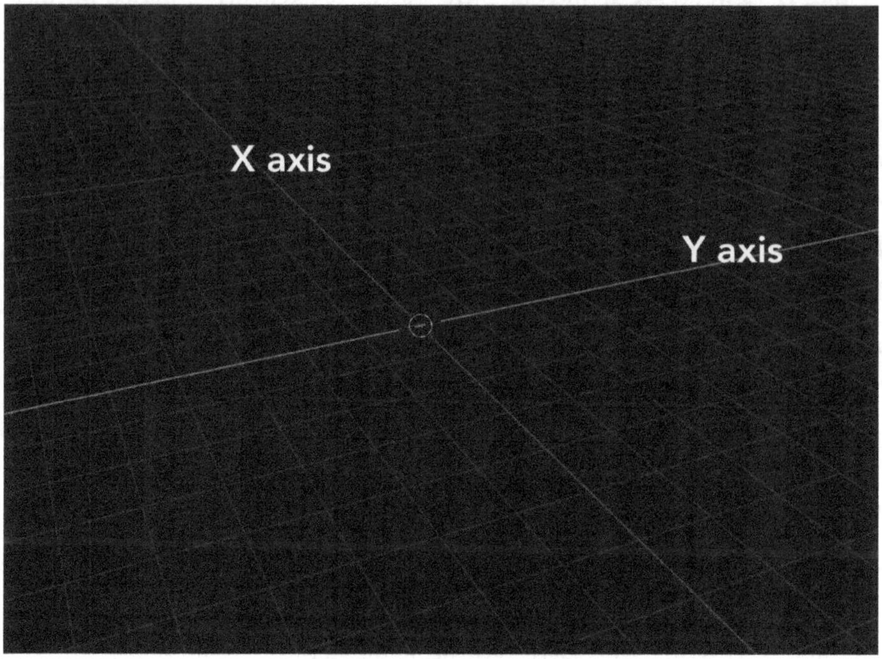

Figure 1.9 – The X and Y axes

As shown in *Figure 1.9*, **X axis** is displayed as red. The green line represents **Y axis**. The color blue is used to represent the Z axis, which runs in the vertical, up-and-down direction. You'll notice there's no blue line representing the Z axis . That's to avoid cluttering the viewport more than is needed.

If you ever need a reminder of any of this, simply look at the little Gizmo in the corner.

Now it's time to learn your first keyboard shortcuts. But before that, you'll need to turn on something called **Emulate Numpad** (if you have an actual numpad on your keyboard, you won't need to do this):

1. Go to **Edit | Preferences**:

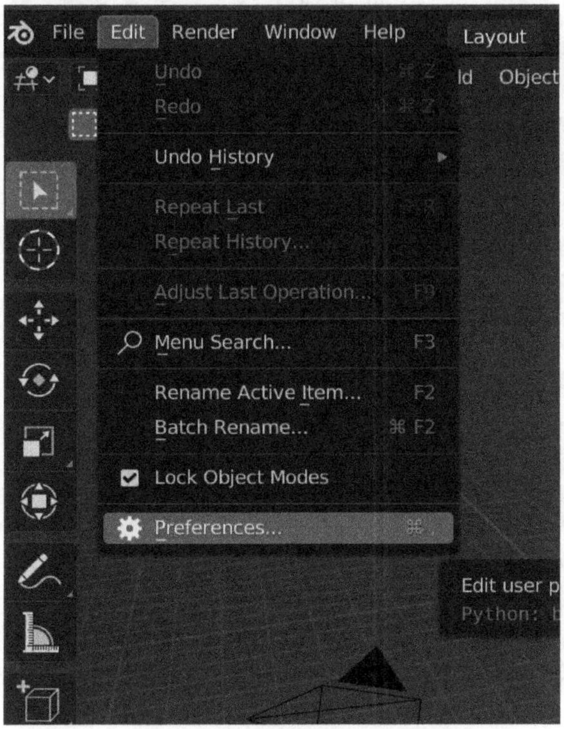

Figure 1.10 – The Preferences menu

2. Find the **Input** tab:

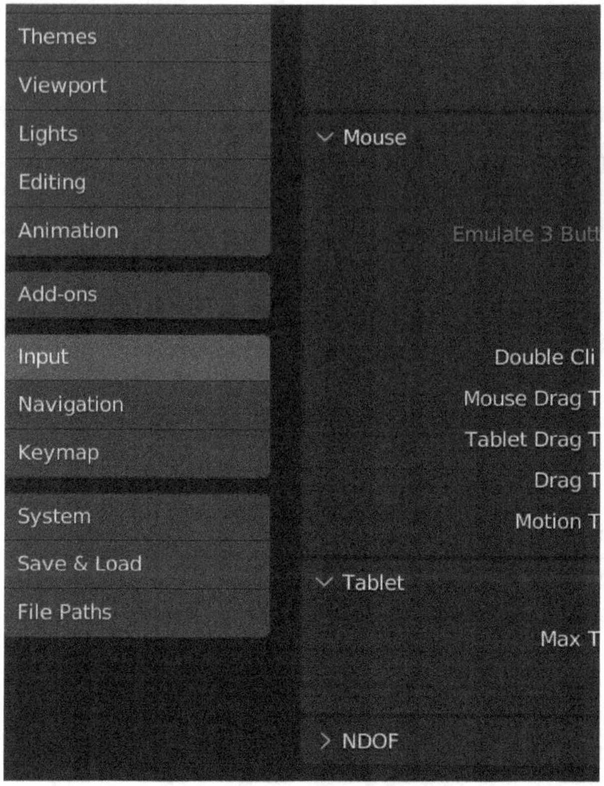

Figure 1.11 – The Input tab

3. Turn on **Emulate Numpad**:

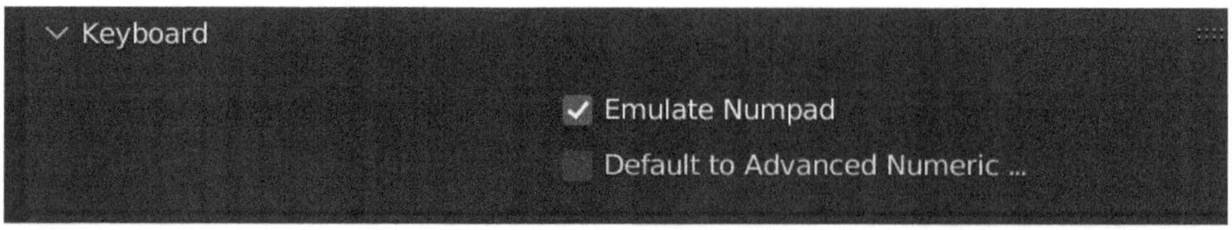

Figure 1.12 – Emulate Numpad

This makes Blender treat your regular number keys as if they were a numpad, which lets you use the viewport shortcuts.

4. Close **Preferences**.

In the viewport, press *1* to get a perfect **front view**, press *3* to get a perfect **right view**, and press *7* to get a **top view**. To see the reverse of these views (back, left, and bottom) press *Ctrl + 1*, *Ctrl + 3*, and *Ctrl + 7*.

There's another way to do this, too: you can click the little red, green, and blue circles on the Gizmo.

Next, you'll learn about the **Orthographic** view mode.

Viewing in Orthographic mode

There are two ways to look at things in 3D. The way you're looking at your 3D Viewport right now is called **Perspective**. Perspective is how we view the real world. The farther away something is, the smaller it appears. It's a very realistic way of viewing things in 3D.

A railroad track is a good example; the further away the rails are, the closer together they appear to be. Take a look at *Figure 1.13*:

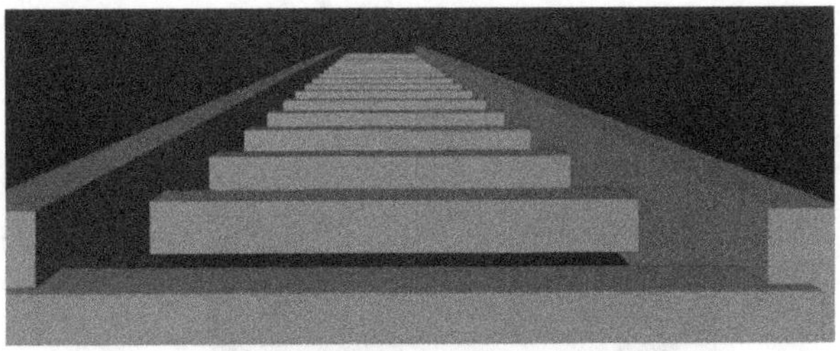

Figure 1.13 – A railroad, viewed in Perspective mode (same as real life)

There's another, different way to view the world in 3D, called **Orthographic**. When you view your Scene in **Orthographic** mode, everything is consistent in size, no matter how far away it is.

To enable **Orthographic** mode, press *5* on your numpad. Here's the same railroad track in **Orthographic** mode:

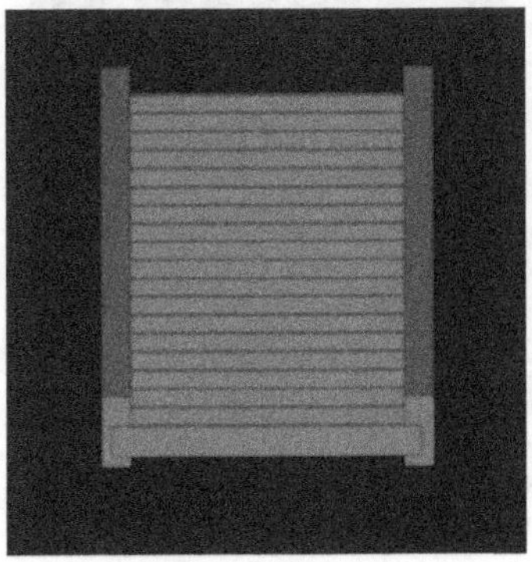

Figure 1.14 – The same railroad in Orthographic mode

This can sometimes be useful when you need to get a better look at something (for example, to get a good look at the overall shape of a model). You probably won't use it much—but it's an option.

Now you know the most important keyboard shortcuts for navigating the 3D Viewport. You'll find these extremely helpful for working quickly and efficiently as we progress.

In the next section, you'll learn some more helpful shortcuts.

Getting to know the UI shortcuts

There are a few more helpful things to know about for getting around in the viewport. You can use keyboard shortcuts to hide and show the toolbar or to control navigation in the 3D Viewport.

The N panel

The **N panel** is the panel that appears when you press *N*. It's sometimes called the **sidebar** or the **side panel**—in this book, I'll be calling it the N panel:

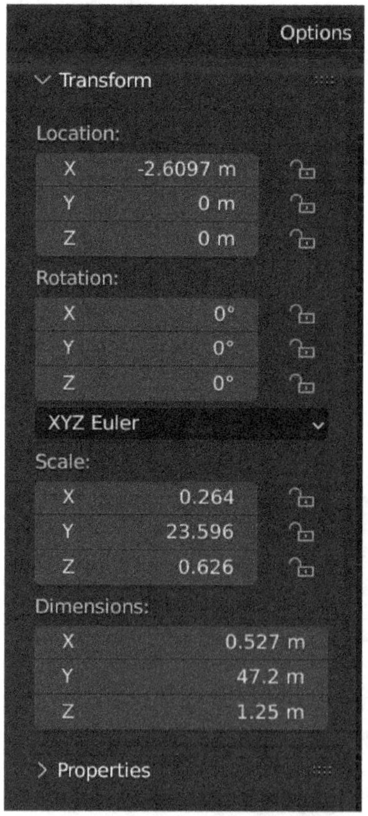

Figure 1.15 – The N panel

This panel gives you quick access to the selected object's position, rotation, and scale values. In *Chapter 3, Creating a Low Poly Tree*, you'll learn how to edit these. The N panel also exists in many of the other editor types (the **Shader Editor**, for example).

To hide the N panel, just press *N* again.

The toolbar

The **toolbar** is a bank of tools down the left-hand side of the viewport. These tools are, for the most part, simple conveniences. They're useful while you're learning Blender, but you'll eventually end up using keyboard shortcuts to work faster.

To show and hide the toolbar, you just press *T*.

There's also a secret way to see the names of all the tools in the toolbar—hover your cursor over the right edge of the toolbar until your cursor turns into a double arrow:

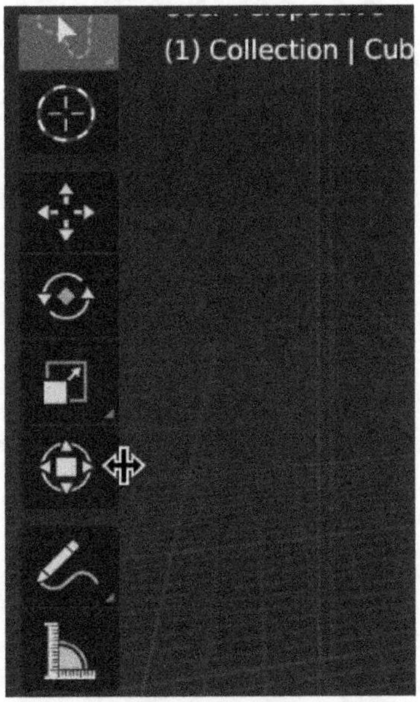

Figure 1.16 – Expanding the toolbar

Now click and drag toward the viewport. Once the toolbar is wide enough, you'll see the tool names, as shown in *Figure 1.17*:

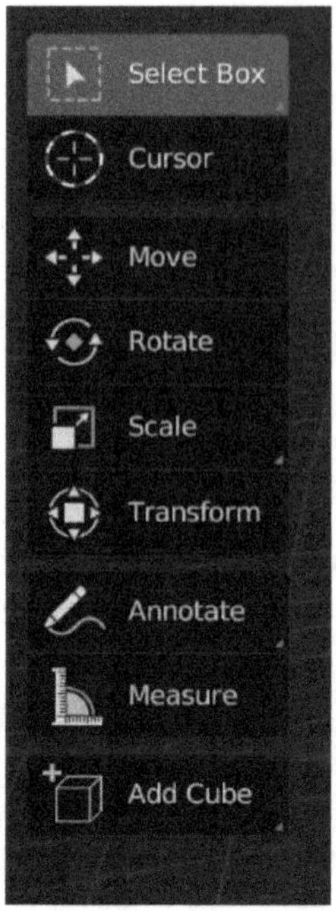

Figure 1.17 – The toolbar

You'll notice the top tool is selected by default. This is the **Select** tool. By default, it's in **Select Box** mode, but you can press *W* to toggle through all the different Select tools:

- **Tweak**, which lets you click and drag objects
- **Box**, which is the default (leave it on this mode for this book)
- **Circle**, which gives you a circle "brush" to select with
- **Lasso**, which gives you a Photoshop-like lasso tool

If, during the course of this book, you find that you're not able to select objects as you expect, it's likely that you ended up with the wrong **Select** tool by accident. Just press *W* to cycle through each tool and get back to the default **Select Box**.

Walk Navigation

There's another, less common way to navigate the viewport in Blender. You can *walk* around in it using the arrow keys, similar to how you would navigate a video game.

To activate it, go to **View** | **Navigation** and click **Walk Navigation** to enter *walk* mode. Use the arrow keys to move around and the mouse to steer. There are a lot of other options—look in the Status bar at the bottom of the window to see them all.

It's a little annoying to go through all those menus every time you want to use **Walk Navigation**, though.

Here's how you can set your own shortcu:

1. Go to **View** | **Navigation** and right-click on **Walk Navigation**.
2. Click **Assign Shortcut**.
3. Press *Shift* + *F* on your keyboard to set it as the shortcut. I picked *Shift* + *F* because it doesn't already do anything.

Now you can turn on **Walk Navigation** simply with the push of a button!

If you get lost

When you're working in the 3D Viewport, you might pan or zoom too far in one direction—and get lost.

If you ever do get lost in the viewport, here's how to un-lose yourself:

1. Select any object in **Outliner** by clicking on it.
2. Press the ~ key to open the **View** menu. The **View** menu is a pie menu—these menus are super-easy to operate. Just move your mouse toward the option you want and then click! In this case, choose the **View Selected** option:

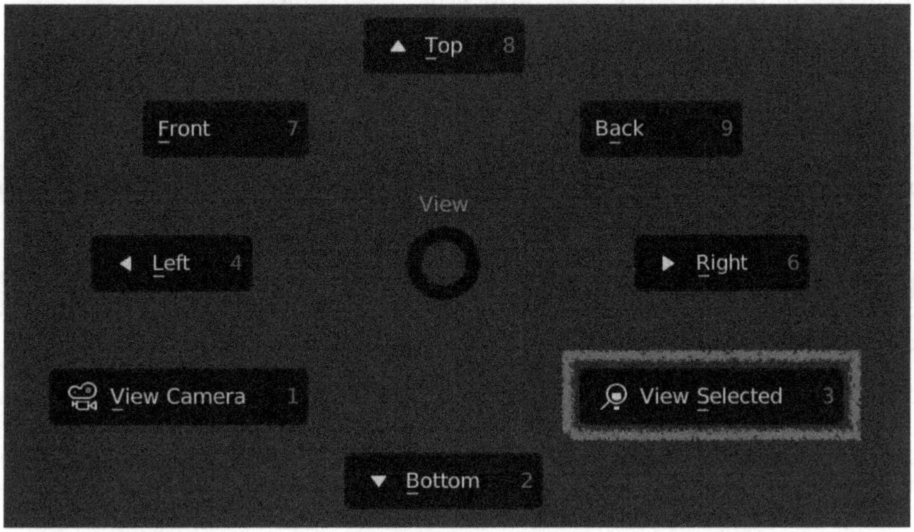

Figure 1.18 – The View pie menu

This will center the view around the object you have selected. This is a really good way to navigate the viewport—and it also works well for finding something you've misplaced!

You don't have to use the mouse to select options in the menu—you can also use the number keys. You'll notice that each option in the **View** pie menu has a small number next to it—pressing that number will select that option.

So, to select the **View Selected** option, you can press ~ then *3*—no mouse needed!

Now you have the ability to re-center the view on any selected object, no matter where you currently are in the 3D Viewport. This is an incredibly helpful technique, especially in larger Scenes.

In the next section, we'll explain those mysterious tabs across the top of the window.

Understanding Workspaces

The tabs across the top of the Blender window (**Layout**, **Modeling**, **Sculpting**, and so on) are called **Workspaces**:

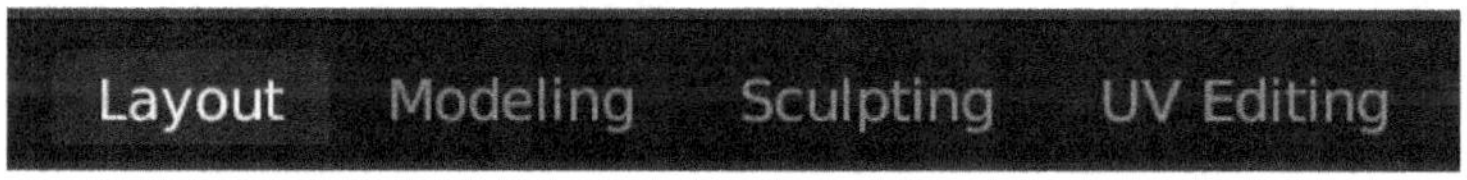

Figure 1.19 – Some Workspace tabs

Workspaces are just different sets of areas, configured for different tasks. For example, the **Layout** Workspace (the one we're in currently) is set up for general Blender work.

Click through the different kinds of Workspaces and have a look!

Any Workspace can do anything

It's important to understand that the Workspaces are only a convenience—and that any Workspace can quickly be configured to perform any task.

For example, switch to the **Shading** Workspace. You'll see a bunch of stuff that you won't recognize. But, just like the **Layout** Workspace, it's all made up of areas. You can easily change the **Editor Type** of any of them, join them, and add new ones.

You could reconfigure this Workspace to look exactly like the **Layout** Workspace if you wanted. Workspaces are very useful, though. They save a lot of time by having things set up and ready to go.

But what if you want a different Workspace? Here's how you can add your own Workspace.

Making your own Workspace

You can make your own Workspace if you want. There are two ways to do it: you can either change an existing one or add a new one. Changing an existing one is easy—just click a Workspace to switch to it, then double-click the name to edit it and name it whatever you want. Now rearrange all of the areas however you like—and you have your own Workspace!

To add a new Workspace, just click the + button at the end of the top bar (you may have to scroll to the side a bit before you can see it) and choose the Workspace you'd like to add (you can also choose to duplicate the current one). Once you have a new Workspace, you can rename and edit it just like any other.

Making your own Workspace is a great way to save yourself the trouble of continuously rearranging areas. However, any changes you make to the workspaces are file-specific. This means that if you open a new file, you won't have any of the Workspaces that you renamed or created.

The next section will explain how to set up your own default Startup file.

Saving your own Startup file

This is something you won't need to do for a while, but when you do need it, here it is. One day, you'll get fearfully tired of setting up Blender *just how you like* it every single time you open a new file.

When that happens, you need to set up your own *Startup file*. A Startup file is like a new set of default settings, so when you open Blender, your new file will be a copy of the Startup file you've made.

Here's how to set up your Startup file:

1. Open a new Blender file.
2. Press *Ctrl* + *S* and save it somewhere.
3. Now, change stuff. Set it up exactly the way you want.
4. Press *Ctrl* + *S* again to make sure your file is saved.
5. Go to **File** | **Defaults** | **Save Startup File**:

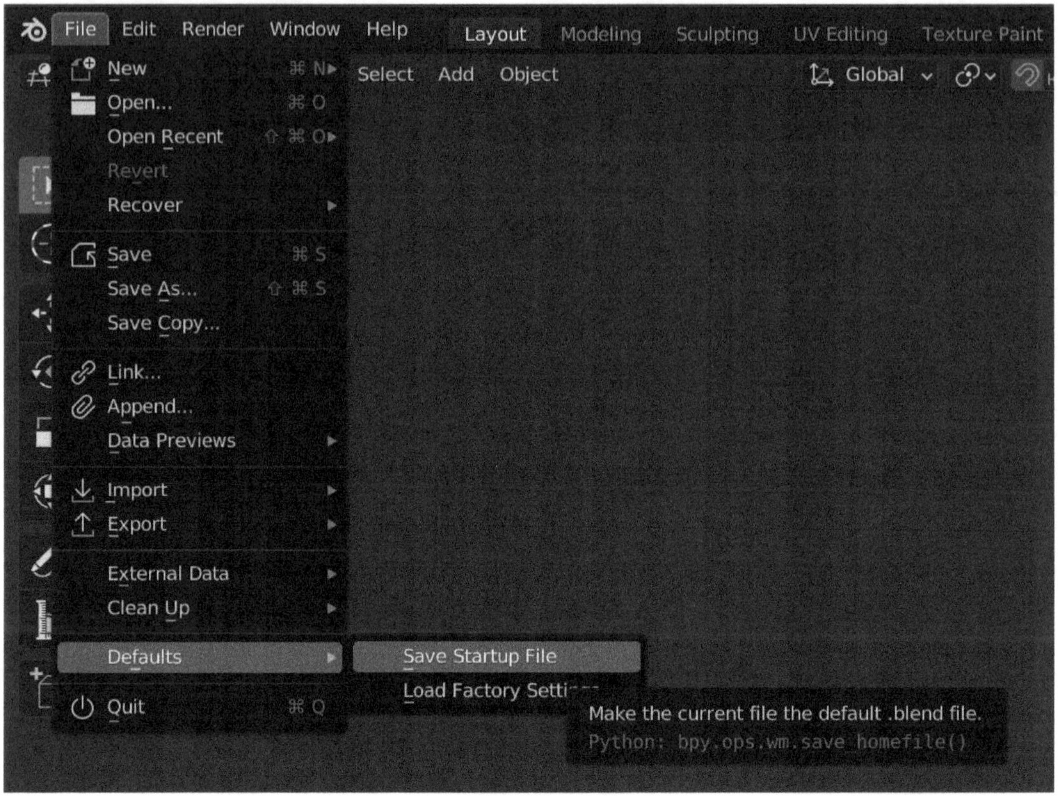

Figure 1.20 – The Save Startup File menu

You've got your own default settings now! If you ever want to change them, simply open your Startup file, change the settings, and press **Save Startup File** again.

If you ever want the default settings back, go to **File | Defaults | Load Factory Settings** to see the original setup again (and you can save that as the Startup file if you want).

Summary

In this chapter, you made it through all the boring stuff. You learned what the different parts of the UI are called and how to add, remove, and switch areas. You learned how to navigate in 3D and what to do if you get lost in the infinity of the viewport.

You learned what Workspaces are and how to make your own. You even learned how to make your own default settings with a Startup file! That's a lot of stuff! If you only remember one thing from this chapter, remember how to navigate in 3D.

Great job making it through this chapter! In the next chapter, you'll learn exactly what low-poly modeling is.

2

Understanding Low Poly Modeling

In this chapter, you'll learn what 3D models are made up of. You'll learn about vertices, edges, and faces, and why they matter.

You'll learn about polygon count and the differences between high poly and low poly modeling. You'll learn about the different use cases for high poly and low poly modeling, and when to use low poly modeling. You'll also understand how low poly is an art style on its own.

By the end of the chapter, you'll have a solid grasp of how 3D modeling works. You'll also understand what *low poly* means.

Here are the main topics we'll be covering in this chapter:

- Understanding meshes
- Smooth versus flat shading
- High poly versus low poly
- Low poly as an art style

Understanding meshes

An object in Blender can be broken into two parts:

- The underlying mesh
- The object's location, rotation, and scale

In Blender, you edit these two things separately. There's **Object** mode for moving, rotating, and positioning objects. Meanwhile, **Edit** mode lets you edit the actual mesh. (*Chapter 3* teaches you all about editing.)

But what is a *mesh*?

A **mesh** is the underlying shape, the *model* part of a 3D model. *Mesh* typically refers to only the 3D shape, though: the term doesn't refer to any of the model's colors, materials, or where it's located in your scene.

Mesh can also be used to mean *any 3D model*—a little bit confusing sometimes, but you'll get the hang of it.

A mesh is made up of three basic components: *vertices*, *edges*, and *faces*.

Take a look at the diagram in *Figure 2.1*:

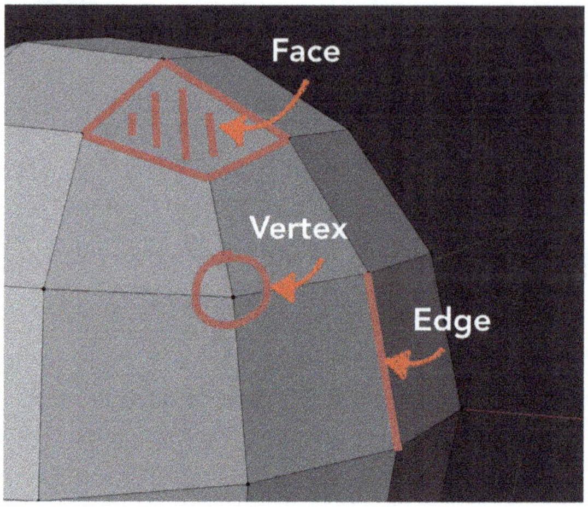

Figure 2.1– Faces, edges, and vertices

These are the different parts that make up a mesh in 3D:

- **Vertices** (or **verts** for short) are single points in 3D space. A mesh is made of tens, hundreds, or even millions of these points.
- **Edges** are lines that connect these points.
- **Faces** or **polygons** are the shapes defined by the edges.

To summarize, a vertex (plural, vertices) is a single point, an edge is a line connecting two points, and a face is a flat polygon or shape that connects multiple edges.

You've just learned about all the important parts of a mesh. Next, we'll talk about smooth versus flat shading.

Smooth versus flat shading

By default, an object will look flat and choppy, like this:

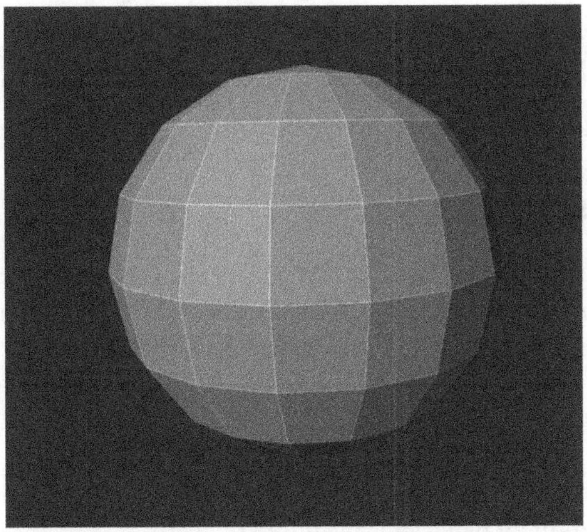

Figure 2.2 – Flat shading

For an object to look smooth and curved, you have to use something called **smooth shading**. Smooth shading makes the flat; hard faces of a mesh *appear* smooth and curved.

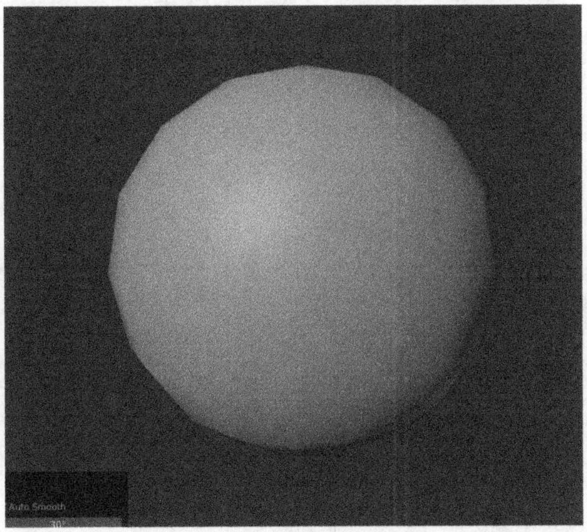

Figure 2.3 – Smooth shading enabled

It's important to note that a smooth-shaded model is no different, structurally, from a flat-shaded model. The smoothness is only an illusion.

Smooth shading is used on any kind of curved, organic-shaped mesh where it's important to have smooth curves. For example, on a human character, you'd use smooth shading. In this book, we'll only be focusing on flat-shaded models. All the easier for you!

You'll often find yourself wanting to change a smooth-shaded model to a flat-shaded one, and vice versa. It's extremely simple. Just select the object, right-click, and choose **Shade Smooth** or **Shade Flat**.

In the next section, we'll take a look at what *low poly* means.

High poly versus low poly

The **poly count** is the number of polygons (or faces) in a mesh. This number is important because it gives a very good idea of the complexity of a mesh. A mesh with eight million polygons is going to be a lot heavier computationally than a mesh with eight hundred polygons.

High poly

A *high* poly count is generally anything in the millions. Meanwhile, a *low* poly count would be anything up to a few hundred. Everything in between is *medium*.

Meshes with high poly counts are referred to as **high poly**. These meshes are generally more difficult to work with because they can slow down Blender a bit (it's hard for Blender to manage 20 million vertices at once!). However, they are still used for some things because of the immense detail they offer. For example, high poly meshes are often used for sculpting, when extreme details are needed, or for professional visual effects projects. More, tinier polygons make for a more detailed model than fewer, bigger ones.

Figure 2.4 is a screenshot of a high poly mesh—can you see all the tiny little faces?

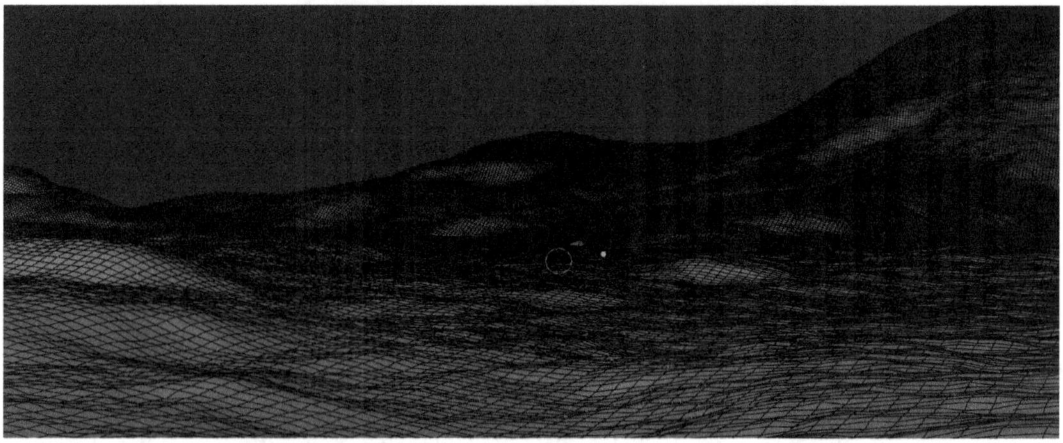

Figure 2.4 – A high poly mesh used to create a landscape

A common use for high-poly models would be in VFX for a film—the dinosaurs in *Jurassic World* are most likely high-poly models (at least in the up-close shots.) This is because it's worth it for extreme, realistic detail (though it's possible to fake details with textures.)

High poly is *not* bad, it's just generally more difficult to work with. High poly meshes are usually created by a process such as digital scanning or sculpting.

Mid-poly

Medium poly meshes are a nice balance. There are enough polygons so that the object can be deformed easily for animation, but not enough to require extra processing power.

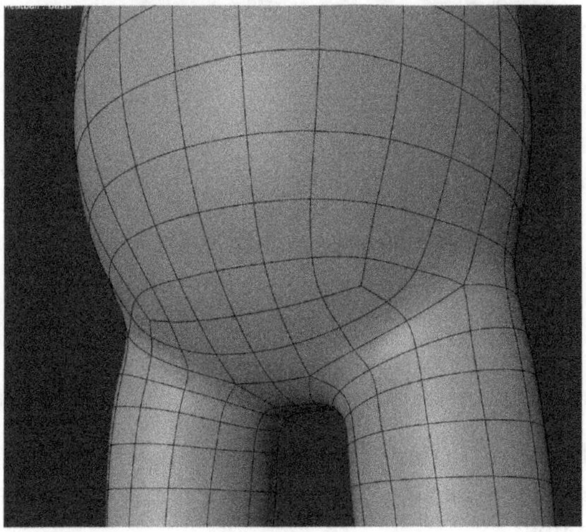

Figure 2.5 – A medium poly mesh

Medium or mid-poly meshes are typically used in animated films as part of a *subdivision* workflow, where the faces are subdivided (divided into smaller faces) at render time, making the model higher-poly. This isn't as complicated as it sounds—in Blender, it's as simple as adding a single modifier to your mesh.

Low poly

Low poly meshes are meshes with very few polygons (relatively.) They generally have a simplistic look to them—which makes them perfectly suited for simple video games or animated sequences.

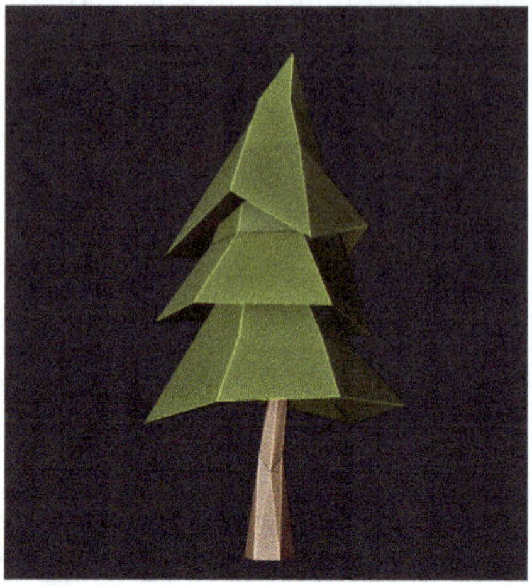

Figure 2.6 – A low poly tree

Low poly meshes use the minimum necessary number of polygons needed to define the desired shape.

Not all 3D models fall exactly into these three buckets. For example, a high-end animated film might use medium-to-high poly models, and a video game modeler might refer to low poly models that are really a bit closer to medium poly.

In general, it's good to keep poly counts in the low-to-mid range, so your computer doesn't slow down too much. It's something you'll rarely have to worry about, though.

Now, I'll explain how low poly works as an art style. (If you got this reference, you're awesome!)

Low poly as an art style

This book is primarily about creating low poly models. We'll be focusing on low poly as an art style—flat-shaded, unsmoothed, minimalistic 3D artwork. Low poly is a clean, simplistic style—but don't be fooled: it's often far more complex than you'd expect.

The goal is to embrace the simplicity of an object. To create something with only the required number of polygons. To simplify as much as possible, but not *too* much. Low poly art is interesting because it is (ideally) a perfect mixture of simplicity and complexity.

We take an extremely simple object and combine it with advanced techniques such as realistic shading, high-resolution rendering, and modern lighting techniques. The result is a visually interesting blend of simplicity and realism.

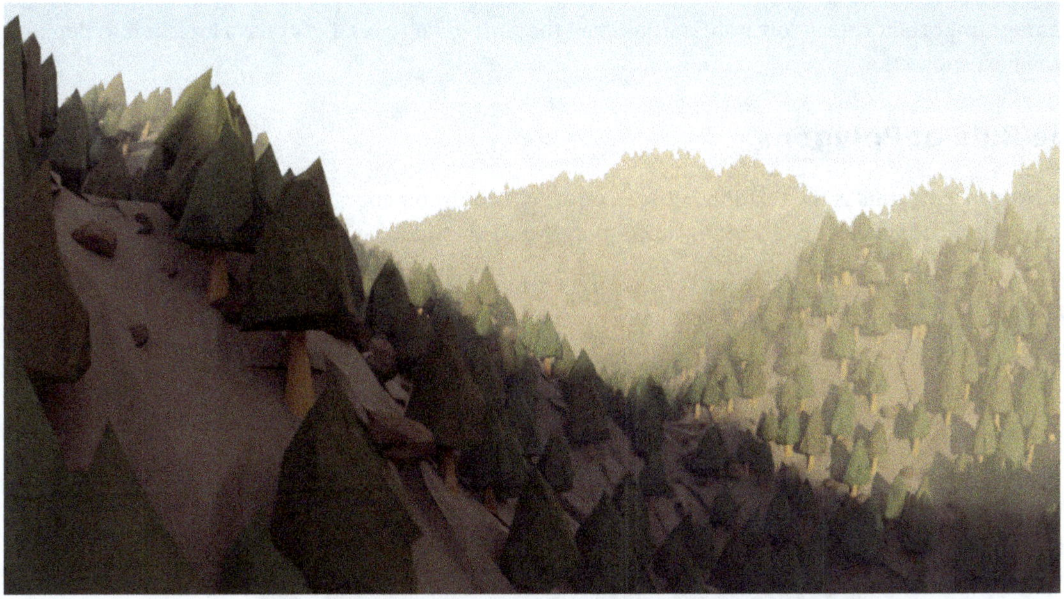

Figure 2.7 – A low poly mountain scene (created in Blender)

And here's an even more stylized low poly render:

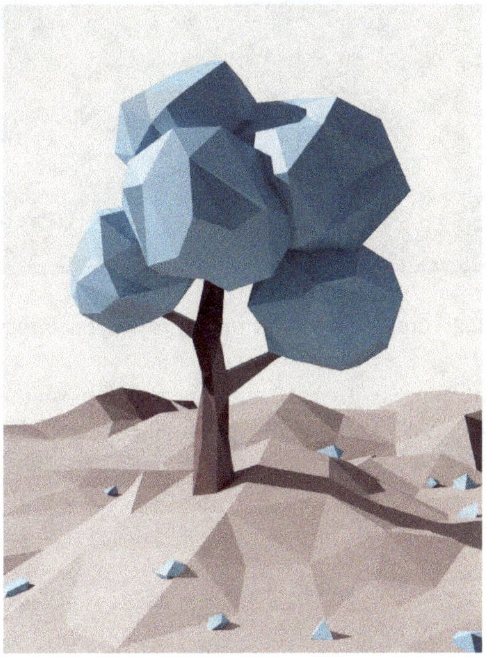

Figure 2.8 – A low poly tree (created in Blender)

The most important rule in low poly is what I call the *Rule of Polygons*. Let's take a look at it in detail in the next subsection.

The Rule of Polygons

The **Rule of Polygons** is the relation between an object's polygon count and its size and importance in the scene. The smaller an object, the fewer polygons it should have.

For example, if you're going to have two different sizes of trees in your scene, you might consider modeling one tree and then simply scaling it down a bit for the smaller versions, like this:

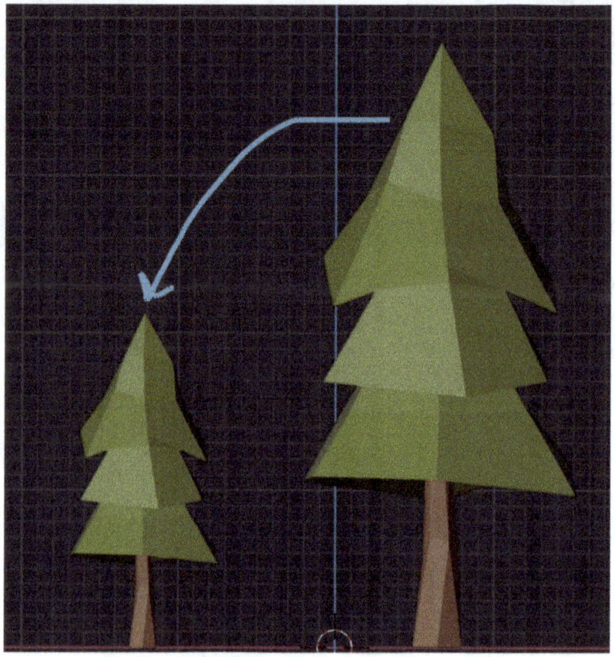

Figure 2.9 – Creating a smaller tree by scaling (incorrect)

However, this breaks the *Rule of Polygons*. That's because the polygons on the little tree are now a little too small, which feels out of scale. As you make the tree smaller, it would look nicer if the polygons stayed roughly the same size. This isn't a hard and fast rule, but it certainly helps a lot of the time.

So, instead of making a smaller version of the tree by scaling it, you make a brand-new, smaller tree model, like this:

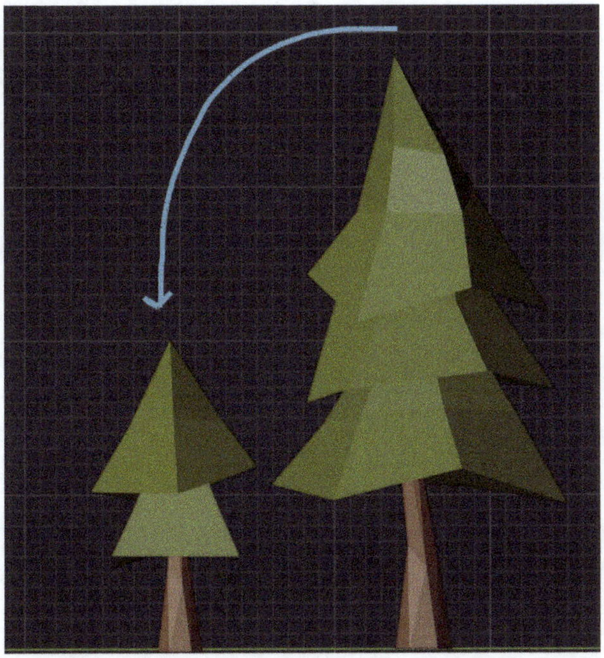

Figure 2.10 – Making a smaller tree from scratch

See how much nicer that looks?

This is not always a hard and fast rule (rules are meant to be broken!) but it'll help a lot if you follow this rule most of the time. Your low poly renders will look more cohesive and professional.

Summary

In this chapter, you learned a bunch of theory—what a mesh is, what vertices, edges, and faces are, and the difference between low, medium, and high poly meshes.

Great job!

If you only remember one thing from this chapter, make sure it's the different parts of the mesh: vertices, edges, and faces.

In the next chapter, you'll finally get to make your first 3D model.

3

Creating a Low Poly Tree

In this chapter, you'll create your first 3D model – a low poly tree. This project will teach you about all of Blender's basic tools, such as how to move and resize objects, and all the basic modeling tools in Blender.

By the end of this chapter, you'll have learned about the following:

- Transforming objects
- Adding, deleting, and duplicating
- Using **Edit Mode**
- Using the **Extrude** and **Inset** tools
- Modeling the tree
- Parenting objects

Transforming objects

It's time to learn how to do some real work in 3D. First up, you'll learn how to move objects around, rotate them, and make them bigger and smaller. In 3D, an object's **transform** is simply its position, rotation, and scale. These values are very easy to edit directly. Here's a simple example to show you how.

In Blender, select the default cube. Press *N* to open the sidebar.

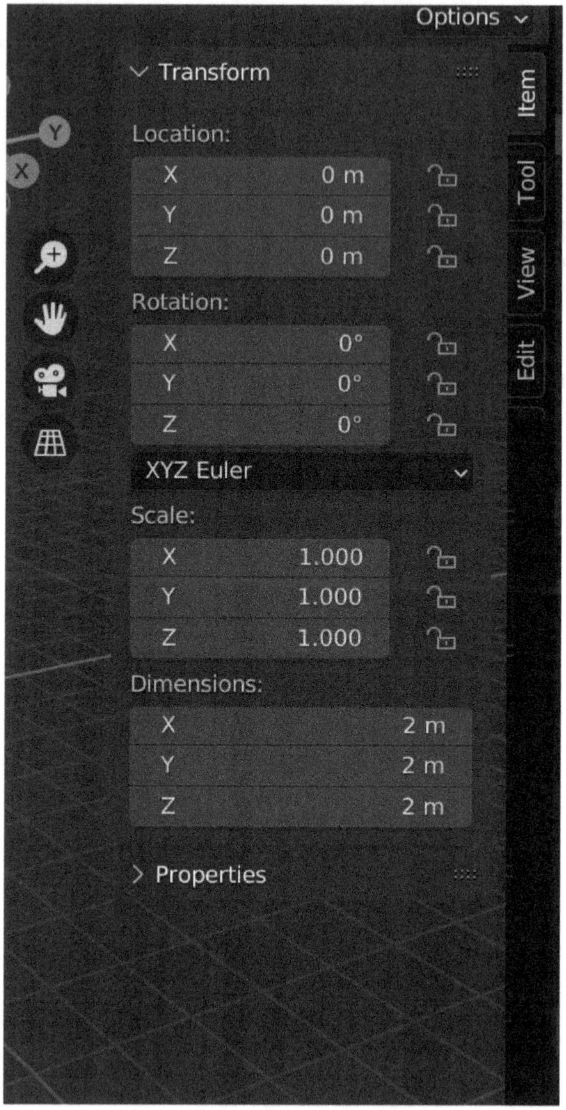

Figure 3.1 – The N sidebar panel

You'll see lots of numbers, divided into categories – **Location**, **Rotation**, and **Scale**. These are all the different values for the location, rotation, and scale, depending on the axis you want to change.

To test this settings out, let's rotate the default cube along the *X* axis:

1. In **Rotation**, click on the **X** value.
2. Type in a new value (for example, `200`). This is the number of degrees that the object will be rotated by.
3. Press *Enter*.

You just performed a manual rotation, so your cube should look like *Figure 3.2* now. This is useful because, sometimes, you'll want to simply set a **Scale**, **Rotation**, or **Location** value to an exact number.

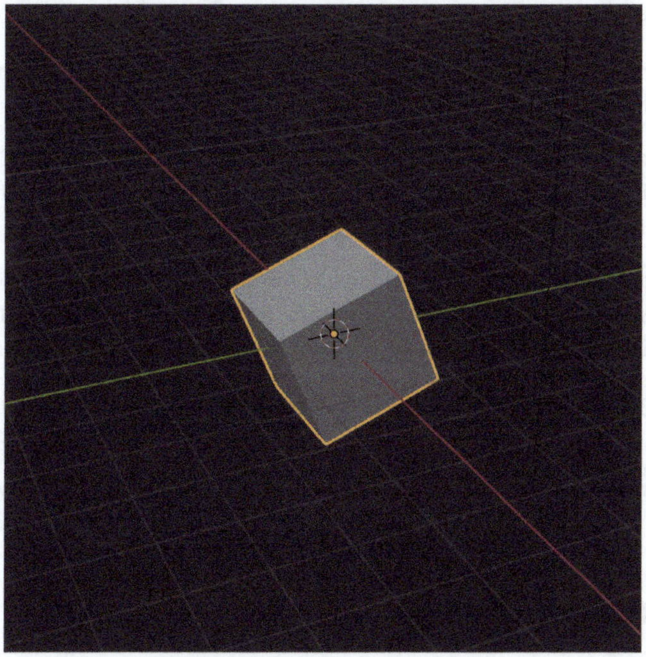

Figure 3.2 – The rotated cube

There's another easier way to edit these values. First, make sure you're not already editing any of the values by clicking somewhere else. Now, click and drag on any of the values with your mouse to *slide* the number higher or lower.

However, there's yet another even easier way to do this – using keyboard shortcuts. Here are the keyboard shortcuts for all the different transform commands:

- *S* to scale an object
- *G* to move an object (think of *G* standing for *grab*)
- *R* to rotate an object

Make sure the cube is still selected and then try these commands out. Press *G* and then move the mouse around – the cube will move too!

There are two things to remember:

- Pressing *Esc* or right-clicking will cancel the command
- Pressing *Enter* or left-clicking will confirm and complete the command

You can also move the cube in a specific direction. While you're moving it (any time after you press *G*), simply press *X*, *Y*, or *Z* to move it along that exact axis. All of this holds true for both the **Scale** and **Rotate** commands as well.

Try the **Scale** command next. When you run this command by pressing *S*, it's a good idea to make sure the mouse is not hovering over the object; otherwise, you won't have much room to scale it.

Pressing *X*, *Y*, and *Z* to scale along a specific axis works here too – try it out. Next, press *R* to rotate the cube. As with scaling and moving, you can use *X*, *Y*, and *Z* to rotate in a specific direction. You can also press *R* twice to rotate in multiple directions at once – try it!

You can also type in exact values to these commands. For example, if you want to move your cube five meters along the *X* axis, press *G* to activate the **Move** tool, then *X* for the *X* axis, and then *5* for the five meters. Don't forget that you need to left-click or press *Enter* to confirm any commands.

If you don't like what you've done, you can reset the location, rotation, or scale. Simply press *Alt* + *G* to reset the position, *Alt* + *R* to reset the rotation, and – you guessed it – *Alt* + *S* to reset the scale.

These controls may seem awkward at first, but as you use Blender, they'll become pretty intuitive for you.

Next, you'll learn how to delete the cube – and add a new one.

Adding, deleting, and duplicating

A cube is nice. But what if you don't want a cube? What if you'd like something else? Deleting and adding objects in Blender is very simple. To add a new object, you just press *Shift* + *A*.

This opens the **Add** menu, which lets you choose a new object to add from a large menu.

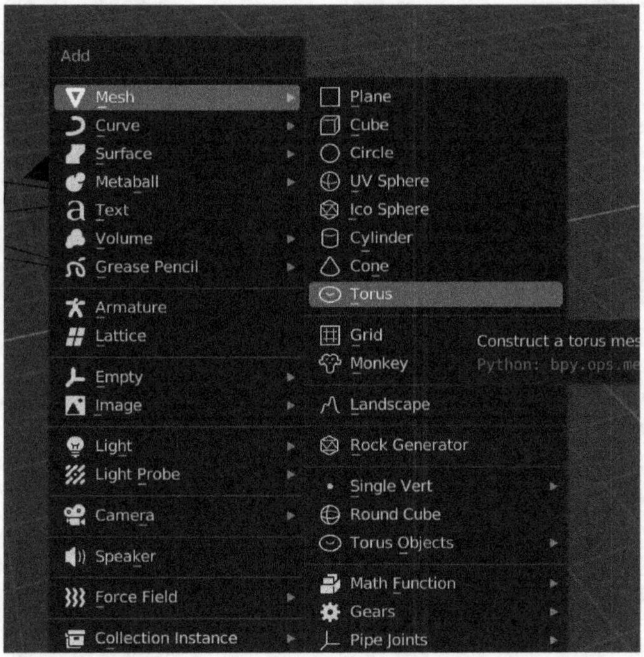

Figure 3.3 – The Add menu

Move your mouse to the **Mesh** category, and you'll see a lot of sub-options appear. These are all the 3D objects you can add to your scene. Pick something new, such as **Torus** (a donut).

New objects appear wherever the 3D cursor is located, which, by default, is the center of the scene. And before you go moving your new object around, pay attention to the small collapsed menu that appeared in the lower-left corner. It's called the *Operator* menu because it shows settings for whatever operator (tool) you just used.

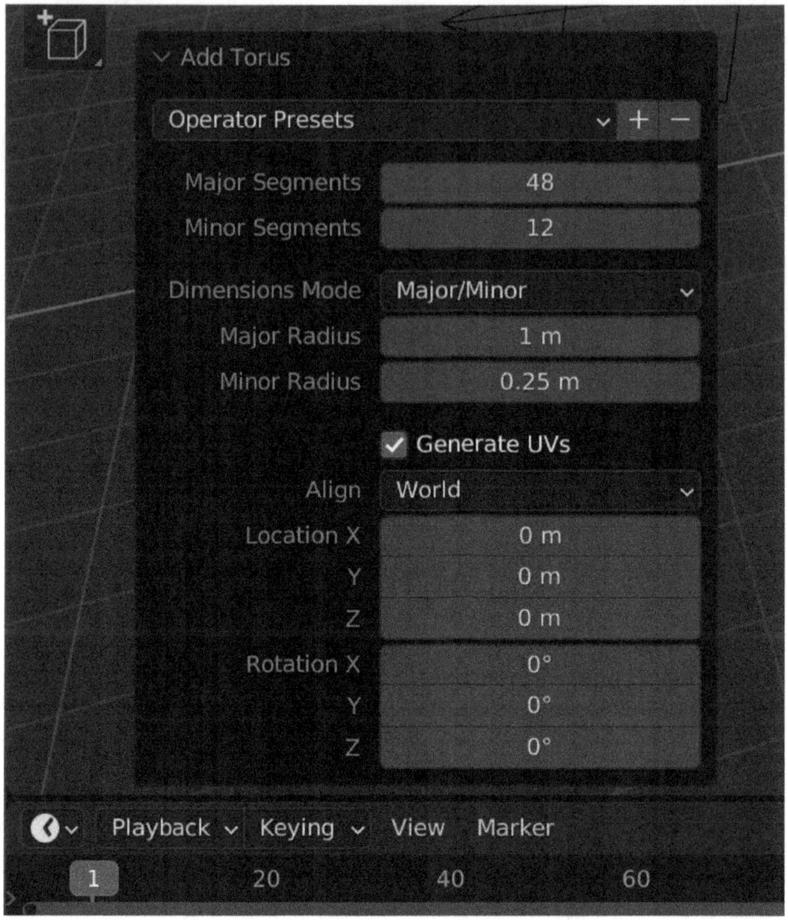

Figure 3.4 – The Operator menu

This menu appears whenever you complete an operation, such as adding a new object (or moving an object.) Open it with this little arrow, and it gives you helpful information and settings related to what you last did.

In this case, it lets you customize the **Torus** object. You can adjust the different values to change the shape, size, and poly count of the torus. This menu is useful, but there's a catch – you can only access it right after you perform an operation. Once you click out of the menu or use another command (such as *G* to move), you won't be able to access the menu anymore, so be careful!

Try adding more new objects – for example, try adding a **Sphere** or **Icosphere** (a sphere made of triangular faces) object.

Now, let's learn how to delete objects:

1. First, you'll need to select the objects you want to delete. You do this by clicking on them. Make sure to hold *Shift* if you want to select multiple objects. For now, let's delete everything. To quickly select everything, simply press the *A* key. (If you ever need to deselect everything, you can press *A* twice.)
2. In Blender, you don't use the delete key for deleting – you use the *X* key. Press it, and then confirm the deletion by pressing *Enter*. Everything's gone!

Now, you know how to make new objects and delete ones you don't need. But what if you want to duplicate an object? The command to duplicate the selected object is *Shift* + *D*. Try it out – add a new object to your scene, make sure it's selected, and then press *Shift* + *D*. If you move your mouse, you'll see that the **Move** command has been automatically activated, and you're now moving the duplicate.

You can cancel that, as usual, by pressing *Esc* or right-clicking. It's important to remember, though, that this only cancels the **Move** operation – *not* the **Duplicate** operation. So, the duplicated object is still there, in exactly the same place as the original. Press *G* to move the duplicate, *R* to rotate it, or... well, you get the idea.

Next, you'll learn how to make changes to the shape of an object.

Understanding Edit Mode

Scaling stuff is nice – but it doesn't get you very far. What if you need to change the shape of the actual mesh?

For that, Blender has something called **Edit Mode**.

So far, you've been working in **Object Mode** – where you work with individual objects. In **Edit Mode**, you work within an object. In this mode, you have access to the same basic tools (such as **Move**, **Rotate**, and **Scale**) but you're working inside the object, editing the vertices it's made up of.

When you're in **Edit Mode**, all the changes you make are inside the object you're editing. If you were to move all the vertices of an object five meters upward in **Edit Mode**, that would *not* affect its **Object Mode** position. This means that if you press *Alt* + *G* to reset the object's position, nothing will happen because the object hasn't been moved at all. Its vertices have been moved within it.

Another thing to remember is that **Edit Mode** changes are permanent. You can use *Ctrl* + *Z* to undo the last few things you've done, but there's no way to reset transforms like you can in **Object Mode**.

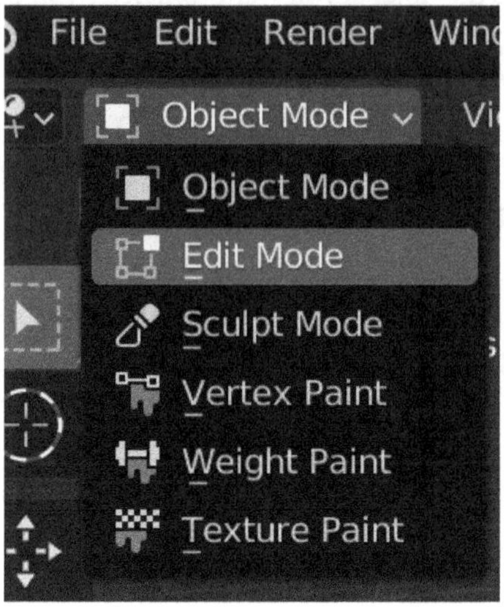

Figure 3.5 – The Mode Switcher

Next, you'll learn how you can use **Edit Mode** to edit objects:

1. Add a new cube to your scene with *Shift* + *A*.
2. It's very easy to enter **Edit Mode** – you select an object and press *Tab*. You'll see the **Mode Selector** in the upper-left corner change from **Object Mode** to **Edit Mode**.

Now that you're in **Edit Mode**, you can edit the mesh. There are three ways to do this – you can edit the mesh's vertices, edges, or faces. The selector in the upper-left corner lets you change between the different selection types – the vertex, edge, or face. You can switch between them by pressing the *1*, *2*, and *3* keys. (However, this only works if you're not using the **Emulate Numpad** setting.) Use the first one, **Vertex Select** mode, for now.

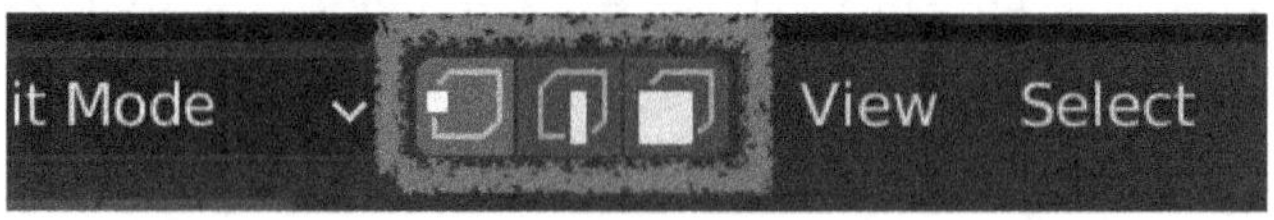

Figure 3.6 – The Selection Mode picker

Selecting vertices is just like selecting anything else:

1. Press *A* to select everything.
2. Press *A* twice to deselect everything.

3. Hold *Shift* while selecting to select multiple vertices.
4. Select a vertex.
5. Press *G* to move it – you're editing the mesh!

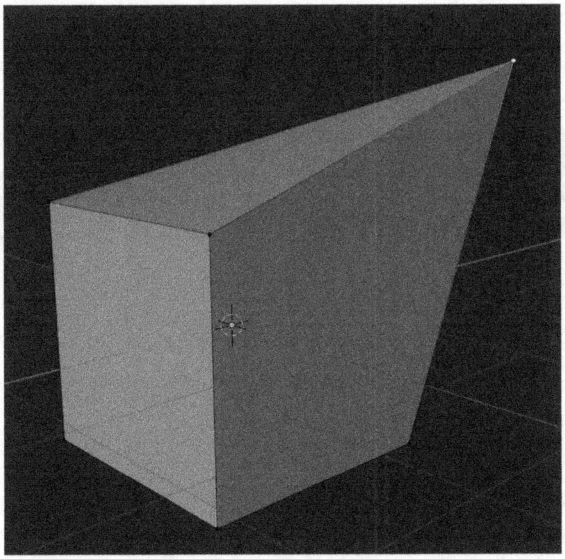

Figure 3.7 – Moving one vertex

All the commands you learned for **Object Mode** transforms work exactly the same way in **Edit Mode**.

Try it all out – select a few vertices and try rotating, scaling, and moving them with *R*, *S*, and *G*, respectively. You can also delete them – press *X* and select **Vertices** from the menu. Now your cube is a new shape.

Next, you'll learn about some new tools that don't exist in **Object Mode**. These are specialized tools for mesh editing.

The Inset and Extrude tools

Now, you know how to change the shape of your cube. But it's still a cube. And you just can't get very far with a cube, no matter how much you move the vertices around. You can make a squashed cube or a stretched cube, but that's about it.

However, with the **Extrude** tool, you can add more geometry (vertices/edges/faces) to the mesh. The **Extrude** tool lets you select a face of your mesh and then *pull* it outward to create entirely new geometry. This is very powerful.

Make sure you're in **Object Mode** (if you're still in **Edit Mode**, press *Tab* to return to **Object Mode**).

Before we try this, let's clean up the scene by deleting everything in it (press *A* to select all and then *X* to delete):

1. Press *Shift* + *A* and add a new cube.
2. Select it, and then press *Tab* to enter **Edit Mode**.
3. Now, you're ready to learn how to extrude. Make sure that the **Selection Mode** option is set to **Face** (see *Figure 3.8*), and then select one face of the cube.

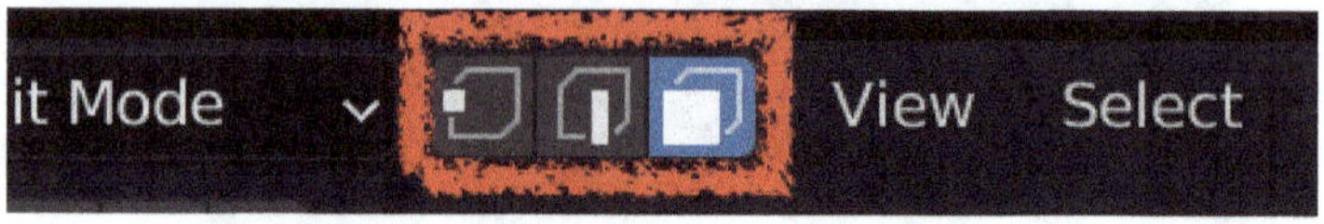

Figure 3.8 – Face Select mode

4. Press *E* to activate the **Extrude** tool. Move your mouse cursor to see what happens.
5. As with other commands, you can press *X*, *Y*, or *Z* to constrain the operation to a particular axis – this gives you more control over the extrusion.

> **Beware of canceling your Extrude operation!**
>
> If you right-click or press *Esc* to cancel the extrude operation, it sets the extruded faces back to their original positions – the extrusion is not canceled. To fix this, you can press *Ctrl* + *Z* to undo the last operation after you cancel.

So, always watch out for canceling your extrusion. You must press *Ctrl* + *Z* to undo an extrusion you don't want – right-clicking is *not* enough.

The **Extrude** tool is extremely powerful. For example (as shown in *Figure 3.9*), you could extrude a face out from your cube, scale that face down, and then extrude from it – the possibilities are endless.

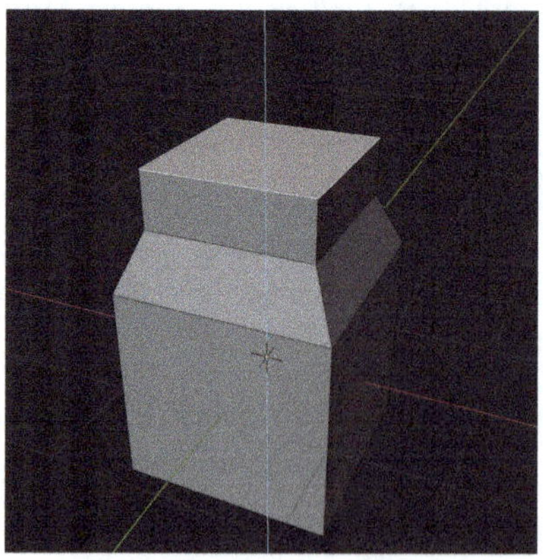

Figure 3.9 – A face extruded, scaled, and extruded again

What if you want to make something more detailed? What if you need more vertices in your mesh? For that, you need to subdivide your mesh. Subdividing breaks one face up into smaller ones. This is something you'll need to do a lot!

Simply press *A* to select all of the mesh's faces, click the **Edge** menu, and then choose **Subdivide**:

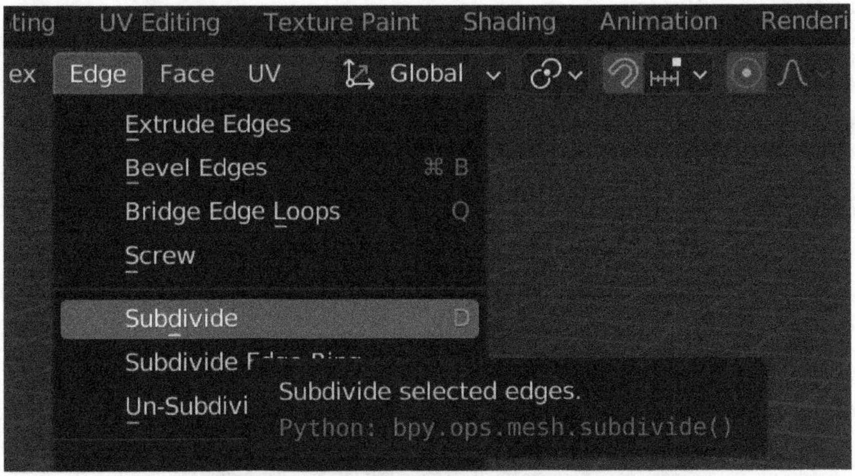

Figure 3.10 – The Subdivide tool

If you open the Operator menu in the lower-left corner of the viewport, you'll see a value called **Number of Cuts**. You can change this to control how many times the mesh is subdivided – but beware! Don't type a huge number into this box – it's easy to go too high (which will crash Blender).

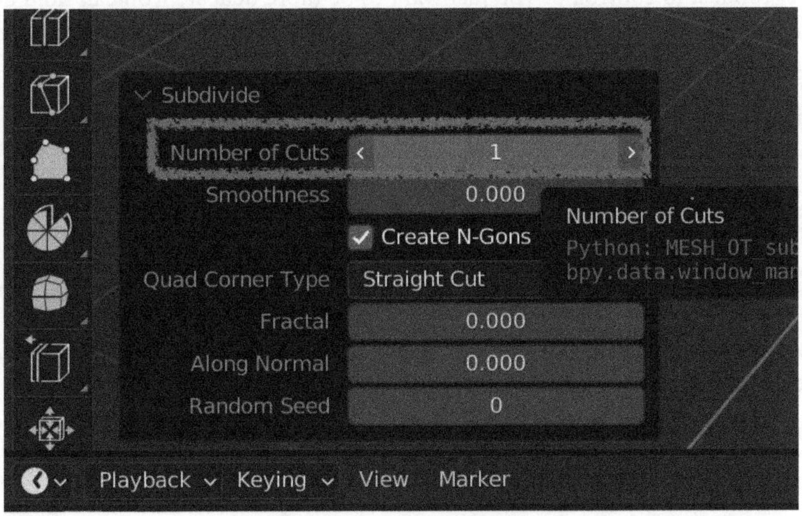

Figure 3.11 – The Subdivide Operator menu

Another type of extruding is called **insetting**. The **Inset** tool allows you to make another, smaller face within an existing face. You'll find this useful all the time – it's a good one to know!

To use the **Inset** tool, simply select a face and press *I* (this is easy to remember – *I* stands for *inset*). This works just like any other operator (tool), and when you right-click or press *Esc* to cancel it, it actually is canceled, as you'd expect.

Here's what the cube looks like after you use *I* to inset a face:

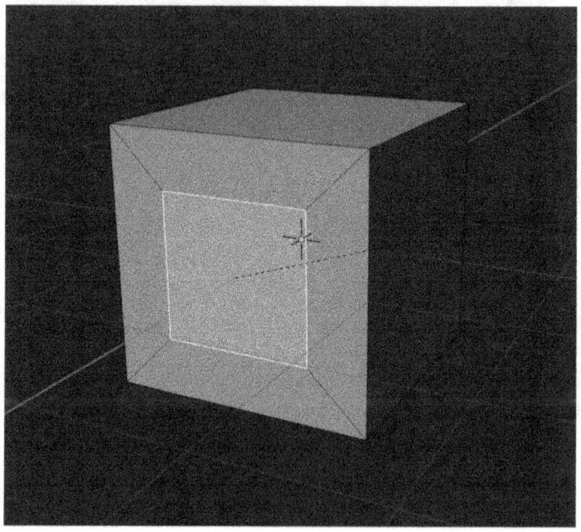

Figure 3.12 – Insetting a face

If the tool moves too fast to control, or you just want to be more delicate, you can hold down *Shift* while you move your cursor. Holding down *Shift* while you do anything in Blender slows the action down and gives you more control.

Next, you'll build your first 3D model – a simple tree.

Modeling the tree

Time for some action!

You're going to build your first project in Blender – a simple 3D tree. You'll use many of the tools and techniques that you just read about. This project is simple, so it's the perfect place to start. Here's what you'll have when you're done:

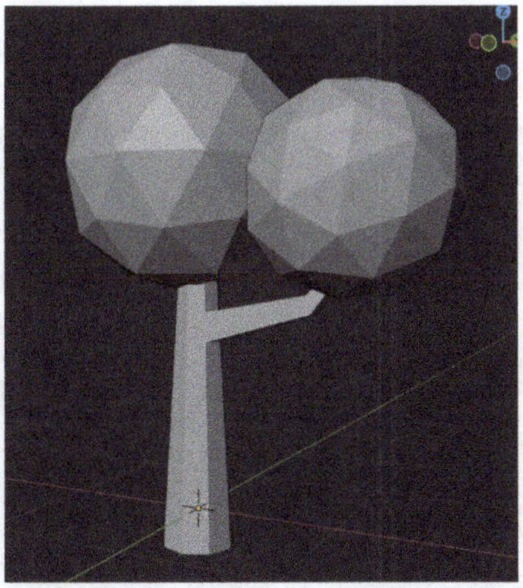

Figure 3.13 – The tree we'll make

We'll start with the easy part – the trunk of the tree.

First, let's get set up:

1. Open a new Blender file.
2. Delete everything in the file.
3. Now, press *Shift* + *A* to add a new **Cylinder** object.

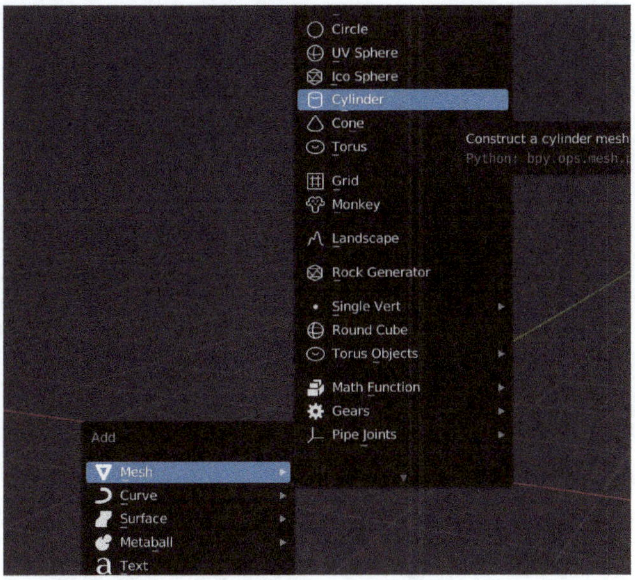

Figure 3.14 – Adding a cylinder

4. Open the Operator menu in the lower-left corner and lower the **Vertices** number to `8`. This cylinder is the beginning of the tree trunk.

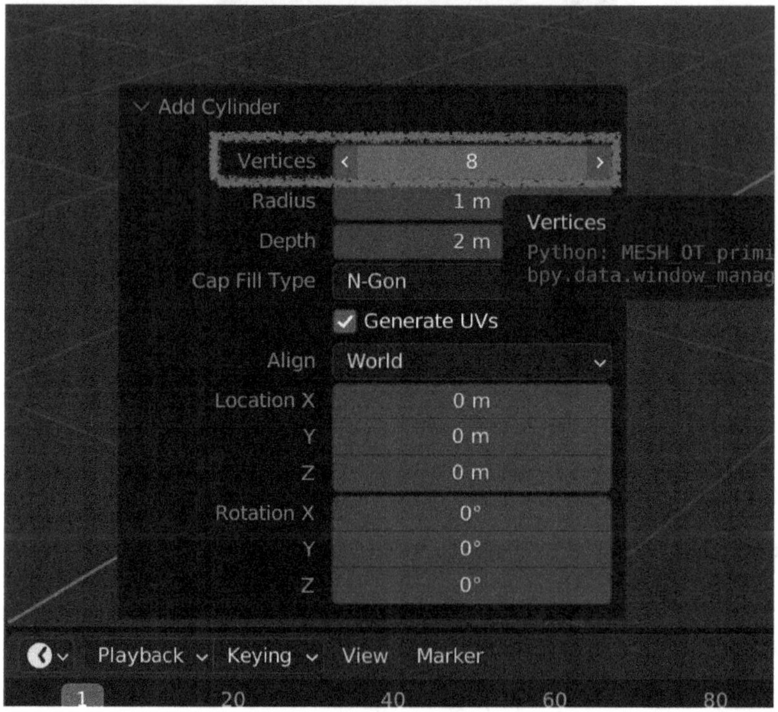

Figure 3.15 – Changing the Vertices count

5. If you take a look at the *N* menu, you'll see that the cylinder is two meters wide. That's one thick tree. Press *S* and scale the cylinder down, until it's around `0.5` meters wide. We could make a big fat tree, but a smaller one will be a little easier to work with.

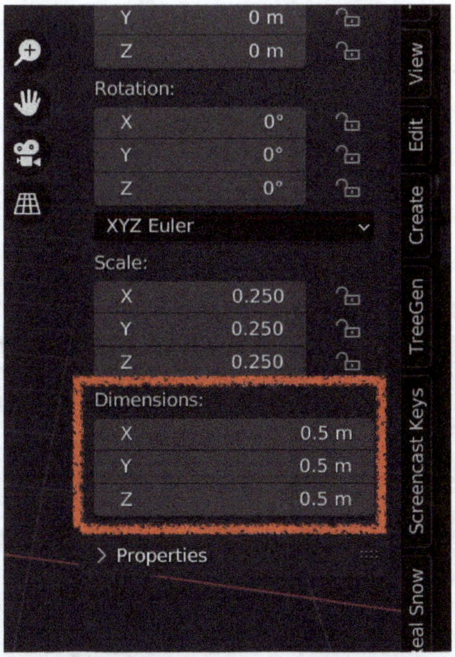

Figure 3.16 – The dimensions you want

The next step is to make the cylinder taller. You'll do this part in **Edit Mode**.

6. Press *Tab* to enter **Edit Mode**. Make sure the selection mode is still set to **Face**, and then select the top face of the cylinder.
7. Now, move this face upward (along the *Z* axis). You already know how to do this – press *G* to move and then *Z* to move the face along the *Z* axis. Move it a few meters up – something like this:

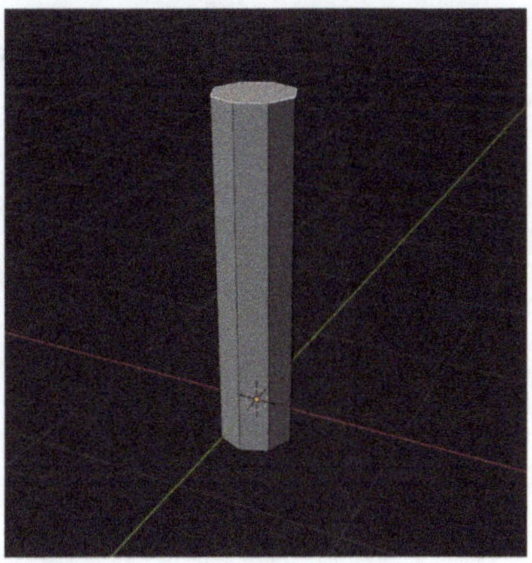

Figure 3.17 – The stretched cylinder

8. The next step is to make the tree trunk tapered – thinner at the top, and thicker at the bottom. This is easy – press *S* to scale the top face down a little bit (it should still be selected).
9. Now, we need to add more geometry, so you'll learn a new tool – **Loop Cut**. This tool allows you to add new *loops* of edges around existing geometry. Press *Ctrl* + *R* to activate the **Loop Cut** tool.
10. Move your mouse around until a yellow loop appears around the cylinder – this is where it'll perform the cut. Scroll (either with a trackpad or a mouse) to increase the number of loops that will be cut.

    A number around `8-10` will work well.

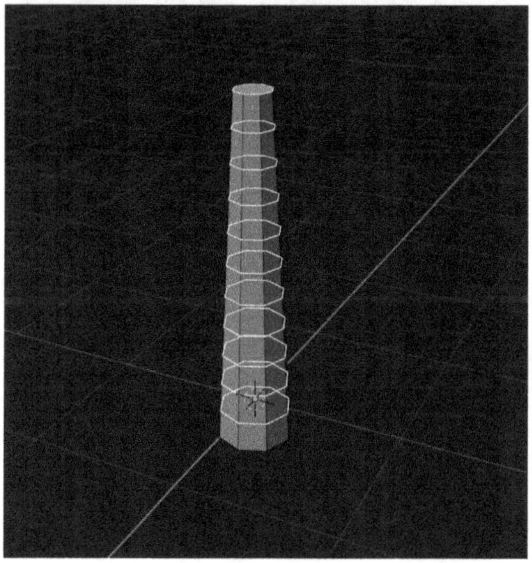

Figure 3.18 – Loop-cutting the tapered cylinder

11. Click twice to confirm the loop cut. You can change the number of cuts in the Operator menu in the lower-left corner if you need to.

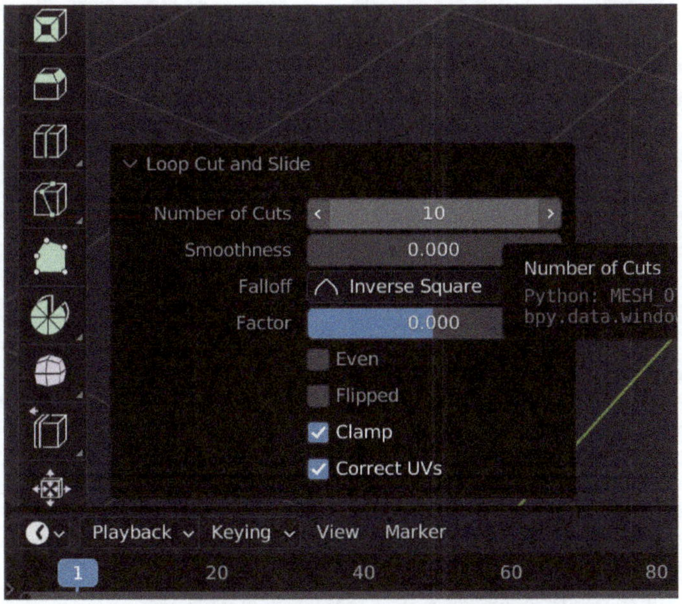

Figure 3.19 – The number of cuts

The tree trunk is almost done! We're going to create a branch next. Press *3* for a right view, and then select two faces near the top of the tree. We're going to extrude the branch out from here.

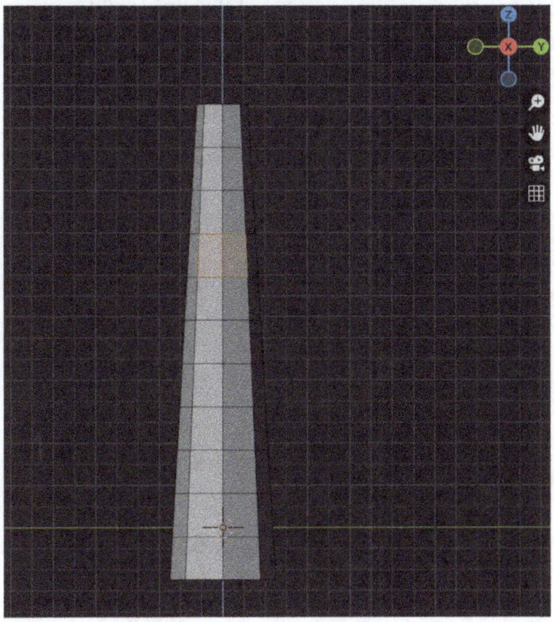

Figure 3.20 – The faces the branch will be extruded from

12. The next step is to extrude the branch. Press *Numpad 1* to go to the front view, and then *E* to extrude the first part of the branch.

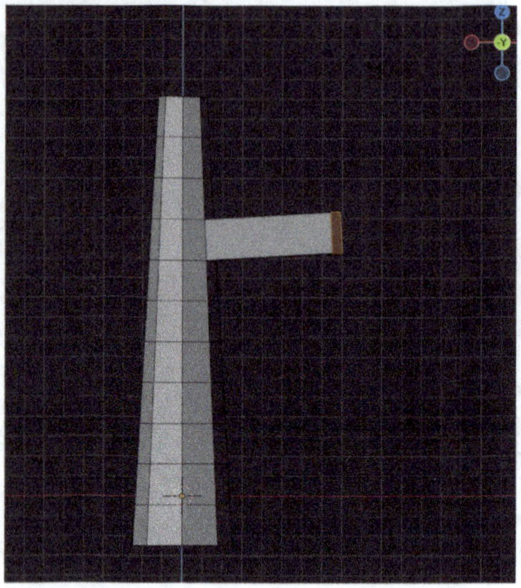

Figure 3.21 – The first part of the branch

13. Press *S* to scale the faces down – this makes the branch tapered. Press *G* and give the branch an upward tilt (by moving the faces upward), and then press *R* to rotate them a little bit.

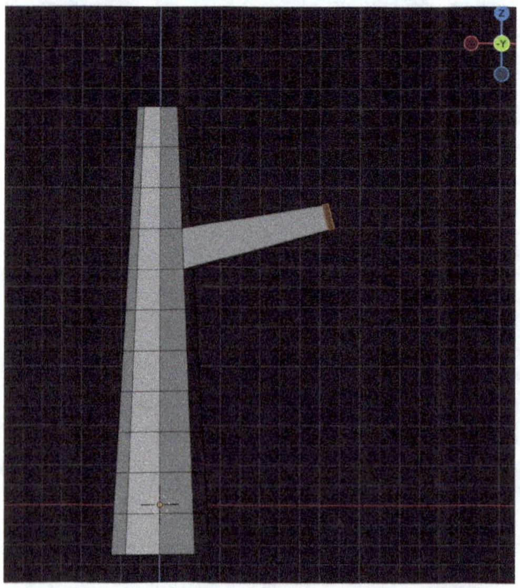

Figure 3.22 – The branch, tapered and adjusted

14. Press *E* to extrude again, *S* to taper the branch again, and then *G* to position it how you like.

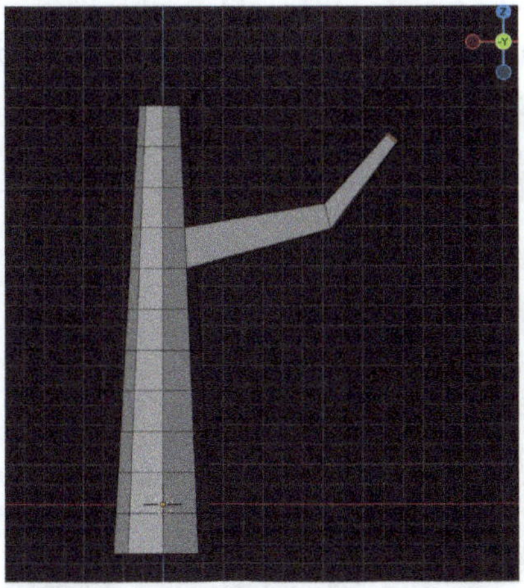

Figure 3.23 – The next extrusion

The trunk is done! Time to make some incredibly simple leaves. For the leaves, we'll use icospheres, which will make a nice bubbly shape:

1. Make sure you're in Object Mode for this part (press *Tab*, but check the Mode Switcher in the upper-left corner to make sure.) Press *Shift* + *A*, navigate to the **Mesh** section of the **Add** menu, and choose a new icosphere. This will be the leaves.
2. Press *1* to view your scene from the front again, and then use *G* and *S* to move and resize your icosphere. The goal is to make it look relatively leafy, like so:

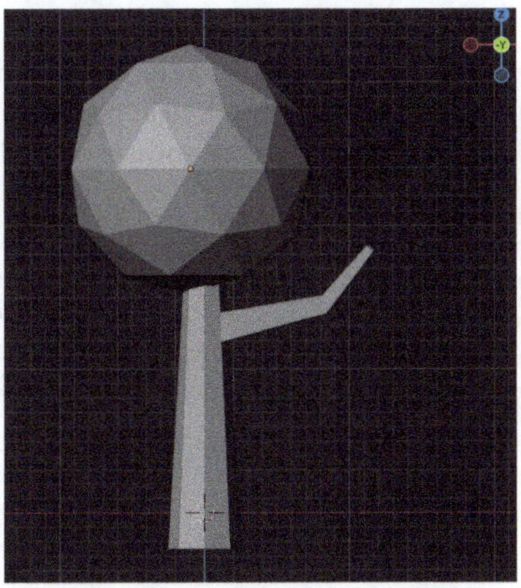

Figure 3.24 – The first part of the leaves

3. Now (making sure you're still in the Front view!), press *Shift* + *D* to duplicate your icosphere. Move your mouse to place the new one to the side so that it's over the branch. You can scale it down a bit, and rotate it so that it looks different from the first one:

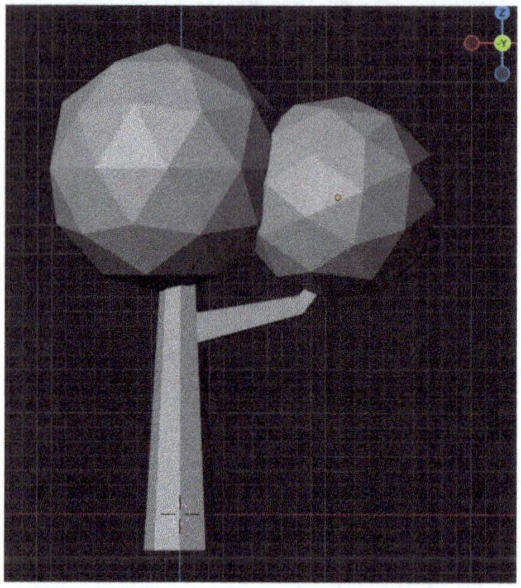

Figure 3.25 – All the leaves

Amazing! Your tree is done! You've completed your first 3D model in Blender. This is a moment to be proud of. Save your file so that you don't lose your work.

Next, you'll learn how to parent objects to each other so that you can move them around as one.

Parenting objects

Parenting objects is a way to connect objects so that they stay together no matter how you move, rotate, or scale them. This will be useful in the case of our tree – right now, if you try to move the tree, you have to have both leaf objects and the trunk selected so that you can move all of it – and that's annoying.

To solve this problem, we will make the leaf objects *children* of the trunk.

Child objects are *connected* to the parent object – no matter what you do to the parent, the child will act as if it's part of it. However, you can still edit and transform the child objects independently of the parent, without any issues. They're still separate objects, but they move/rotate/scale with the parent as if they were connected. This is very helpful.

This is a simple process:

1. Select the objects you want to become the children (both leaf objects).
2. Select the object you want to parent them to (the trunk object).
3. Press *Ctrl* + *P*, and choose **Object (Keep Transform)**. This option makes sure that the object stays in place and does not move when parented.

Done! You'll see a faint dotted line that indicates the parent-child relationship. So now, whenever you move the trunk object, the leaves come with it – much less annoying.

You can always un-parent the object again by selecting it and pressing *Alt* + *P*, which is **Clear Parent**. Then, the object will be un-parented.

Summary

In this chapter, you learned all about real 3D modeling. You learned how to move, rotate, and scale objects in 3D. You learned about **Edit Mode**, how to use basic modeling tools to edit objects, and how to parent objects to each other.

That's a lot! However, if you only remember one thing from this chapter, remember that you just made your first 3D model, and it wasn't that hard!

In the next chapter, you're going to learn about something cool – modifiers.

Part 2: Modeling and Shading for Low Poly

In this part, you'll learn about more modeling techniques and try out some new Blender features, such as modifiers. You'll learn how to use materials to give your models color, and you'll get to model a low poly mushroom.

This part has the following chapters:

- *Chapter 4, Exploring Modifiers*
- *Chapter 5, Creating Low Poly Mushrooms*
- *Chapter 6, Understanding Materials and Shading*

4

Exploring Modifiers

In this chapter, you're going to learn about modifiers. Modifiers are powerful because they allow you to make edits and changes that are not permanent until you apply them. When you use modifiers to edit an object, you can go back and edit your modifiers at any time.

Modifiers also simplify and automate tasks such as modeling symmetrical objects or duplicating an object many times. For example, if you want a symmetrical object, you can create half of that object and add a **Mirror** modifier, which will generate the other half of the object for you.

In this chapter, we'll cover the following:

- Understanding what modifiers are
- Learning about the **Array** modifier
- Learning about the **Mirror** modifier and how to use it to build a low poly chair
- Learning about the **Bevel** modifier
- Learning about the **Solidify** modifier

What are modifiers?

Modifiers are a non-destructive tool. When you use a modifier to do something, it can always be undone again or edited until the modifier has been applied.

There are many different kinds of modifiers. Each one performs a single specific task. You work with modifiers in the **Modifier** tab of the **Properties** panel.

Blender has tons of useful modifiers, but in this chapter, we'll cover the **Array**, **Mirror**, **Bevel**, and **Solidify** modifiers.

Now, let's build a small example to see the **Array** modifier in action. You'll use the **Array** modifier to make a bunch of duplicates of the default cube. So, follow along:

1. Open a new Blender file and select the default cube.
2. Now, click the blue wrench icon in the **Properties** panel to open the **Modifiers** tab.

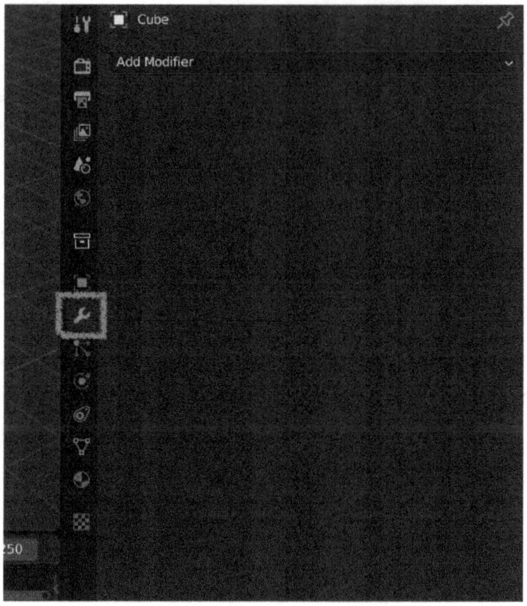

Figure 4.1 – The Modifiers panel

The blank space is called the **modifier stack**. This is where you can see all the modifiers currently affecting your object. It's empty right now.

3. To add new modifiers, click the **Add Modifier** button at the top of the stack. This will open the **New Modifier** dropdown, which displays all of the available modifier options.
4. Choose the one labeled **Array**. This modifier generates a set number of duplicates of your object.

You'll see that the **Array** modifier has now been added to the modifier stack. There are a few basic controls to understand here. At the top, next to the name of the modifier, are the visibility options. These allow you to control whether the modifier is visible in **Edit Mode**, in the viewport at all, or at render time.

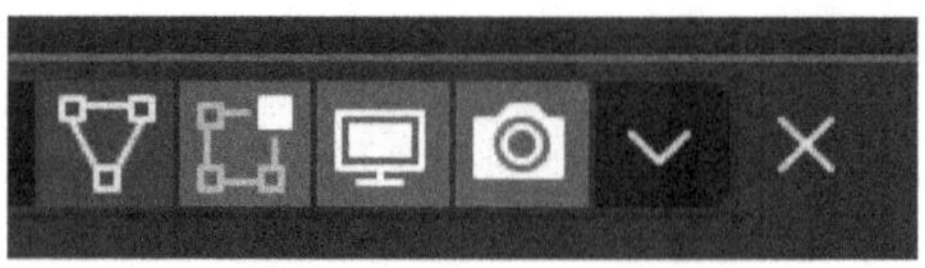

Figure 4.2 – The modifier visibility options

The small arrow menu beside these buttons is the **Apply** menu. You can use this menu to move the modifier up or down the modifier stack, duplicate it, or apply it. You can also click and drag the dots in the corner of a modifier to move it around.

Once a modifier is applied, it becomes permanent and is removed from the stack. You cannot edit the modifier ever again once it is applied, so it's always good to make sure you know what you're doing before you hit **Apply**. If you're worried it will break your model, simply hit *Shift* + *D* to duplicate it and move the duplicate somewhere out of the way, so you always have it if you need it.

Now you know how the modifier stack works and how you can add and remove modifiers. Next, you'll learn how to configure the **Array** modifier.

The Array modifier

Now, let's learn more about the **Array** modifier. The **Array** modifier is one of the most useful modifiers. It duplicates an object over and over again, in a straight line, as many times as you want. You'll commonly use this modifier for anything repetitive, such as a fence or a wooden bridge. You can also pair it with a **Curve** modifier to create a line of objects along a curve, though that's not covered in this book. The **Array** modifier is extremely simple to use.

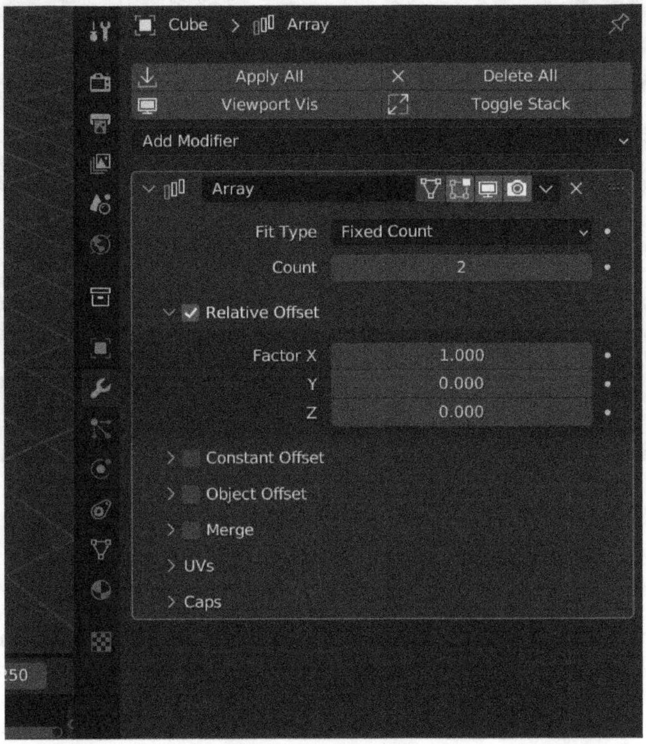

Figure 4.3 – The modifier stack with an Array modifier in it

The **Array** modifier is great for creating rows, lines, or grids of objects. The **Count** value allows you to control how many duplicates are created. The values in the **Relative Offset** section allow you to control how far apart the duplicates are on the X, Y, and Z axes.

And that's really all there is to it! Play around with it to get the hang of how it works, then add a second **Array** modifier.

Each modifier in the stack acts on the results of the previous one. So the new **Array** modifier will create duplicates of whatever the first **Array** modifier created.

For example, if you set up the first **Array** modifier with a **Relative Offset** value for **X** of `2` and a **Count** value of `10`, then set the second **Array** modifier with a **Relative Offset** value of **Y** = `2` and a **Count** value of `10`, the second one will array the results of the first one and you'll have a grid of 100 cubes, as shown in *Figure 4.4*.

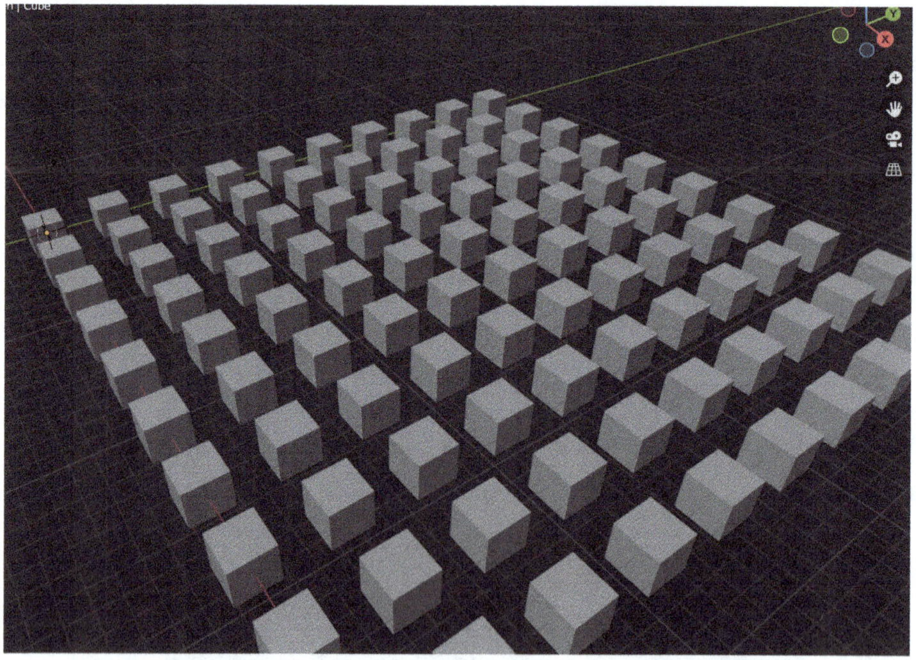

Figure 4.4 – Cube field made with two Array modifiers

Cool, right?

It's important to remember that the 100 cubes are still treated as one object. You can still select it and hit *Tab* to enter **Edit Mode**, but you'll only be editing the original cube.

Next, you're going to build a simple chair. You'll learn how to use the **Mirror** modifier in the process.

The Mirror modifier

The **Mirror** modifier is incredibly useful because you'll often want to create symmetrical 3D models.

Without the **Mirror** modifier, you'd have to try to make your 3D model symmetrical by hand, constantly trying to keep it the same on both sides. That would be difficult and error-prone. It would take a long time to finish your model.

With the **Mirror** modifier, you don't have to do any of that. You simply build half of your model, and the **Mirror** modifier copies it to create the other half of the model. This keeps it perfectly symmetrical.

This modifier is used for all sorts of awesome things—almost anything symmetrical can be created with a **Mirror** modifier, such as a full character or a battle vehicle.

The **Mirror** modifier is simple to use. You'll understand it best if you build an example project, so let's put together a simple chair.

Building a low poly chair with a Mirror modifier

You're ready to use modifiers to build something. You'll be building a simple chair. Along the way, you'll learn how to use the **Mirror** modifier to keep things symmetrical.

Here's what you'll be making:

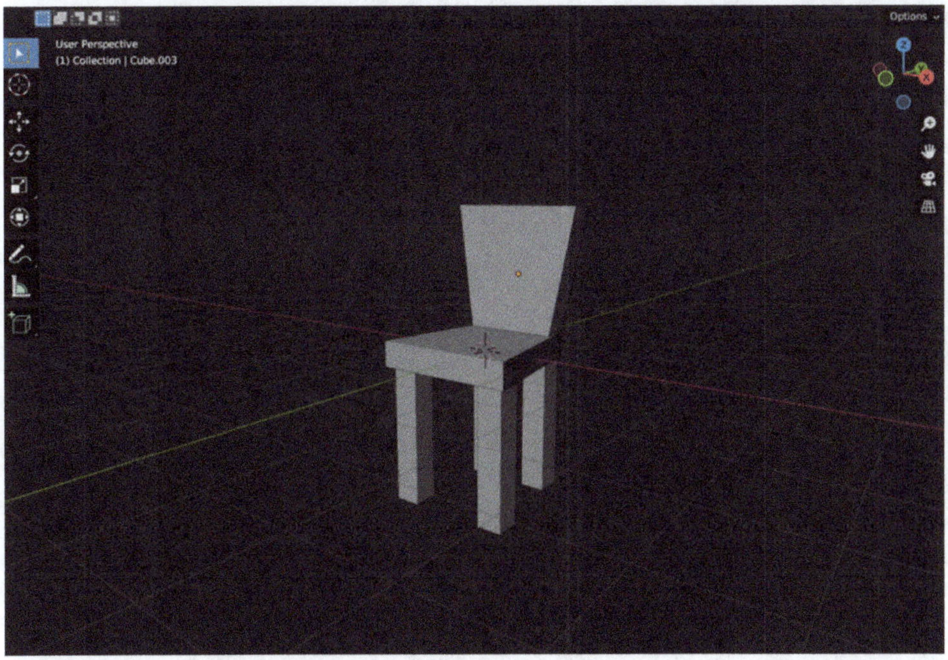

Figure 4.5 – The chair you'll make

Let's start with the seat.

The seat

To build the chair's seat, follow these steps:

1. Open a new file in Blender.
2. Select the **Camera** and the **Light** and press *X* to delete them. You don't need these right now, and it'll be simpler to work without them in the way.
3. Keep the cube, however. This will become the seat of the chair.
4. Select the cube and press *Tab* to go into **Edit Mode**.
5. Make sure you're in the **Face Select** mode (the control in the upper-left corner of the 3D viewport, near **Mode Switcher**).

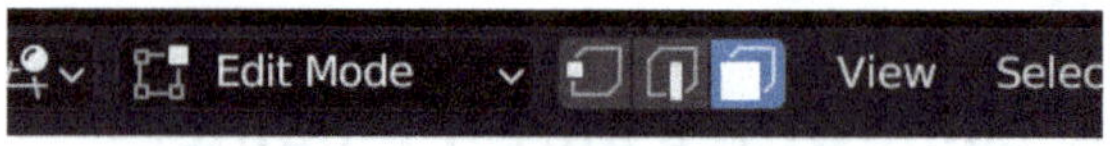

Figure 4.6 – Face Select mode

6. Now, press *Numpad 1* to view the cube from the **front**.

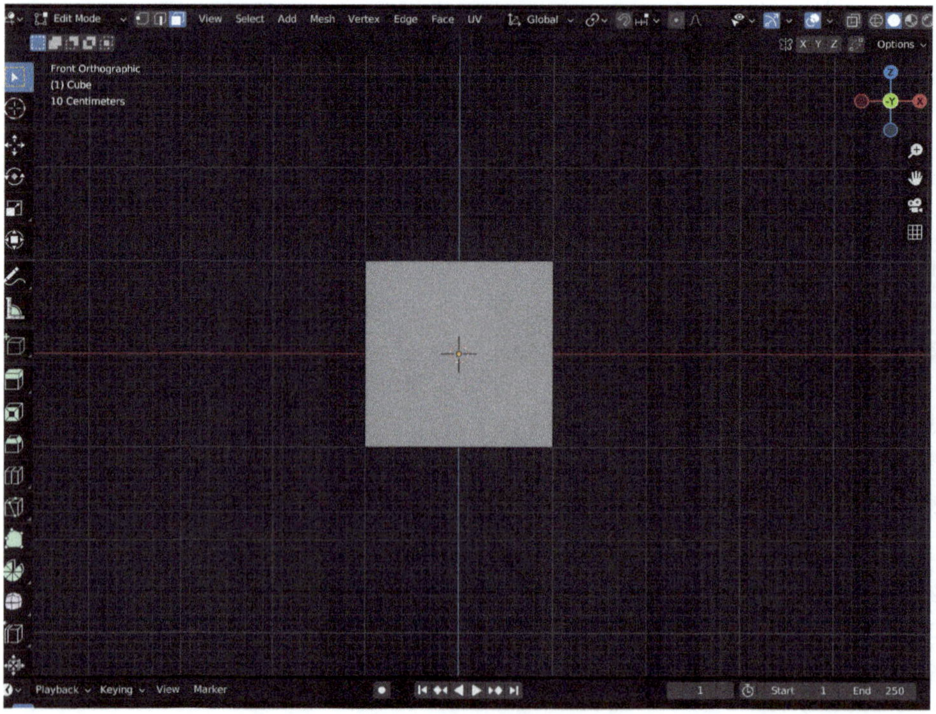

Figure 4.7 – The cube from the Front view

7. Press *A* to select everything, then *S* and *Z* to squash it on the Z axis. The goal is to make it thinner, more like a chair seat.

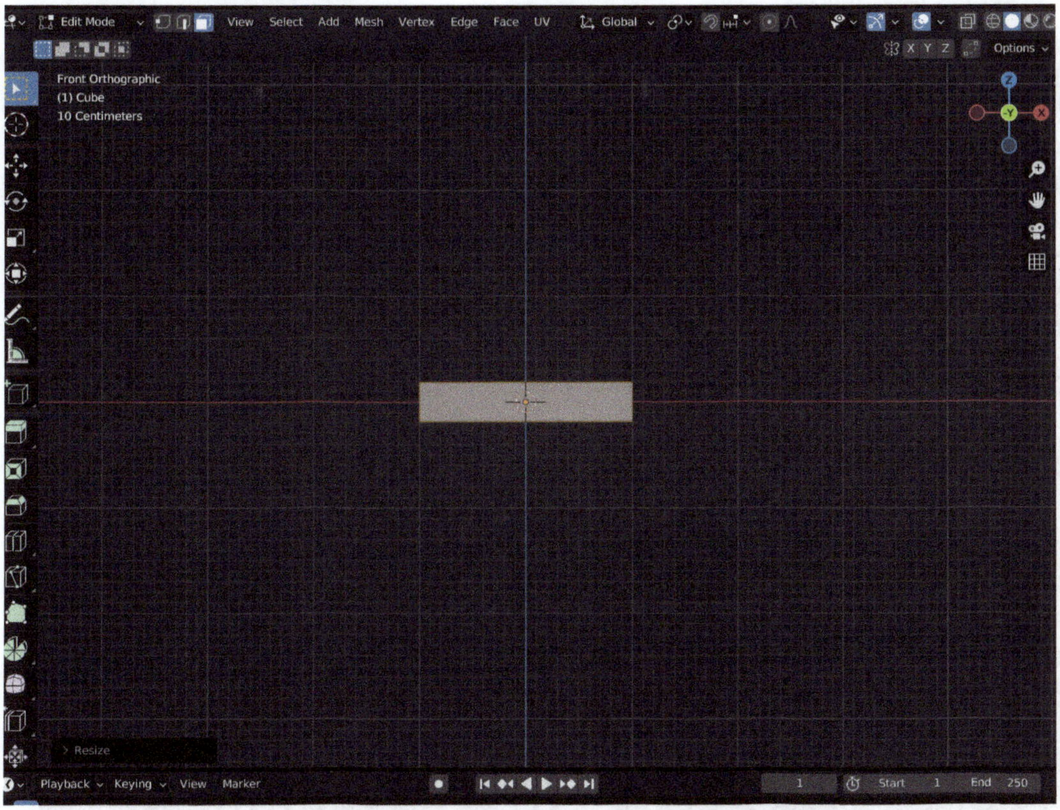

Figure 4.8 – Squash the cube to make it thinner

8. Now select the back face of the cube (it's okay to leave the **Front** view). Press *7* to get the **Top** view and then scale the selected face down on the X axis by pressing *S* then *X*. The goal is to create a tapered shape.

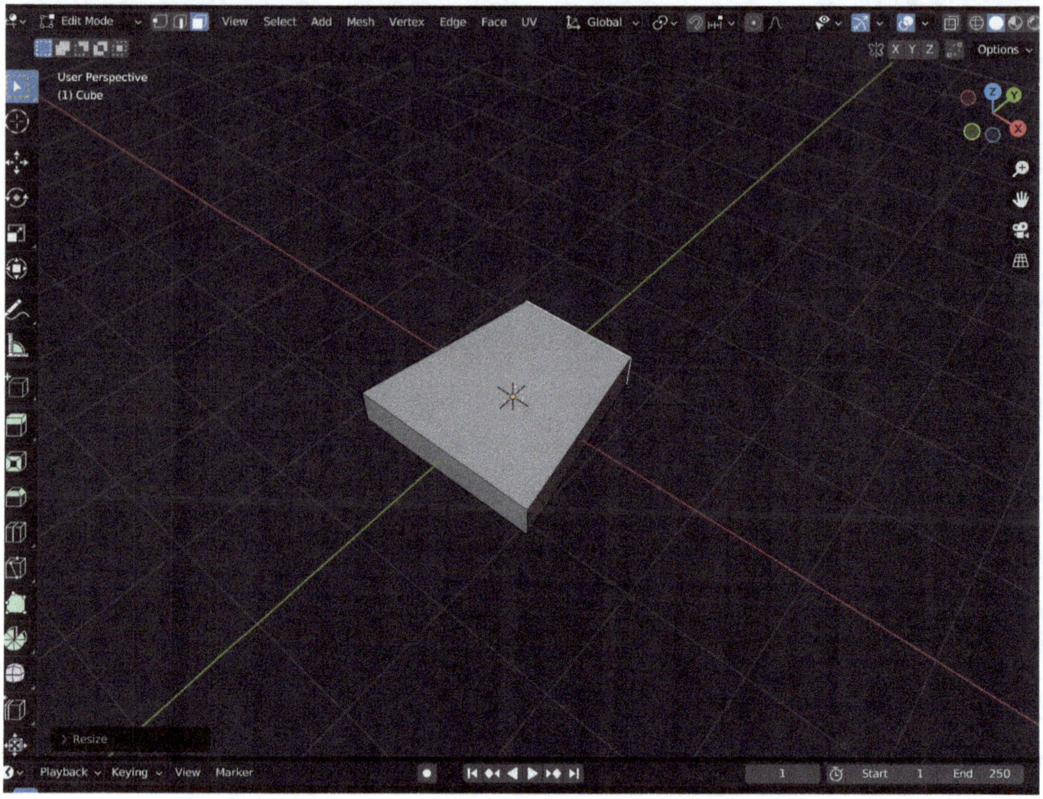

Figure 4.9 – Scale one face on the X axis to taper the chair seat

That's it for the seat. The next step is the legs of the chair.

The legs

To make the legs the same on both sides, you'll use the **Mirror** modifier:

1. First, hit *Tab* to leave **Edit Mode** and go back to **Object Mode**.
2. Now, press *Shift* + *A* and add a new cube.
3. Select the new cube and open the **Modifiers** tab (blue wrench icon in the **Properties** panel).
4. Click **Add Modifier** and select **Mirror** to add a **Mirror** modifier to your cube.

The **Mirror** modifier gives you a lot of options.

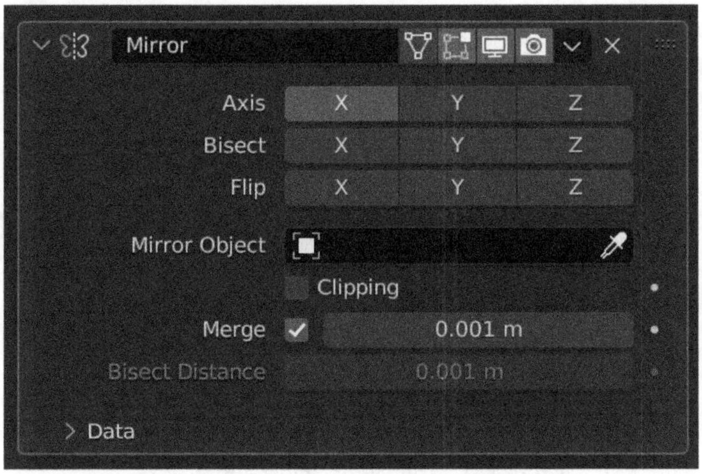

Figure 4.10 – The Mirror modifier

The **Axis** controls let you control which direction the object is mirrored in. **Mirror Object** lets you choose an object for it to be mirrored around. **Mirror Object** will be used as the point of symmetry for the cube. The point of symmetry is the center point around which the object will be mirrored.

The **Clipping** checkbox is useful when you've deleted half of a model and added a **Mirror** modifier—when you turn on **Clipping**, the vertices in the center automatically get welded together, and can't be pulled apart again.

If you don't choose a **Mirror Object**, the object's origin will be used as the point of symmetry. (The origin is the little yellow dot you see when you select any object. It's the point that an object rotates and scales around.)

Your chair legs will use the chair seat as the **Mirror Object**.

Here's how to set that up:

1. Click the **Mirror Object** field and choose the chair seat object (probably still called **Cube**).

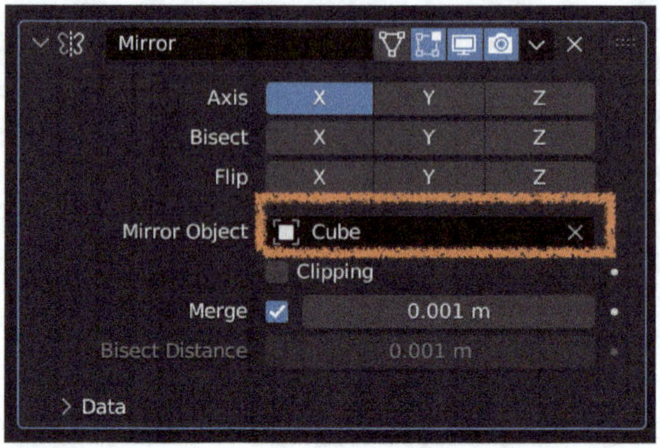

Figure 4.11 – The Mirror Object option

2. Now, if you hit *G* and move the cube, you'll see that there's a symmetrical duplicate on the other side of the chair seat.

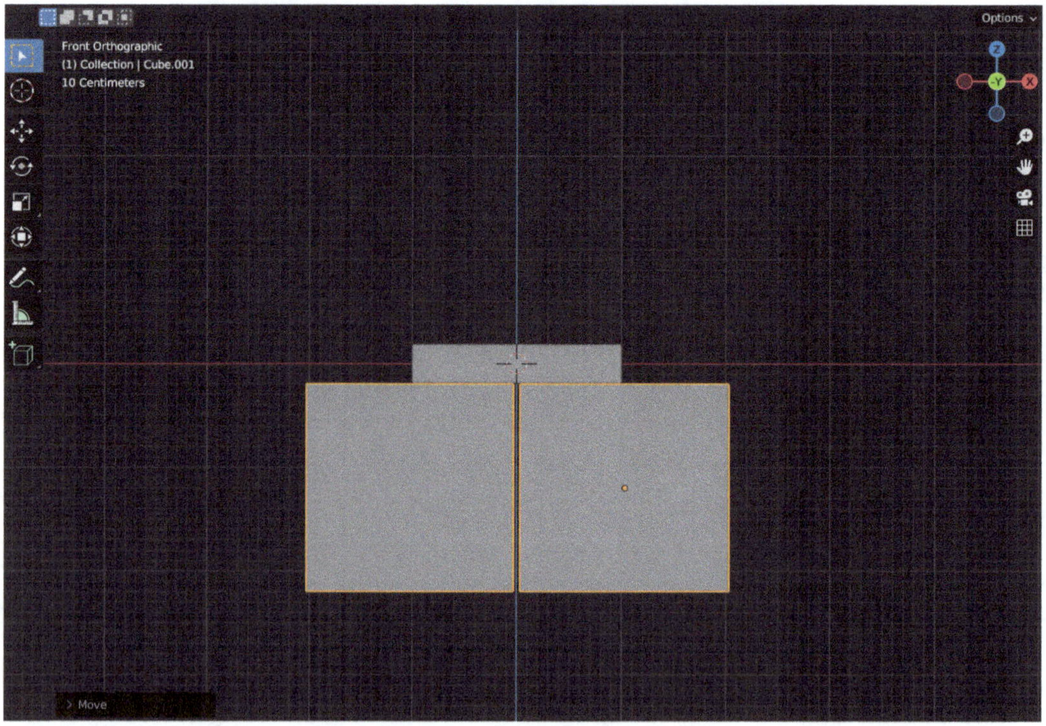

Figure 4.12 – Positioning the mirrored cube (which will become your chair leg)

3. Hit *1* again for the **Front** view and use *G* to position the cube somewhere near the edge of the chair seat.
4. Next, press *Tab* to go into **Edit Mode** and hit *A* to select all of the vertices. Press *S* to scale it. You just need to make the object thinner, so press *Shift* + *Z* to make the scaling affect all axes except Z (so X and Y).
5. Scale the object down until it's about as thin as a chair leg should be, then hit *Enter* to confirm.

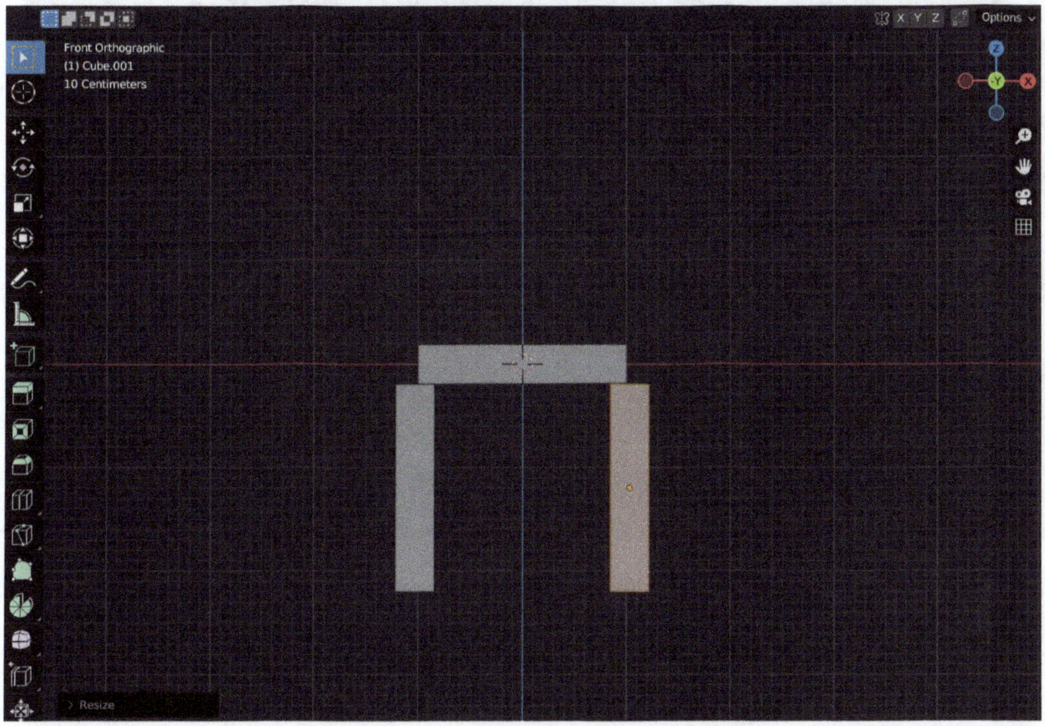

Figure 4.13 – Scaling the cube in Edit Mode

The next step is to put the leg in the right place (in **Object Mode**:

1. Hit *Tab* to leave **Edit Mode**.
2. Hit *G* then *Z* to move the leg down so it just barely touches the seat. Now, you need to move it into the corner of the chair seat.
3. Press *7* to return to the **Top** view and press *Alt* + *Z* to turn on **X-Ray** mode. This makes all of your objects see-through. This is amazingly useful when you're trying to put something where you want it.

4. Now, just press *G* and position the leg in one of the corners of the chair seat.

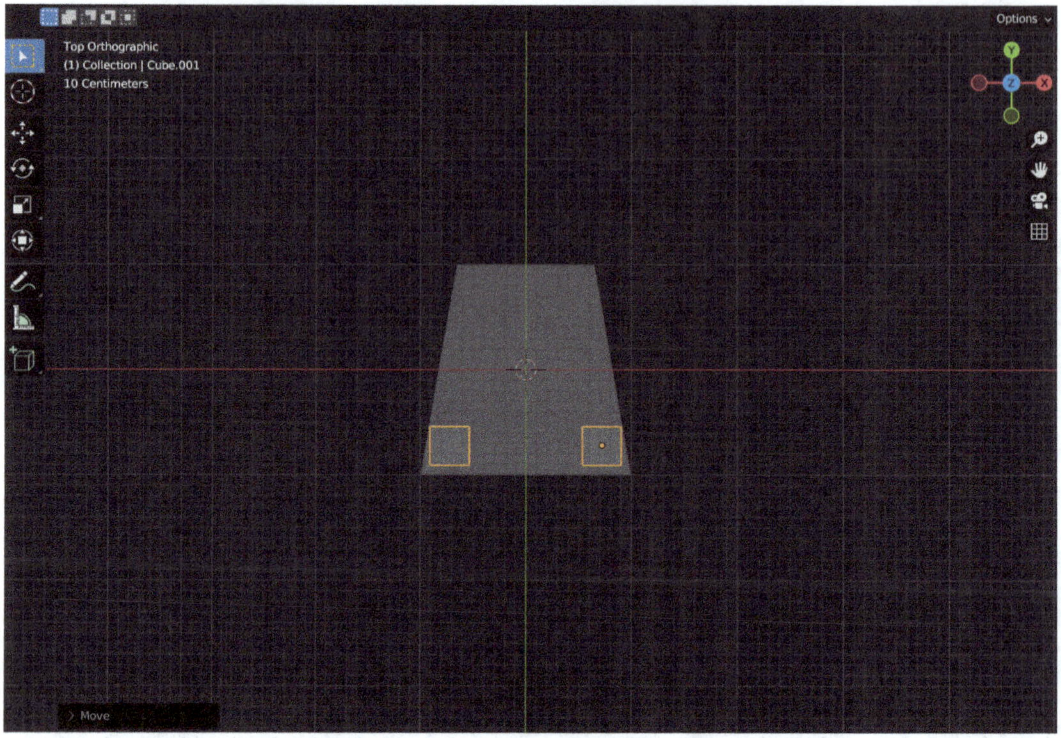

Figure 4.14 – Positioning the legs from the Top view

Perfect!

It's time to make the remaining two legs, and this will be easy: you can just duplicate the one you already have. Simply press *Shift* + *D* and move your mouse cursor to position the leg in the open corner of the chair.

When you have duplicated it, you have also duplicated the **Mirror** modifier, so it's already mirrored for you.

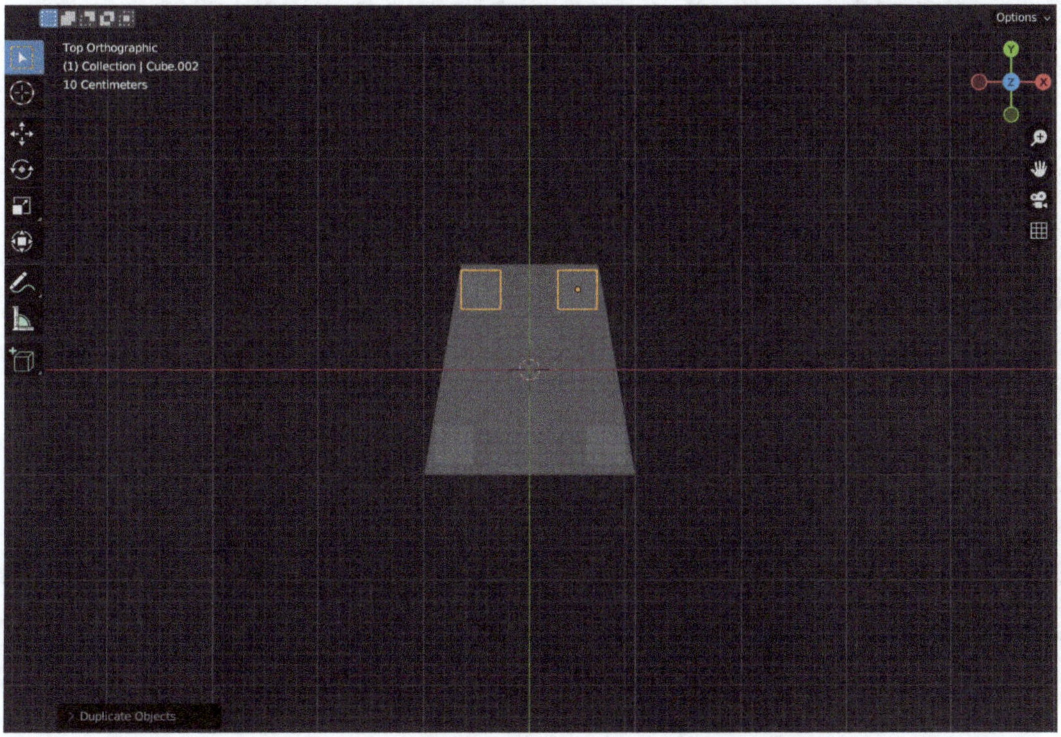

Figure 4.15 – Duplicating the front legs to make the back legs

Now that you have the legs where you want, you can turn off the X-Ray mode by pressing *Alt* + *Z* again.

And the legs are done! Now, the last step is to make the back of the chair, and then you'll be done!

The back

The back of the chair is extremely simple. To create it, you just need to duplicate the seat with *Shift* + *D*, and then use *G* and *R* to position it. It'll help if you use the **Right** view.

Here's what it'll look like when you're done:

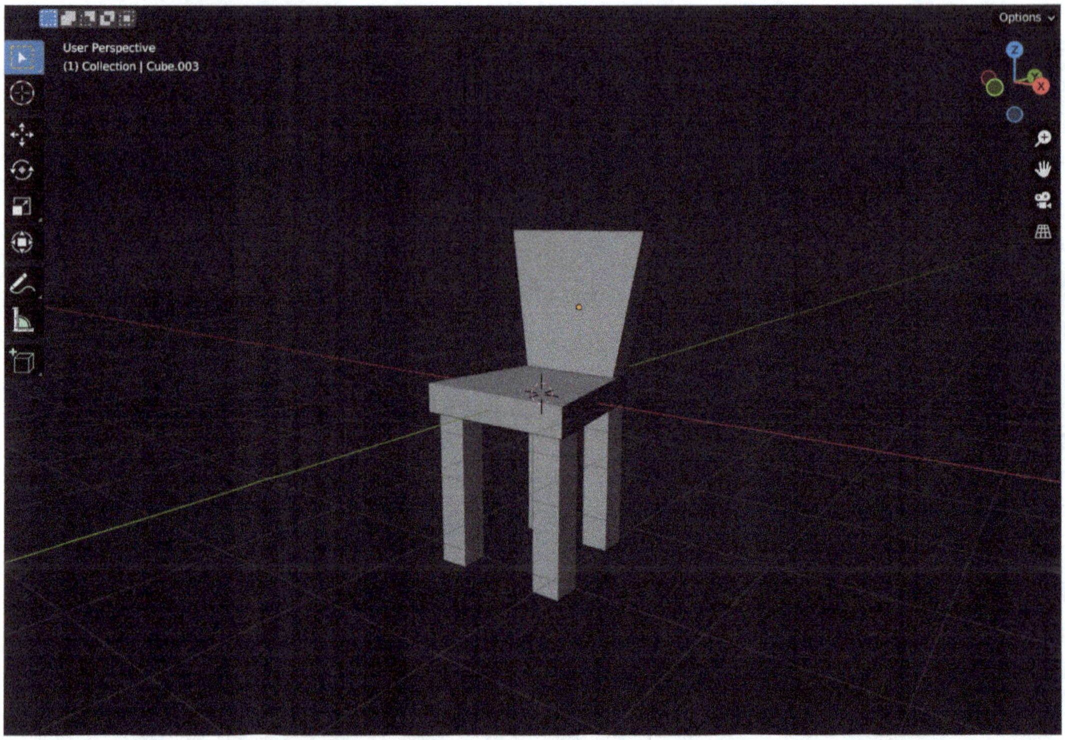

Figure 4.16 – The back is the same as the seat

That's it for the chair! Great job!

In the next section, you'll learn about another modifier: the Bevel modifier.

The Bevel modifier

The **Bevel modifier** is the exact same thing as the **Bevel** tool (*Ctrl* + *B*) but in the modifier form. It's like using the **Bevel** tool on your entire mesh. You have controls for the number of segments and how strong the bevel is. You also get a **Threshold** value, which controls which edges get beveled.

The Bevel modifier is really great when you need to soften up the edges of an object a little bit—it helps you lose the hard, sharp edge that you have by default. In low poly modeling, you won't find yourself using this very often. Still, it's a good tool to know about. You'll use this most often when trying to recreate real-world objects. In real life, even the sharpest objects (such as the edge of a knife) have a slight roundness or bevel. Nothing real has perfectly sharp edges like objects in Blender have.

Let's try out the **Bevel** modifier:

1. Again, open a new Blender scene and select the default cube.
2. Navigate to the **Modifier** tab and click the **Add New** button.
3. Choose **Bevel**.

Here's what the modifier looks like:

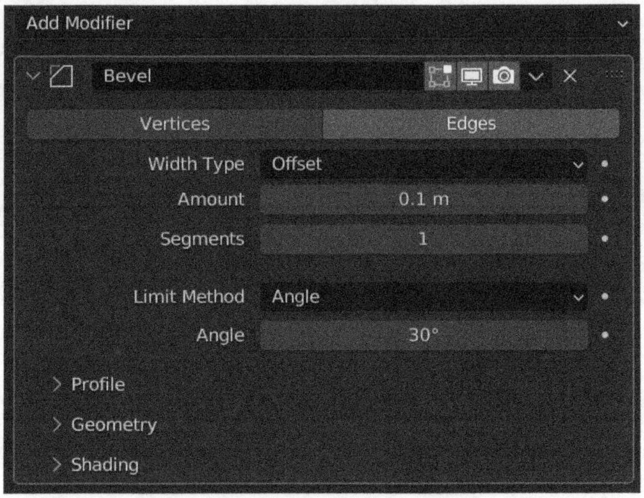

Figure 4.17 – The Bevel modifier

There are a lot of options here but you only need to focus on three main ones (even now, I still have no idea what half of those options do. I've never needed them!):

- **Amount**: This one is simple—how much bevel do you want? This adjusts how large the bevel effect is on the object.

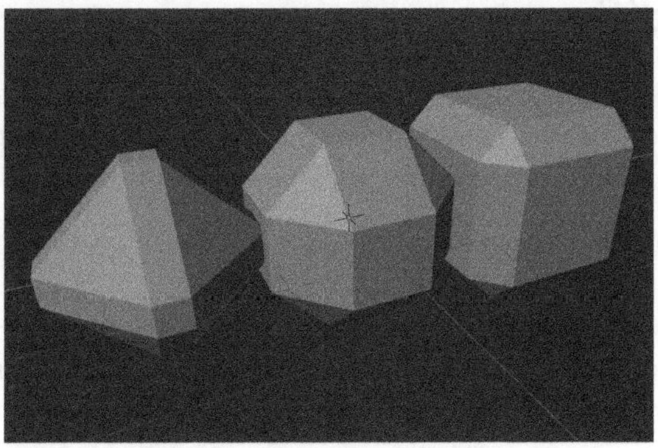

Figure 4.18 – Different bevel amounts

- **Segments**: This controls how many different segments the bevel is made up of. More segments have a smoother look, while fewer are choppier.

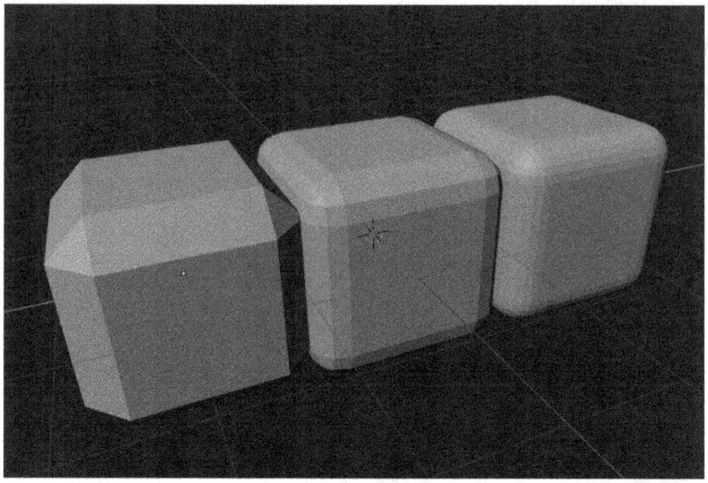

Figure 4.19 – Beveling with more or less segments

- **Angle**: This is the threshold angle. Any angle greater than this will be beveled; any less will not be. This is useful if you have a mesh with both sharp and smooth edges as it allows you to bevel only the sharp parts.

  The default of 30° is usually a good starting point—only change it if you need to.

Those are the three most useful settings on the **Bevel** modifier. You can get quite a lot of different bevels by adjusting these settings.

Next up is the **Solidify** modifier. This one is good to know about—even if you don't use it that often.

The Solidify modifier

The **Solidify** modifier is a bit like the **Extrude** tool in **Edit Mode**. It simply adds thickness to the mesh it is applied to. This can be useful when you have an object (for example, a cup) that is only made of faces (and is thin, such as a plane). The **Solidify** modifier adds some quick thickness for you.

Let's test out the **Solidify** modifier on a plane so you can see how it works:

1. Delete the default cube in your scene.
2. Press *Shift* + *A* and add a new **plane** instead. A plane is just a single, square face; it is infinitely thin—a great test subject for the **Solidify** modifier.
3. Open the **Modifier** tab, click the **Add New** button, and choose **Solidify**.

Here's what the **Solidify** modifier looks like:

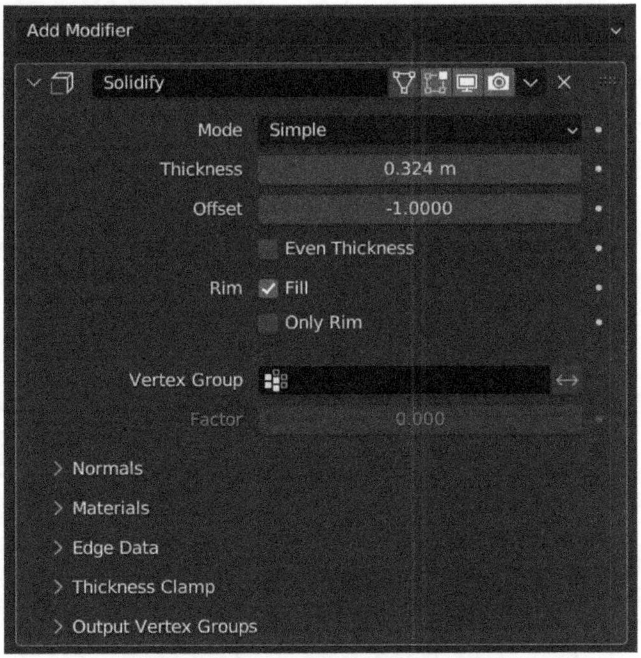

Figure 4.20 – The Solidify modifier

This modifier has one important setting: **Thickness**. This simply adjusts how thick it is. Negative values will simply make the extrusion happen in the opposite direction.

That's all you need to know about the **Solidify** modifier to use it well.

You've learned a lot about modifiers! Time for a recap of what you've learned.

Summary

In this chapter, you learned all about modifiers in Blender. You learned about what modifiers are and how they work non-destructively on your mesh. You also learned how to use some specific kinds of modifiers—namely, the **Bevel**, **Array**, **Solidify**, and **Mirror** modifiers.

These are the most fundamental and useful modifiers, but it doesn't mean they're the only ones you'll ever need. There are tons of other modifiers, but they're not covered in this book—there's just not enough space!

In the next chapter, you're going to learn how to make some low poly mushrooms. And don't ask why I picked mushrooms.

5

Creating Low Poly Mushrooms

In this chapter, you're going to build another complete model in Blender – a mushroom. You'll start with basic shapes and work toward a more complex form. You'll learn how to triangulate your model to improve the low poly look, and how to use the **Merge** tool to adjust your model's polygons by merging vertices.

You'll also learn how to create multiple variations of the same model.

In this chapter, you'll learn how to do the following:

- Base your model on a reference image
- Start your model with basic shapes
- Edit your mesh for an ideal low poly look

We'll start with reference images. Referencing is a vital step in the 3D art process – it guides your project and makes it much easier to figure out what you need to do.

Setting up reference images

Whenever you're creating a new 3D model, you need reference images or art. Reference art can be anything – from a crude sketch to a real photograph.

Reference art simply gives you an idea of what you're making. If you have an actual shape to follow, a guideline to make your model, it'll turn out a lot better. However, this doesn't mean you can't make new things up as you go along (which I do all the time). It just means that you need to start with a clear idea of what it is you're going to be creating.

Your reference can be anything at all. Photos work great, but if it's something you can't get a picture of, a simple sketch will help you work out what it's generally supposed to look like. Let's learn how to use sketches in the next section.

For the mushroom, you'll just use a simple sketch. Feel free to look up some additional references if you need a better idea of what a mushroom looks like.

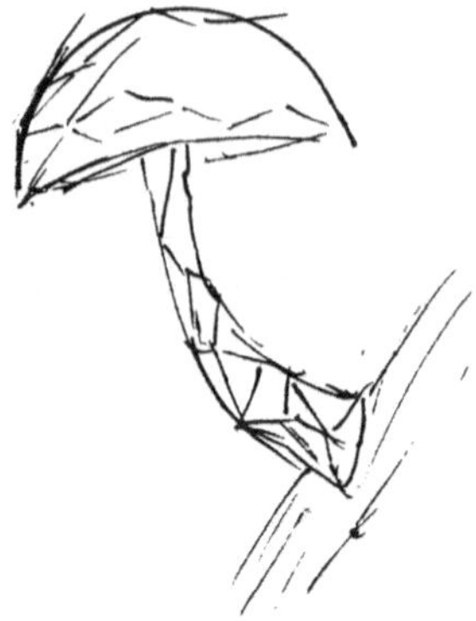

Figure 5.1 – The rough mushroom sketch (made on a sticky note)

Of course, whenever possible, it helps a lot to look at the real-life version of your subject. This is especially true for more complex subjects. However, since our subject is simple, a sketch will work just fine.

It's possible to import your reference into Blender so that you can look at it as you build your model. However, ours is so simple that we won't need to do that. The reference is just here to give us an idea of what it is we're creating.

Now that we have our reference, the next step is to block out the model with basic shapes.

Working from basic shapes

With 3D modeling, it's a good idea to start simple. This lets you work out the basic shape of your model without having to worry about the details.

The shape you start from is a matter of opinion. Most shapes can be made into other shapes, but sometimes, starting with the right primitive shape can be a timesaver.

It's *possible* to start from any shape, but that's not always the best option. You want to start out with a shape that's similar to the thing you're trying to make. That way, you have to do as little work as possible.

So, try to choose a primitive shape that makes sense for whatever it is you're making.

In this case, it makes a lot of sense to start from a cylinder, since the mushroom you're making is mostly round.

So, let's begin!

Creating the mushroom top

First, have a good look at the reference sketch (or make your own) so that you know what you're making. Next, open up a new Blender file:

1. First, delete all the default objects. Simply press *A* to select everything and then *X* to delete it all.
2. Next, add a new cylinder. Press *Shift* + *A* to open the **Add** menu, navigate to the **Mesh** section, and choose **Cylinder**.
3. Before you do anything else, you need to tweak the settings in the **Operator** menu (this menu shows you settings related to the last command you ran: Open up the menu and change the **Vertices** setting from 32 to just 8.

Now, our cylinder is much blockier. This will help create the low poly look we're going for (see *Figure 5.2*).

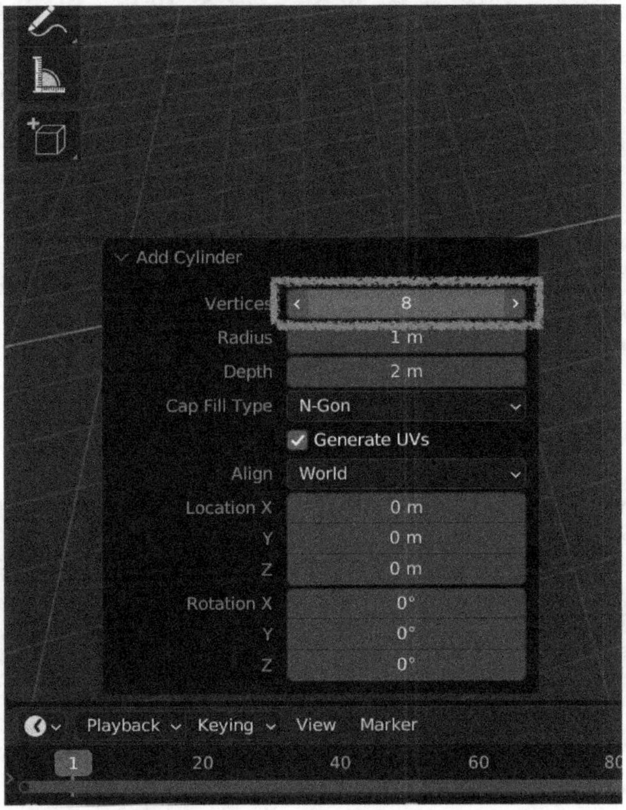

Figure 5.2 – Setting Vertices to 8 for a simple cylinder

Now that we have a mesh to start from, we'll create the top of the mushroom. But first, let's name our object:

1. Select the object, press *F2* (*Fn* + *F2* on a Mac), and type `Mushroom` into the `Object Name` box (see *Figure 5.3*).

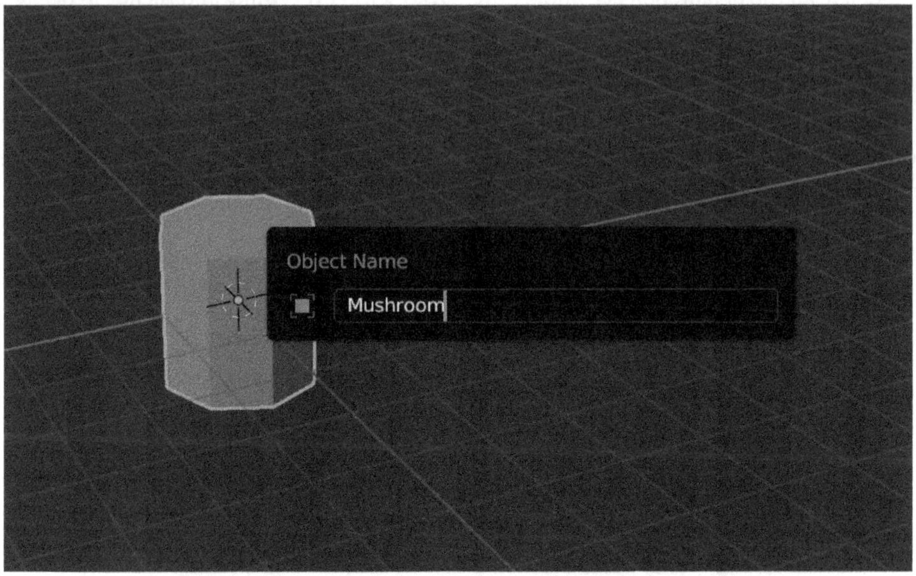

Figure 5.3 – Renaming the cylinder

2. With the `Mushroom` cylinder selected, press *Tab* to enter **Edit Mode**.
3. Make sure **Selection Mode** is set to **Face Select**.

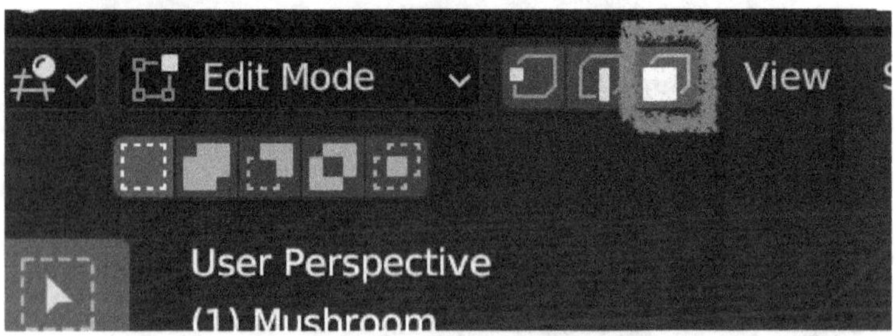

Figure 5.4 – Face Select Mode

4. Now, select the top face of the cylinder, press *S*, and scale it down to taper the cylinder. You should get something like this:

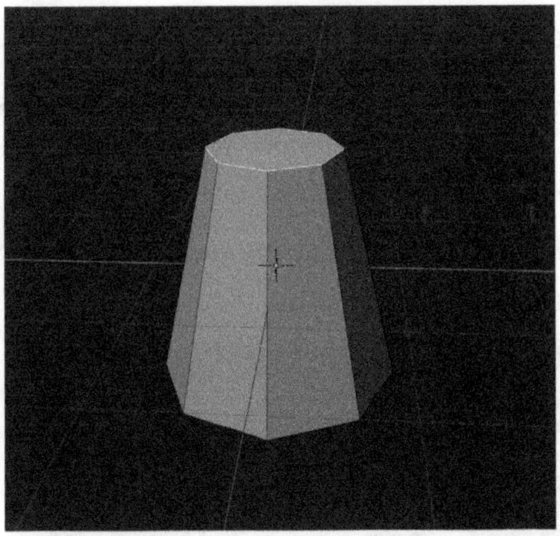

Figure 5.5 – Scaling the top face

5. Select the bottom face, and scale it a little bigger to make the taper even more pronounced, as shown in *Figure 5.6*.

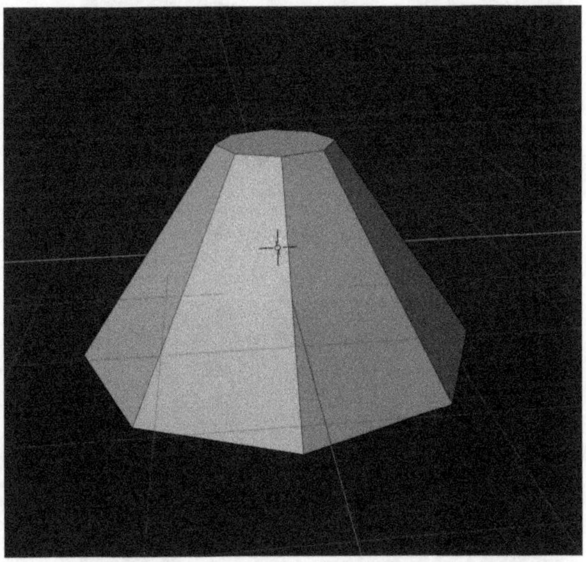

Figure 5.6 – Scaling up the bottom face

Now, you have a rough mushroom top.

Building the mushroom stem

Next, you need the mushroom stem. You could create this part by adding another cylinder, but it'll be simpler to extrude it out of our existing mushroom top. Before you can do that, though, you need to *hollow out* the mushroom top. Let's see how:

1. Press *Tab* to return to **Edit Mode**, and make sure you're still in **Face Select** mode.
2. Select the bottom face of the mushroom and press *I* to inset it. Do so just a little bit (see *Figure 5.7*).

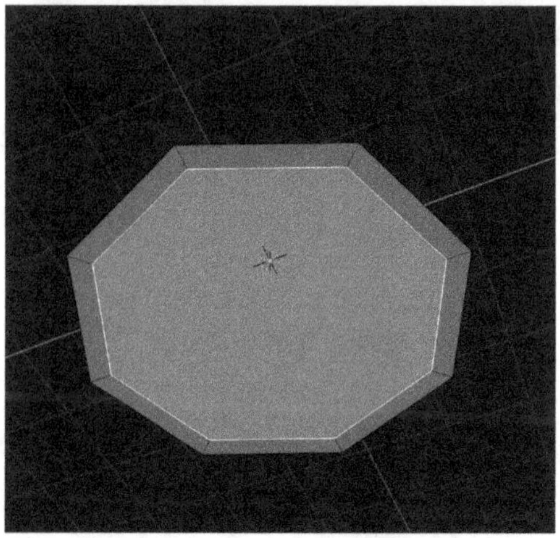

Figure 5.7 – Insetting the bottom

3. Press *E* to use the **Extrude** tool, and then extrude your selection inward, into the mushroom top. Your result will look like this:

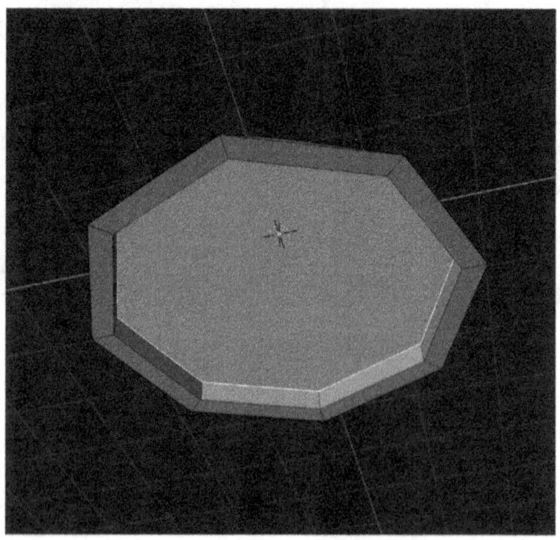

Figure 5.8 – Extruding inward

4. Now, press *3* for the **Right** view.
5. Press *Alt* + *Z* to change to **X-Ray** mode, and use *G* and *S* to position and scale the face you just extruded. The goal is to get something like this:

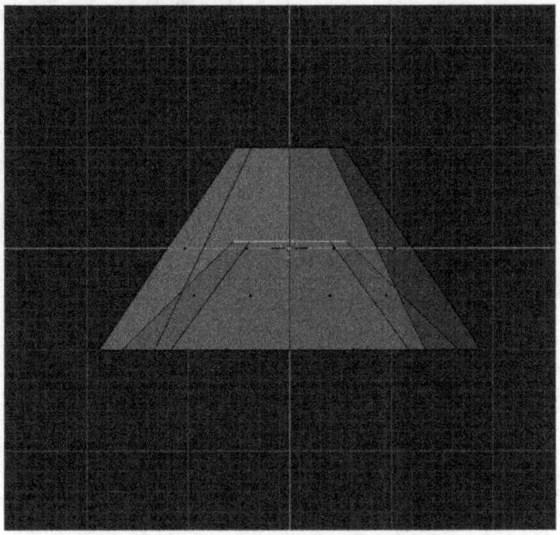

Figure 5.9 – The Front view, in X-Ray mode – scaling and positioning the extruded face

Now that the mushroom top is finished, you can extrude the stem. Make sure you're in the **Right** view or the **Front** view for these steps:

1. Press *E* to extrude the face again, and move it downward. Scale it down slightly. This will create a thinner part of the stem, which is more interesting than a totally straight, even stem.

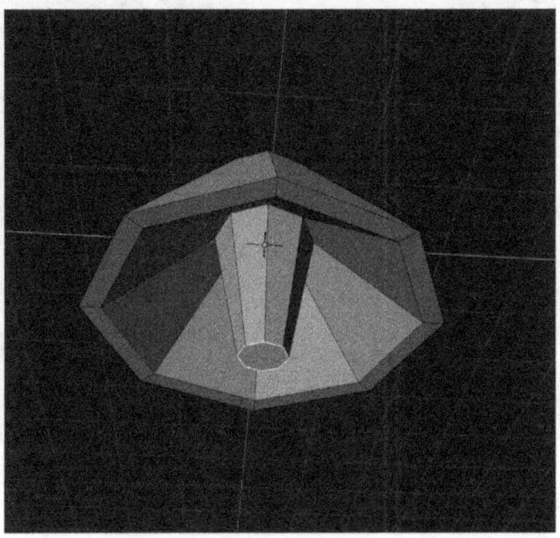

Figure 5.10 – Extruding the start of the stem from the middle

2. Press *E* again and extrude the rest of the stem.

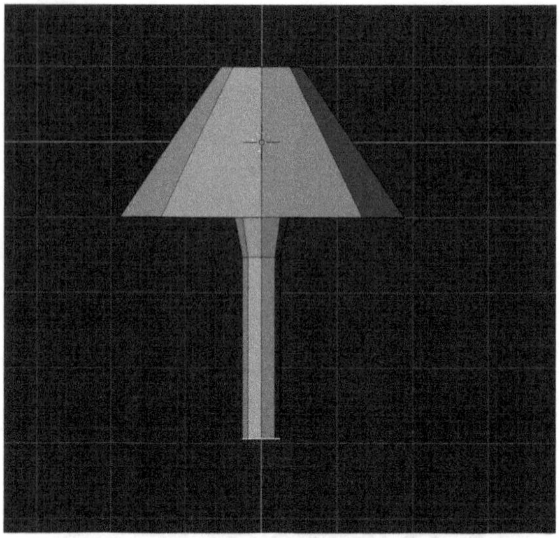

Figure 5.11 – Extruding the full stem

3. Press *S* to scale the bottom face so that it tapers outward again.

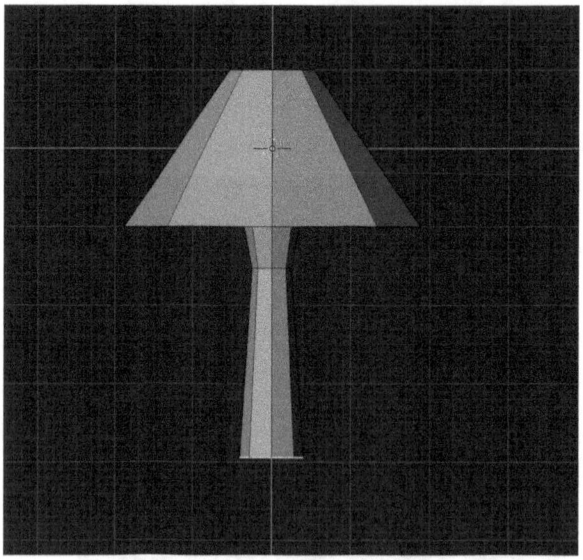

Figure 5.12 – Scaling the bottom of the stem to taper it

Now, we have a rough shape for the mushroom. Next, we'll work on making it a bit more detailed.

Adding details to the mushroom top

Now, you have a very crude blob that looks something like a mushroom. It's time to add some more detail to the top so that it looks a little more curved. To do that, you're going to use the **Loop Cut** tool. The **Loop Cut** tool lets you add new loops of edges around your model:

1. In **Edit Mode**, press *Ctrl* + *R* to activate the **Loop Cut** tool. Hover your mouse over the mushroom until you see a yellow line across the top of it.

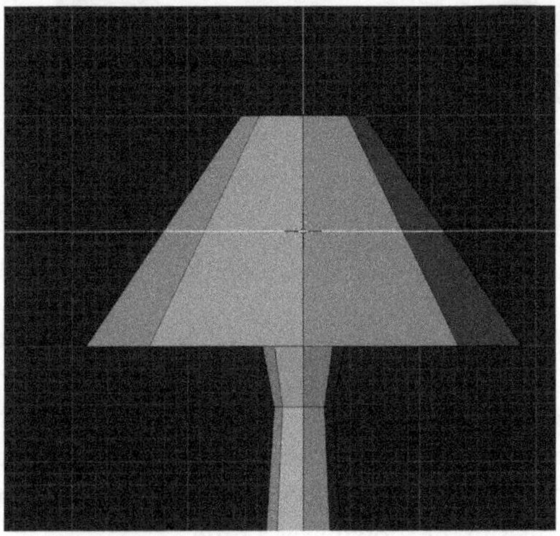

Figure 5.13 – The yellow selection ring shown by the Loop Cut tool

2. Scroll up and down to adjust the number of cuts. A number around 3 or 4 will be best for this, since we're keeping the model simple.

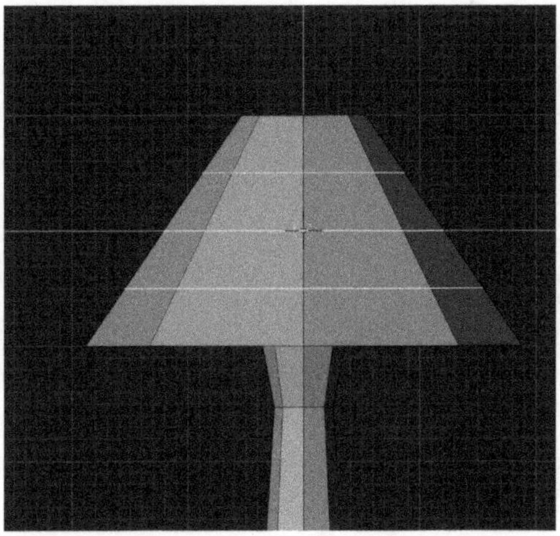

Figure 5.14 – Scroll to adjust the number of cuts

3. Click once to confirm the cut. You will then enter the **Slide** phase. Right-click to cancel the slide so that the cuts are left in the default, centered position.

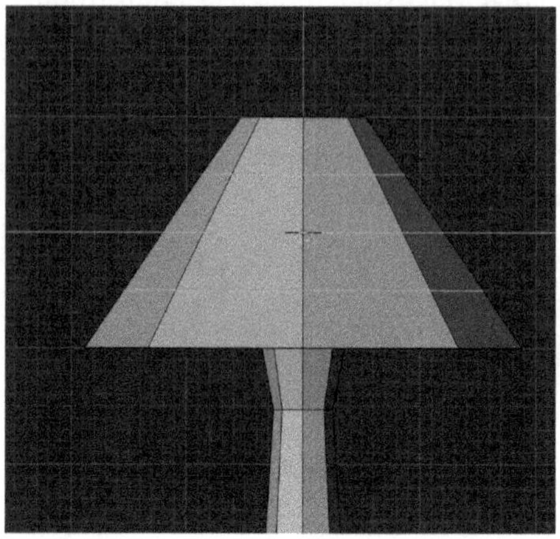

Figure 5.15 – Click to confirm the cuts, and then right-click to leave them in place

4. Now that you have edge loops, you can shape the mushroom. Switch to **Edge Select** mode and press *Alt* + *click* on an edge to select the entire edge loop. This might take a few tries. Try *Alt* + *click* on different edges if you can't get the loop the first time. Alternatively, you can just press *Shift* + *select all* of the edges in the loop one at a time.
5. Scale the edge loop you've selected using *S*.

You'll do this to each edge loop in turn to form the curved mushroom shape. Just select each edge loop (*Alt* + *click*), and use *S* to scale it bigger or smaller. It might help to use the **Right** view (*3*) as you work. Here's what you want to end up with:

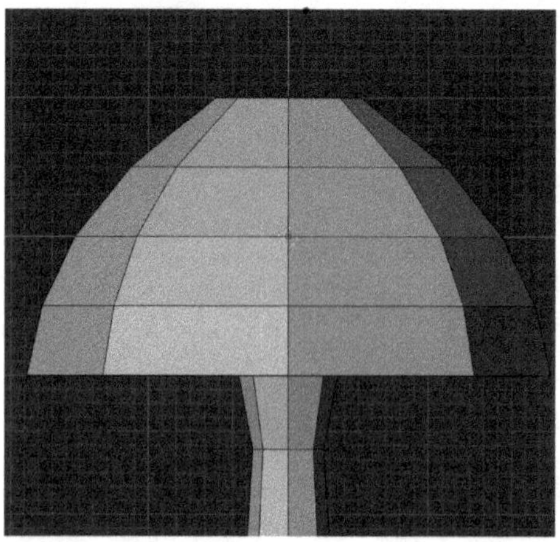

Figure 5.16 – The rounded mushroom top

Now, you have a curved mushroom top!

Adding details to the stem

In our reference, the stem is slightly curved. This adds a really neat look to the mushroom. To accomplish this, we'll do two things – first, we'll add more edge loops along the stem so that it can be bent. Then, we'll use the trusty *R* (rotate) and *G* (grab/move) keys to give the stem a bit of a curve by moving the new edges around:

1. Press *Ctrl* + *R* to activate the **Loop Cut** tool.
2. Move your mouse around until you see a yellow line around the stem. This is where the cut will happen.
3. Scroll (with two fingers on a trackpad or with a mouse wheel) to change the number of cuts. Four or five cuts should work fine.
4. Click once to confirm the cut and start sliding your new edges, and then right-click to cancel the slide (this will keep the new edge loops).

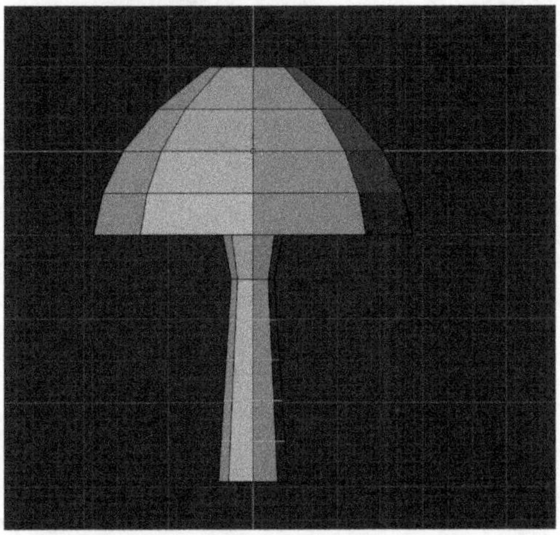

Figure 5.17 – Loop cuts for the stem

5. Make sure you're still in the **X-Ray** view mode (*Alt* + *Z*), and press *3* to enter the **Right** view.
6. Press *Alt* + *click* the bottom edge loop to select it with **Loop Select** (since you're in **X-Ray** mode, you can also click + drag across the edges to select them).
7. Now, press *G* to move the edge loop around and *R* to rotate it. Place it off to the side a little.

Now, you need to adjust the rest of the edge loops on the stem. This will take some time, but it's not too bad. Simply go one loop at a time, moving and rotating them (or scaling too) to your preference.

There's also a quicker way to do this – press *O* to enable **Proportional Editing**. **Proportional Editing** lets you perform normal operations, such as rotating and scaling, but it affects everything within a certain radius instead of just the selected items. In this case, you'll use it for rotation. Once you've enabled **Proportional Editing**, you can start an operation as you normally would (in this case, you want to rotate, so select the very end of the stem in **Face Select** mode, go to the **Side** view, and then press *R* to rotate). You can scroll to adjust the **Proportional Editing** radius, which controls what is affected.

Whether you do this task manually or with **Proportional Editing**, you want to end up with a shape similar to this:

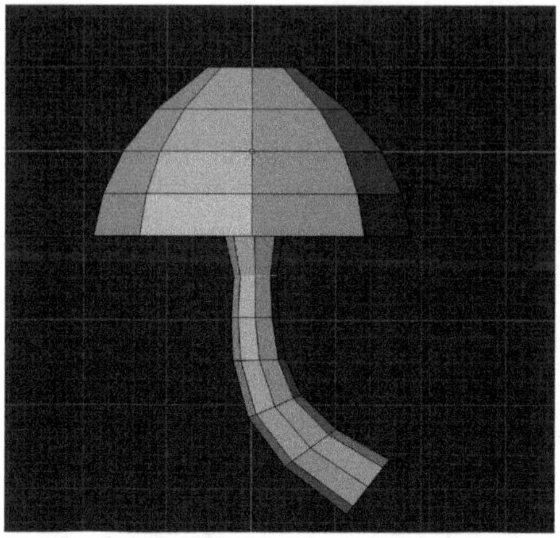

Figure 5.18 – The curved stem

It'll look nice if you rotate the mushroom top a bit, to:

1. Switch to **Vertex Selection** mode (still with **X-Ray** on, in the **Right** view), and click and drag across the mushroom top to select it all.
2. Rotate the top slightly.

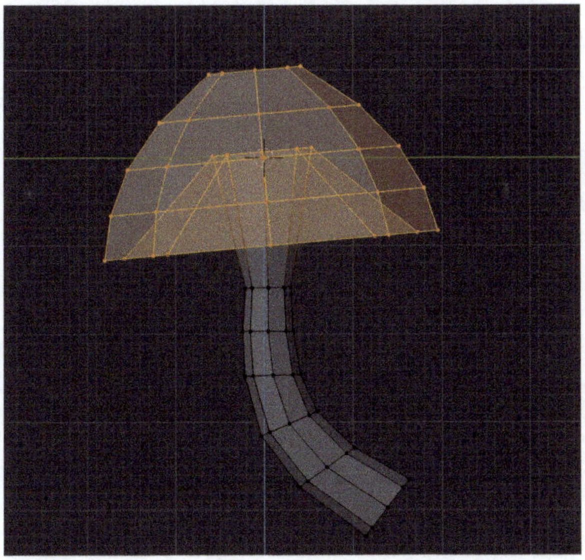

Figure 5.19 – Selecting the top in X-Ray and rotating it

Now, we have the complete basic shape of the mushroom. However, it's still made of very even, regular polygons. In the next section, you'll learn how to tweak your model to make it look more interesting.

Fine-tuning the model

Our model could be considered done. It checks all the boxes – it's mushroom-shaped and low poly. However, it's still a very blocky, regular shape. It's boring and uninteresting to look at.

We can take it a step further with something I call *artistic modeling*.

We'll mess with the way the faces are positioned, how they're shaped, and how many vertices they have. We'll achieve a slightly more visually pleasing look, or at least something a little more interesting, using these techniques.

The first step is *triangulation*. But first, you need to learn some terminology.

Faces have different names depending on how many sides they have:

- A three-sided face is often called a *triangle*, or just a *tri*
- A face with four sides is known as a *quad*

- All faces with five or more sides are simply called *n-gons* (the word comes from *polygon*, with *poly* replaced by *n*, which means an arbitrary number of sides)

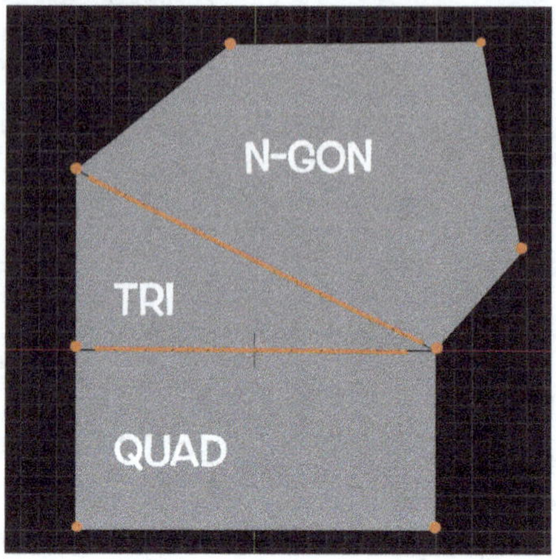

Figure 5.20 – Types of faces

Each type of face has different pros and cons. The *n*-gons can only be used when they are perfectly flat – they don't bend well. Quads are ideal for a subdivision workflow, which involves subdividing a model further at render time.

The thing to remember about both quads and *n*-gons is that it's important to keep them flat. If they're bent, Blender won't know how to display them because it's a physical impossibility.

Triangles are often used in extremely high-poly meshes for 3D sculpting, and mesh-generating tools such as photogrammetry software commonly output meshes made of triangles.

Triangles have the advantage that they cannot be bent. You can't skew or bend a triangle – it's the most basic face shape possible. This makes triangles very well-suited for low poly models. They are also the simplest possible shape, which adds to the simple effect of your art.

I like to use a combination of tris and quads on my low poly models. It's always different, though, and it really comes down to artistic choice. As you get better at low poly, you'll start to see how you can use geometry and face sizes and shapes to accentuate or highlight different parts of your model, or add or remove details.

However, before we turn our quads into triangles, let's randomize our mesh a little so that it looks less regular. Don't overdo this – really:

> **Note**
>
> This isn't something you'll always want to do to a low poly model. This randomizing/messing-up step is only something you do when you're trying to create an artistic low poly style, as we are here. If you were making low poly models for games or animations, you wouldn't want to mess it up like this – you would want it to be all quads. However, for an artistic scene, I think this slightly messed-up style looks really nice. If you're making models professionally or for anything other than an artistic scene, don't do this.

1. First, make sure you're in **Edit Mode**. It helps to be in **X-Ray** view for this step. You can turn it on with *Alt* + *X*.
2. Make sure you're in **Edge Select** mode. Select any edge loop on your mushroom mesh.
3. Now, pan and orbit around until the selected edge loop is roughly parallel to the viewport, as shown in the following figure, so that you're looking *through* the edge loop. This will make it easier to rotate.

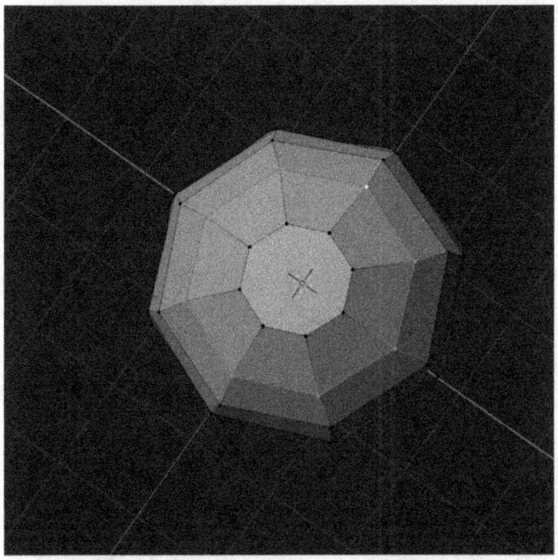

Figure 5.21 – Randomly rotating a loop

4. Now, press *R* to rotate the selected loop – just slightly, but enough to add a little randomness.

Do this to a few more edge loops. The goal is just to add just a little randomness while keeping the shape. Here's what you should end up with:

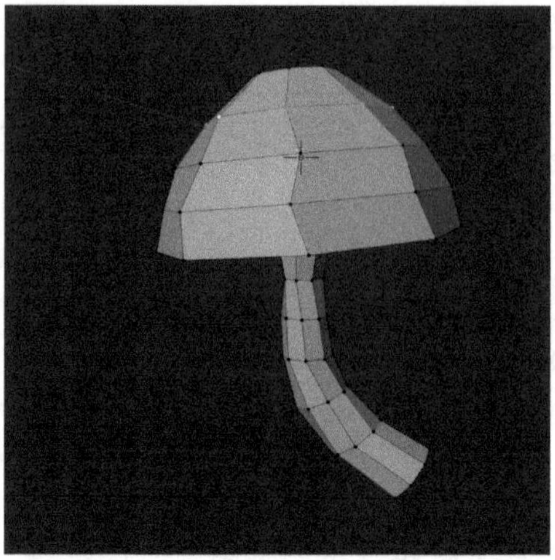

Figure 5.22 – One loop rotated randomly

Now, switch to **Face Select** mode and turn off **X-Ray** (*Alt* + *X*). You're going to do the same rotation trick but with some random faces. This helps break up the even pattern a bit more. Here's what your mushroom should look like after this:

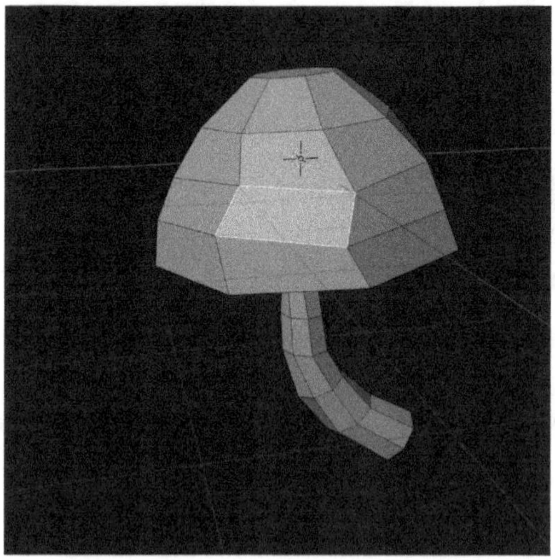

Figure 5.23 – Randomly rotating a face

Now, you have added some randomness to your mesh. Let's now turn all of our quads into triangles. Press *A* to select everything, and then press *Ctrl* + *T* to *triangulate*. This breaks every selected face up into triangular ones.

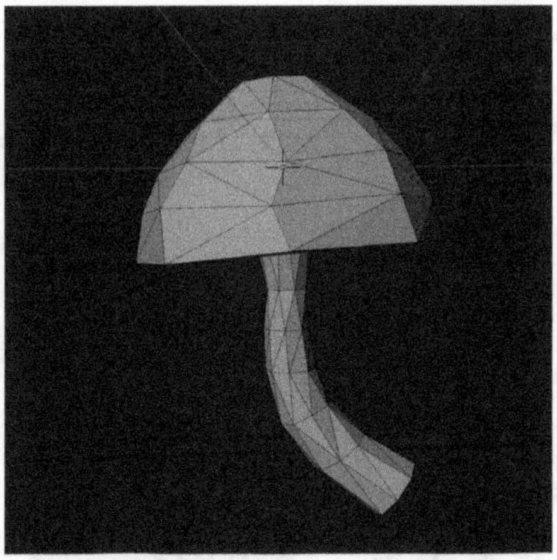

Figure 5.24 – Complete triangulation

Now, our model is very triangular-looking. You want to keep most of the triangles, but you can make things more interesting by joining a few of them together to make bigger faces here and there.

Simply select two triangles and press *F* to join them into one quad. It's best to join ones that are on the same plane (i.e., flat in relation to each other) so that you don't have any bent quads.

If you want to un-join a quad, you can switch to **Vertex Select** mode, select two vertices, and press *J* to add a new edge to connect them to each other (splitting a quad into two triangles).

Here's what I have after joining some triangles back together to form quads:

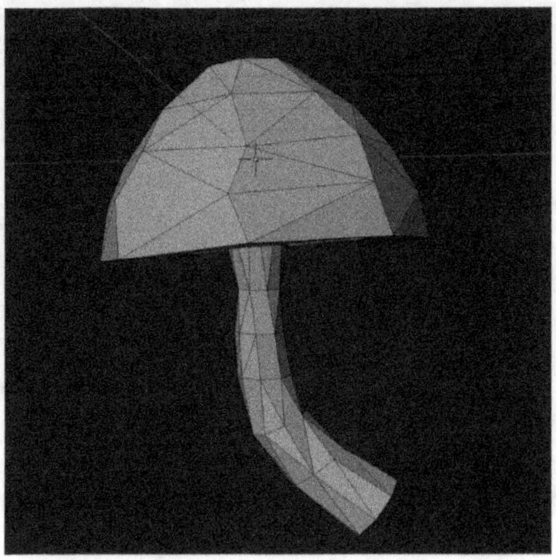

Figure 5.25 – Joining a few triangles back into quads for variation

There's another neat thing you can do to combine vertices – switch to **Vertex Select** mode, select two vertices, press *M* for the **Merge** tool, and pick **At center**.

Now, those two vertices are one. This is just another way to add some randomness. Remember that you shouldn't do this everywhere, just here and there, to keep things interesting. Here's where I joined some vertices:

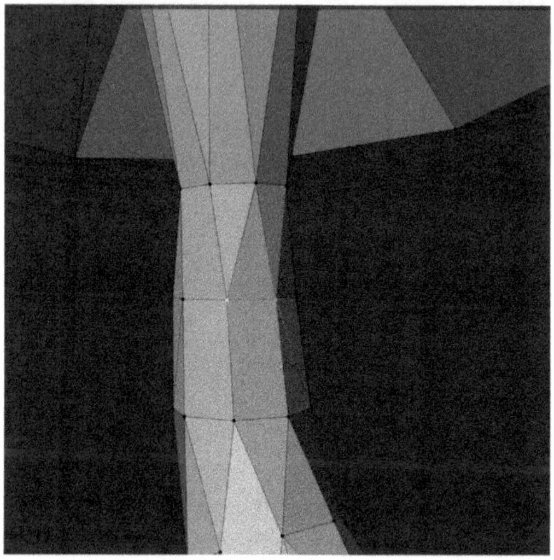

Figure 5.26 – Before the merge

And after we merge, we get something like this:

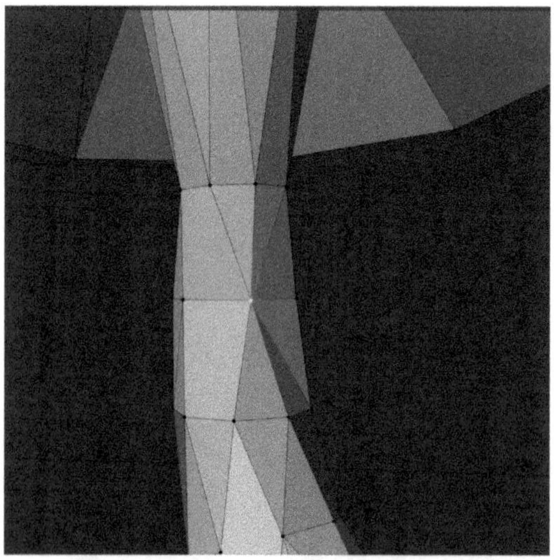

Figure 5.27 – After the merge

You've quickly learned a lot of new techniques and great ways to add a little bit of variation to your mesh, which really helps with the low poly look.

However, make sure you don't overdo this. A randomization technique like this is best used subtly, in moderation. Also, sometimes, you won't even need to do any of this – you might already like the way your low poly model looks. It's an artistic choice and is up to you, depending on what you like.

These are just options.

Here's the final mushroom:

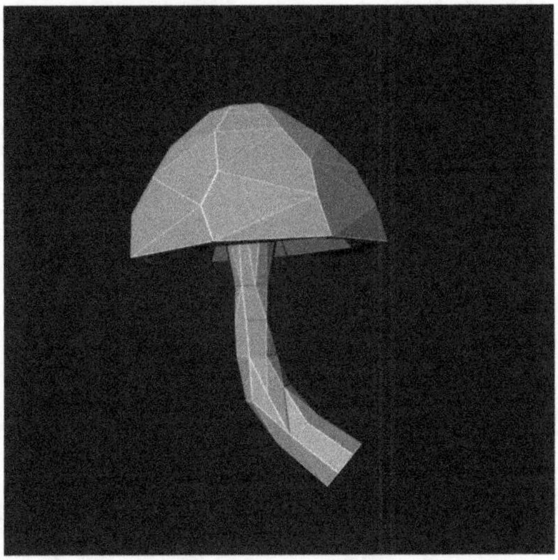

Figure 5.28 – The final mushroom

Great work!

Summary

In this chapter, you built your second low poly model – a mushroom. You learned what reference art is and why you should use it. You learned how to start your model from simple shapes. You learned how to turn faces into triangles for artistic effect, too.

You also learned how to make artistic adjustments to a model for the ultimate low poly look.

If you only remember one thing from this chapter, remember that it's always extremely helpful to start working from a reference.

In the next chapter, you'll learn what materials are and how you can use them to add color to your mushroom.

6
Understanding Materials and Shading

Tired of everything you make being drab and gray?

In this chapter, you'll learn how to add color to your models using materials. First, you'll learn about materials and how they work. Then you'll learn about a new workspace: the **Shading** tab. You'll learn how easy it is to make your own materials, and you'll set up materials for your mushroom and your tree.

Here's what you'll be able to do by the end of this chapter:

- Create materials for your models
- Edit materials to get the colors you want
- Understand the basics of the **Shader Editor**
- Add multiple materials to one model

You'll start by learning what a material is, and what it does. Then you'll move on to creating your own materials.

Understanding materials

Before you can understand materials, you need to learn a little about how 3D rendering works in Blender. The whole process is done by a complicated piece of software called a **rendering engine**. There are two different rendering engines in Blender: one is called **Eevee**, and the other is called **Cycles**.

The rendering engine does all the hard work of rendering. It calculates what your 3D scene looks like from the point of view of a camera. It simulates the effect of light emitting from a source (like the default one we always delete) and calculates how that light would bounce around the scene, what it would illuminate, and what would remain in shadow.

But light reacts differently with different objects. For example, light hitting a smooth, shiny mirror reflects perfectly off of it, but light hitting a piece of stone reflects differently since the stone is rough. See *Figure 6.1* to know the difference:

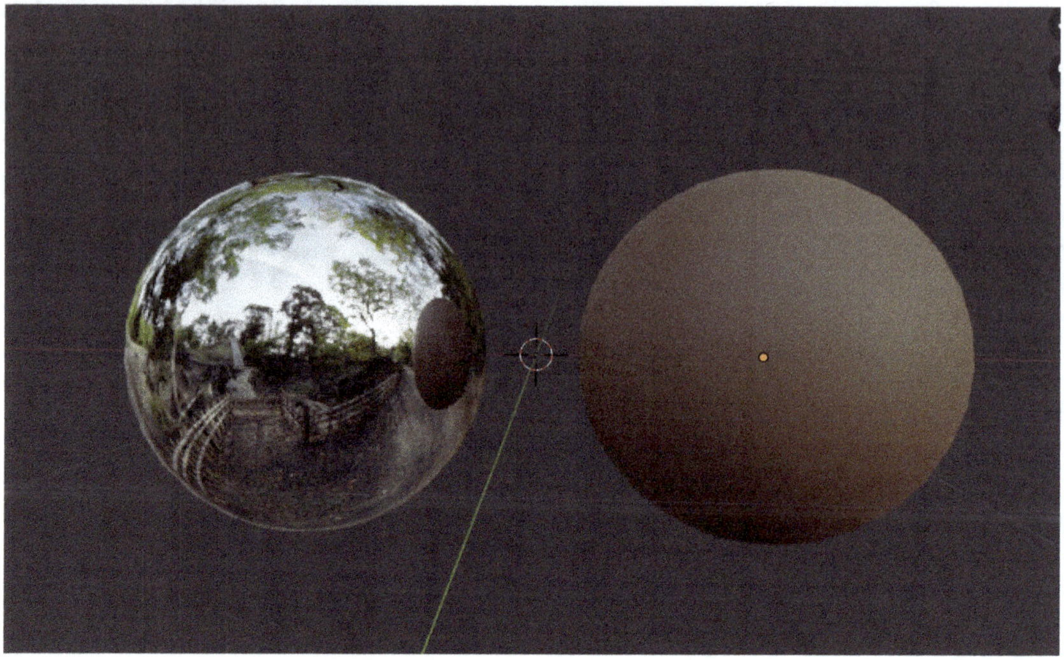

Figure 6.1: Shiny versus rough material

This is where materials come in. Materials decide how light is going to react with a particular object.

The material defines all the physical properties of an object's surface. An object's material controls the color of the object, how rough the object is, how shiny it is, how metallic it looks, whether it is transparent, and more.

Since materials are so important, you'll want to know what the look is that you're going for. If you're going to create a rock material, for example, you should go outside and pick up a rock. Is it rough? Shiny? When you're creating more complex materials, referencing real objects like this is important. In this book, we're only going to deal with extremely simple materials, so references aren't as important as they would be if you were trying to create realistic materials.

Materials don't show up in the viewport by default. You need to have lights set up in your scene for the rendering engine to be able to render your materials because you can't see anything without light.

In the last part of this book, you'll learn how to add your own lighting.

For now, Blender provides a quick solution to this problem: **Material Preview** mode. This lets you view your materials using the Eevee rendering engine with a bunch of convenient, default lighting setups. You can't create final renders in **Material Preview** mode, but it's great for developing your object's material.

This all happens in the **Shading** workspace, where you'll use the **Shader Editor** program to create your materials.

The Shader Editor

In this section, you'll learn how the Shading workspace is laid out and what the different parts are. You'll make your first material and understand the gritty details of how materials work. You'll also create your first material.

The Shading workspace is where you'll be working in this chapter. *Shading* is the process of creating and working on materials for objects.

Open up a new Blender file and switch to the Shading workspace by clicking the **Shading** tab at the top of the window.

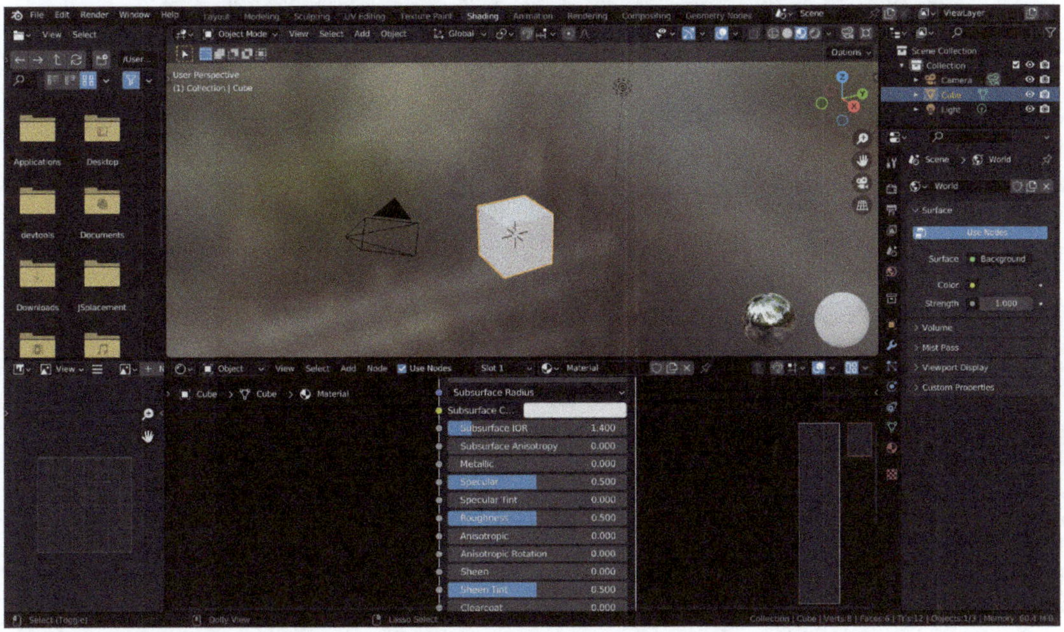

Figure 6.2: The Shading tab

The Shading workspace is divided into six parts. In the middle is the 3D viewport. It looks a little different than usual since it's set to **Material Preview** mode. Below the 3D viewport is the **Shader Editor**. This is where you'll use building blocks called **Shader nodes** to build materials.

On the right-hand side, there are the **Outliner** and **Properties** functions as usual. It's much easier to have them here than to have to switch back to the **Layout** workspace whenever you need them.

On the left-hand side, there are two areas: an **Image Editor** for viewing images, and a file browser. We're not going to use these areas for anything at all, so it's best to get them out of the way. Hover over the upper-left corner of the 3D viewport until your cursor becomes a little cross, then drag your mouse toward the file browser to join the areas.

Get rid of the Image Editor area by joining the **Shader Editor** area into it.

Now we're ready for action!

The **Shader Editor** is one of Blender's node editors. In a node editor, you connect blocks called nodes to create things. In this case, you're creating materials.

There's already a default material open in the editor. You can see its name at the top, in the **data-block** menu.

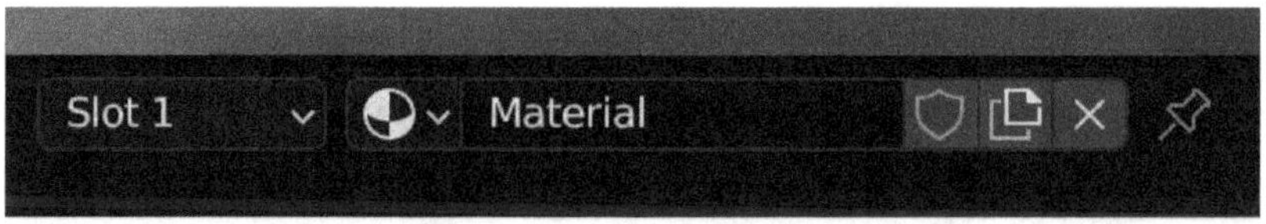

Figure 6.3: The data-block menu at the top of the Shader node window

The buttons beside the material's name are also important. The drop-down list beside the name lets you choose which material is currently assigned to this object. When you open the drop-down menu, you see a list of all the materials in the scene, and you can choose any of them.

Any object can use any material, regardless of how many other objects are already using that material. It's perfectly fine for many objects to have the exact same material assigned to them. When you edit a material that is assigned to multiple objects, it is updated across all of those objects.

The **X** button removes the material (unassigns it) from the object. If a material exists but is not assigned to any object, it is said to have 0 *users*. Any material in the dropdown with a **0** beside its name has 0 users. This can be dangerous because when you close your Blender file, any materials with 0 users will be deleted.

Sounds annoying, right?

There's a very simple solution. It's the little **shield** button beside the material name (see *Figure 6.3*). This button is called the **Fake User** button. It assigns a fake user to the material so that it can never have 0 users and won't be deleted. When you make a material in Blender, it's a good idea to turn this on (unless you *want* the material to get deleted).

The button beside the **Fake User** button (see the stacked file icon in *Figure 6.3*) is the **Duplicate** button. It simply makes a copy of the current material and assigns it in place of the current one. This is very useful when you need multiple versions of a material. For example, if you had a shiny copper material and you needed a shiny gold material, you could simply duplicate the copper material and change the color to make your gold.

One last thing: the **Pin** button.

The **Shader Editor** changes to show the materials and settings for whichever object is currently selected. But what if you don't want that? What if you need to select a different object and still see this object's material?

Just click the **Pin** button to the right of the material name (*Figure 6.3*). It *pins* the current material into the editor. Changing the selection won't change what's shown. Just don't forget to unpin it when you're done so the node editor goes back to showing nodes for the selected object.

Navigation in the **Shader Editor** is very similar to navigating the **3D viewport**. Scroll on your trackpad (or use the middle mouse button) to pan. To zoom in and out, just pinch in and out on your trackpad (or hold *Ctrl* and scroll.) On a mouse, just use the scroll wheel.

It's all the same as the viewport.

Next, you'll learn about the default nodes you see in the editor. Most importantly, there's the big one: **Principled BSDF.**

Nodes in Blender

Nodes are like *pieces* of materials. They're simple, modular building blocks that each perform a specific function. You connect their sockets to build more complicated materials. There are two default nodes in the **Shader Editor**: **Principled Shader** and **Material Output**. For simple projects, like the ones in this book, you won't need any more nodes than these.

Let's start with the **Principled BSDF** node.

The Principled BSDF node

The **Principled BSDF** node is the most useful shader node. **BSDF** stands for the **Bidirectional Scattering Distribution Function**, and it's a *program that calculates how light bounces off a surface.*

It's not too hard to see why BSDF exists. Shader nodes are the only kind of node you can connect to the **Surface** output.

The **Principled BSDF** node has a lot of inputs, as shown in *Figure 6.4*:

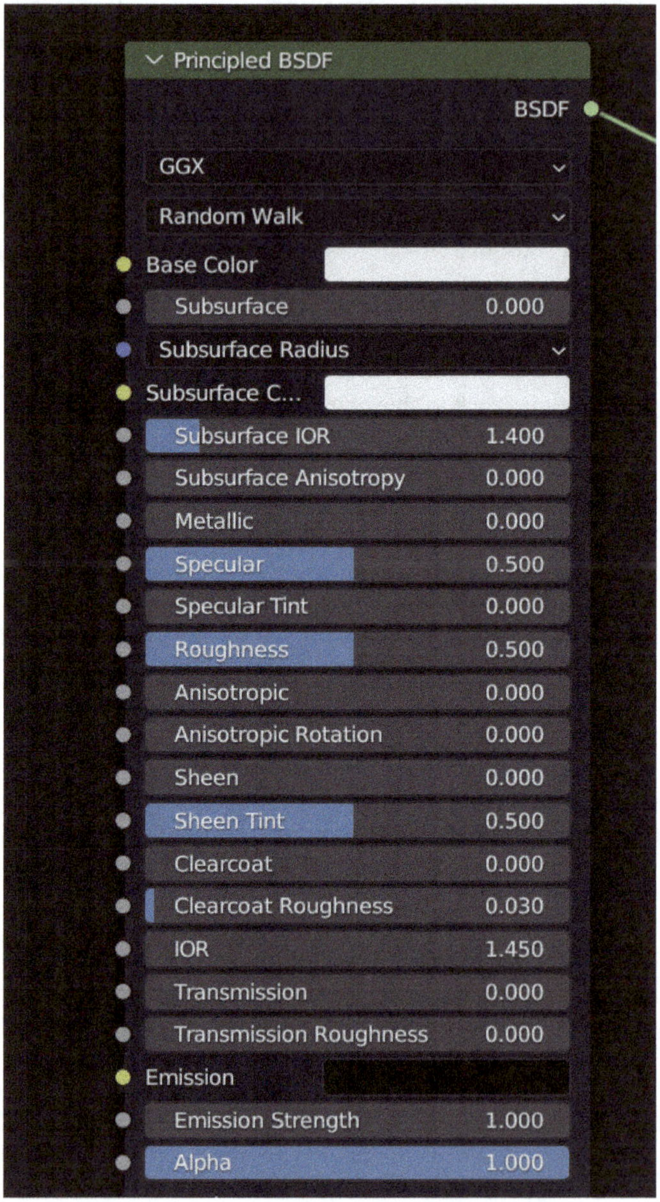

Figure 6.4: The Principled BSDF node

However, most of the time, you'll only be focusing on the following three inputs:

- **Base Color**: The main color of your object.
- **Metallic**: This controls how *metallic* (made of metal) your material is. A value of `1` means that the material is fully metallic, such as gold, and a value of `0` means that the material is not metallic at all, such as plastic.
- **Roughness**: This value controls how shiny the material is. A value of `0` makes it perfectly shiny, like a mirror, and a value of `1` means it's perfectly rough.

Using different combinations of these three inputs, you can make your material look like a *lot* of different things. Here are a few different combinations you can try:

- **Make a mirror**: Base color black, metallic `1`, roughness `0`
- **Make shiny plastic**: Metallic `0`, roughness `0`
- **Make gold**: Base color orangey-yellow, metallic `1`, roughness `0-0.1`

As shown in *Figure 6.4*, the little dots on the side of each node are called **sockets**. There are input sockets on the left-hand side of a node, and output sockets on the right-hand side.

To connect two nodes, you click and drag an output socket from one node to an input socket on another.

The Material Output node

The **Material Output** node is always last in your material or **node tree**. It has three input sockets, but the most important is the first one: the **Surface** input.

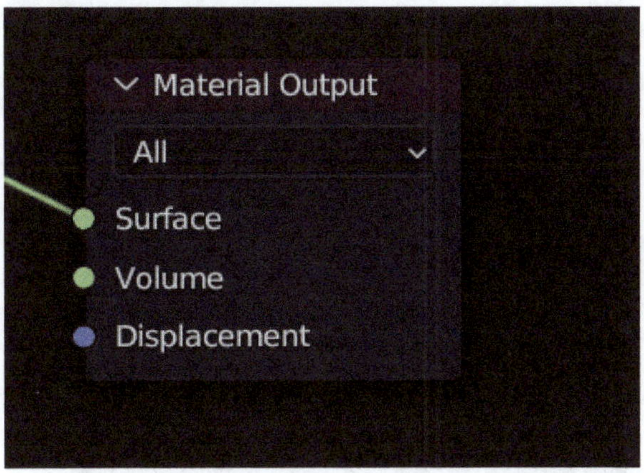

Figure 6.5: Material Output

This input is green, which means that you need to connect a shader to it. From there, the shader goes right out onto the object's surface.

A *shader* is a program that defines what the surface of an object looks like, and how each face is displayed at render time. In Blender, shaders are represented by nodes that are colored green in the **Shader Editor**.

As you've no doubt discovered, there are limitless possibilities. For now, we'll leave it at that, but there'll be more complex materials in later chapters of the book.

Next, you'll build the materials for your low-poly tree, the one you built back in *Chapter 3*.

Materials for the tree

Time to improve your boring gray tree!

Now that you know how materials work, this will be pretty simple:

1. First, find and open the `.blend` file where your tree is saved.
2. Now, select the leaves option. Switch to the **Shading** tab.
3. Click the **New** button at the top of the **Shader Editor** to make a new material. Name it `Leaves`. (If there is already a default material there, simply rename that one.)
4. Now we need to adjust the **Principled BSDF** node. First, change the **Base Color** setting to a nice leafy green.
5. Leave the **Metallic** value at its default of `0`, but raise **Roughness** to `0.7` or `0.8` so the leaves aren't too shiny.

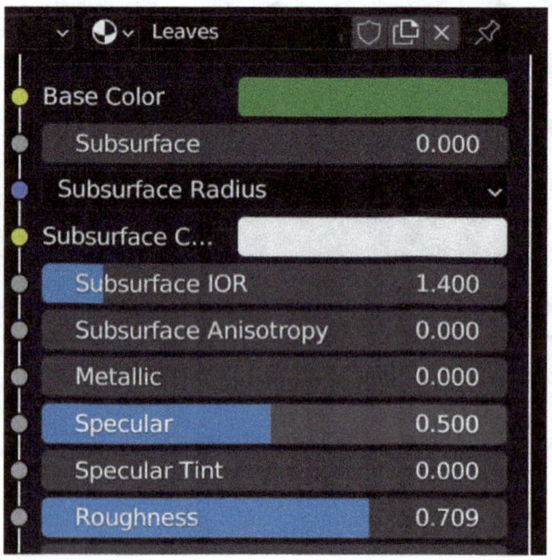

Figure 6.6: Node for the Leaves material

That's all for the `Leaves` material. Now we need to apply this material to the other leaf objects so all the leaves are the same color. This is easy:

1. Select any leaf object.
2. Click the material drop-down menu and choose your new `Leaves` material.

Now the `Leaves` material is assigned to that leaf object too. You can repeat this process for the other leaf objects. Just select one and assign the material. Select another, assign the material, and so forth.

Next up is the tree trunk. This will be simple:

1. Select the tree trunk.
2. If it already has a material assigned, we need to get rid of it. Press the **X** button beside the name of the current material (if there is a current material). This removes that material from the object.
3. Now click the **New** button to create a new material for the object. This will give you a new material with the default nodes ready to go again. Name the new material `Trunk`.
4. Again, this is not a complicated material. Change the **Base Color** setting to brown. Brown can be a little hard to find in the color picker, so simply slide the brightness slider down so all the colors are darker, then choose a brown color from the red/orange section.
5. Tweak the level of roughness. Tree bark isn't very shiny, so for our simple tree bark, something like `0.5` or `0.8` should work great.

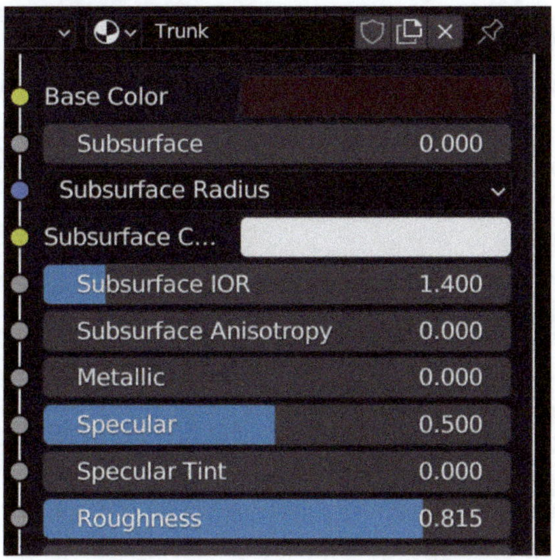

Figure 6.7: Node for the Trunk material

Now the tree's materials are complete! Great work.

Next, we'll set up materials for the mushroom (the one you made back in *Chapter 5*).

Materials for the mushroom

Creating materials for the mushroom will be a little more challenging than for the tree since the mushroom is a complete object and needs different materials on different parts of the object. You want to put a red material on the top of the mushroom and a different color on the stem.

Blender makes this possible using something called **material slots**. Each slot holds one material. An object can have as many slots as it needs.

Each slot is assigned to a set of faces. The slot's material will be applied to those faces.

For our exercise, our mushroom will have two slots. One slot will have a red material, and it'll be assigned to all of the faces that form the top of the mushroom. The second slot will be assigned to the stem part of the model, and it'll use a different material.

Open up the Blender file for the mushroom you built in *Chapter 5*.

First, we'll set up two different material slots on the mushroom. One slot will include the top of the mushroom, and the other slot will be the stem. Once you have those slots set up, you can assign a different material to each slot:

1. We'll start in the **Layout** tab.
2. Open the **Material** tab of the **Properties** panel. At the top, you'll see the slot list. By default, every object has just one slot, but you can create as many as you need.
3. Press the + button in the slot list to make two slots. Don't worry about which materials are in which slots yet; we're just creating the slots for now.

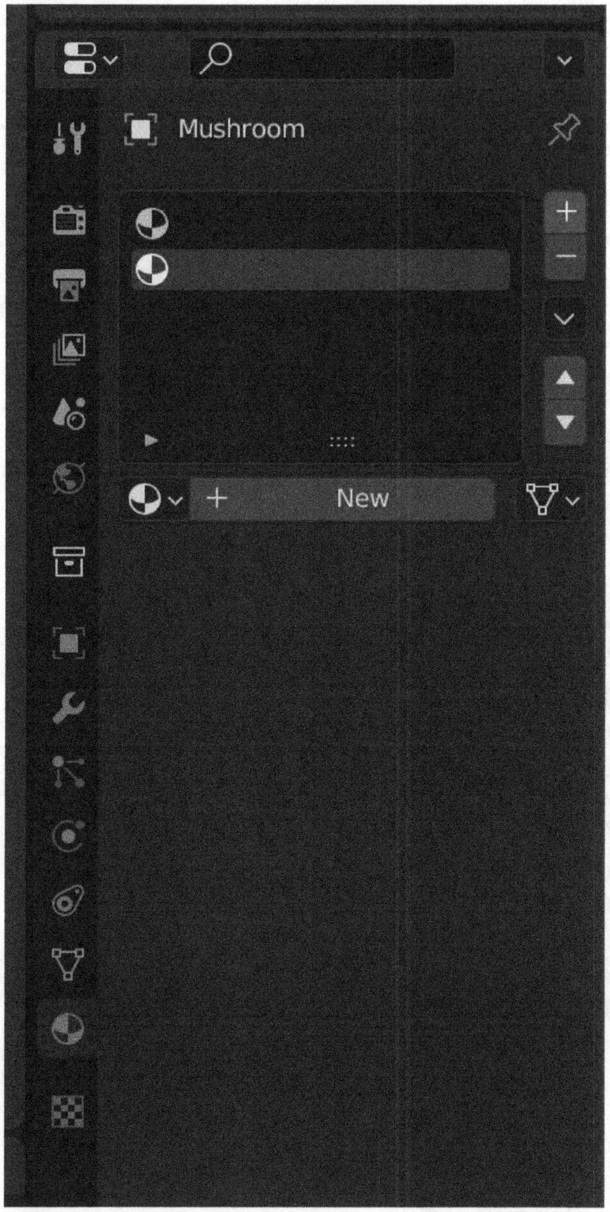

Figure 6.8: The Material Properties tab in the Properties panel

4. In the viewport, press *Tab* to enter **Edit** mode.
5. Change the selection mode to **Face**.
6. Now, select all of the faces on the model by pressing *A*.

7. In the **Material** panel on the side, select **Slot 1**.
8. Click the large **Assign** button under it to assign **Slot 1** to the selected faces. Now the entire mesh is assigned to **Slot 1** and the entire mesh is using one material. Next, you'll change some parts of the mesh to use a different material.
9. Now, press *Alt* + *A* or *A* + *A* to deselect everything.
10. Select all of the faces on the stem of the mushroom, so we can assign **Slot 2** to those. A quick way to do this would be to select the face on the bottom of the stem and then press *Ctrl* + on the keyboard to expand the selection. You'll still have to hold *Shift* and select/deselect a few faces to get it exact.

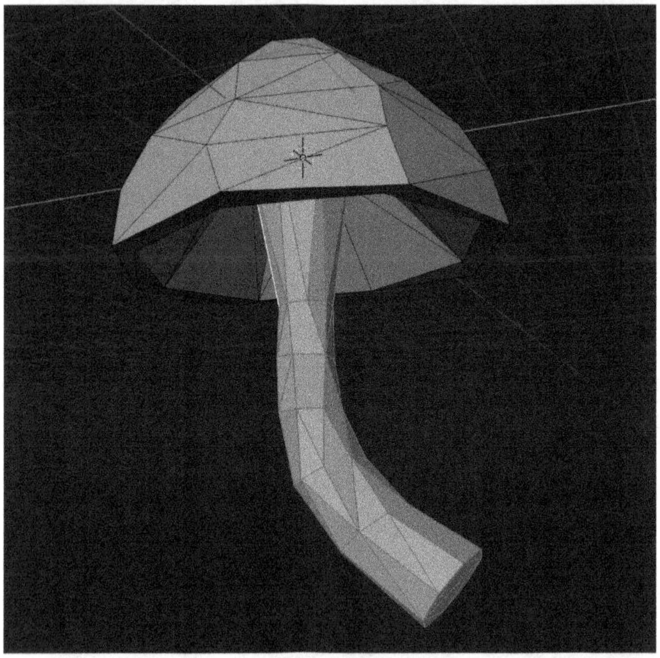

Figure 6.9: The stem, all selected

11. Now you have the entire stem selected. Select **Slot 2** and press **Assign**. This will assign all of the stem faces to **Slot 2**. They won't be assigned to **Slot 1** anymore.
12. Press *Tab* to get out of **Edit** mode.

Now the slots are done and ready for materials. All you have left to do is set up the two materials, one for each slot. You'll do that part in the **Shading** workspace. These materials will be simple, just like the ones for the tree:

1. Switch to the **Shading** tab.
2. Select the mushroom.
3. To work with the slots in the node editor, you'll notice that there's a **Slot** menu at the top, next to the material name. You can switch this to whichever slot you'd like to work on.
4. Make sure the **Slot** menu is set to **Slot 1**, and click the **New Material** button. Name the material `Mushroom Top`. (If there's a default material there, just rename it.)
5. Now adjust the material. Make it red and maybe a bit rougher.

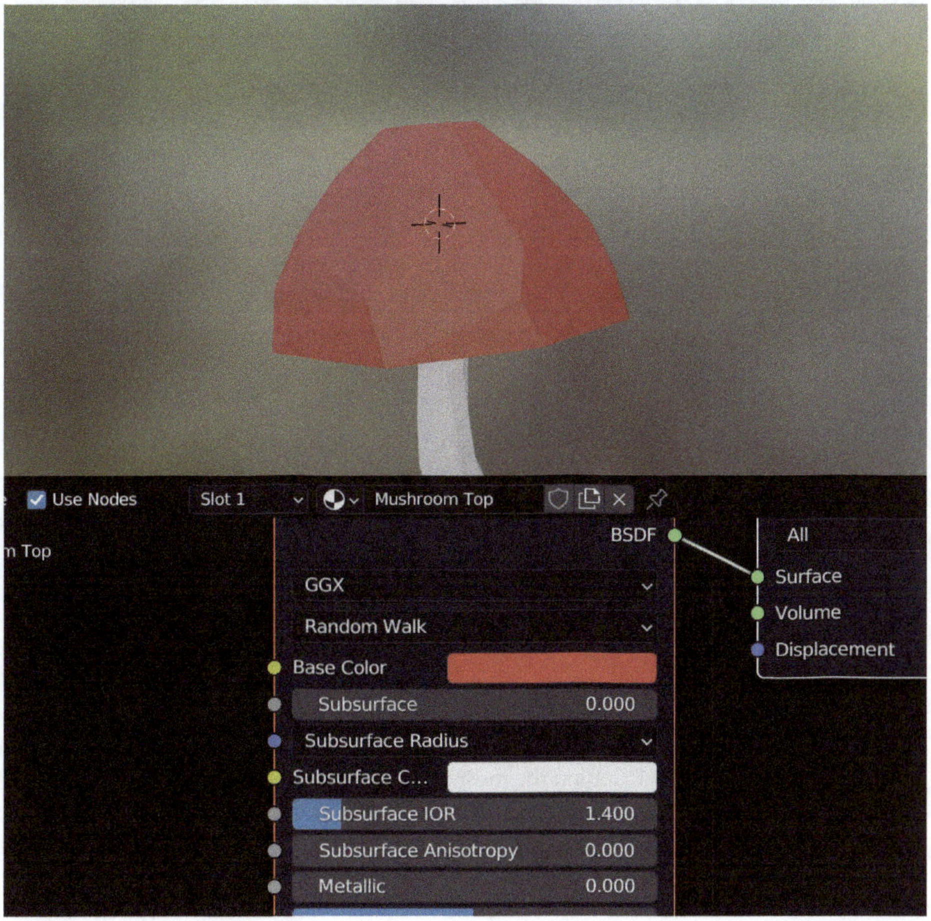

Figure 6.10: The Mushroom Top material in Slot 1

Time to create a material for the mushroom stem in **Slot**:

1. Change the **Slot** menu to **Slot 2**.
2. If there's already a material assigned, press *X* to unassign it, then press **New**. Otherwise, just press **New**.
3. Name the new material `Mushroom Stem`.
4. Choose a tan color and increase the roughness. If these materials seem inexact, it's because they are, but it doesn't really matter right now. It depends on the situation and the artist's (your) choice.

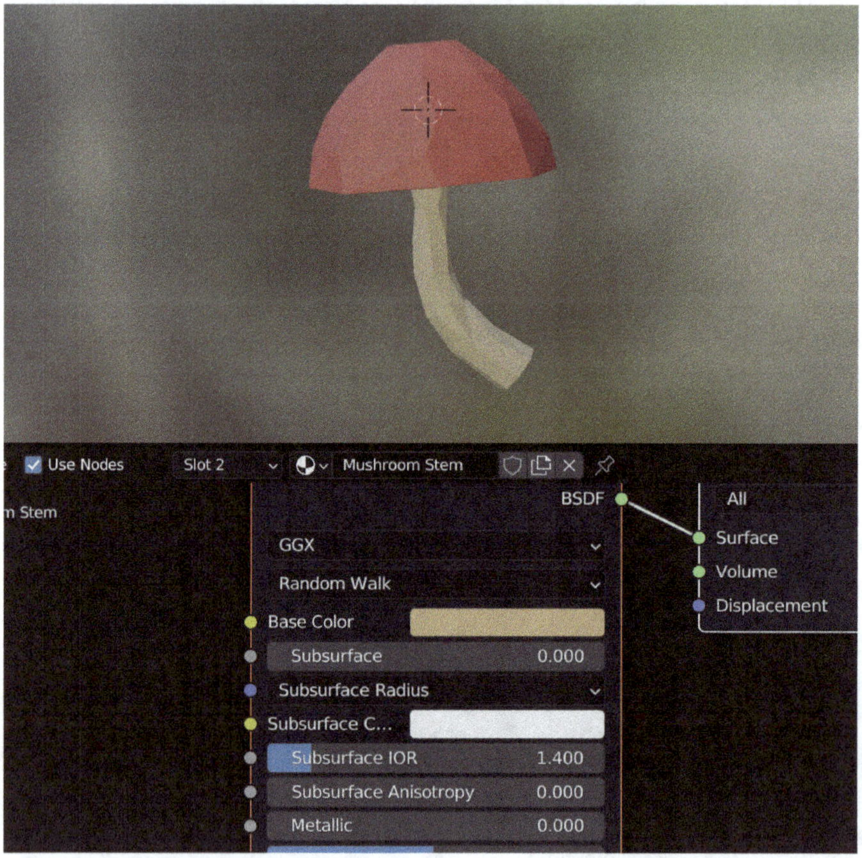

Figure 6.11: Setting the mushroom stem's material

That's it! Now you have a lovely, full-color mushroom.

You've learned a lot. Let's recap.

Summary

In this chapter, you finally added color to your drab, gray 3D models. You learned what materials are and how to set them up in the **Shader Editor**. You learned how to edit and build simple materials using the **Principled BSDF** node.

You even learned how to assign materials to different faces of an object.

That's a lot!

If you only remember one thing from this chapter, make it how materials work: *each object has material slots, and each slot holds a material.*

In the next chapter, we'll dive back into modeling and teach you how to make some low-poly vehicles.

Part 3: Creating Your Own Assets

Assets are complete, reusable 3D models. In this part, you'll model several different objects, learning new things as you go. You'll create simple models, such as buildings, but you'll also create more advanced projects, such as a tractor and a kangaroo. At the end of this part, you'll learn how to bring all your models together into an asset library for easy access within Blender's Asset Browser.

This part has the following chapters:

7

Creating a Low Poly Tractor

Time for a challenge!

In this chapter, you're going to build a tractor in Blender. This is the most complex project yet—but don't worry, it's not so bad.

We'll break the tractor up into separate pieces to simplify the modeling process. We'll build each piece and put them together as we go. The end result will be awesome!

When it's all done, we'll create materials for it.

In this chapter, you'll do the following:

- Build a simple tractor model from scratch
- Learn how to use the **Mirror** modifier
- Learn how to use double **Mirror** modifiers for parts such as wheels to mirror them twice
- See an example of breaking a concept into pieces for modeling

We'll start by taking a look at what we'll be making.

Breaking it down

Before we start modeling, let's take a look at the tractor we'll be making.

When you're working with a complex model like this one, it's difficult to know where to start. I've found a useful trick to solve this problem: break the subject into small, easy-to-manage pieces.

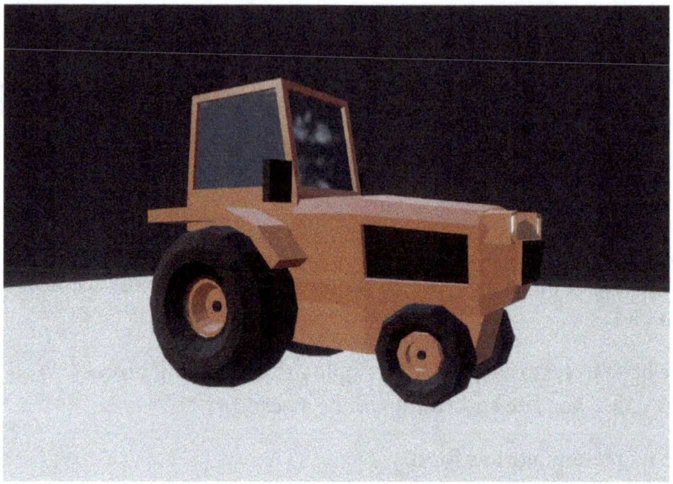

Figure 7.1 – The tractor we'll build

This tractor is pretty easy to break up. I've highlighted the main parts of the model here:

- The wheels
- The engine
- The body
- The cab
- The details (headlights, mirrors, lights, wheel hubs, etc.)

Next, let's dive in and model all the main parts of the tractor.

Adding the main parts

In this section, you'll learn how to model each of the main parts in dedicated subsections. We'll put the parts together as we go.

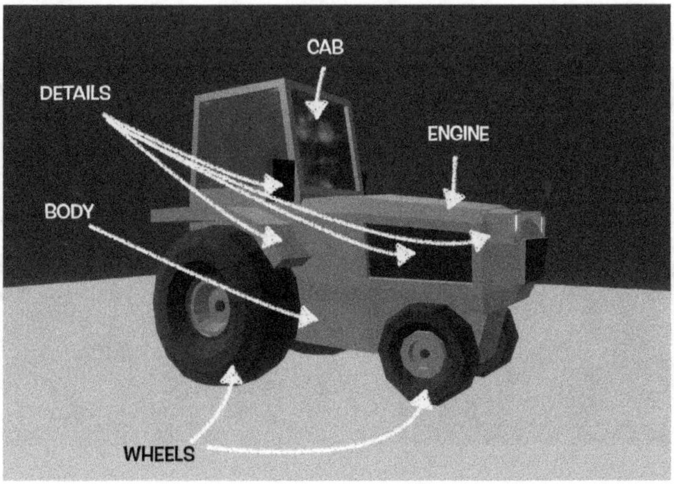

Figure 7.2 – The different parts of the tractor. We'll model them all separately

Figure 7.2 shows all the main parts of the tractor—we'll go through them one at a time and model them.

The wheels

The first of the main parts we'll work on is the wheels. First up are the big back wheels.

The back wheels

We'll start with the big back wheels. We don't have to start with those, but the rest of the tractor relies on the size and shape of the big back wheels, so it makes sense to start there.

The big wheels are one of the more complicated parts of the tractor—you'll be using extrude, loop cut, inset, and most of the other tools you've learned about.

If we make the wheels first, we'll have a nice guideline for the scale and position of the other parts. We'll use a **Mirror** modifier to make the wheels on both sides identical. Then we'll use another **Mirror** modifier to make a second wheel by copying the first.

Let's get started! First, we need to get Blender set up:

1. Press *A* to select everything, then *X* to delete it all. Next, we're going to turn on the **Cavity** setting. This highlights the edges of objects and makes things easier to look at.

2. Open the view options menu with the arrow button shown in *Figure 7.3*:

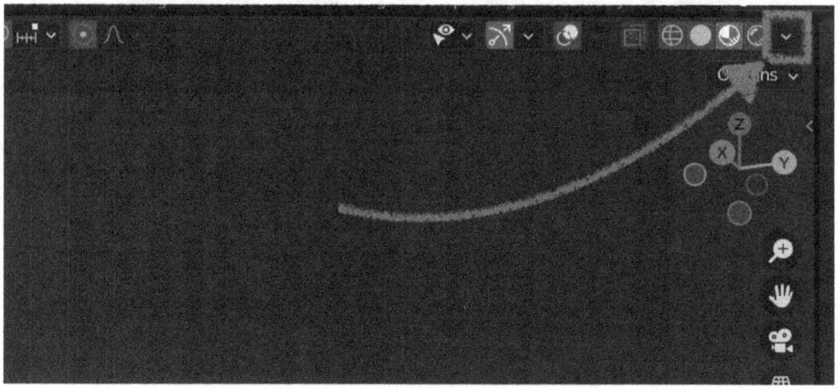

Figure 7.3 – The viewport display options

3. Now hit the **Cavity** checkbox to enable it. Nothing will change since there's nothing in the scene yet.

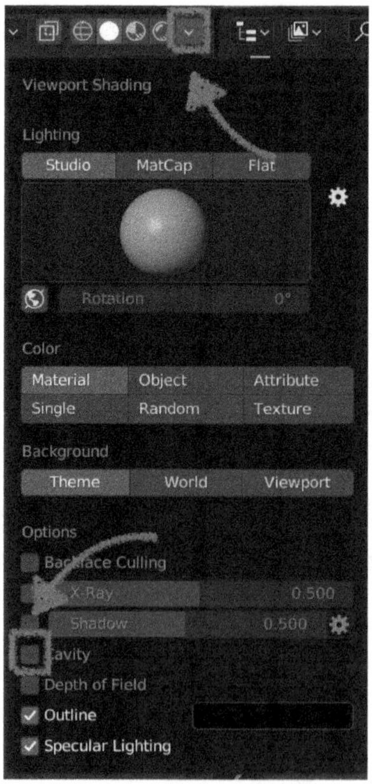

Figure 7.4 – The Cavity setting

We'll start modeling the wheel with a cylinder, since it's the closest thing to a wheel shape already. The default cylinder has too many faces—we want ours to be simple:

1. Press *Shift* + *A* and choose **Mesh** | **Cylinder**.
2. Open the **Operator** menu and change **Vertices** to `16` instead of `32`.

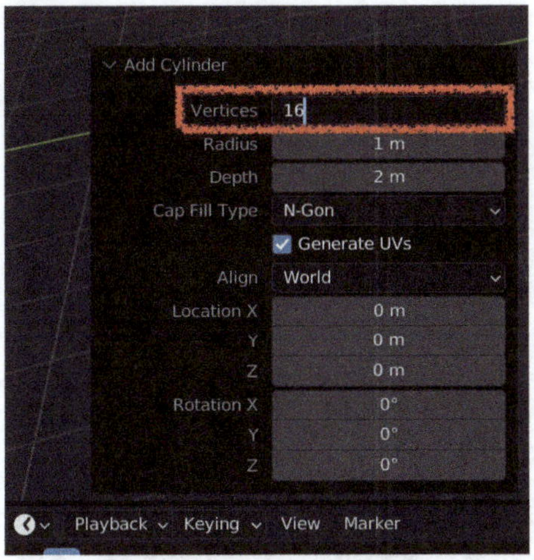

Figure 7.5 – Adding a cylinder

See how the edges of the mesh are all highlighted in a lighter color? That's due to the **Cavity** setting.

Now we can turn the cylinder on its side. We don't want to rotate the object, because that'll make the **Mirror** modifier confusing later:

1. *Tab* into **Edit Mode** and press *A* to select the whole mesh.
2. Press *R* to rotate then *Y* and *90* to rotate it exactly 90 degrees on the Y axis.

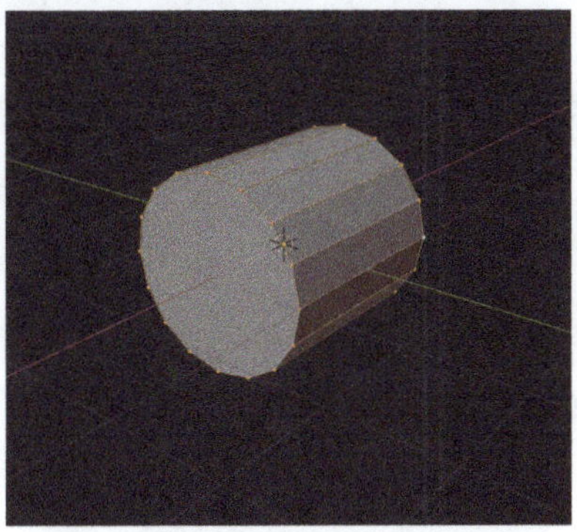

Figure 7.6 – The positioned cylinder

The next step is to add a **Mirror** modifier to the cylinder to make it automatically symmetrical. Before we mirror it, though, we'll need to remove half of it:

1. Enter **Edit Mode**.
2. Press *Ctrl* + *R* to turn on the **Loop Cut** tool.
3. Hover over the cylinder until you see the new edge loop in yellow.
4. Click to confirm the cut location, then right-click to exit **Slide** mode.

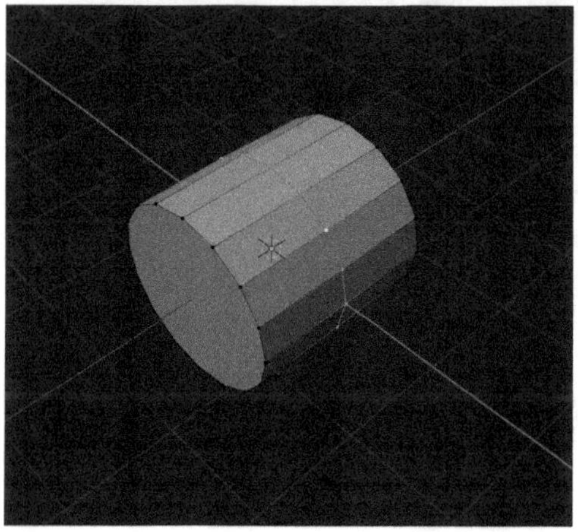

Figure 7.7 – Cutting the cylinder

Now we have a new loop of edges across the middle of the cylinder. We can select one of the end faces and delete those vertices:

1. Press *Ctrl* + *3* to enter **Left** view.
2. Switch to **Face Select** mode in the selection mode picker.
3. Select the big round face.
4. Press *X* and choose **Vertices** to delete all the vertices.

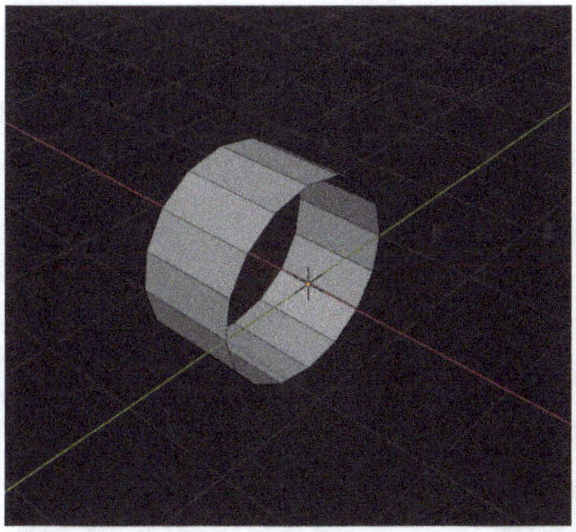

Figure 7.8 – Half of the cylinder removed

The next step is to add the **Mirror** modifier. This will be easy. Simply open the **Modifiers** tab of the **Properties** panel and hit **Add Modifier**. Pick **Mirror**. The modifier won't work perfectly right away—there'll be a small gap between the two sides of the mesh.

To fix this, adjust the **Merge Distance** value, which controls how close together vertices have to be before they get merged. It's the small number beside the **Merge** checkbox. If you increase it to `0.1`, the gap should close up.

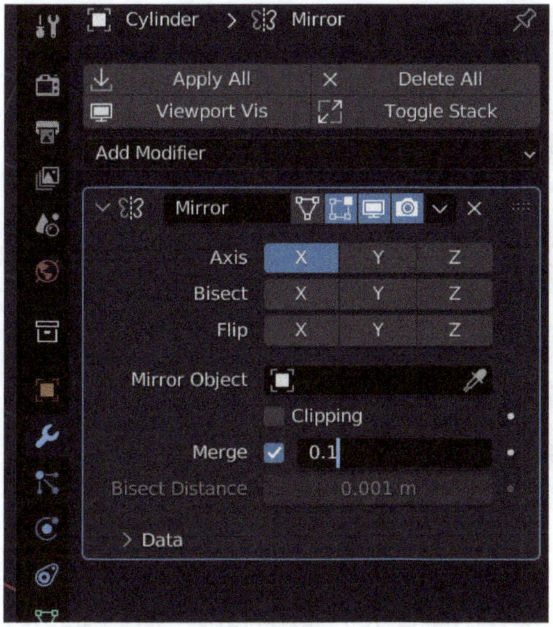

Figure 7.9 – The Mirror modifier

Now, we can work on shaping the wheel:

1. Select the big face and move it on the X axis (using *G* and *X*). See how the **Mirror** modifier keeps it symmetrical? Move it inward until your cylinder is thinner, like this:

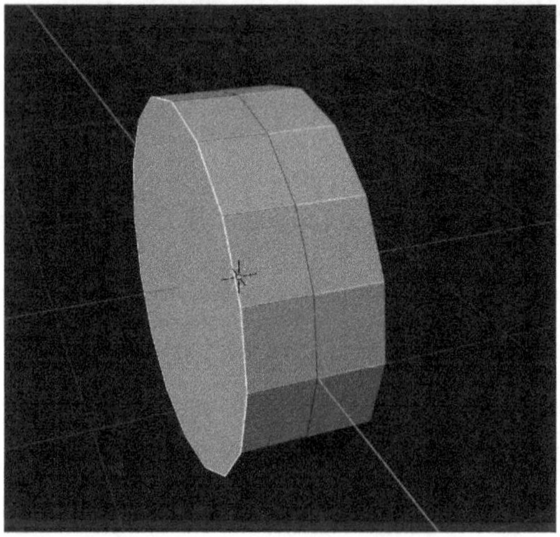

Figure 7.10 – The first extrusion

2. Press *E* to extrude the face out—not too far, but something like this:

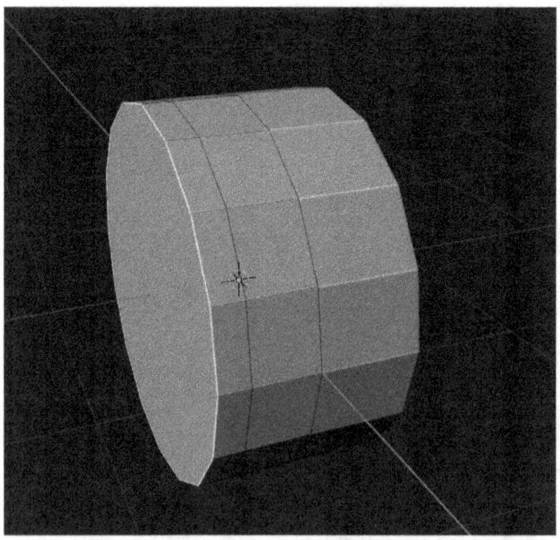

Figure 7.11 – The second extrusion

3. Press *S* to scale the new face down. This tapers the tire—it's starting to look like a wheel!

4. Press *I* to inset the face. Just make it a little smaller than the existing face. You can always adjust the size of the inset face using *S* if you need to.

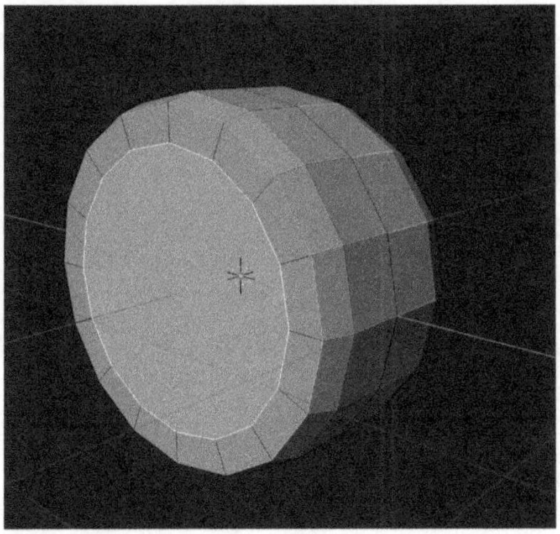

Figure 7.12 – The face after being scaled and then inset again

5. Press *G* and *X* to pull out the new face.
6. Press *I* to inset the face again.
7. Press *I* again.
8. Press *G* and *X* again to move the face inward. See how simple it is to make interesting shapes, using just the extrude, inset, and move tools?

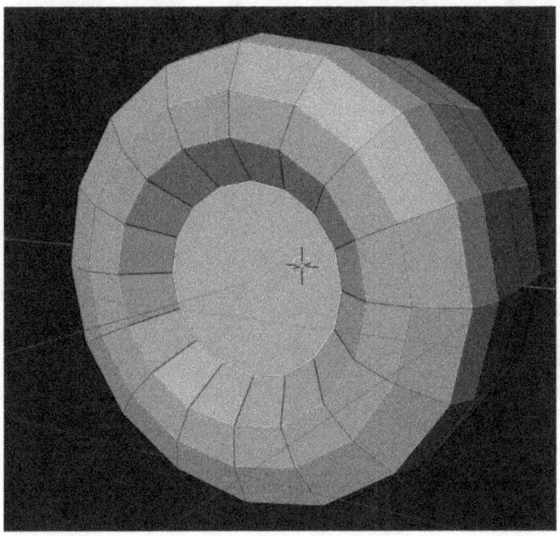

Figure 7.13 – The face after another inset, moved inward and scaled

9. Now, inset, extrude inward, inset again, and extrude inward again. Scale the face down to taper the last part.

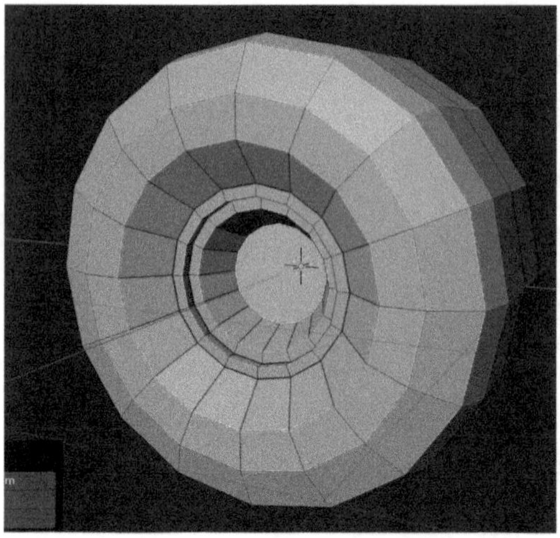

Figure 7.14 – Adding detail with more insetting and extruding

10. The last part requires insetting and extruding outward to make a little protruding bolt or axle.

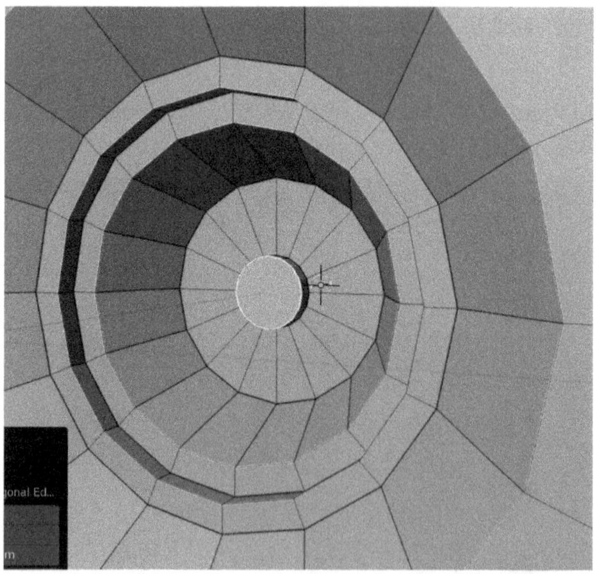

Figure 7.15 – Extruding the axle stub

Great job! We have mostly finished with the wheel now.

It's supposed to look a bit cartoony, but it looks a little too thick. I'll show you how to adjust it:

1. Hit *1* to see the wheel from the **Front** view.
2. Press *Alt* + *Z* to activate the **X-Ray** view.

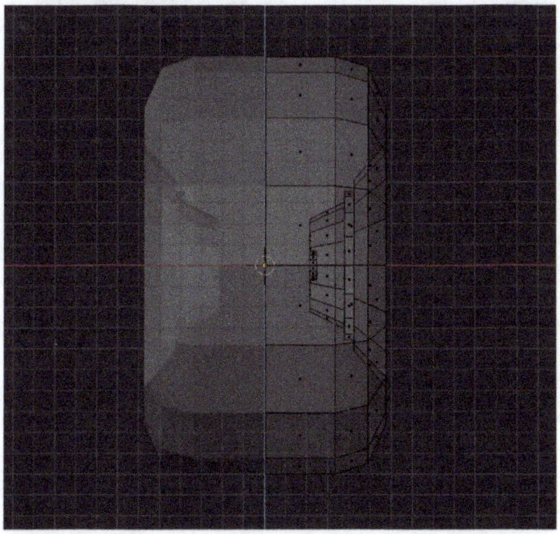

Figure 7.16 – Front view in X-Ray mode

3. Switch to **Vertex Select** mode and click and drag to select all but the center vertices.

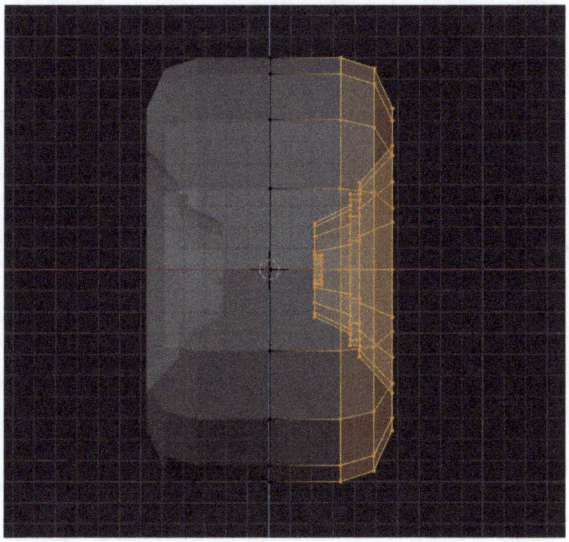

Figure 7.17 – Selecting all but the center vertices

4. Press *G* and then *X* and move the selected vertices inward a bit.

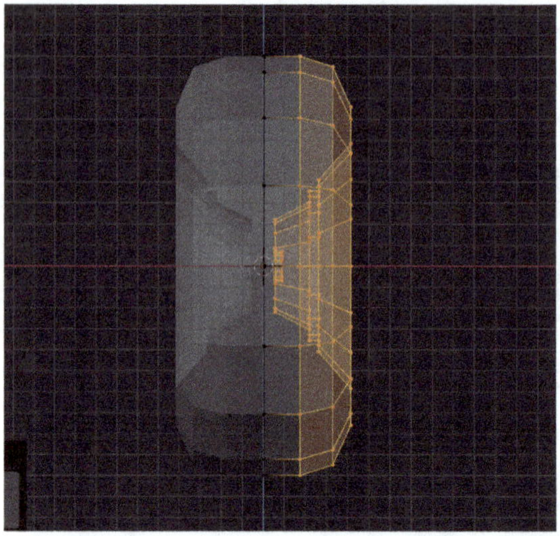

Figure 7.18 – Moving the vertices inward to make the tire thinner

Perfect! It looks much better now.

We only have one wheel right now, and we're going to need two of these. To solve that problem, we're going to add a second **Mirror** modifier. This modifier will mirror the entire wheel so that we have two.

Before we can mirror it, though, we'll need an object to mirror it around:

1. Make sure you're in **Object Mode**.
2. Press *Shift* + *A* and pick a cube. This cube will be the body of the tractor—it's also our mirror object.
3. Select the wheel again (if you can't see it, select it in the Outliner).
4. Open the **Modifiers** tab and add a new mirror.
5. Click in the **Mirror Object** field and select the cube.

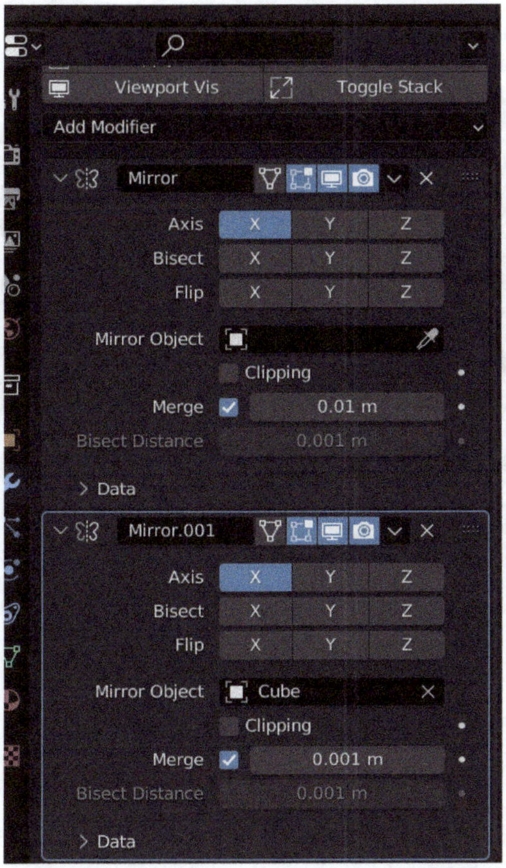

Figure 7.19 – The second Mirror modifier

6. Press *G* and then *X* and move the wheel out along the X axis. There are two now!

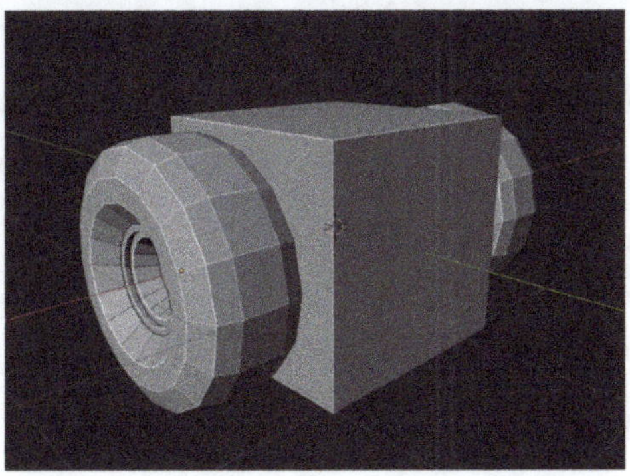

Figure 7.20 – The twice-mirrored wheel

That's it for the mirroring. The last little step is to name the wheel. Double-click the cylinder in the Outliner and name it `Big Wheel`.

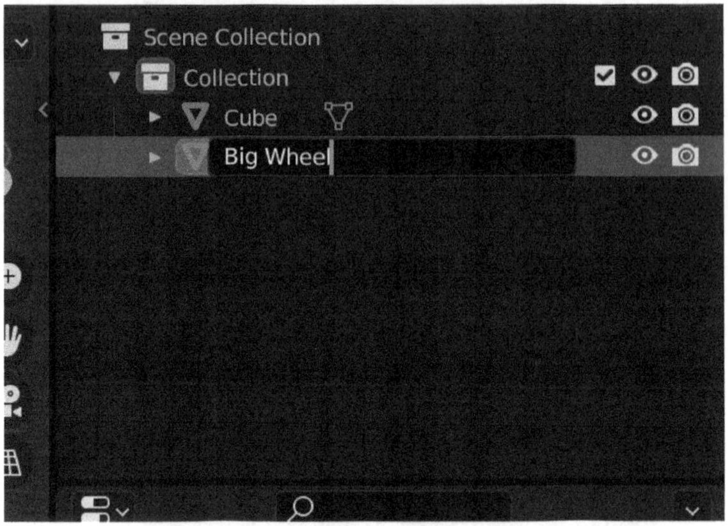

Figure 7.21 – Naming the wheel

Next, you'll make the smaller front wheels.

The front wheels

The front wheels are different from the back ones. They're a lot smaller, and it would look strange to scale the back wheels down to that size (remember the *Rule of Polygons* we discussed in *Chapter 2*?). We'll build the new, smaller wheels from scratch so they don't look funny.

The process is very similar to that for the back wheels, so it should be a breeze for you.

Start with a cylinder again. Make sure you're in **Object Mode**, then hit *Shift* + *A* and select **Mesh | Cylinder**. In the **Operator** menu, set **Vertices** to `10`.

Now, we'll put the cylinder in (roughly) the right place:

1. Press *G* and then *Y* and slide it out in front of the cube.
2. Now we need to rotate it. *Tab* into **Edit Mode**.
3. Press *A* to select everything.
4. Press *R*, then *Y*, then *90* to rotate it 90 degrees on the Y axis.
5. *Tab* back to **Object Mode**.
6. Press *3* for the **Right** view.
7. Use *G* to position the cylinder at the same level as the back wheel.

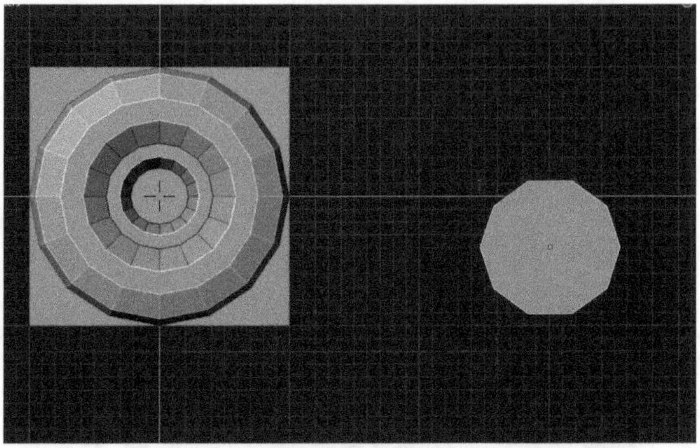

Figure 7.22 – A cylinder to start the front wheels

Now we need to chop it in half and add a **Mirror** modifier again. The steps are exactly the same as they were for the other wheel:

1. *Tab* into **Edit Mode** on the new cylinder.
2. Press *Ctrl* + *R* to loop cut it. Make a cut across the middle. Click to confirm, then right-click to cancel the slide.

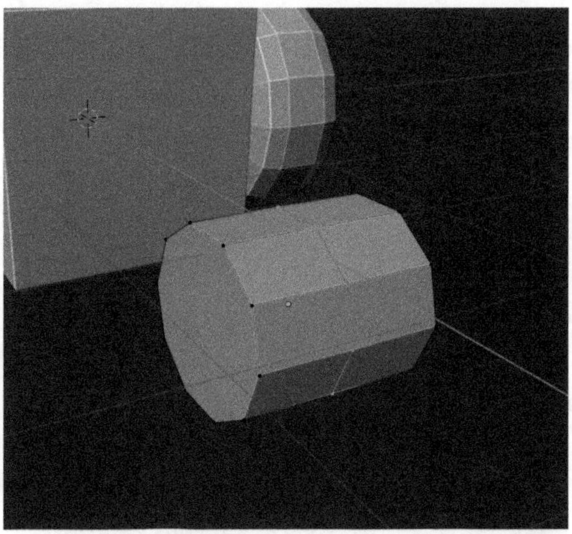

Figure 7.23 – Cutting the cylinder in half again

3. Switch to the **Face Select** mode.

4. Press *Ctrl* + *3* to go to the **Left** view.
5. Select the big face and press *X* | **Vertices** to delete it.

   Now you have this:

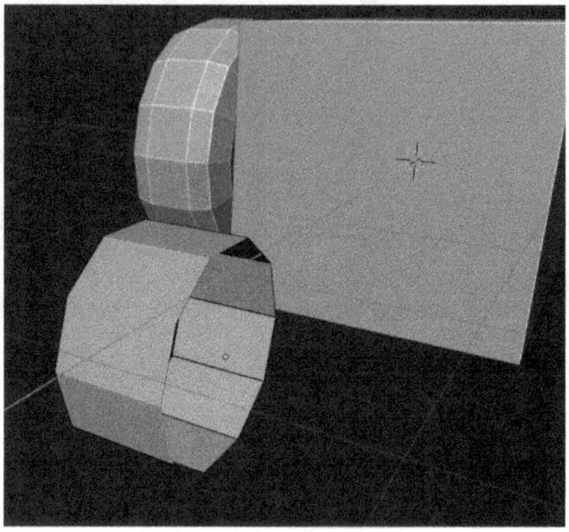

Figure 7.24 – The half cylinder

6. In the **Modifier** tab, hit **Add New** and pick **Mirror**.

Successfully mirrored! Now we just have to model the wheel shape. We'll make this wheel a little simpler than the back one:

1. Select the big face at the end of the cylinder.

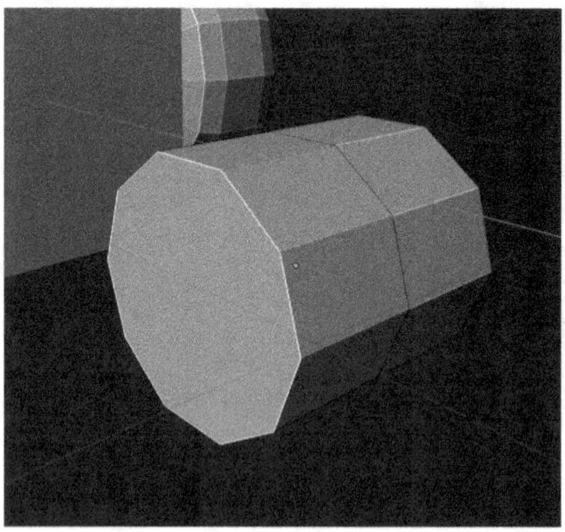

Figure 7.25 – Select this face

2. Press *G* and then *X* and slide it inward to make the cylinder thinner.

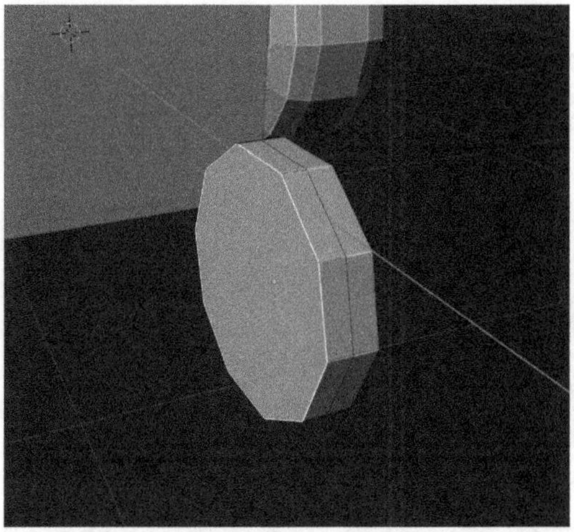

Figure 7.26 – Move it along the X axis

3. Hit *E* to extrude it out, then *S* to scale it down.

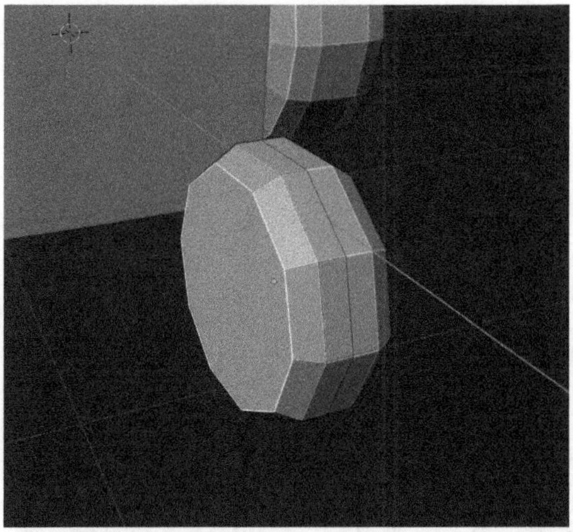

Figure 7.27 – Scale it down

4. Hit *I* and inset the face.

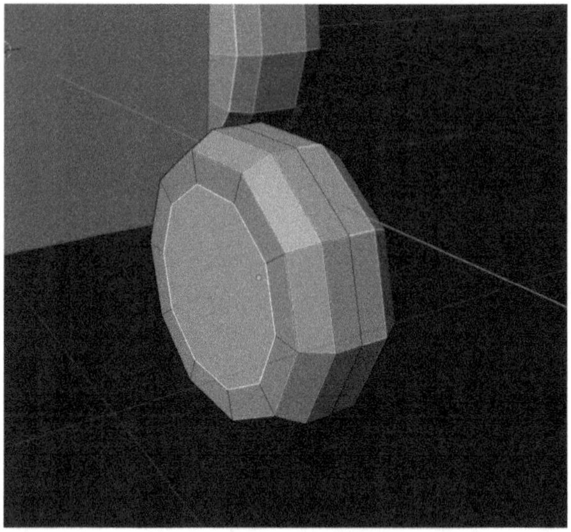

Figure 7.28 – Inset the face

5. Press *E* and extrude it inward.
6. Use *S* to scale the face. You can move it in and out as needed using *G* and *X*.

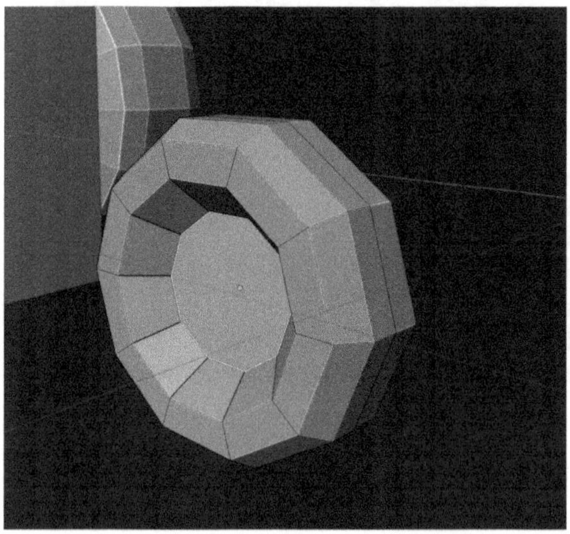

Figure 7.29 – Extruded inward and scaled

7. Extrude it out a little with *E*.

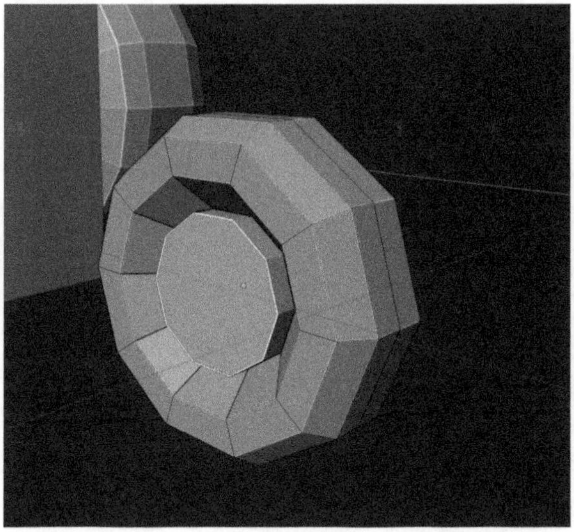

Figure 7.30 – Extruding the center

8. Press *I* to inset, then *E* to extrude inward.

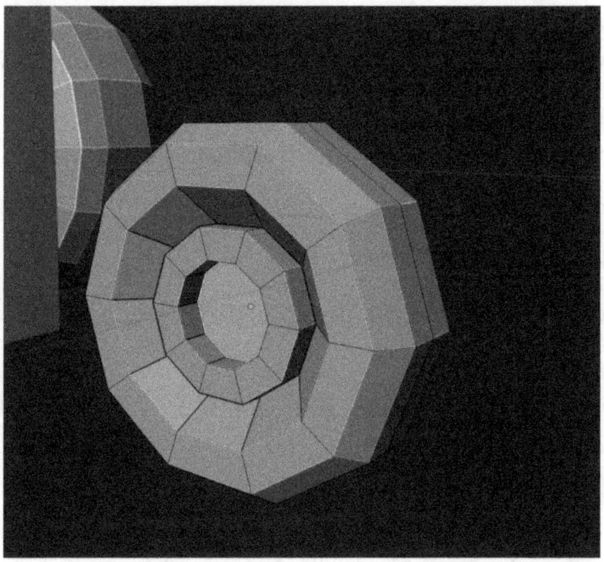

Figure 7.31 – Insetting and extruding inward

9. Inset and extrude one more time to make a small bolt/axle sticking out in the middle.

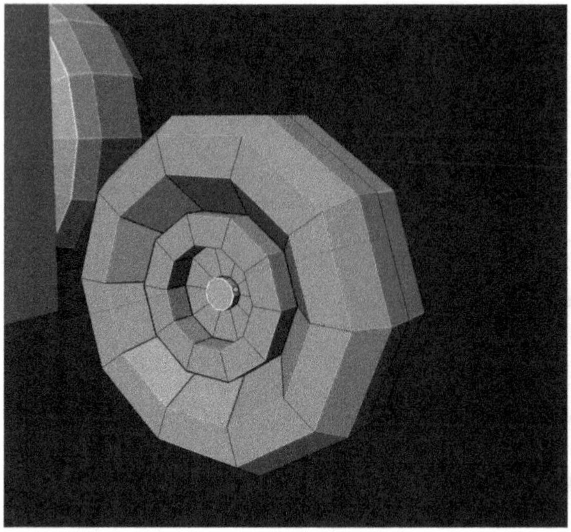

Figure 7.32 – One last inset and extrude

10. *Tab* back into **Object Mode**.

Great work! You've completed the modeling part! Now we'll add a second **Mirror** modifier. It's super simple: just hit the **New Modifier** button in the **Modifier** panel, then set the mirror object to the same cube we used for the back wheels.

If you hit *G* and *X*, you can move your two new wheels around.

One last step: name the object `Small Wheels`.

You just did a lot of work!

You learned how to use cylinders to model wheels—with **Mirror** modifiers and lots of insetting and extruding. Well done!

Next, we'll position the wheels just how we want, and build the body piece they'll connect to.

The body

The body is the part the wheels will be attached to. The engine and the cab will also sit on top of it. We'll make the body out of a cube. Since it's a really simple model, we won't need to use a **Mirror** modifier. It'd be overkill.

To make this part, we'll just start with the cube that we already have in the scene, the one we've been using as a mirror object to model wheels.

Double-click it in the Outliner and rename it `Body`.

The actual modeling will be really simple. First, get ready:

1. *Tab* into **Edit Mode** on the cube.
2. Press *3* for the **Right** view, and turn on **X-Ray** with *Alt* + *Z*.
3. Change to **Vertex Select** mode.

Now we can rearrange the vertices of the cube. Since we're viewing the cube in **Right** view, we're only seeing the front vertices of the cube. If we select one vertex and press *G*, we're only moving the front one—but we want to move both the front and back vertices.

Since we're in **X-Ray**, you can click and drag across any vertex to select both front and back vertices. Then, you can hit *G* to move them around.

We'll use this trick a lot in the rest of the modeling process:

1. Click and drag across one of the vertices of the cube to select both vertices in that location.
2. Press *G* to move the vertices. You'll need to do this for all the vertices of the cube—your goal is to end up like this:

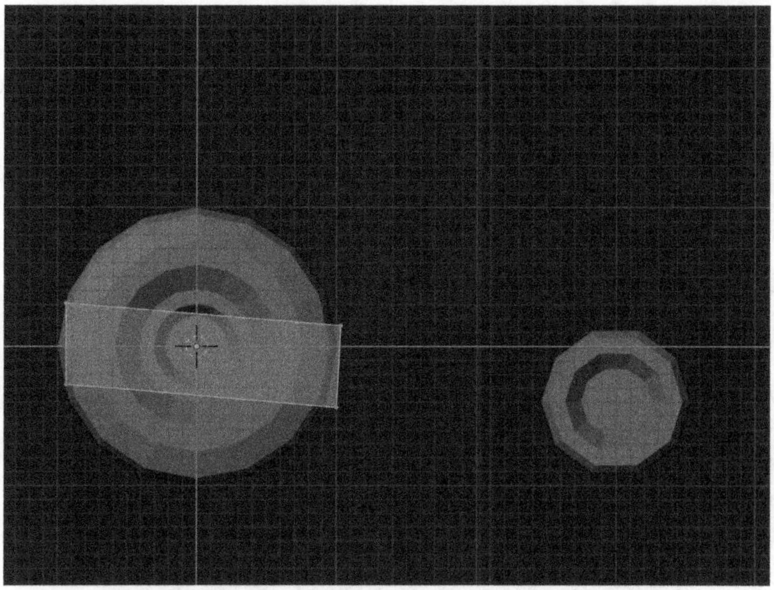

Figure 7.33 – Shaping the cube in X-Ray in the Right View

3. Next, click and drag across the front to select the whole front face of the cube. Press *E* to extrude that face out.

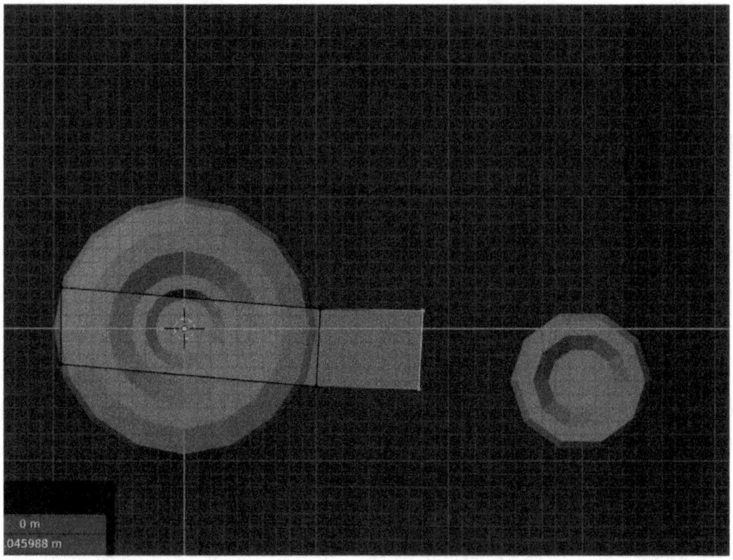

Figure 7.34 – Extruding the body

4. Extrude it again.
5. Time for some tweaking: adjust the vertices to shape the profile of the body.
6. We need more mesh in the back, between the big wheels. Select the middle-top-back face by dragging across its vertices.

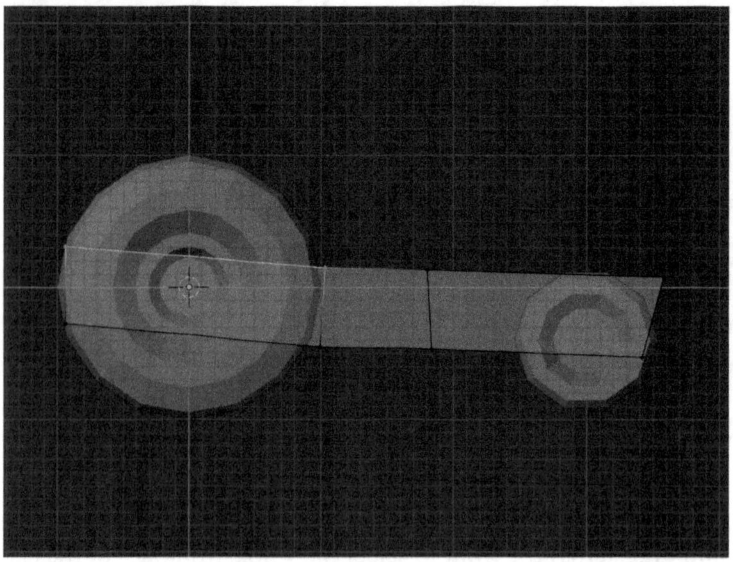

Figure 7.35 – More extruding

7. Now, extrude it upward with *E*.

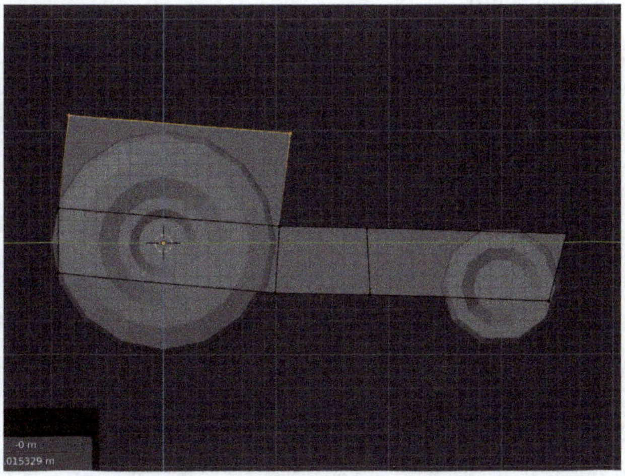

Figure 7.36 – Extruding the rear part

Now, the body looks nice from the side, but it's still just a perfect rectangle if you view it from the top (press *7*). We're going to fix that next:

1. Press *7* for **Top** view. Make sure **X-Ray** is still on.
2. *Tab* into **Edit Mode**.
3. First, the whole thing is too wide. Let's make it thinner. Press *A* to select all and then press *S* and then *X* to scale it on the X axis.

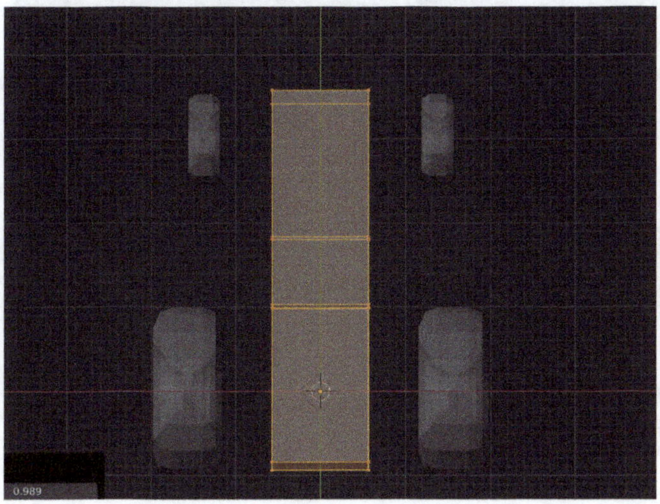

Figure 7.37 – Top view

4. It also seems a little too long. Click and drag over the front vertices to select them, then use *G* and *Y* to move them back a little.

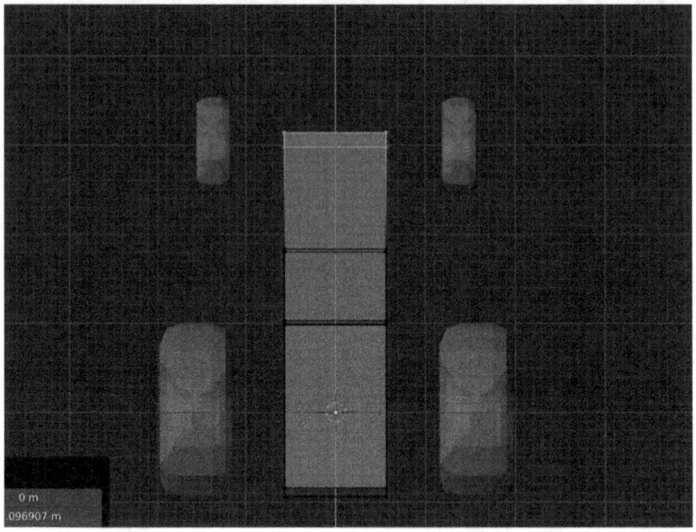

Figure 7.38 – Shortening the front

5. We're going to taper the front, so it's thinner than the back. First, we'll add an edge loop so that only the very front part gets tapered. Press *Ctrl* + *R* and add a new edge loop.

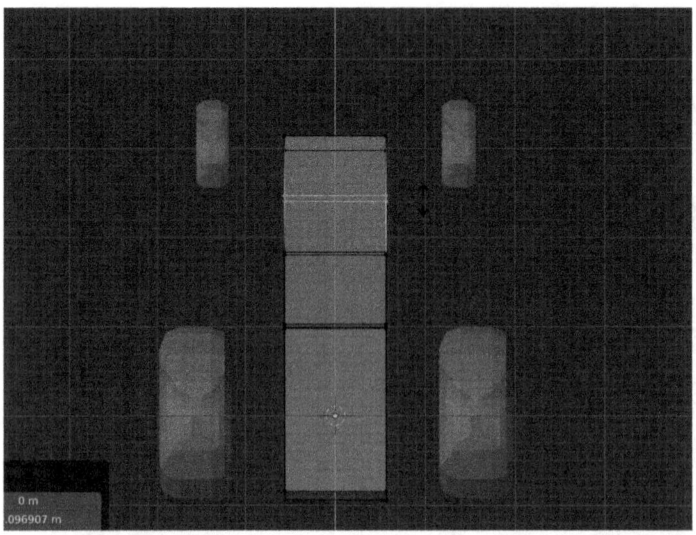

Figure 7.39 – Adding a new loop

6. Slide the loop back a little and then click to confirm the loop cut.
7. Now, click and drag over the front vertices and use *S* and then *X* to make the front thinner.

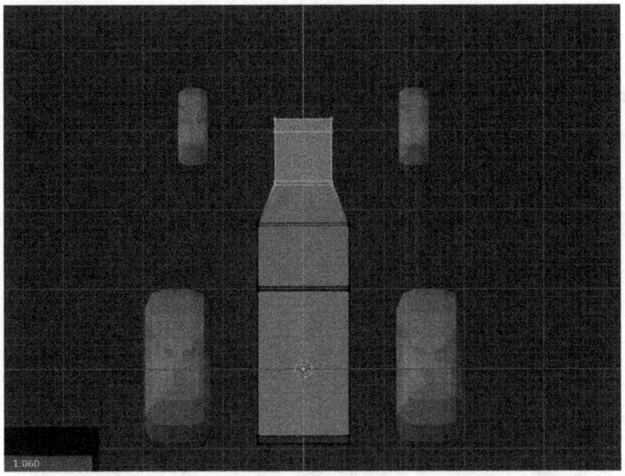

Figure 7.40 – Squashing the front part

That's it for the modeling part of the body. You can *Tab* out of **Edit Mode** now. Feel free to make any additional tweaks to the mesh—it's all up to you. If you can make it better, do it!

Press *Alt* + *Z* to exit **X-Ray** mode. Let's put the wheels where they belong. Simply select a wheel and move it along the X axis until it's almost touching the body mesh. You can also move them in the Y direction to get them where they belong.

The final wheels and body setup should look like this:

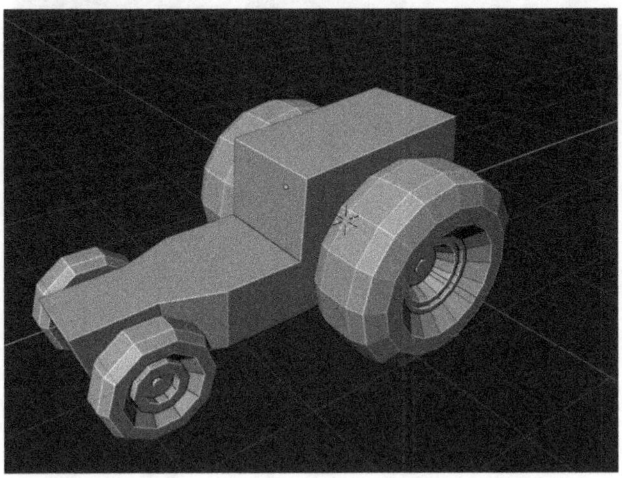

Figure 7.41 – The wheels and the body

Great job on the body! The next part we'll make is the big engine piece. It's a fairly simple job—it's mostly a big cube, with a few changes.

The engine

The tractor's engine is a simple, mostly cubical shape, so it won't be too hard to make. We'll start out with a cube. Before we do the extruding and shaping, we'll cut the cube in half and add a **Mirror** modifier to make things easier.

Let's start by adding a cube and repositioning it:

1. First, make sure you're in **Object Mode**.
2. Then, press Shift + A and choose **Mesh | Cube** to get a new cube. In the Outliner, rename the cube to Engine.
3. Let's get the cube out where we can see it. Press 3 for the **Right** view and hit G to reposition the cube like this:

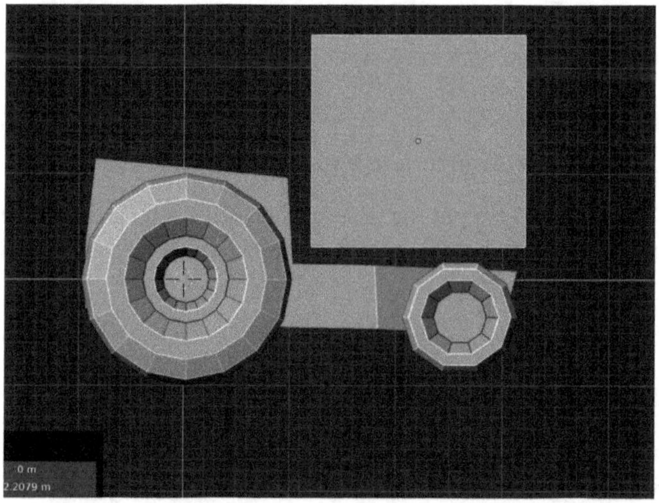

Figure 7.42 – The start of the engine

Now, we can slice it in half and add a mirror, just like we did for the wheels:

1. *Tab* into **Edit Mode**.
2. Press *Ctrl* + *R* and make a cut right across the center of the cube. Click to confirm, then right-click to cancel the slide operation.

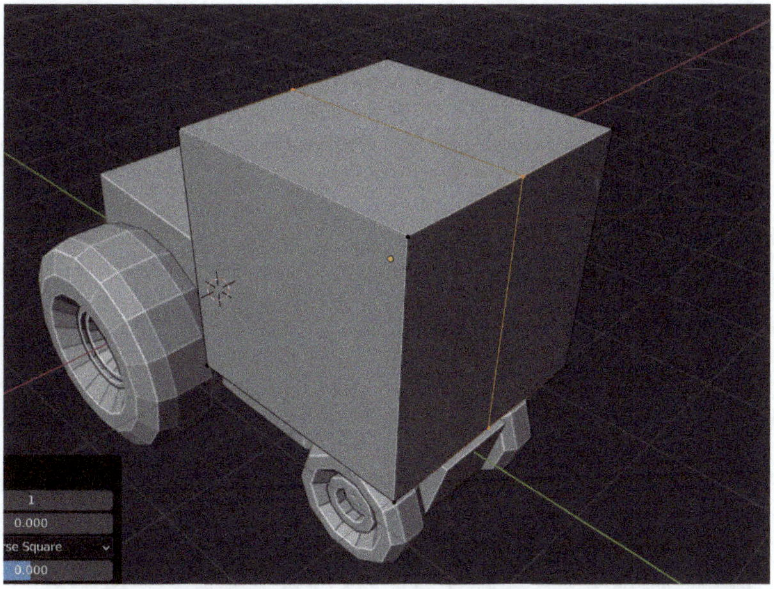

Figure 7.43 – Adding a single loop

3. Switch to **Face Select** mode.
4. Press *Ctrl* + *3* for the **Left** view.
5. Select the face and press *X* | **Vertices** to delete those vertices.

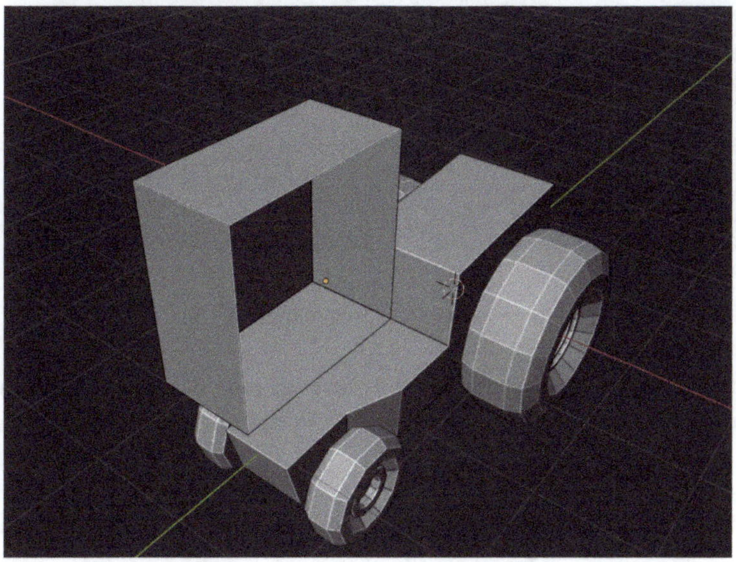

Figure 7.44 – Deleting half of the cube

6. Hit **Add Modifier** in the **Modifier** tab and pick **Mirror**.

It's mirrored! That was easy.

Now we can work on creating the basic engine shape. We'll use the same technique we used when we were modeling the body:

1. *Tab* into **Edit Mode**.
2. Turn on **X-Ray** with *Alt* + *Z*.
3. Press *3* for the **Right** view.
4. Switch to **Vertex Select** mode.
5. Click and drag over the corner vertices and position them, one at a time, using *G*.

Your goal is an engine-like shape. It's okay if the shape overlaps the wheels; we'll be fixing that later. You should get something like this:

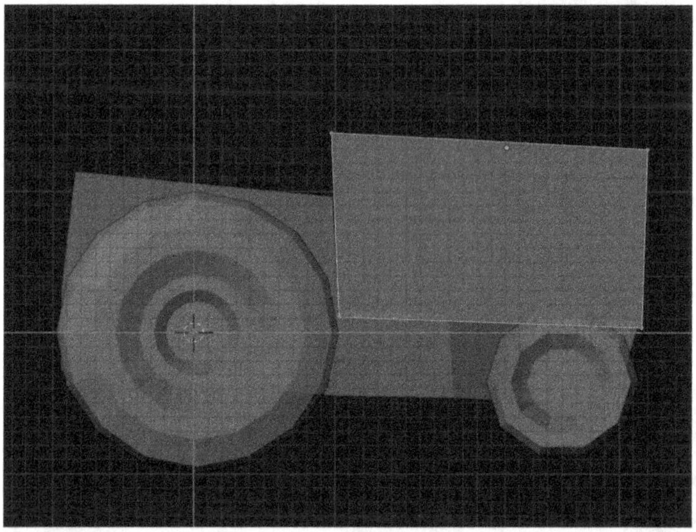

Figure 7.45 – Shaping it manually

We need a more detailed shape. Let's start by adding an edge loop near the front using *Ctrl* + *R*. A little more adjusting and it's looking much better. Let's taper it, from the **Top** view:

1. Press *7*, then click and drag to select the front corner vertex.
2. Press *G* and then *X* and move the vertex inward (since it's mirrored, this is a lot like scaling it).

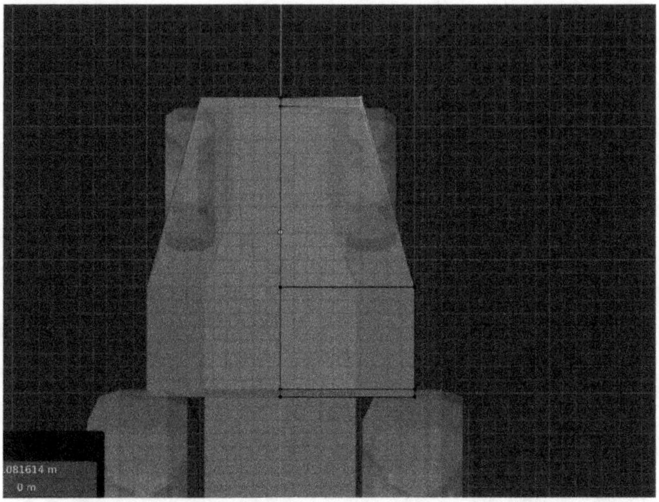

Figure 7.46 – Adjusting the front

Let's adjust the back of the engine, too.

3. Select the back outside vertices and adjust them using *G* and then *X*.

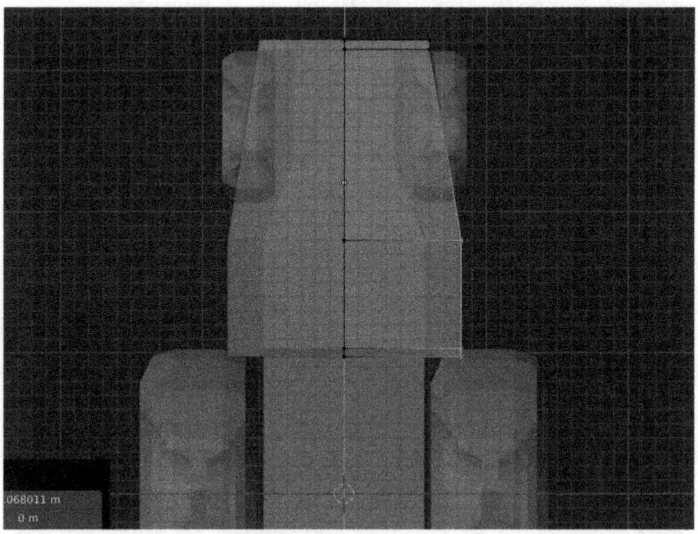

Figure 7.47 – Making the engine thinner

We're going to add two loop cuts long-ways across the engine, one at the bottom and one at the top:

1. Hit *3* for **Right** view.
2. Press *Ctrl* + *R* and make a cut at the top, then do it again for a cut at the bottom.

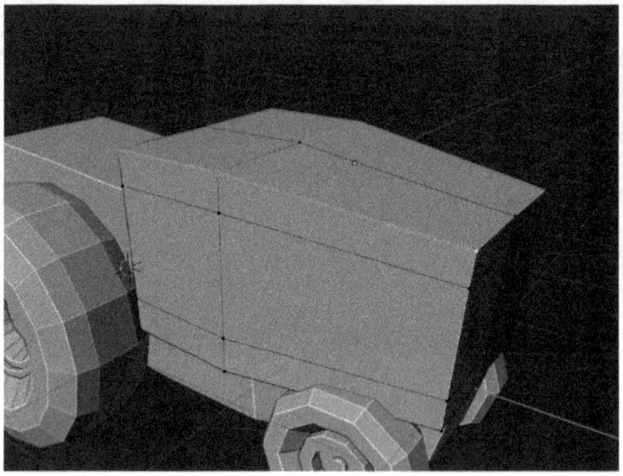

Figure 7.48 – The new cuts

Now we'll taper the edges by moving the top and bottom vertices inward:

1. Press *Alt* + *Z* to exit **X-Ray** mode.
2. Select the top corner vertices.
3. Use *G* and *X* to move them inward. You can also move them down a tiny bit (using *G* and *Z*).

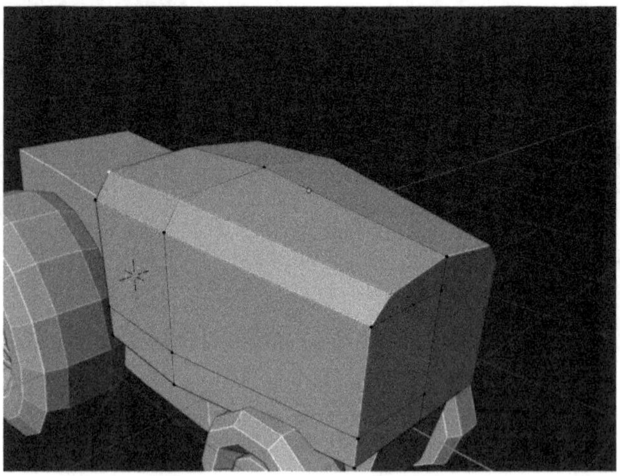

Figure 7.49 – Adjusting the shape

4. Now select the bottom three vertices and move them inward with *G* and *X*.

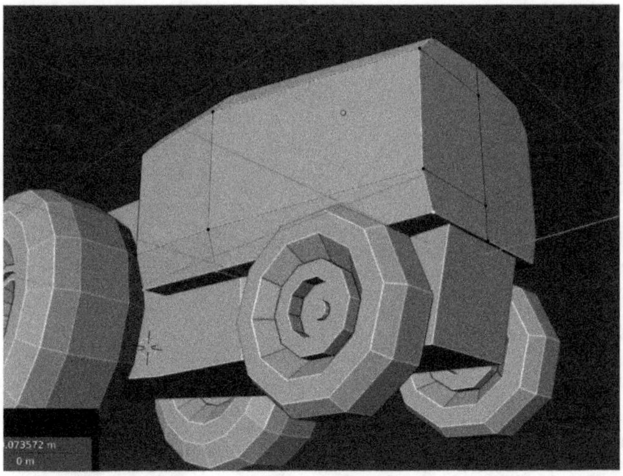

Figure 7.50 – Adjusting the shape some more

5. The engine still hits the front wheels, so switch to **Face Select** mode and select the face highlighted in the following figure.

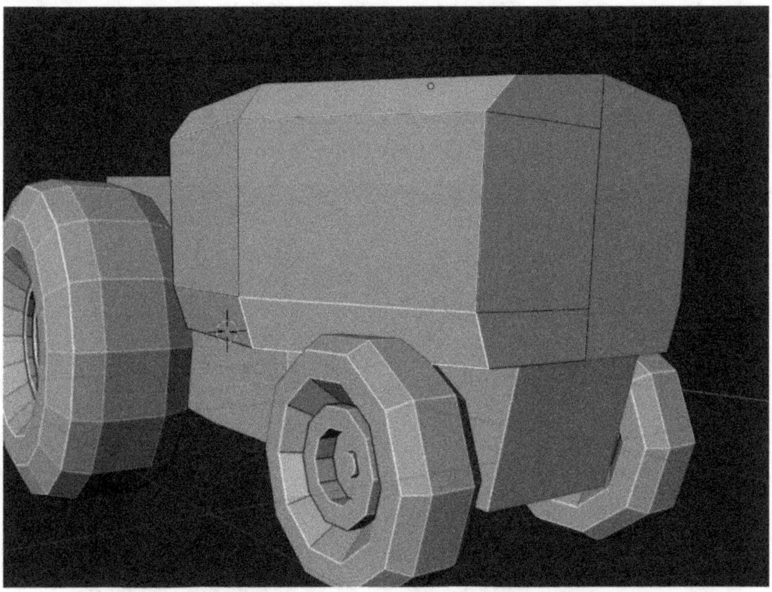

Figure 7.51 – Select this face

6. Move the face inward using *G* and *X*. Move it inward until it no longer intersects with the wheel (at least mostly—a tiny bit of intersection won't be noticed).

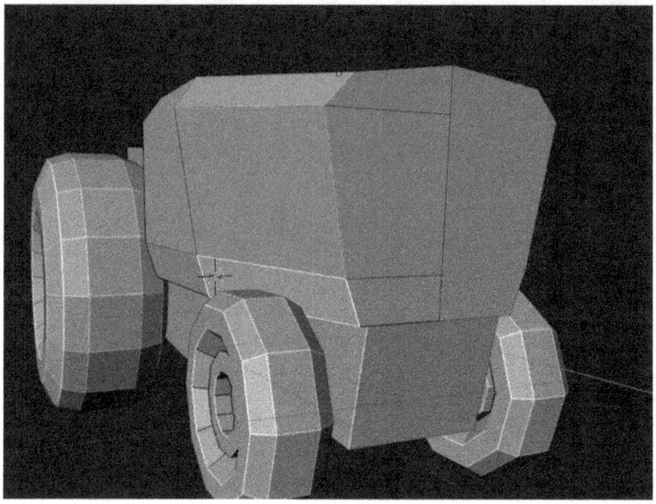

Figure 7.52 – Move it inward to avoid intersecting the wheel

Let's add another edge loop to add more definition to the front of the tractor:

1. Press *Ctrl* + *R* and make a loop near the front.
2. Go back to **Right** view and **X-Ray** mode. Select the front vertices of the tractor and move them forward so that the engine hangs over the edge of the body.

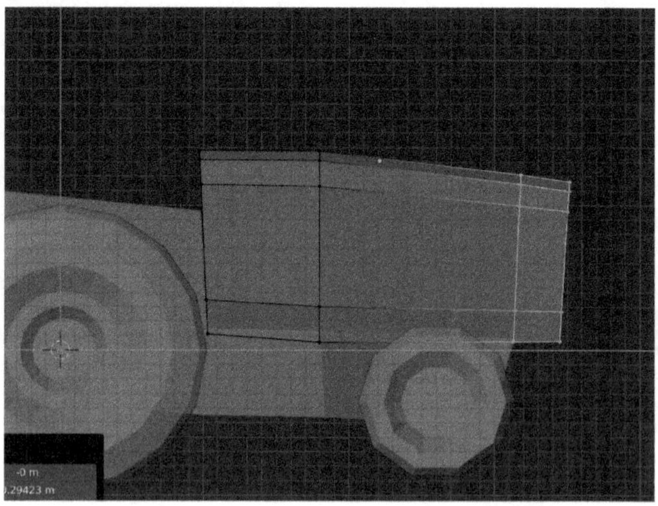

Figure 7.53 – New loop and stretched front

Now we'll taper the front of the engine:

1. Select the front four corner vertices and move them inward with *G* and *X*.

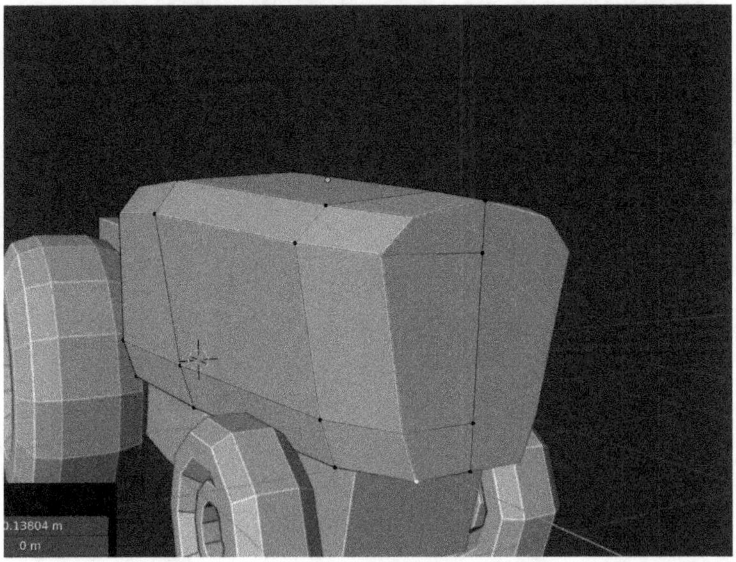

Figure 7.54 – Tweaking the shape more

2. Now select the front top face and move it downward. Then select the front bottom face and move it upward.

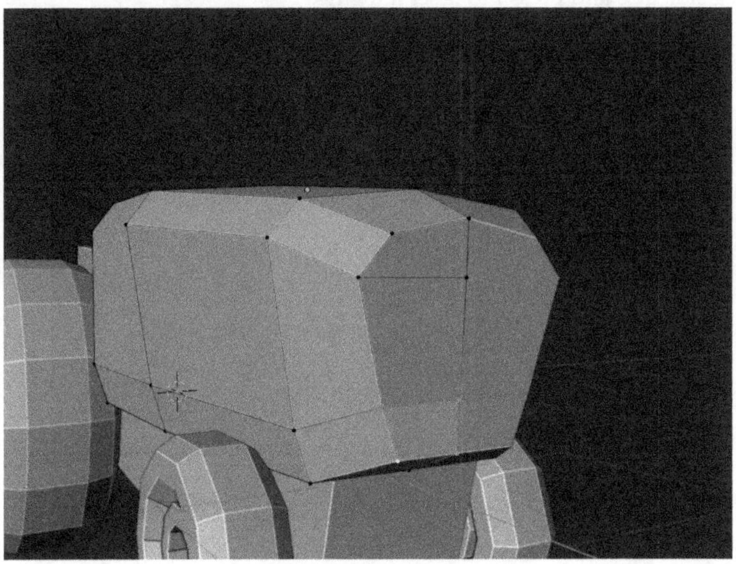

Figure 7.55 – Tapering the engine

3. Select the top and bottom two vertices and pull them back a little with *G* and *Y*.

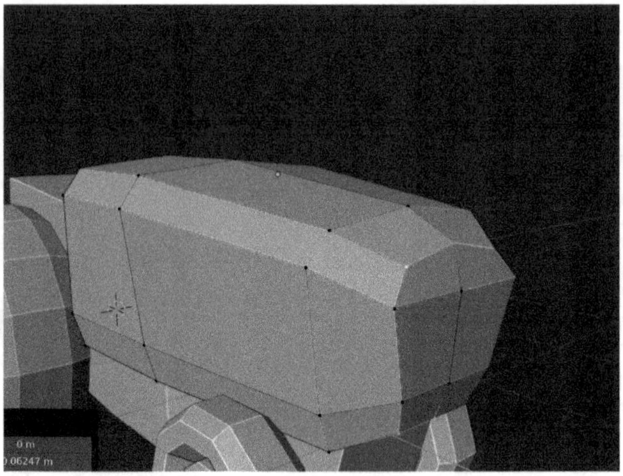

Figure 7.56 – Rounding the shape

All right! That's it for the basic shape. It's really looking like an engine now!

The next step is to inset and extrude a few faces to add some *panel* details that will help make the model interesting. This part will be super easy since we already have the mesh mirrored:

1. In **Edit Mode**, switch to **Face Select** mode.
2. Select the big side face and press *I* to inset it a little.

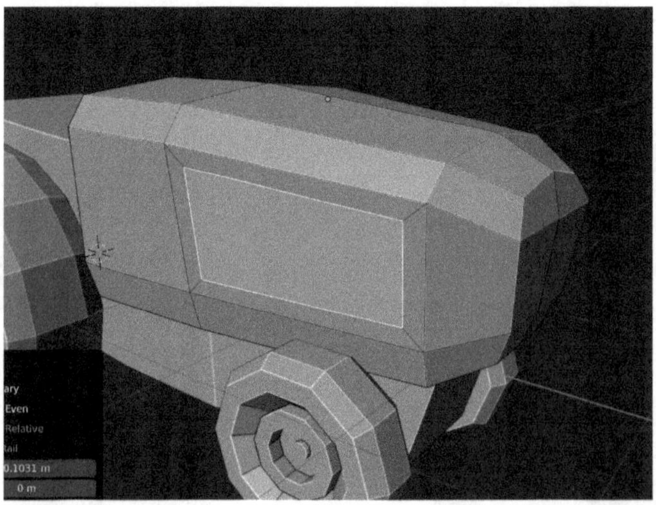

Figure 7.57 – Insetting a panel

3. Now hit *E* and extrude it slightly inward.

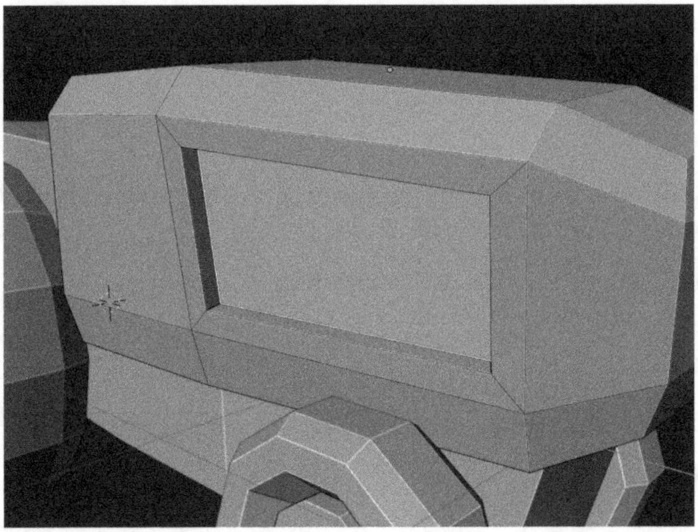

Figure 7.58 – Extruding it

4. Now select the front face of the engine and extrude it out just a little with *E*.

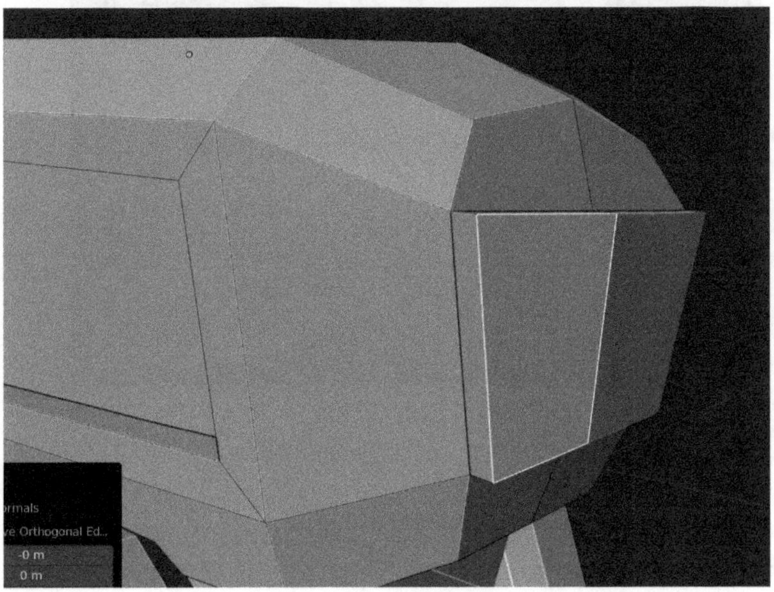

Figure 7.59 – Extruding a front detail

Looks a little more interesting now, right?

We're all done with the engine. The next thing we need is a place for the driver to sit: a cab. Since it's no fun to sit out in the hot sun, we'll make a nice, roomy glass cab.

The cab

The cab is where the driver sits—it's a pretty important part of the tractor. Thankfully, it's a really simple shape. It's not much more than a modified cube.

This means it'll be nice and easy to model. We'll start with a cube, of course. And this time, since it's such a simple shape, we won't even need to mirror it.

Let's get started!

1. Make sure you're in **Object Mode**, then press *Shift* + *A* and pick **Mesh** | **Cube**.
2. Press *3* for **Right** view.
3. Use *G* to put the cube roughly where the cab will go. It already looks pretty cool!

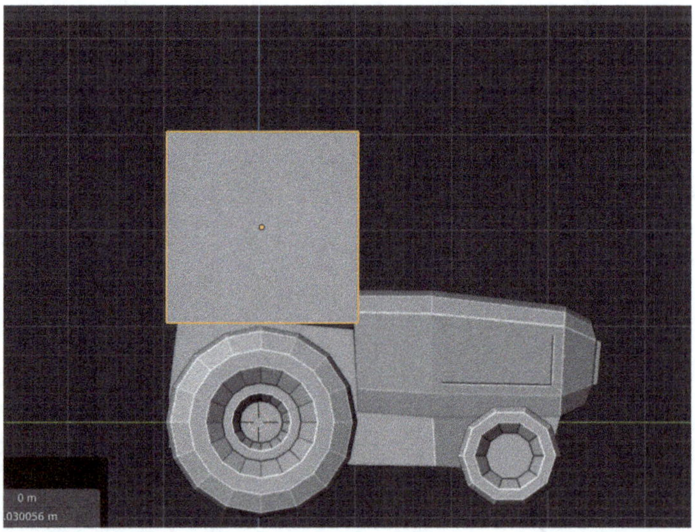

Figure 7.60 – The beginnings of the cab

4. Now *Tab* into **Edit Mode**. Switch to **Vertex Select** mode.
5. Enter **X-Ray** mode with *Alt* + *Z*.
6. Click and drag across the vertices to select both, then use *G* to move. Your goal is this shape:

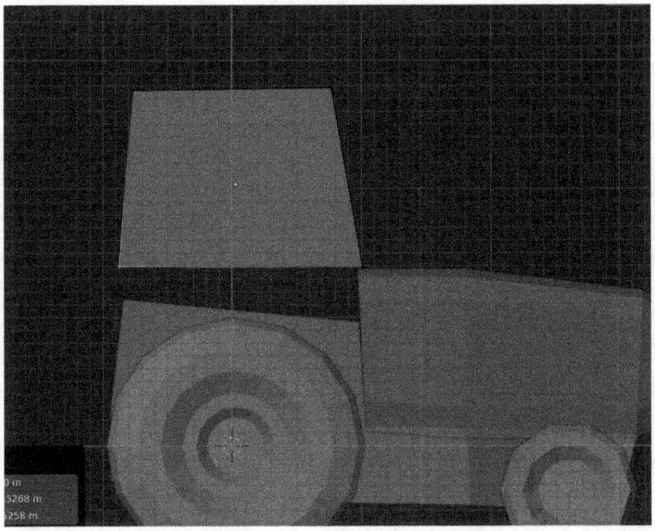

Figure 7.61 – Adjusting vertices manually

7. Now select the bottom vertices and extrude them downward with *E*.

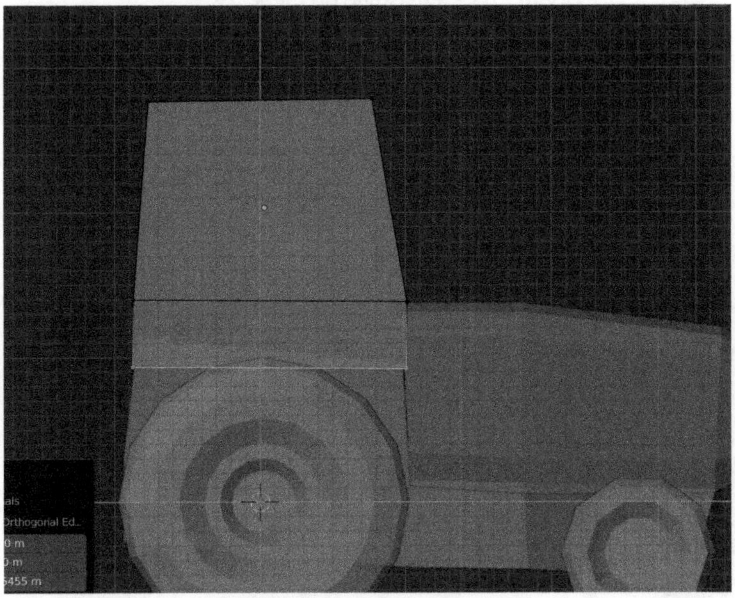

Figure 7.62 – Extruding downward

8. Turn off **X-Ray**. Select everything with *A* and use *S* and *X* to scale everything down on the X axis.

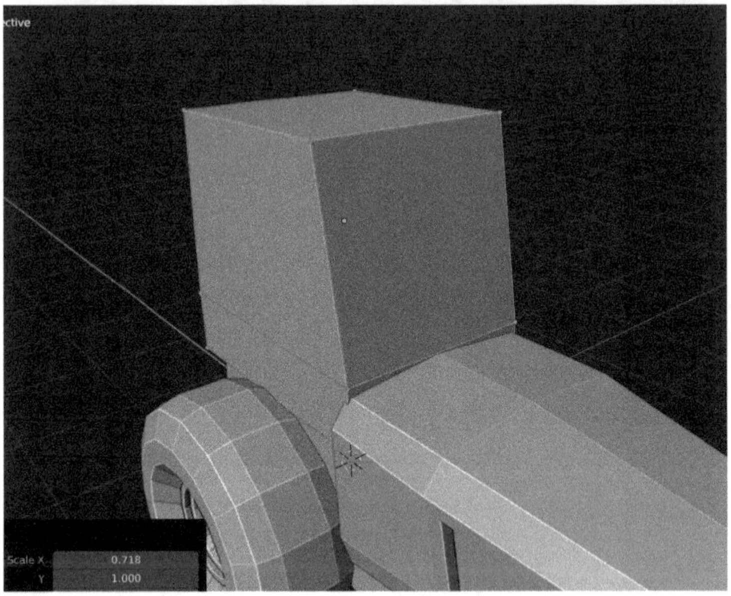

Figure 7.63 – Squashing on the X axis

9. Switch to **Face Select** mode and select the front and side faces.
10. Press *I* to inset them. You may need to press *I* twice so that it works on individual faces.

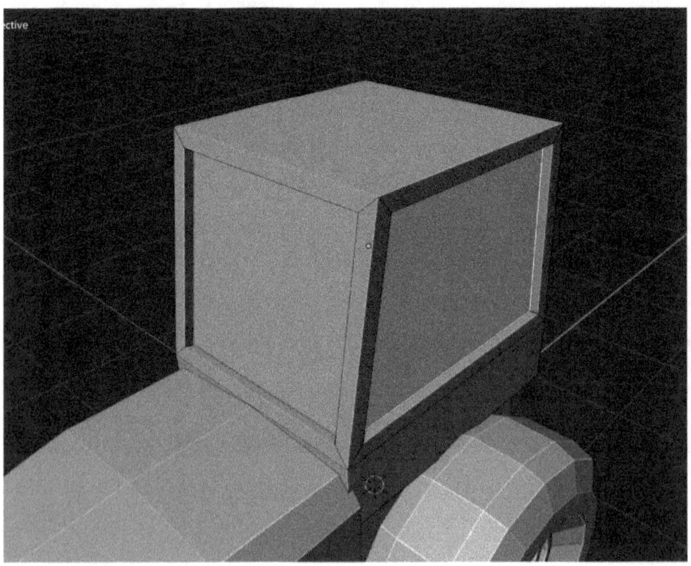

Figure 7.64 – Insetting the windows

11. Press *Alt* + *E* to open the **Extrude** menu. Pick **Extrude Individual Faces** and extrude them inward just a little bit to make windows. This operation is different from normal extruding because it extrudes each face in its own direction, instead of all the faces in the same direction.

Amazing! That's it for the cab. Rename the mesh from `Cube` to `Cab` in the Outliner.

You just modeled the body, the engine, and the cab—that was a lot of work, and you practiced a lot of valuable modeling techniques, such as manually positioning vertices in **X-Ray** mode.

Next up is adding some extra details.

Adding the details

Adding details to the tractor will make it a much more interesting model. The details will really help the tractor look more like a tractor. It'll also make it more fun to look at.

We're going to add the following details:

- Axles
- Wheel hubs
- Mirrors
- Headlights

Most of these are pretty easy, so this should be quick.

Wheel axles

We'll start by adding the wheel axles:

1. In **Object Mode**, press *Shift* + *A* to add a new cylinder.
2. Rotate the cylinder 90 degrees on the Y axis, and scale it down until it's small enough to serve as an axle.
3. Scale it on the X axis to make it longer.
4. Press *3* for the **Right** view (enter **X-Ray** mode if you want). Position the cylinder at the center of the wheel to serve as an axle.
5. Duplicate the cylinder to make a front axle.
6. If either axle protrudes through the wheels, select it and scale it down on the X axis to fix it.
7. Now rename the cylinders `Back axle` and `Front axle`.

Here's the final axle:

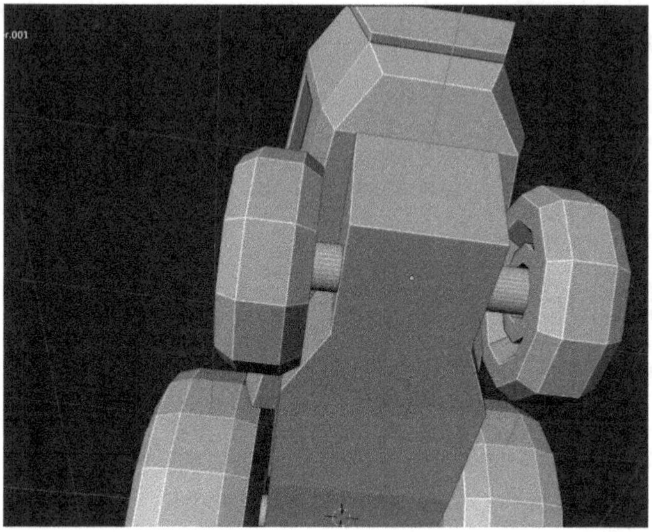

Figure 7.65 – The axles

And here's a view of both, in **X-Ray** mode:

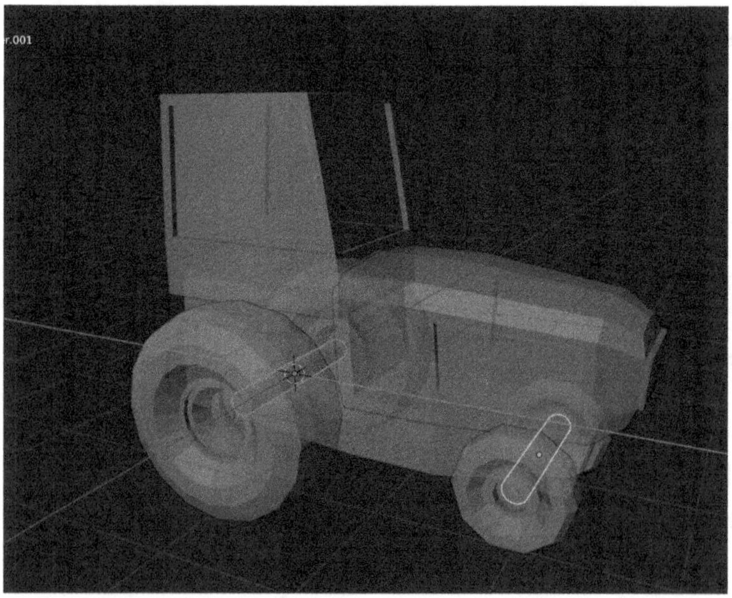

Figure 7.66 – The axles, in X-Ray mode

Well done! The axles are complete! Now, let's make some wheel hubs to go over the back wheels.

Wheel hubs

We'll make the back wheel hubs next. This is an extremely simple mesh, and it'll start with a plane:

1. Press *Shift* + *A* to add a plane.
2. Press *3* for **Right** view and *Alt* + *Z* for **X-Ray** mode.
3. *Tab* into **Edit Mode**.
4. Switch to vertex select.
5. Click and drag across vertices to select both, then position them using *G*, like this:

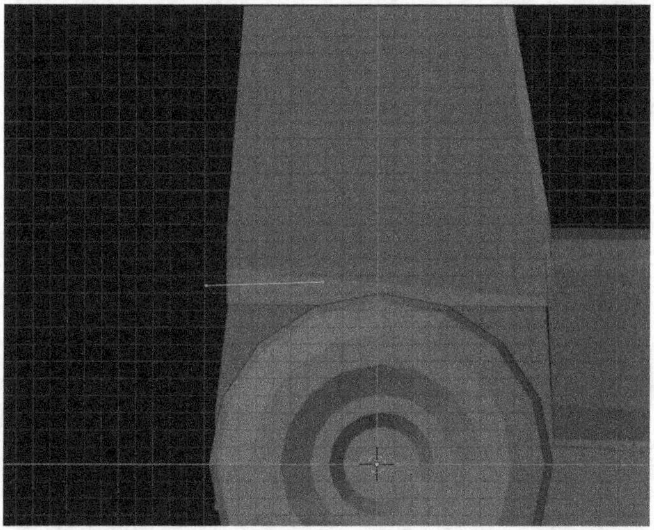

Figure 7.67 – A plane positioned manually, in X-Ray

6. Select the front two vertices by dragging across them.

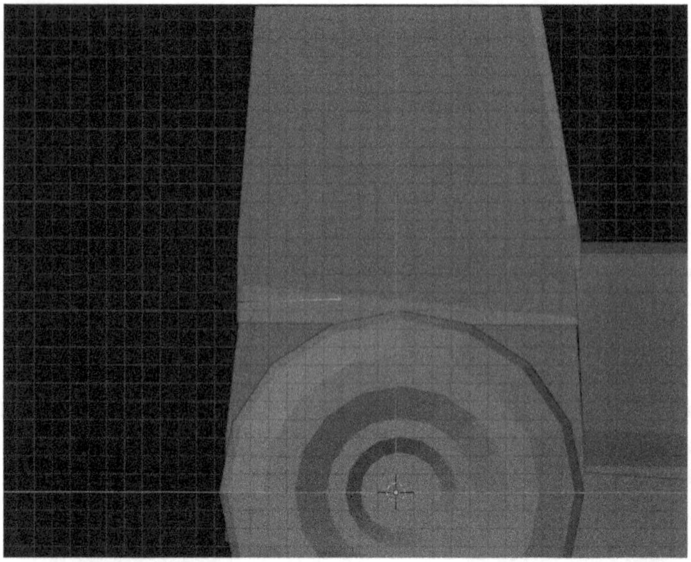

Figure 7.68 – Click and drag to select these front vertices

7. Press *E* to extrude them out. Do this three times in total, moving along the wheel as you go (stay in **Right** view as you extrude!).
8. Turn off **X-Ray** mode. Press *A* to select everything, and then *S* and *X* to make it wider.

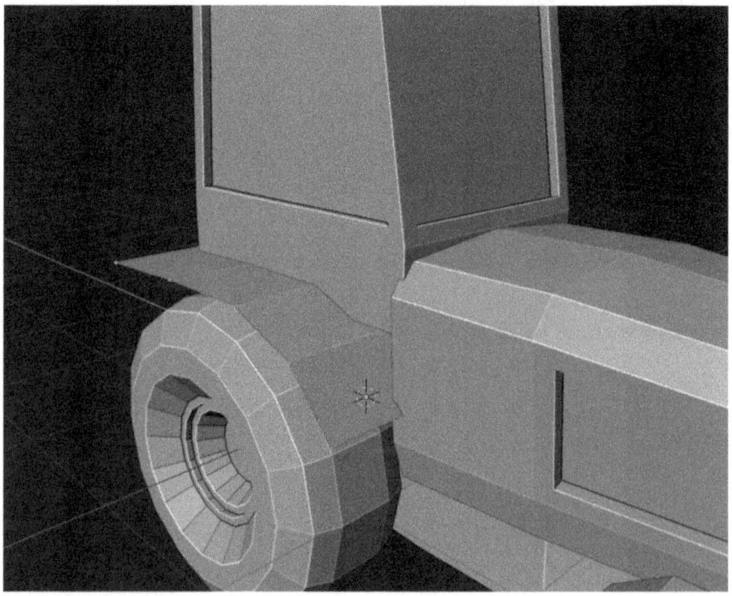

Figure 7.69 – The extruded shape, scaled very wide on the X axis

9. We just need to make it thicker now. Open the **Modifier** tab and add a **Solidify** modifier. This modifier is amazing for things like this—it's like an automatic **Extrude** tool.
10. Adjust the thickness on the modifier to a number such as `-0.15`.

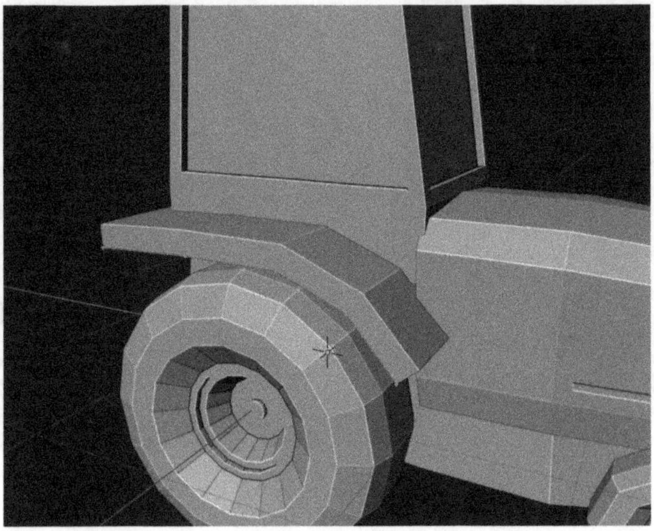

Figure 7.70 – Thickness from a Solidify modifier

11. Tweak the mesh as you wish.
12. Rename the object to `Hub`.

The wheel hubs are now complete. Excellent work! Next up are the rearview mirrors.

Mirrors

Mirrors are fairly simple—they're just a cube, mirrored:

1. Add a new cube. Name it `Mirror` and give it a **Mirror** modifier.
2. Pick the body as the mirror object. (If you click the eyedropper, you can use it to select the object you want from the viewport.)
3. Position, rotate, and scale the cube until it looks nice and mirrory.

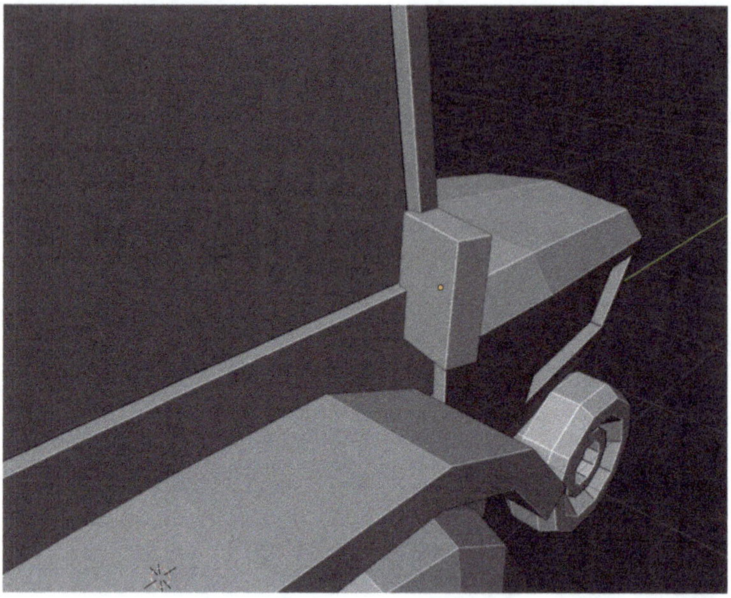

Figure 7.71 – The mirror, a cube

Since it's mirrored (a mirrored mirror!), it'll look the same on both sides.

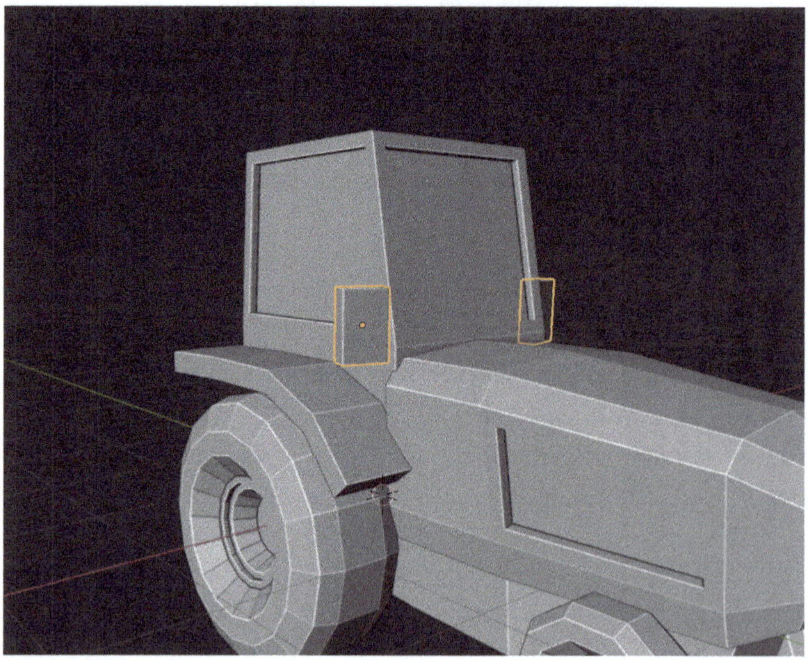

Figure 7.72 – Both mirrors

Now, let's add the headlights.

Headlights

The headlights are very similar to the mirrors. To make them, we'll start by duplicating the mirror object:

1. Select the mirrors and press *Shift* + *D* to duplicate. Right-click to leave the duplicate in place.
2. Rename the object `Lights`.
3. Press *Alt* + *R* to clear the rotation.
4. Position and scale the cube to make a headlight.

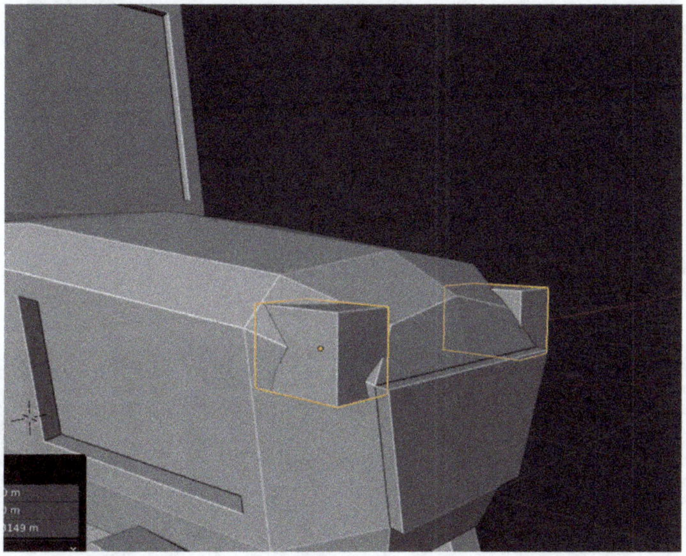

Figure 7.73 – A cube for the headlights

5. In **Edit Mode**, tweak the shape a little to make them look nicer.

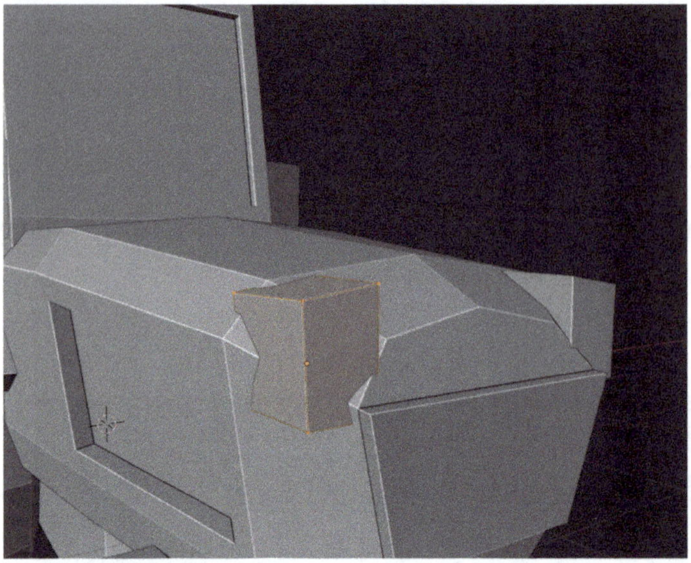

Figure 7.74 – Shaping it manually

6. Switch to **Face Select** mode. Select the front faces of the headlights.
7. Inset the faces, then extrude them inward.

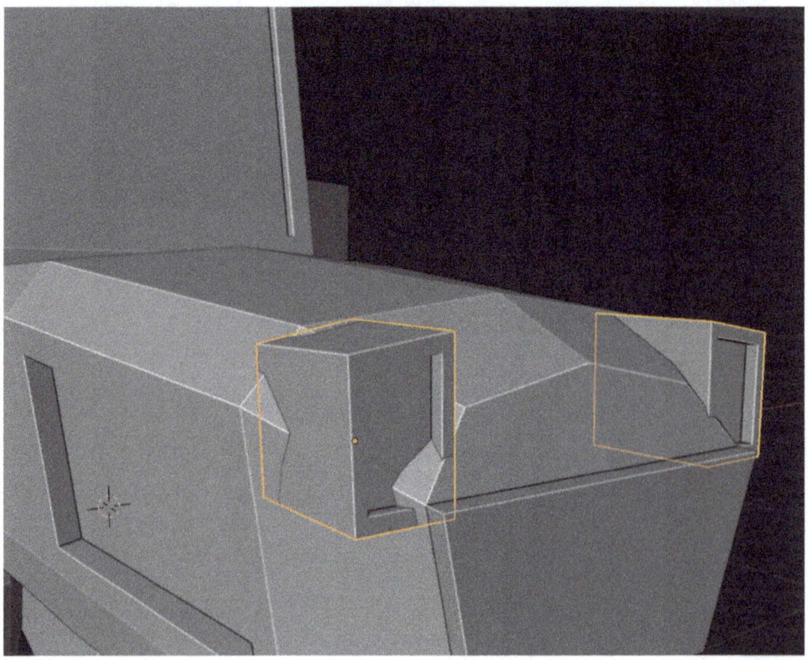

Figure 7.75 – Inset and extrude the front as a bit of detail

Now we can parent all the objects to one object. Let's make the engine the parent, since it's easy to select. Press *A* to select everything, then press *Shift* and select the engine.

Press *Ctrl* + *P* and select **Keep Transform** to parent everything to the engine. Now, when you move the engine, the whole thing moves with it.

Our tractor model is almost done! Just a little way to go and it'll be complete! Next up we have materials.

Adding materials

The final step before we can call our tractor done is to add materials to it. It'll look awesome when we're done!

First, we'll make the material that'll cover most of the tractor: a basic orange color. Switch to the **Shading** tab and take the following steps:

1. Select the `Engine` object.
2. Press the **New material** button at the top of the Shader Editor.
3. Name the new material `Orange`. Change the base color to orange and lower the roughness to make it a little shinier.

Now we need to assign this material to the other parts of the tractor. This is very tedious. There's a really helpful add-on that can make this process way faster. It's not a default Blender functionality (though it should be), but the add-on is included with Blender, so all we have to do is enable it.

Open **Preferences (Edit | Preferences)** and navigate to the **Addons** tab. Search for **Material Utilities** and check the box to turn it on.

Let's use the add-on!

1. Select the cab.
2. Press *Shift* + *Q* to use **Material Utilities**.
3. Go to **Assign Material | Search**, then pick the `Orange` material.
4. Press **Assign**.

This will assign the material to whatever object is currently selected. Select everything but the wheels and assign the `Orange` material.

Let's make a dark material for the wheels.

Select a wheel object, select **New Material**, and name it `Wheels`. Adjust it to be a dark rubber material by making the base color black and the roughness `0.9`.

Assign the `Wheels` material to the other pair of wheels.

Now *Tab* into **Edit Mode** on a wheel and select only the middle wheel faces. We'll set these to orange to make the wheel more interesting. You can do this using the *Shift* + *Q* shortcut (it works on faces too!)

Do the same for the other set of wheels.

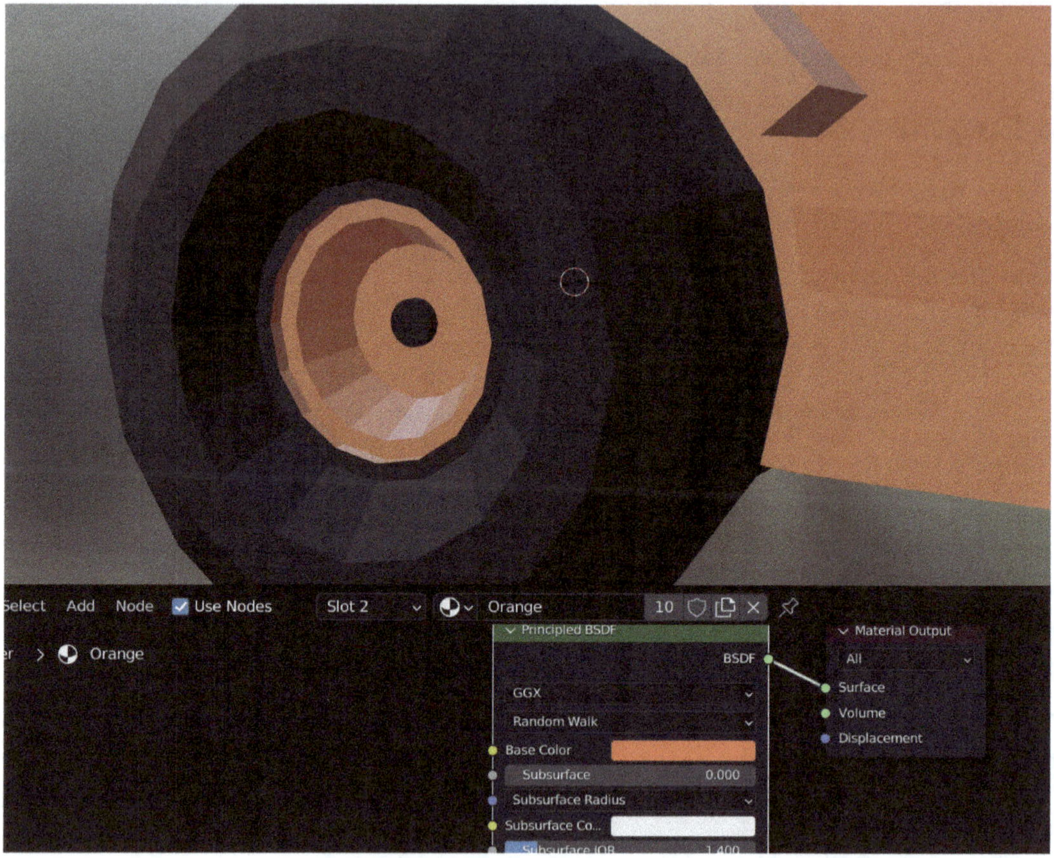

Figure 7.76 – Adding materials

Almost done!

Let's add some black to the engine panels. Select the extruded faces in **Edit Mode**, press *Shift* + *Q*, and assign the `Wheels` material to them.

Assign it to the mirrors too.

Let's make a new material for the windows. Select the windows in **Edit Mode**, press *Shift* + *Q*, and choose **New Material**. Name it `Windows`.

Shift + *Q* will automatically put the new material in a new material slot on the object. Adjust it to a dark bluish color, with a roughness of `0` to make it look shiny, like a window.

The final material is the headlights. *Tab* into **Edit Mode** and select the front faces of the headlights, then use *Shift* + *Q* to create a new material there called `Lights`.

In the `Lights` material, you can delete the principled node by pressing *X*. We're going to use a different kind of shader, an emission shader, instead. The emission shader makes an object emit light, which is cool for anything that glows or is a light.

1. Press Shift + A in the Shader Editor (where the nodes are) and choose **Shader** | **Emission.**
2. Plug it into the surface output.
3. Adjust the color to a gentle yellow and the strength to whatever you like.
4. Open the **Render** tab in the **Properties** panel and turn on **Bloom**. This will make your headlights glow.

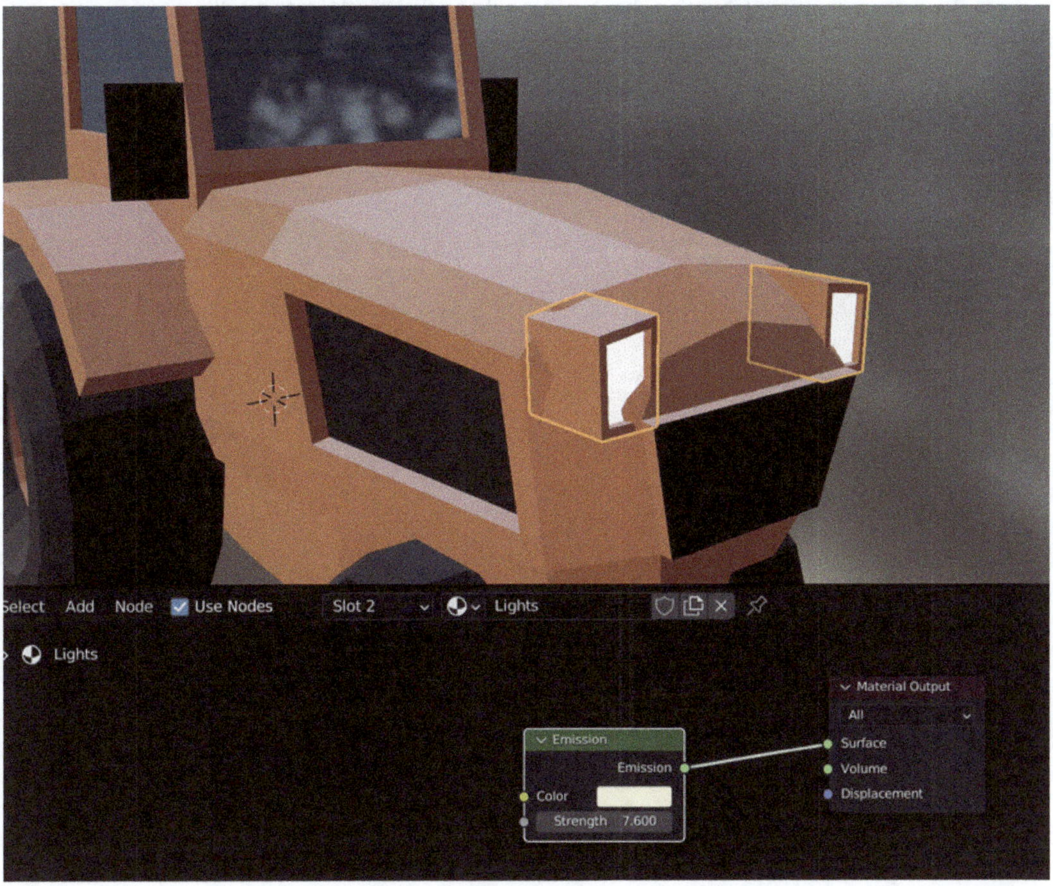

Figure 7.77 – The material for the headlights

And that's it. You've just built an entire tractor, from scratch, in Blender.

Great job!

Summary

In this chapter, you learned how to build an entire 3D tractor from scratch. You learned how to break a concept into pieces for modeling. You also learned how to make low poly wheels, and how to use **Mirror** modifiers to speed up the process.

You also learned about the emission shader for making things light up.

Great work!

If you only remember one thing from this chapter, it should be that the **Mirror** modifier can save you a ton of work. It's a good idea to use it whenever you're making something complicated and symmetrical.

In the next chapter, you'll learn about creating environment components in low poly—trees, rocks, grass, the works!

8
Low Poly Environment Modeling

It's time to make some useful landscape assets, such as trees, grass, and rocks. In this chapter, you'll learn how to make all of those assets, and even how to create multiple variations of them.

This chapter will be good practice for you since there are a lot of simple modeling tasks.

By the end of this chapter, you'll understand the following:

- How to create simple low poly plants
- How to make low poly rocks
- How to use the Proportional Editing tool

You'll also have a bunch of completed low poly models.

To start, we'll go over the specifics of what we're making.

What we're making

In this chapter, we'll be building a lot of small, different projects. Since you're getting pretty good at navigating Blender, I won't always name the keys you need to press. I might tell you to *go to the Right view* or *move the top face upward in the Z direction* without telling you which keys to press.

You're getting good at this.

Here's what we'll be making. It's a fairly long list:

- Grass
- A tall tree
- A branching tree

- A rock
- A flat rock
- A flower

For most of these objects, you'll also learn how to create a few different variations of the model so you don't have a forest full of totally identical trees or a garden of identical flowers.

We'll start simple. In the next section, you'll model grass.

Modeling low poly grass

First, let's model grass. This will be really simple: we'll just make a few grass shapes and then duplicate them to make a clump. Then, we can duplicate that clump, edit it a little, and have a whole different clump of grass!

Grass is easy to model. We're going to start with a cylinder:

1. Press *Shift* + *A* and choose **Mesh** | **Cylinder**.
2. In the **Operator** menu, change the **Vertices** number to `3`.

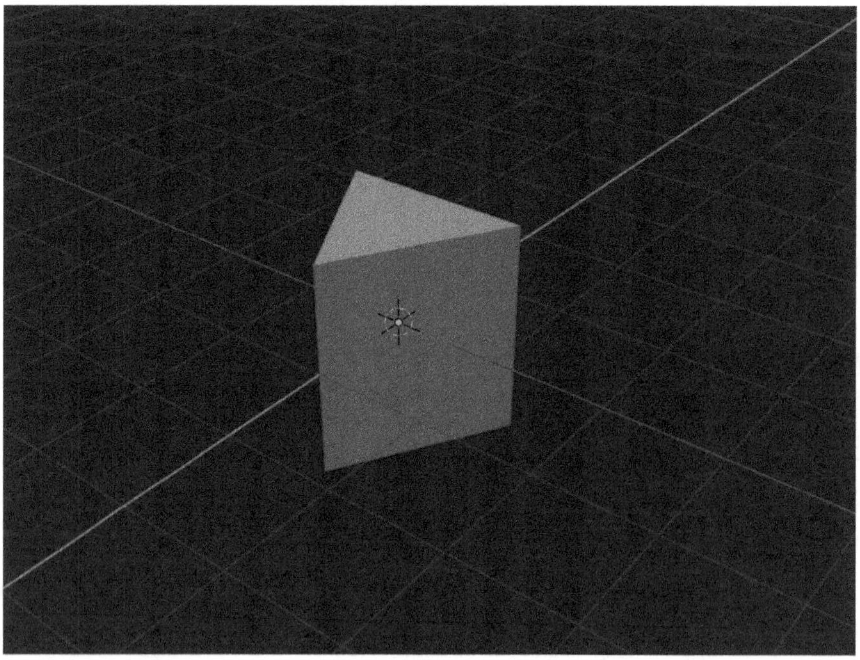

Figure 8.1 – The new cylinder

With only three vertices, this shape is more of a *tall triangle* than it is a cylinder. This is perfect for making our grass. We're going to taper this cylinder, then give it a slight bend or curve to make it more organic-looking.

Once we have a single blade of grass, we'll just duplicate and adjust it a few times to make a clump of grass. When the clump is ready, we'll make a few copies and adjust them individually to make *different* clumps.

Then, we'll join each clump into a single object, and you'll have a few different grass clumps to choose from. Follow these steps:

1. Select your cylinder and enter **Edit Mode**.
2. Hit *A* to select everything.
3. Hit *S* to scale everything down smaller (you don't want a monster blade of grass).
4. Select the top face of your cylinder.
5. Move it upward along the Z axis to make the cylinder tall.
6. Scale it down to taper the cylinder.

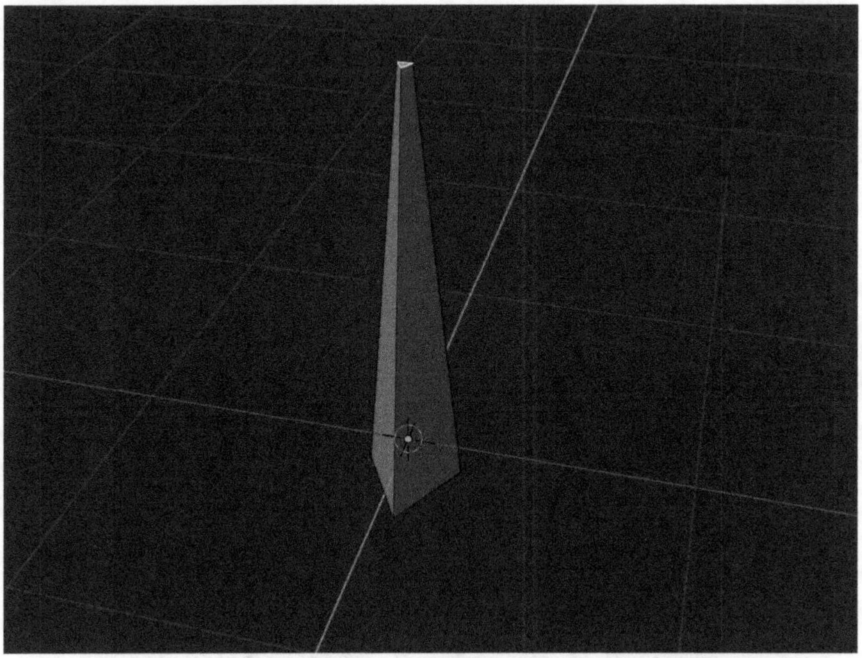

Figure 8.2 – Tapering the cylinder

7. Press *Ctrl* + *R* and add four new edge loops along the cylinder. These new edges will allow you to add a bit of a curve to the cylinder.

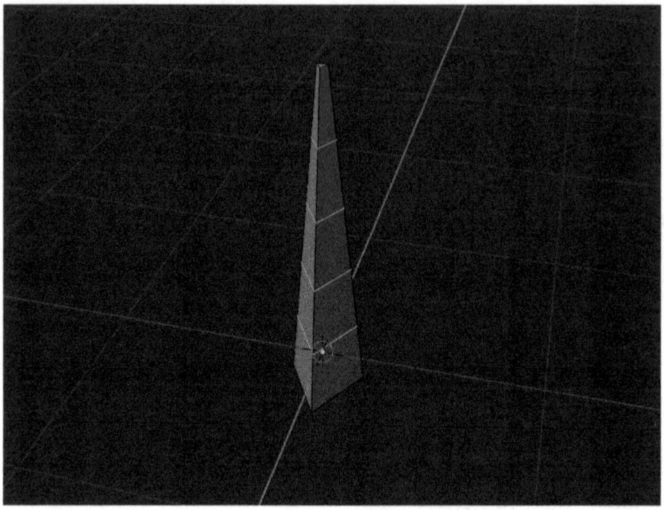

Figure 8.3 – Adding loops

8. Select the top face again and press *M* to activate the **Merge** tool. The **Merge** tool merges several vertices into one. Choose **Center** to merge the vertices at the center. Now your grass is pointy!

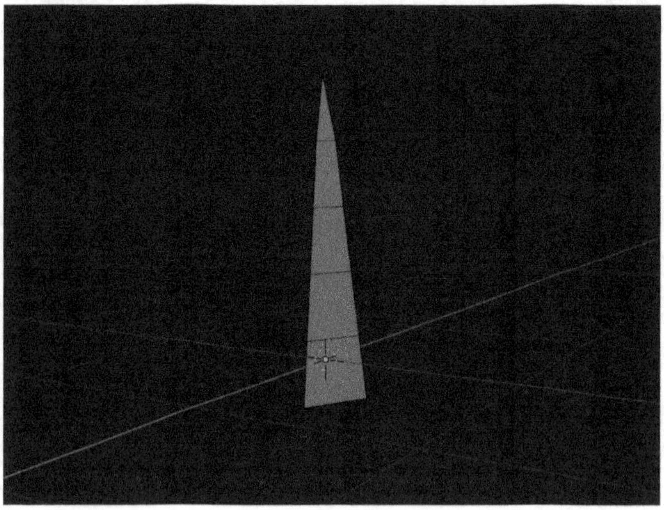

Figure 8.4 – Making a point

That's the basic grass blade shape. The next step is to bend it a little. We'll do that from the **Right** view in **Edit Mode:**

1. Press *3* for the **Right** view and *Alt* + *Z* to turn on **X-Ray** mode.
2. Switch to **Vertex Select** mode.
3. Click and drag across vertices to select them.
4. Select the top vertex and move to the side a bit.

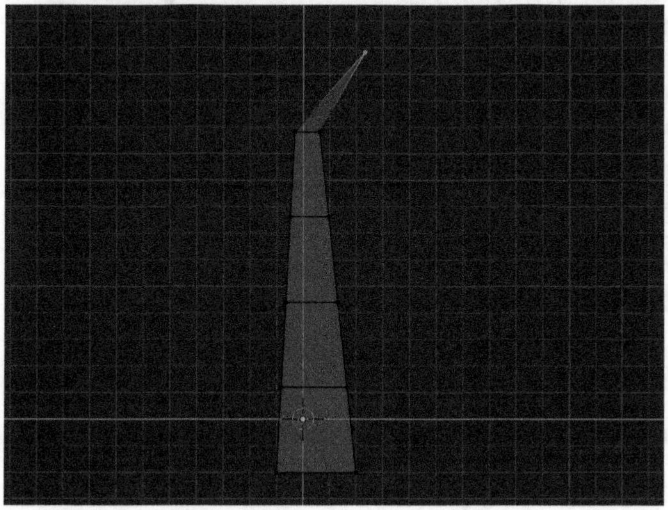

Figure 8.5 – Moving the point

5. Now, select the next loop (by clicking and dragging) and use *G* to move it over a little.
6. Use *R* to rotate it if you need to.

Do this for all of the loops to create a simple curve in the blade of grass. You can also scale the loops if you like, to change how thin or thick the grass is at that location.

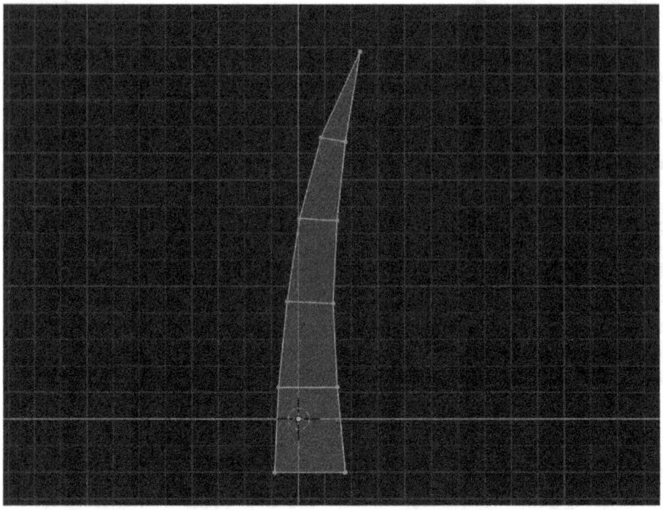

Figure 8.6 – The final bent grass

Now, the grass blade is curved and it's looking great. Exit **X-Ray** mode to get a good look at it. Next, we're going to twist the blade a little bit, to add some interest.

To twist the blade, you'll use **Proportional Editing**. This is a powerful tool. When you have it enabled, any operation you do (rotate, for example) will affect everything within a certain distance from the selected vertices.

This distance, or *falloff radius*, is shown as a white circle on your screen. You can adjust it by scrolling.

The hotkey to enable **Proportional Editing** is *O*. Follow these steps:

1. Press *O* to turn on **Proportional Editing**.
2. Select the top vertex of the grass.
3. Press *R* and *Z* to rotate it on the *Z* axis. This will twist the whole blade of grass in a very cool way.
4. Scroll to adjust the **Proportional Editing** radius, and move your mouse to rotate more or less. The goal is just to use a gentle twist.

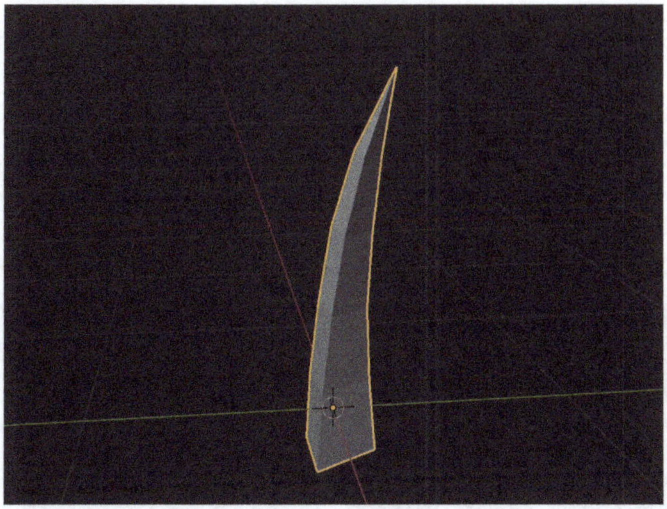

Figure 8.7 – With a slight twist added

Now, your blade of grass is ready. Next, we'll use this one blade to make a *clump* of grass:

1. Press *Tab* to get out of **Object Mode**, and press *O* to turn **Proportional Editing** off again.
2. To make a clump, hit *7* for the **Top** view.
3. Press *Shift* + *D* to make a duplicate of the grass. Position it near the first one. Make a few of these (four or five).

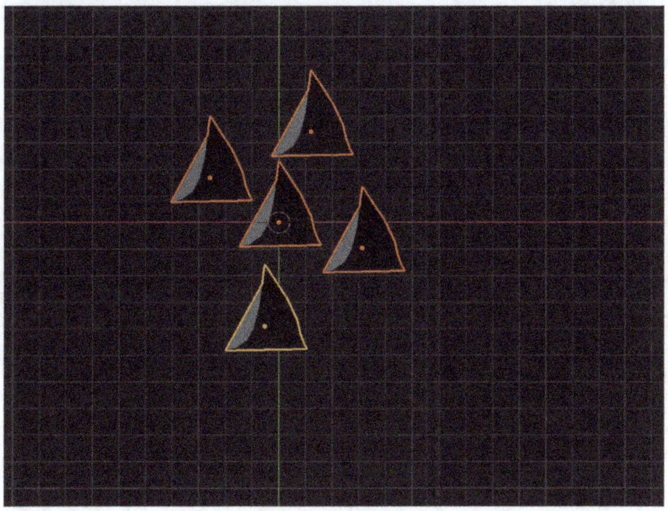

Figure 8.8 – Duplicating in the Top view

4. Now select the blades of grass, one at a time, and rotate each one a *random* amount so they won't look so identical.
5. Next, you'll add some random scale.
6. Simply select a blade and press *S* to scale it down.
7. It works well if you leave one or two bigger blades and make the rest a lot smaller. Once you're done scaling, check to make sure that the bottom of the grass is at the same general level (use *G* and *Z* to move any piece up or down as needed).

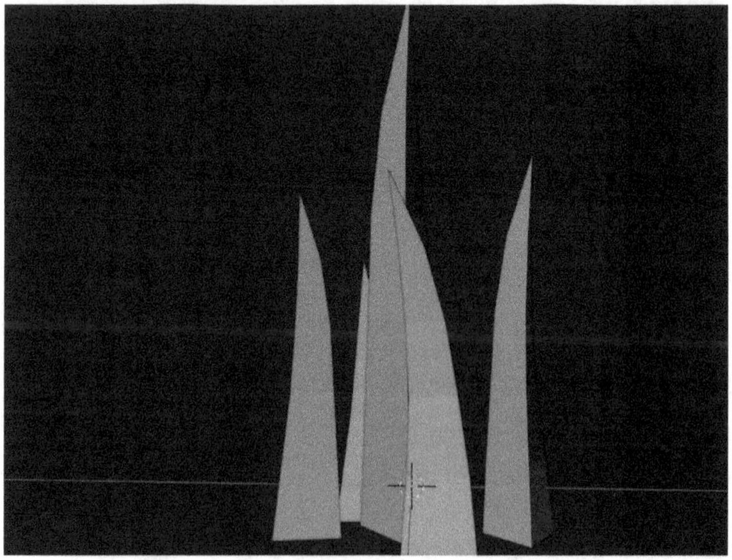

Figure 8.9 – Adding rotation and scale variation

8. Once you have the clump looking good, select the entire clump and press *Shift* + *D* to duplicate it. Move it out of the way along the *X* axis. This will be a new clump. Delete one of the grass blades and modify the scales and rotations some more.
9. There, you have a brand-new clump!
10. Now select all the blades in one clump and press *Ctrl* + *J* to join them into a single object. You can *move* the clump around easily now, without having to select each separate blade of grass.

Do the same thing for the other clump.

Two complete clumps! Nice work! Now, give them names in the outliner: `Grass Clump 1` and `Grass Clump 2`.

The last step is the material. You know how to set that up now—just make it a nice green color. And make sure it's not too shiny. (Remember to hit *Z* + *2* to see your materials in **Material Preview** mode.)

Remember, you can always change the material later—it's no big deal.

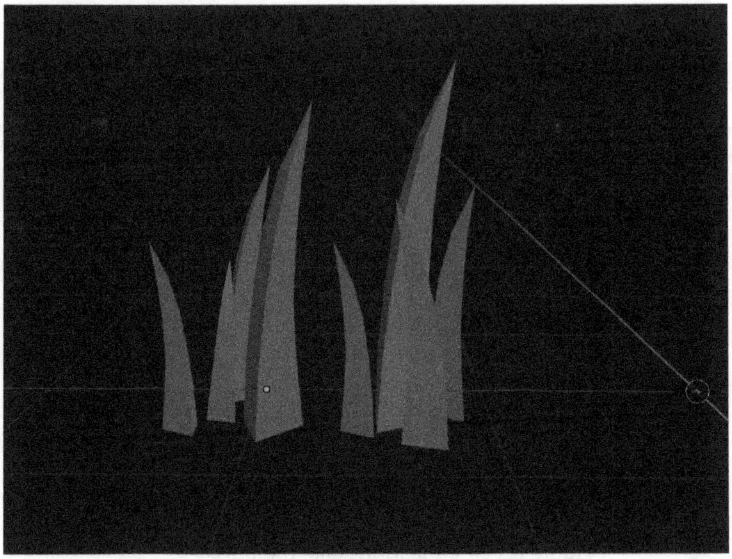

Figure 8.10 – Duplicating the whole clump

Now, select your two grass clumps and move them off to the side to make some room for the next thing: a flower. You can also click the tiny eyeball next to the grass objects in the outliner to hide the clumps.

Making low poly flowers

The flowers are very similar to the grass. They won't be that hard to make; you'll start with a triangular stem just like the grass, then add a simple squashed icosphere for the bloom.

Make sure you're back in the **Solid View** mode (hit *Z* + *6*).

First, add a cylinder. In the **Operator** menu, change the number of vertices to `3`, if it's not already.

Now you need to thin the cylinder out and taper it, exactly like the grass. The steps are almost identical:

1. Select your cylinder and enter **Edit Mode**.
2. Hit *A* to select everything.
3. Hit *S* to scale everything down smaller. (You don't want a monster flower stem, so make it pretty thin.)
4. Select the top face of your cylinder.
5. Move it upward along the *Z* axis to make the cylinder tall.
6. Scale it down to taper the cylinder.

7. Press *Ctrl* + *R* and add four new edge loops along the cylinder. These new edges will allow you to add a bit of a curve.

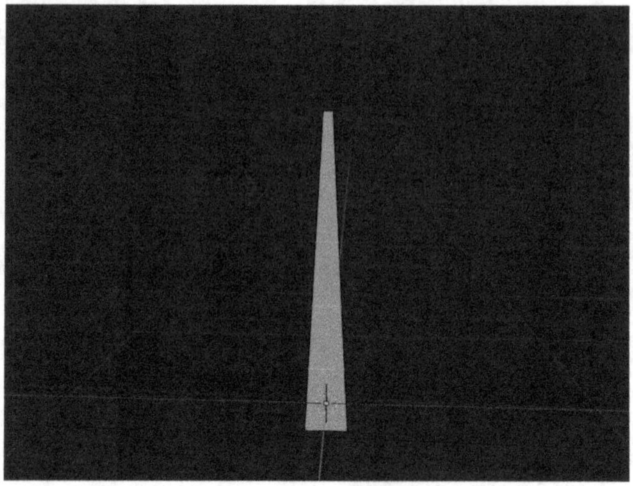

Figure 8.11 – Edge loops (like the grass)

Now we need to bend the stem. Do it just like you did for the grass blade:

1. Get into **Edit Mode**, and turn on **X-Ray** mode(*Alt* + *Z*).
2. Click and drag to select vertices and reposition and rotate them to form a gentle bend. It's best to work in the **Front** or **Right** view for this part (press *1* or *3*).
3. When you're done, the stem should look like this:

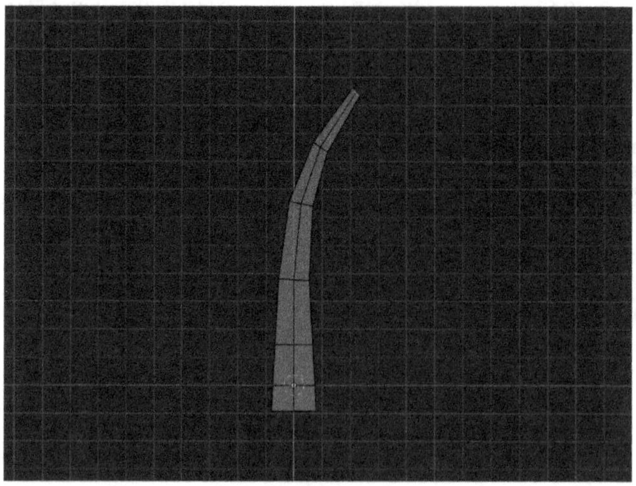

Figure 8.12 – Bending the stem

The last step for the stem is to add a little twist. It's not needed, but it adds a little interest. It may be a little too complex for some scenes, but it should do fine for yours:

1. Turn on **Proportional Editing** with *O*.
2. Select the top vertex, and rotate it a little on the Z axis to twist the stem.

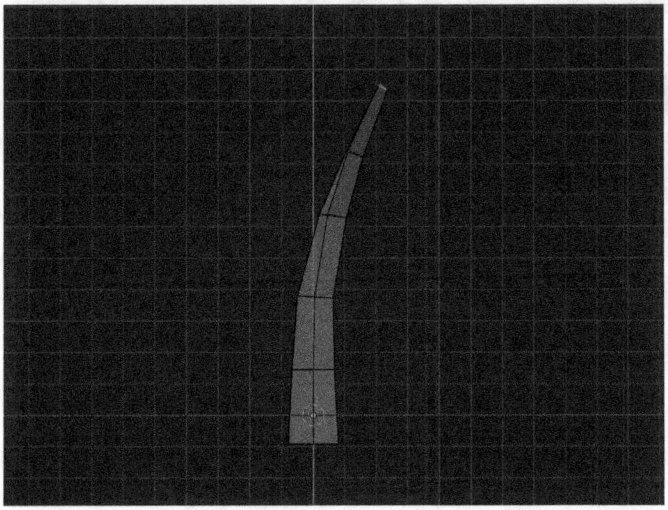

Figure 8.13 – Twisting the stem

The process is just like what you did to make the grass blade. That's the complete flower stem. Now, let's make the bloom part, the actual *flower*.

Since the bloom part is so small, it'll be really, really simple—just a single icosphere:

1. Press *Tab* to go back to **Object Mode**.
2. Press *Shift* + *A* and add a new icosphere.
3. In the **Operator** menu, change the subdivisions to `1`. This gives you a simpler sphere, with much fewer faces.
4. Scale it *way* down.
5. Use *S* to squash it on the *Z* axis.

6. Rotate it so that it's at an angle, like a flower, then position it at the end of the stem, like this:

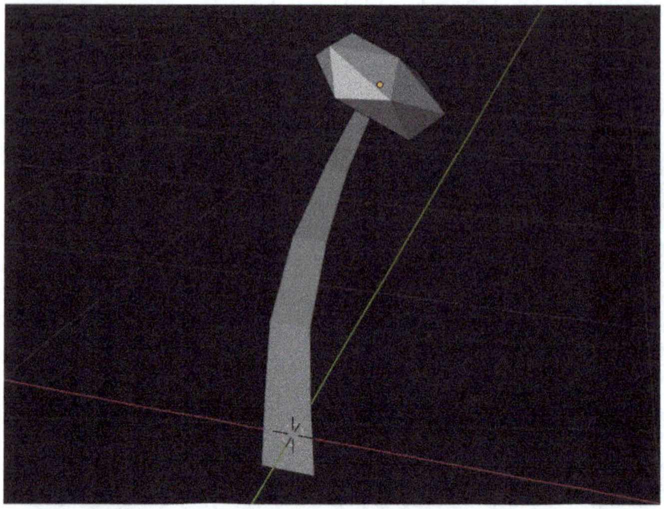

Figure 8.14 – Adding the bloom

It's a simple flower. Possibly a little ugly too. Feel free to change it up!

There's not much left! All you have to do now is set up materials. Give the flower a bright color, such as red or pink, and make the stem green.

I did my flower in pink:

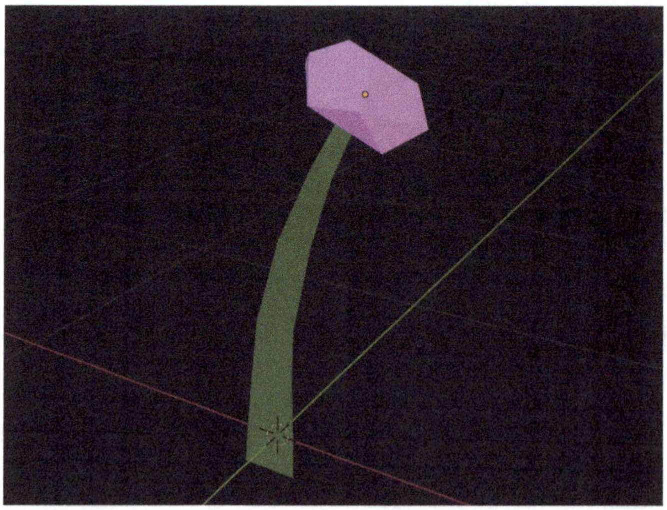

Figure 8.15 – Flower after adding materials

Once you have the materials all set up, you can join the objects together. Just select them both, then press *Ctrl* + *J* to join them.

When you join two objects with different materials, the new object has two material slots, one for each material. For the flower, one slot will be assigned to the bloom part, and another to the stem (since they both had different materials). If you want to come back later and change the material for the flower, you can easily switch out that slot's material.

The flower is done. Move it off to one side so it doesn't get in the way of your next project: rocks.

Modeling low poly rocks

Rocks are really simple to build—especially low-poly ones. We're going to make two kinds of rocks: a fairly normal boulder and a flatter one.

The process here is a bit different. You'll start with a mesh, then mess it up and randomize it. You'll use the **Knife** tool to add new edges and vertices, and **Proportional Editing** to shape it.

Let's start by making a basic rock shape to build upon.

Creating the basic rock shape

Here's how you model the basic rock shape:

1. Add an icosphere.
2. In the **Operator** menu, change the subdivisions to `1`, for the simplest possible sphere.
3. Press *Tab* to go into **Edit Mode**.
4. Switch to **Vertex Select** mode.
5. Turn on **Proportional Editing** by pressing *O*.
6. Now, you need to flatten the bottom of the sphere. Select one of the bottom vertices and move it upward with *G* to flatten the bottom of the icosphere. (Don't worry about making this perfect; just aim for mostly flat. It's a rock after all.) Remember that you can scroll to adjust the **Proportional Editing** radius.

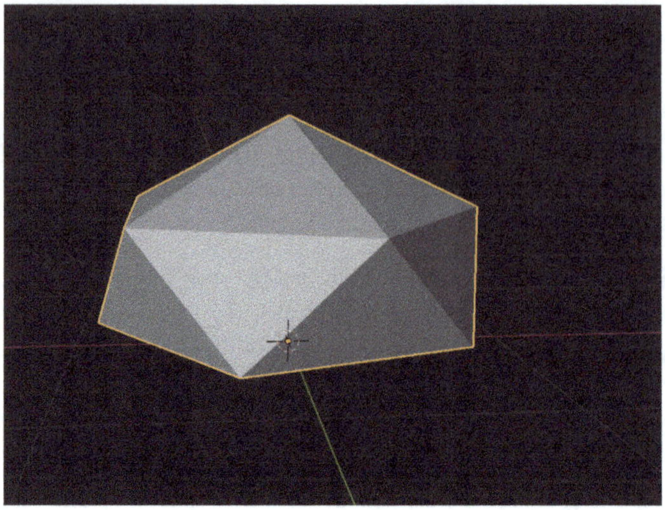

Figure 8.16 – Starting the rock

This is our basic rock shape. Let's mess things up a little bit now. I call this process *randomizing*, but it's a bit of an art. You're trying to get a random, rocky shape, but you want that shape to make you think of a *rock*. Not a pile of garbage or a beach ball, but a rock. Rocks typically have some big, flat sides, but also some more detailed parts, so you want some big faces and some smaller ones.

You'll have no idea what you're doing here. That's OK. You have to do it to know what you're doing. The more you do stuff like this, the better you get at it.

You don't have to try to follow exactly what I'm doing here. I'll show you how it's done and how to fix certain problems you might run into.

Just have fun!

Creating a boulder

Let's create a normal boulder. I don't like to use **Proportional Editing** for this part, so press *O* or click the **Proportional Editing** button to turn it off. Then, follow these steps:

1. Select any vertex.
2. Press *G* to move that vertex somewhere new.

This is how we'll reshape the sphere into a rock. Our first goal is to make it slightly less rounded because that's too perfect for a rock. I like a slightly stretched shape. It'll be tedious, but going one vertex at a time will give you more control over the result.

Make sure that you continually view your rock from different angles so that you have a coherent idea of what's happening.

Here's what I ended up with. You can see how the shape is a little longer now, and how some of the faces are stretched into big flat surfaces:

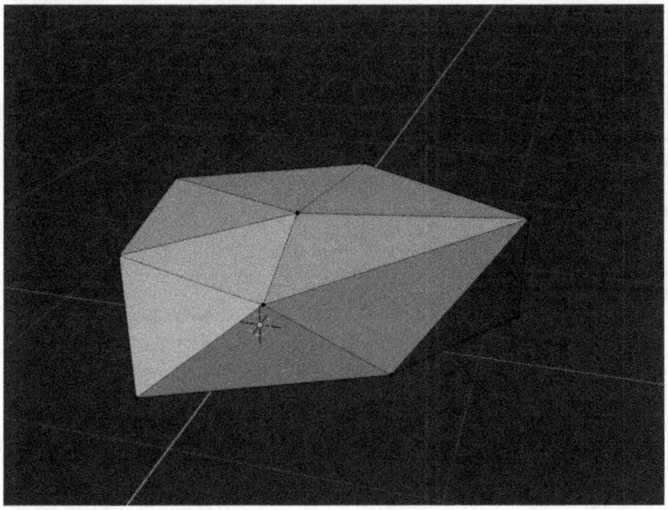

Figure 8.17 – Tweaking the shape

Now we get to do the fun part: use the **Knife** tool. The **Knife** tool lets you click anywhere to cut new vertices into your mesh. It creates nasty, weird faces—and that's just fine on a low poly rock. To use **Knife**, press *K*. Then, follow these steps:

1. Click anywhere on an edge of the mesh to add a new vertex. Now you can see a red line where the cut will happen.
2. Click on another edge to add another vertex—new vertices will be added wherever the cut intersects an edge.
3. When you like what you see, hit *Enter* to confirm it (or *Esc* to cancel and try again if you're not happy with it).
4. I like to add my new cuts in places where I wish I could bend a face but can't—the cut will allow you to move that new part.

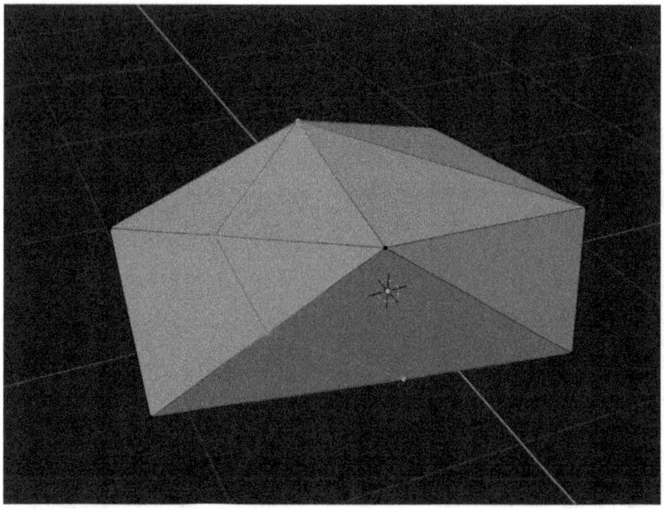

Figure 8.18 – Cutting new vertices with the Knife tool

5. Now you have new vertices—use *G* to position them how you like, or leave them as they are.

I selected my new vertices and moved them outward, to add a new dimension or facet to my rock.

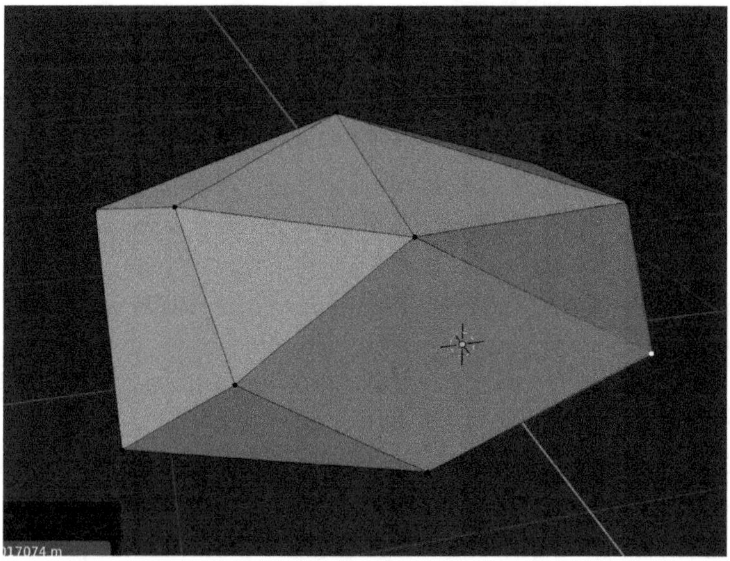

Figure 8.19 – More tweaking

Here's a problem: this resulted in a crazy face that is impossible. It connects these four vertices in a seemingly impossible way—we don't want an illusory rock. To fix this, we can turn this one face into two faces, by connecting *vertex A* and *vertex B* (see *Figure 8.20*). To do that, just select the two vertices and press *J* to join them. Keep an eye out for impossible faces like this—they're confusing but easy to fix.

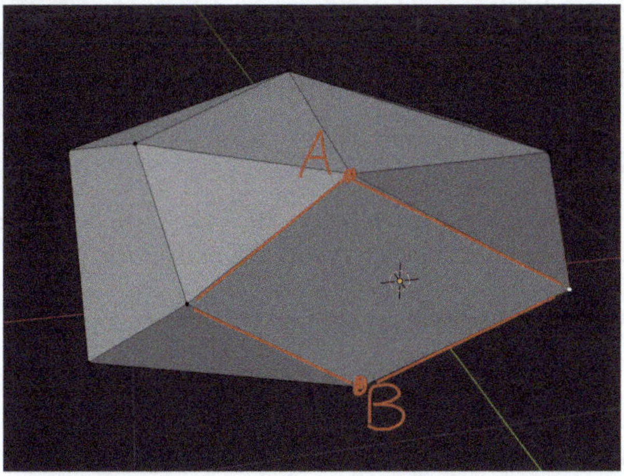

Figure 8.20 – This face is impossible. We will split it into two triangles

Another difficulty you might run into is too many vertices, as in *Figure 8.21*. I don't want all of these here, but if I delete one, there'll be a hole in the mesh. To solve this, you can merge them using the **Merge** tool. Select the vertices you want to merge together, then press *M*. The **Merge** tool gives you several options for where the new vertex should be located: at the location of the first one, last one, or centered between them all. I like to pick **Center**.

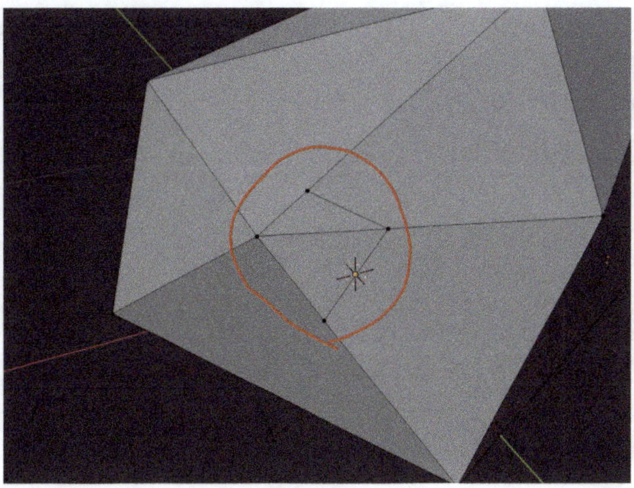

Figure 8.21 – This is a mess, so let's merge it into one vertex

Now, work at it until you are happy with your rock. It'll be hard, and you might not like it the first time. That's fine—you'll get better at this kind of thing as you do it more.

That was a lot of work. Great job making it through. You just learned a ton of things: how to use the **Knife** tool, how to solve the impossible face problem, and how to use the **Merge** tool.

Now, give it a good name (I called mine `Rock`—couldn't think of anything better). Duplicate it and move it to one side. We'll leave the duplicate alone but change the original rock into a new, flatter version.

Creating a flat rock

To make the flat version, we'll simply squash the duplicate rock. It will be extremely easy. We'll just use the same technique we used earlier to flatten the bottom of the rock:

1. Press *Tab* to get back into **Edit Mode**.
2. Press *O* to turn on **Proportional Editing**.
3. Select a vertex or two on the top of the rock.
4. Press *G* + *Z* to move them down and squash the rock (scroll to adjust the **Proportional Editing** radius).

Now that your rock is squashed, you're done! You have two complete rocks. If you want more rocks, it's really easy. Just duplicate one of your existing rocks, press *Tab* to go into **Edit Mode**, and reshape it some more. You could start from scratch again if you like.

Materials are simple. Make a nice gray, and turn the roughness up all the way (rocks are *not* shiny (though you may find yourself needing a shiny rock, someday…). You could even take it up a level and use a different shade of gray for different rocks.

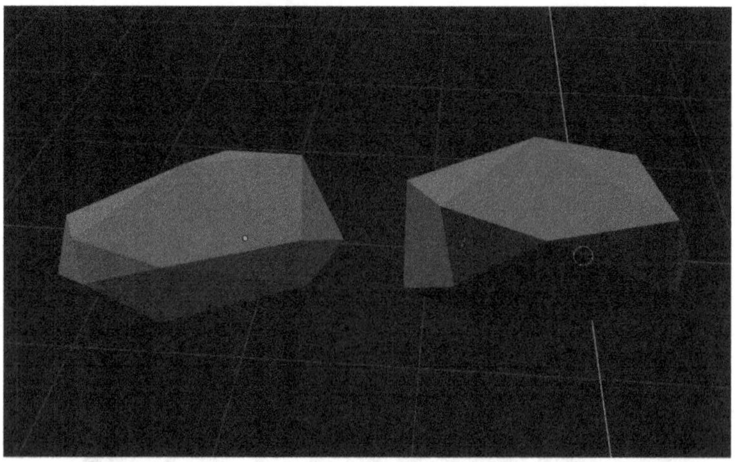

Figure 8.22 – The final rocks

That's it for the rocks! Select them, hit *G*, and slide them along the *X* axis to get them out of the way for the next project: trees.

Creating low poly trees

"But Samuel, I already made a tree!"

Yes, but the one in *Chapter 3* was just to get you started.

The ones we'll build here are way better. Not more realistic—these are still stylized, low-poly trees. But still, they're a step up from what you made earlier.

This means they'll be harder to make, too. So buckle up!

We're going to make two different kinds of trees: a tall, pointy type of tree, and a wider, branching tree.

Both of these trees will use the same tree trunk, based on a cylinder. This means that you'll only have to make the trunk once—less work! Let's begin.

Creating the trunk

Making the trunk is simple. It all starts with a cylinder:

1. Add a cylinder.
2. In the **Operator** menu, change the vertex number to `8`.
3. *Press Tab* to go into **Edit Mode**.
4. Press *A* to select everything, then *S* to scale it down pretty small, like this:

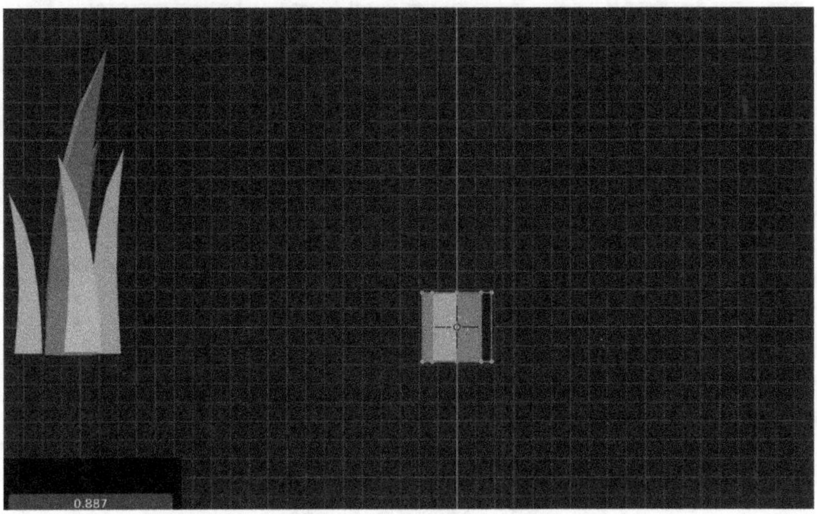

Figure 8.23 – The cylinder that will become the tree trunk

5. Select the top face and move it up on the *Z* axis. Go pretty high—this is a tall tree.

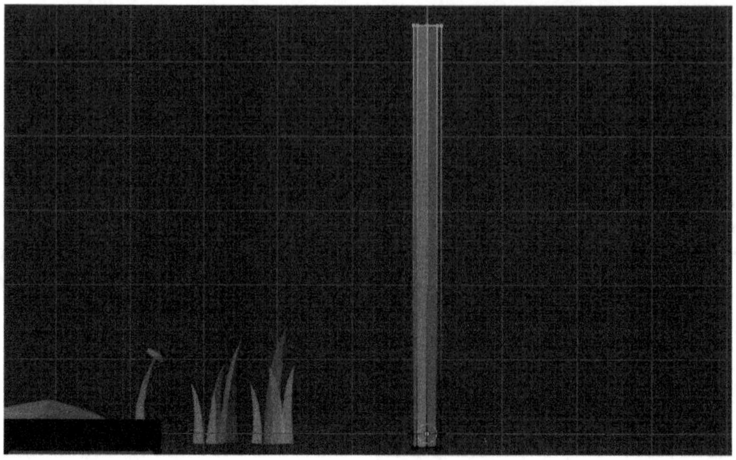

Figure 8.24 – Stretching it

6. Press *Ctrl* + *R* and scroll to add new edge loops. I added four.
7. Now, switch to **Vertex Select** mode, and enter **X-Ray** view.
8. Select one of the edge loops by dragging over the vertices, then either move it a little bit, rotate it, or scale it. Just do something to it, enough to add some randomness—but not too much.

Repeat for the other loops, tweaking them just a little, to add some interest to the overall shape. Here's what I ended up with:

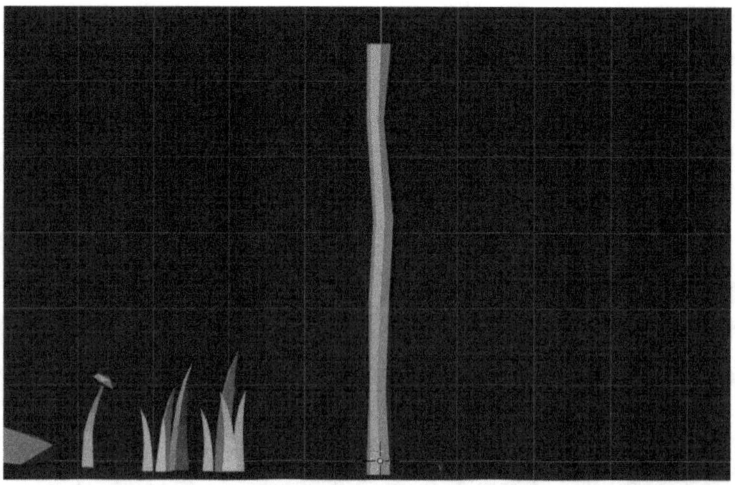

Figure 8.25 – Adding randomness

That's it for the trunk!

Now, let's turn it into two different kinds of trees. The first kind, the tall tree, is very simple.

Creating a tall tree

Before you start with the tall tree, duplicate the trunk (in **Object Mode**) and move it off to one side so that you can still use it for the second tree.

Now, let's make the leaves:

1. In **Object Mode**, add an icosphere. Change the subdivisions to `1`.
2. Position it at the top of the tree trunk using *G*.
3. *Press Tab* to go into **Edit Mode**.
4. Turn on **Proportional Editing** with *O*.
5. Select a vertex on top, and move it upward to stretch the sphere.
6. Adjust the sphere's shape by moving individual vertices. The goal is to get a shape like this: wider at the bottom and thinner at the top.

You can use **Proportional Editing** or turn it off; a bit of both might be needed. Try scaling the top with **Proportional Editing** to taper it. Here's my result:

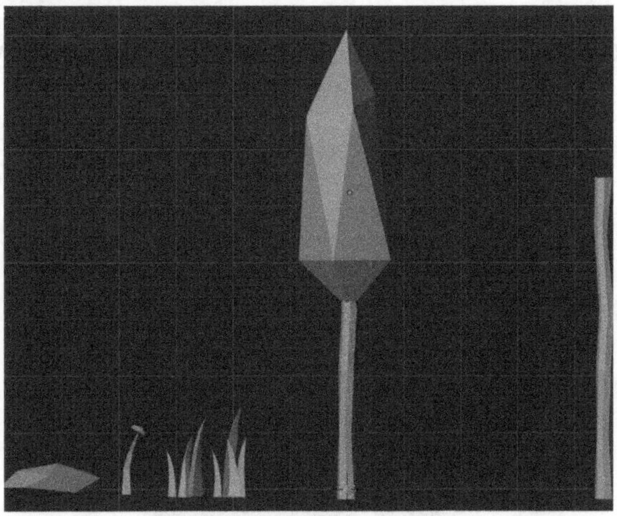

Figure 8.26 – The top of the tree

Now, you have the leaves for the tall tree. Time to set up some materials—again, this is really easy. I'm not going to show you how to do it—you already know how. Make a green one for the leaves and a brown one for the trunk.

Join the trunk and leaves together when you're done setting the materials, and name the new object `Tall Tree`.

Now, it's time for the branching tree!

Creating a branching tree

This one's not much harder. Before you make the leaves, though, let's improve the trunk. We'll build this tree from the trunk we duplicated earlier. The first thing you need to do is add some branches, which we'll make out of cylinders:

1. Press *Shift* + *A* and add a new cylinder.
2. In the **Operator** menu, set the vertex number to `8`.
3. Scale the cylinder *way* down.
4. You don't want tiny branches, so the cylinder needs to be taller. Press *S* and *Z* to stretch it on the *Z* axis.

   That's it for the branch.
5. Press *G* to move the branch object. Position it like a tree branch, sticking out of the tree trunk (it helps if you work in the **Right** or **Front** view, so you can line them up easily).
6. Now, duplicate the branch and position it somewhere else. If you're feeling extra creative, you can press *Tab* to go into **Edit Mode**, hit *Ctrl* + *R* to add a new loop, and add a little bit of a bend in the middle of the branch by moving the new loop down a little bit. Whatever you like.

Here's what mine looks like:

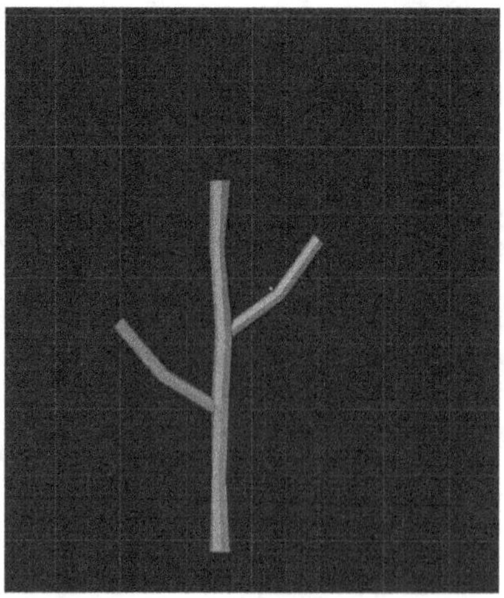

Figure 8.27 – Adding branches

Now all we need is the leaves. Follow these steps:

1. Press *Shift* + *A* to add a new icosphere, and, as usual, set the subdivisions to `1` in the **Operator** menu. This will give us a simple shape to start with for making the leaves.
2. Press *Tab to go* into **Edit Mode**.
3. Select one of the bottom vertices of the icosphere.
4. Turn on **Proportional Editing** with *O*.
5. Press *G* and *Z* to lift the bottom of the sphere (just like you did for the rocks). You want to indent it a little, like this, to make a concave surface:

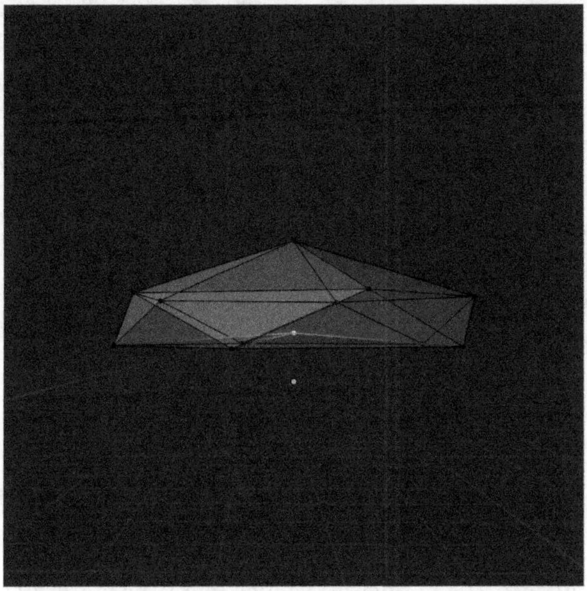

Figure 8.28 – Making a treetop (a lot like the rocks)

6. *Press Tab* to go back to **Object Mode**.
7. Now use *G* + *Z* to move the leaf object *above* the tree. Use the **Top** view (*7*) and position the leaf objects at the end of a branch.
8. Then, press *Shift* + *D* and move the duplicated leaf object to the end of the other branch. Duplicate it again for the top of the tree.

Do all of this in the **Top** view. We'll fine-tune the positions next.

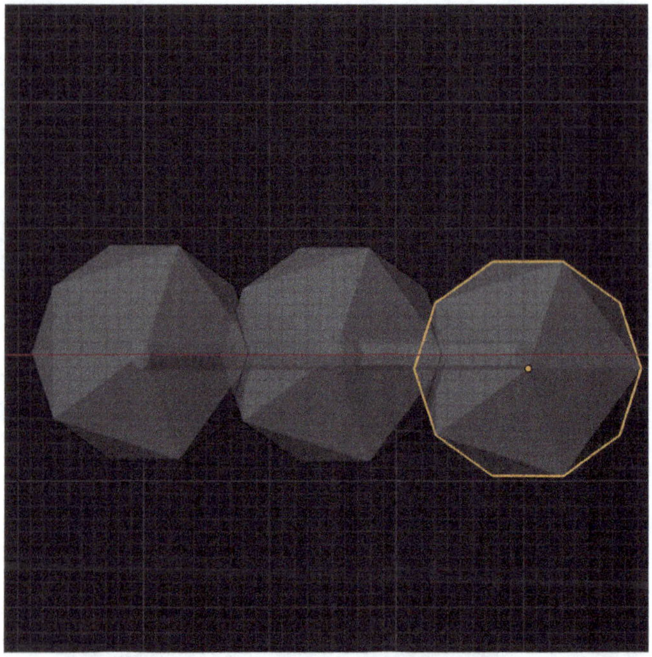

Figure 8.29 – Positioning in the Top view

Now, look at the model from other angles and move your leaf objects downward until they're sitting where you want them. You'll most likely have to adjust and tweak them with *G* and *R* to get them just right. Also, try making some of them bigger and some smaller by scaling them with *S*.

You can also rotate them on the *Z* axis so you can't tell that they're identical. You can tilt them a little to one side, too—try using **Trackball rotation** (*R R*) to do this.

Check your model from all sides to make sure it looks nice and nothing is intersecting where it shouldn't.

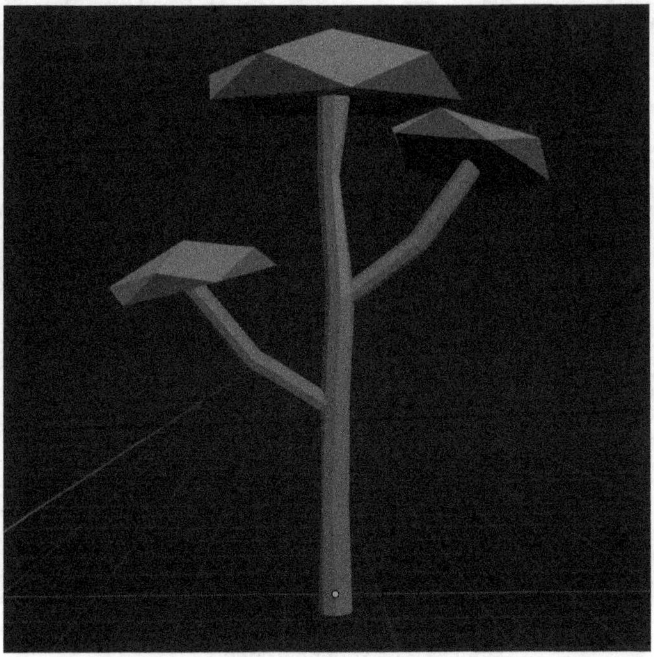

Figure 8.30 – The complete tree

Set materials for each object—the same materials you used for the last tree (if you want, you can also make new, different ones).

If you want multiple variations of the tree, simply select the whole setup, hit *Shift* + *D* to duplicate, and then press *X* to move it out along the *X* axis. Adjust the branches, rotate the leaves, add more branches or leaves—and it's a whole different tree!

Select all the parts of the tree and press *Ctrl* + *J* to turn them into a single object. (Do this after you set the materials, so you don't have to worry about making slots and assigning them.)

You've done it! That's it for the trees.

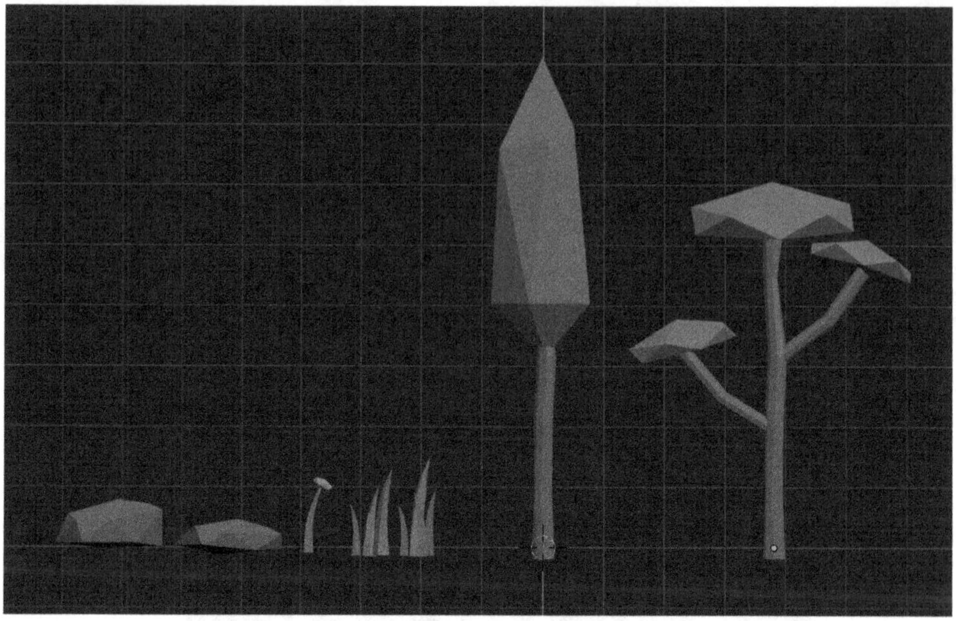

Figure 3.31 – Your new lineup

Now, you have a whole set of completed low poly assets.

Summary

In this chapter, you created nature itself from nothing at all. You learned how to build different kinds of low poly plants: trees, flowers, and grass. You learned how to make multiple versions of one model.

You made some simple rocks, too.

Good job!

In the next chapter, you'll enter the complex world of building low poly animals.

9

Modeling a Kangaroo

So far in this book, we have trees, rocks, and even grass: all the pieces we need to build a world. But, who lives here?

In this chapter, you'll learn how to build a low poly animal. You'll follow step-by-step instructions to build a low poly kangaroo from scratch.

The instructions in this chapter will be specific to the kangaroo, but also generalized enough that you can apply the same steps to any other animal. What you learn here will still apply.

By the end of this chapter, you'll have achieved the following:

- Know how to import reference images
- Understand where to start when modeling an animal
- Have a firm grasp of the steps you'll need to follow to model any animal in low poly
- Have a sweet low poly kangaroo model

You'll start by learning how to import your reference images.

Why modeling animals is hard

Modeling low poly animals is *not* easy. I started learning how to model animals just for this book—and I still have a long way to go. My animal models are *not* perfect. But if I can do it, so can you. This chapter will be one of the tougher ones. However, with a little effort and a lot of practice, you'll be making some pretty cool animals in no time.

Practice is key here. Some of the process involves using more complex techniques – using tools such as the **Knife** tool to cut out edges where you think they're needed. This will be difficult in the beginning, but will get easier the more you do it.

The steps in this chapter will be both specific *and* generalized. You'll learn how to build a kangaroo with some example images. But the same steps will apply to building most other animals.

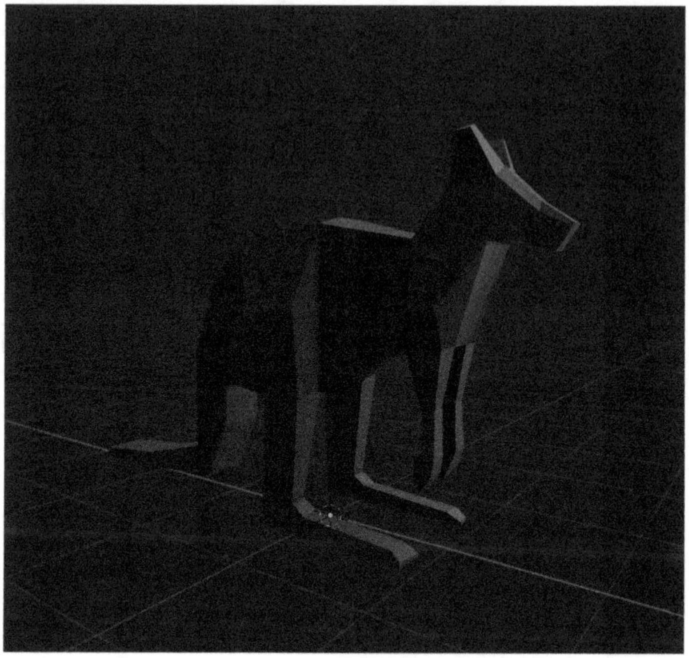

Figure 9.1 – The final result: a low poly kangaroo

I'm no expert at modeling animals—but I was able to turn out a decent result. You will be able to too.

So, even though I'm not an expert, I can still manage a decent animal. And if I can, so can you.

The best way to get good at it is to do it over and over and over again (which I recommend… though maybe make some animals other than kangaroos!).

We'll start with reference images: how to bring one into Blender and how to set it up.

Reference images

Reference images are pictures of whatever it is you're trying to make.

These could be artwork that you made yourself, pictures off the internet, or pictures you took yourself. It's often really hard to know what an animal will look like in low poly—try searching for low poly art of that animal online. There's a good chance someone else has already done it, and you can get a general idea of what you might be trying to make.

Searching for a reference image

For reference, it helps to have pictures from multiple angles: one from the front, one from the side, and one from the top. This way you'll have clear references from all sides of your model.

For example, for the kangaroo, I found the following picture online when I searched `kangaroo blueprint image`.

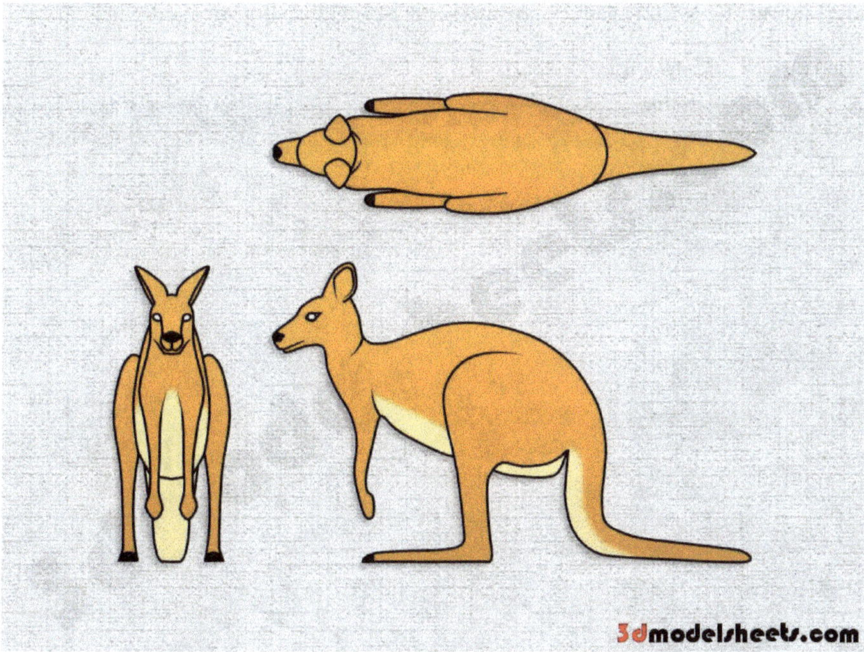

Figure 9.2 – Reference images of a kangaroo used in this chapter (image from: seamless-pixels.blogspot.com)

The best reference art for modeling simple low poly animals is just plain, simple line art. You can usually find an image like the one in *Figure 9.2* by searching *"[animal] blueprint image."*

Once you have your image, getting it into Blender is *really* easy.

Importing and setting up the reference image in Blender

It's best to build your models in Blender so that the **Front** view (when you press *1*) shows the *front* of the object. This way, the **Right** view (when you press *3*) will also show the side of the object.

To make this happen, you just need to line up your reference images in the following way before you start:

1. Press *1* to go to the **Front** view.
2. Now drag your reference image into Blender. The reference image will be aligned with whatever view Blender is currently using—in this case, the **Front** view.
3. Press *G* to move the reference so that the front view of the reference image is sitting against the *ground*. It doesn't have to be exact—this image is just a guideline after all.

Here's what you want to end up with:

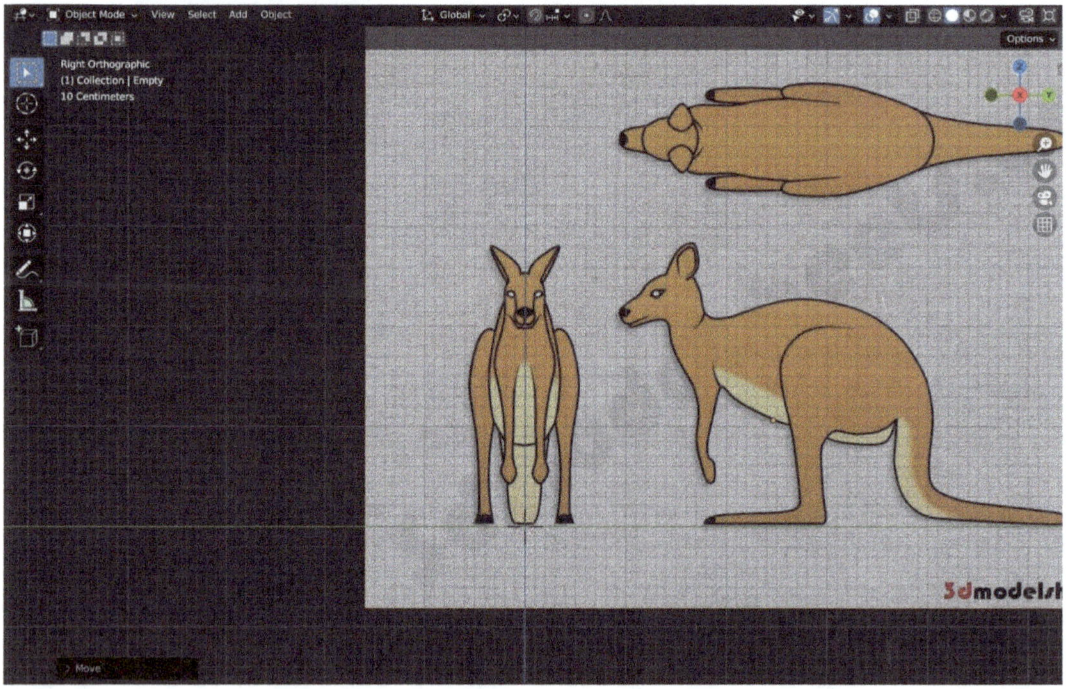

Figure 9.3 – Importing the reference image in Blender

The image will be too bright, so you need to lower the opacity and make it a bit transparent:

1. Select the reference image and click the **Image Settings** option that appears in the **Properties** panel.
2. Check the **Opacity** box to enable the opacity setting.

3. Click + drag the **Opacity** slider and lower the opacity to around **0.05** or less so that you can just about see the picture, like this:

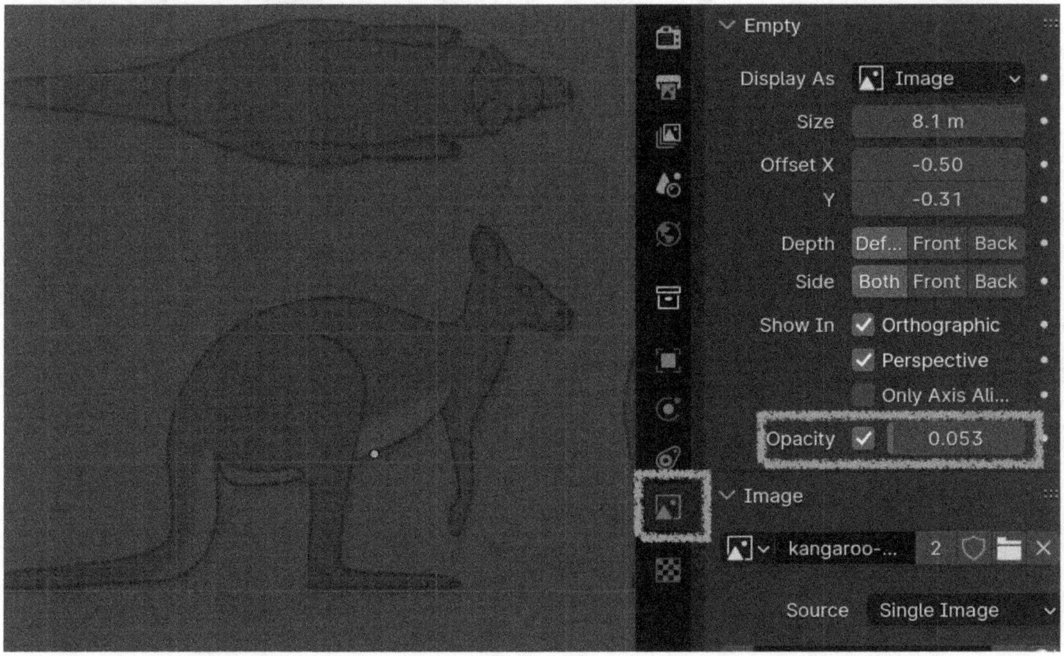

Figure 9.4 – Lowering the opacity of the reference image

4. Name that image `Front`.

Now you need the side view image:

1. To get that, just duplicate your reference image with *Shift* + *D*, then right-click to leave the duplicate in place and press *R*, *Z*, and *90* to rotate it 90 degrees. (If your reference image ends up backward (mine did) just press *R*, *Z*, and *180* to flip it around.)

> **Note**
>
> If you have a different image for the side view, just press *3* to go to the **Right** view and drag in your side view image. It'll be perfectly lined up to the Right view. If it's not, you can always press *Alt* + *R* to clear its rotation and rotate it manually.

2. Use *G* to move the reference image until it's centered and sitting on the floor. And don't forget to name the image `Side`. (If it's a different image (not a duplicate) use *S* to scale it so it roughly matches the other one.)

Here's what mine looks like:

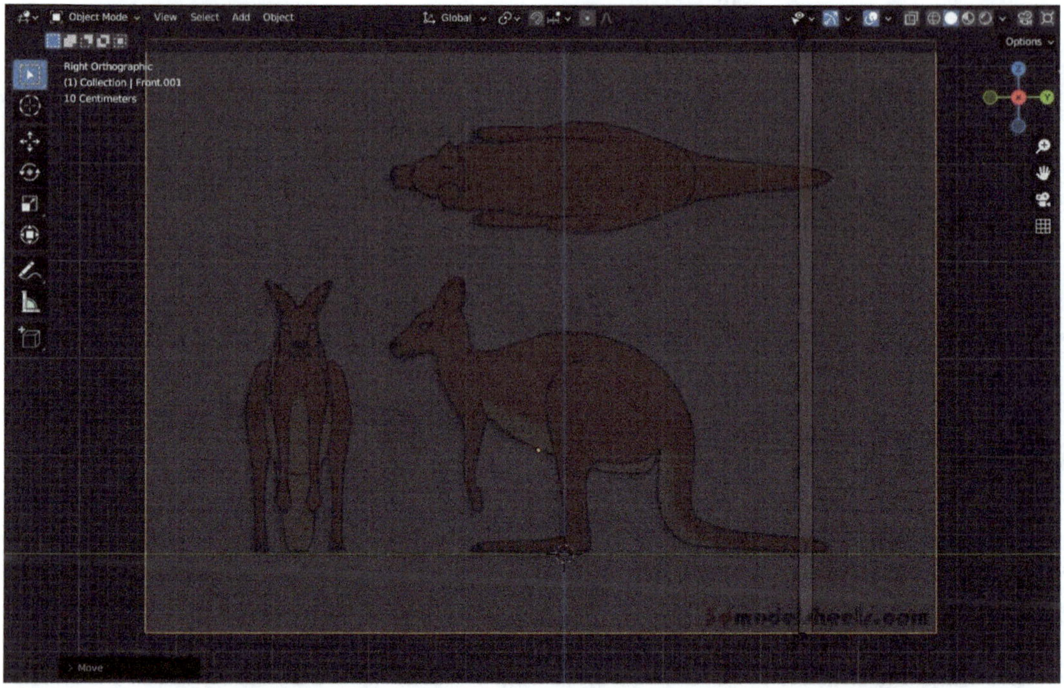

Figure 9.5 – Positioning the side image

> **Another note**
>
> This looks messy, as you've probably noticed. Your scene is full of kangaroo pictures, since each image has three different angles on it. For example, the front view image also shows the side and top (which you need to ignore), and the side view image also shows the front and top (which you need to ignore). If this is confusing for you, you can cut the image up in an image editor like Photoshop and have a single clean image for each view angle. It's up to you.

Next, we'll build the rough outline of the animal's body by extruding a plane.

Modeling the body

We'll make our animal starting from a plane. It's fairly simple.

First, go to the **Right** view (*3*) and add a new plane. Press *Shift* + *A* and choose **Mesh** | **Plane** from the popup.

Now we'll shape the plane into the rough shape of the animal's body, head, and tail (not the legs):

1. *Tab* into **Edit Mode** on the plane.
2. Make sure you're in **Vertex Select** mode, so you can adjust individual vertices.
3. Press *A* to select everything.
4. Press *R*, *Y*, and *90* to turn it vertical on the Y axis.
5. Switch to **X-Ray** by pressing *Alt* + *Z*.

Here's what the plane looks like so far:

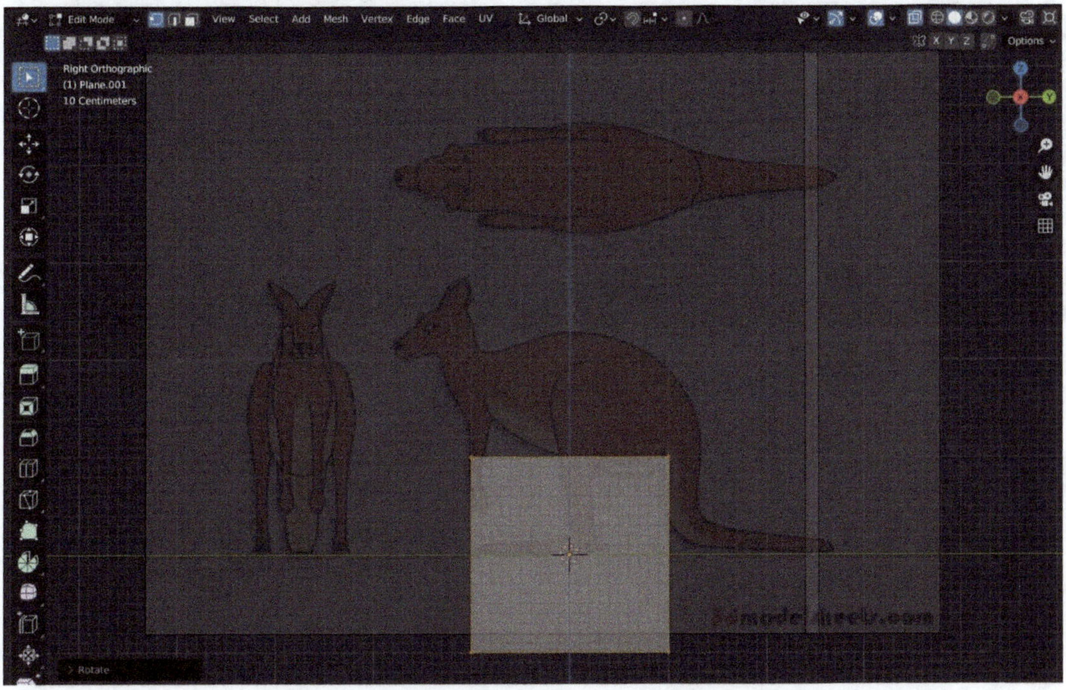

Figure 9.6 – Adding a plane

6. Now select each vertex, and move them one at a time to position your plane as follows:

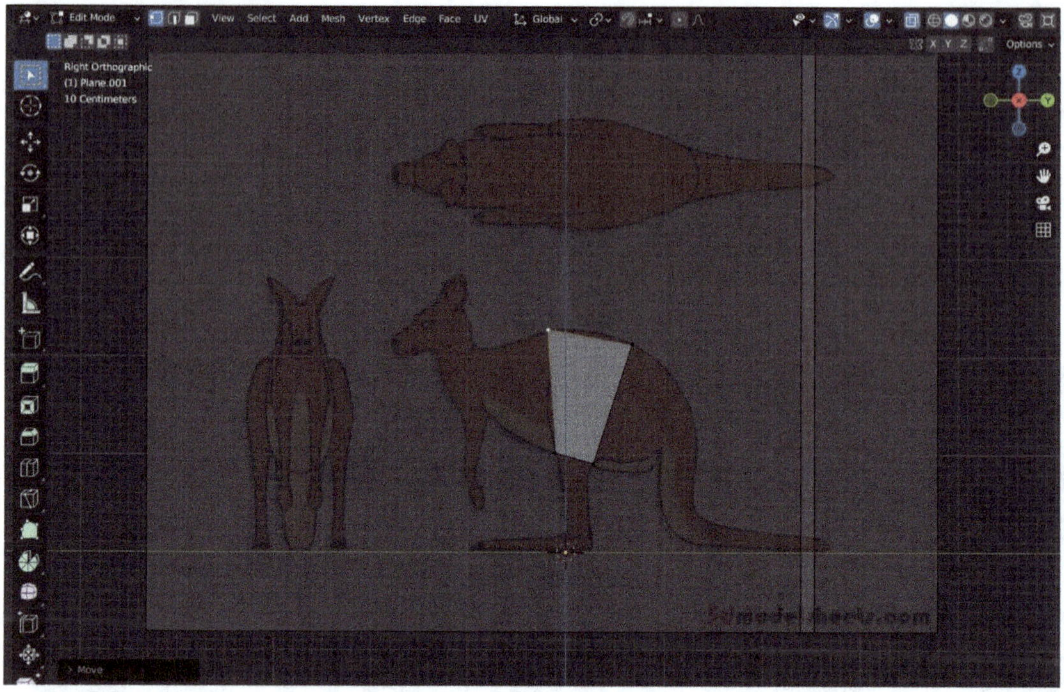

Figure 9.7 – Starting to build the body

As you work, you'll try to follow the shape of the kangaroo's body. Since you're going to extrude the legs later, it helps to make some of the faces line up with the positions of the legs.

7. Now select two vertices on one edge of the plane, press *E* to extrude, click to confirm, then manually position them again.

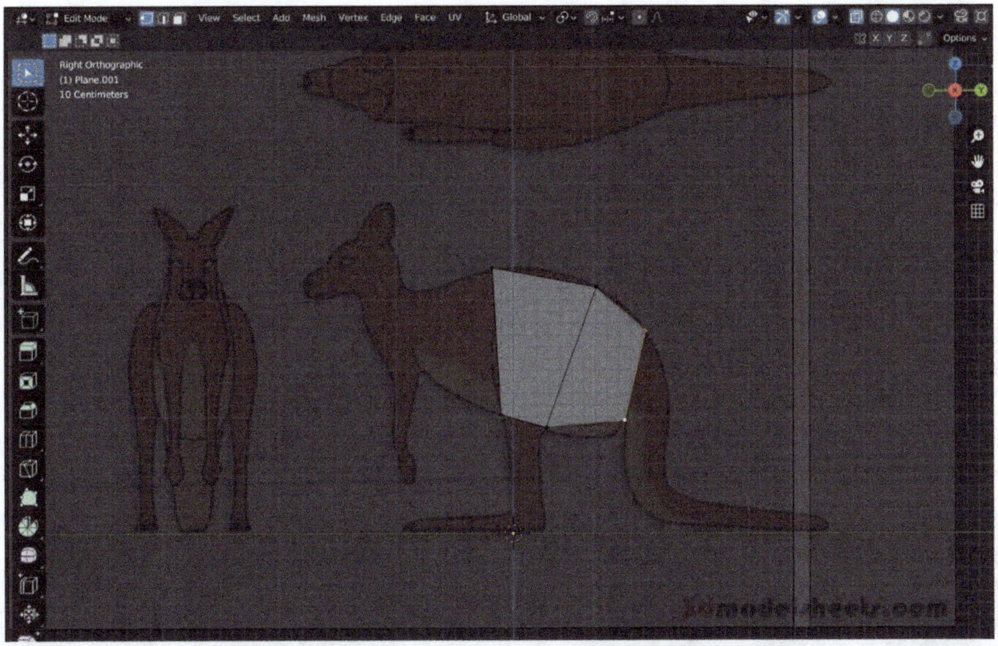

Figure 9.8 – Extruding more faces

Continue like that for the whole body. Here's what you'll have when you're done:

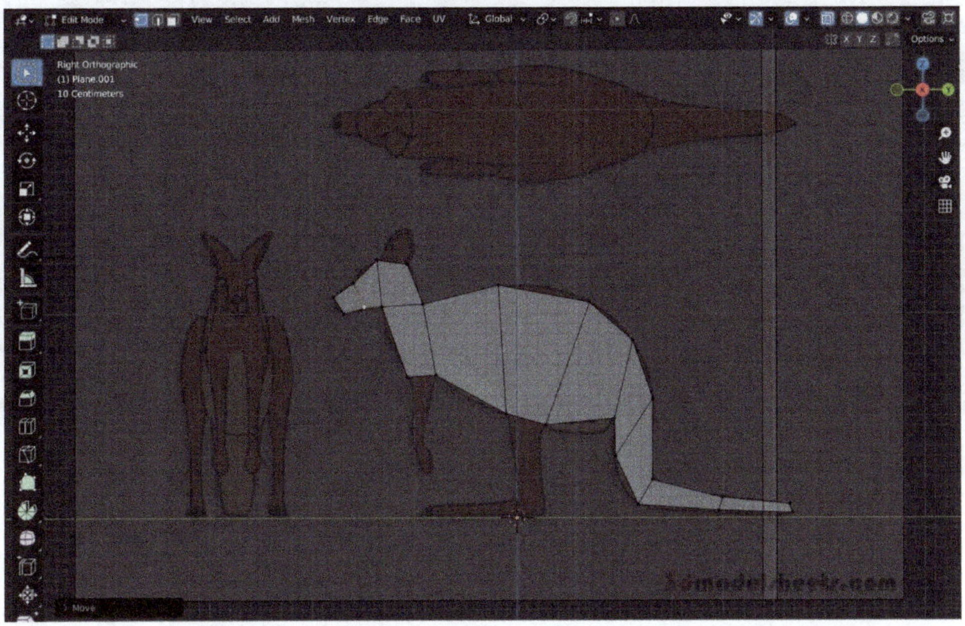

Figure 9.9 – The complete body shape

Notice how the mesh lines up with the ears and the legs so we can easily extrude those later.

Now you have the rough outline of your animal. Next, we'll extrude the outline outward to add thickness, and use a **Mirror** modifier to keep it symmetrical.

Extruding and mirroring the body

We'll be using the **Mirror** modifier again, just like we did for the low poly tractor in *Chapter 7*. It should be pretty easy for us to mirror the mesh we have. First, we'll extrude the mesh out along the X axis to give it some thickness, and then we'll add the **Mirror** modifier:

1. In **Edit Mode**, press *A* to select everything.
2. Press *E X* to extrude it along the X axis (view it from the front to see super clearly).
3. Bring it out a little, to somewhere just before the kangaroo's eyes, to give it some thickness:

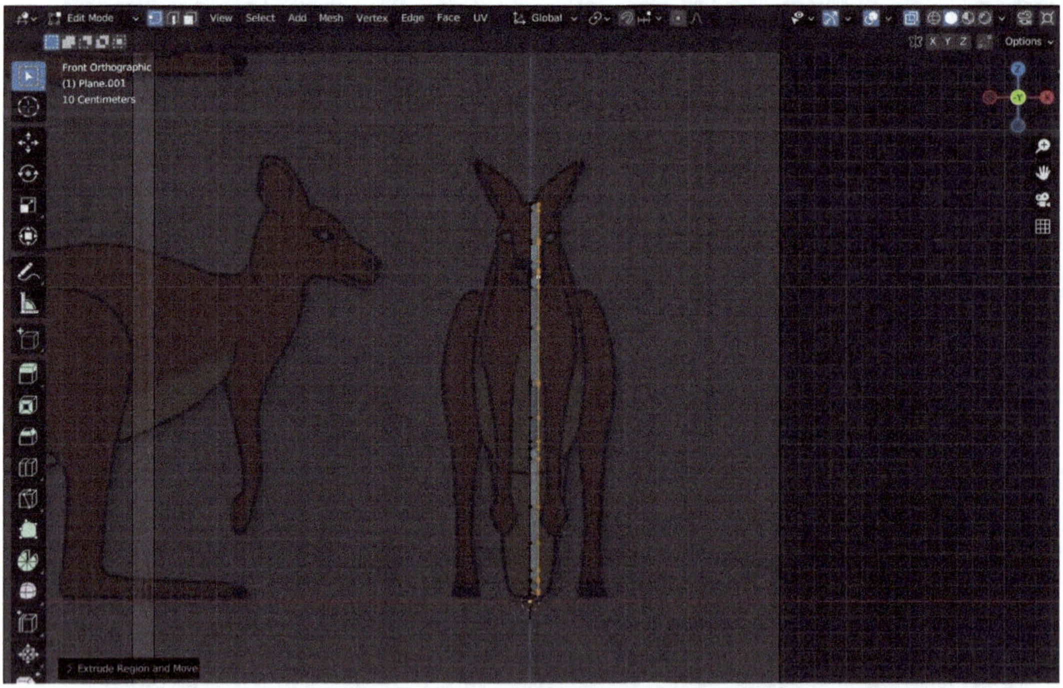

Figure 9.10 – Adding some thickness

4. Extrude it again, a little further. Here's what we have so far, from the Front view:

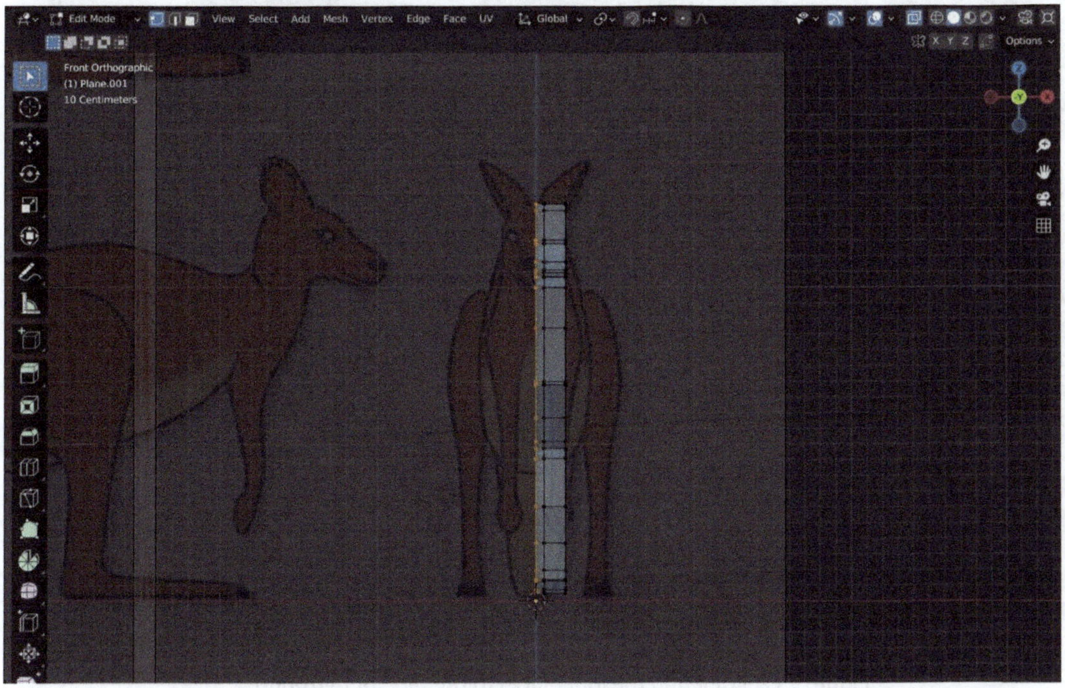

Figure 9.11 – Adding another layer of thickness

5. Now we need to delete the innermost faces so that we can mirror the mesh. Click and drag across these vertices (the ones selected in *Figure 9.12*) to select them, then press *X* and pick **Faces**.
6. The next step is to add the **Mirror** modifier. Open the **Modifier** panel, click **New**, and pick **Mirror**.

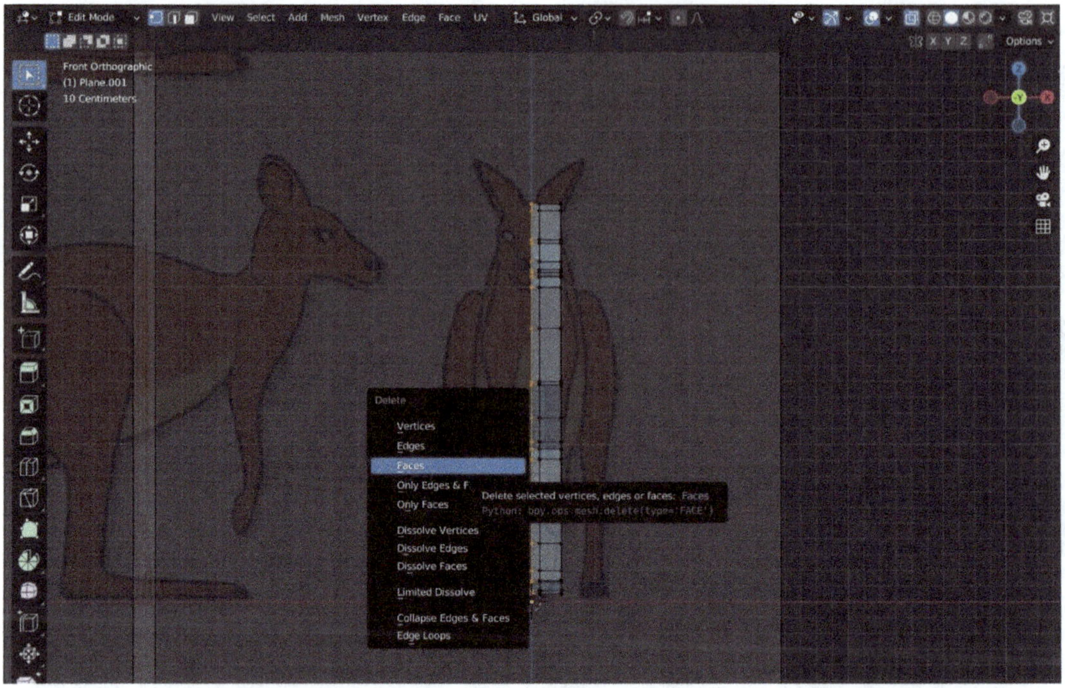

Figure 9.12 – Deleting the inner faces to prepare for mirroring

7. Make sure that the **Clipping** setting is **ON** in the **Modifier** panel. This setting makes it so that vertices in the center can't be moved away from the center (which is nice).

Now you have the body mesh mirrored. The next step is to refine the model.

Making legs

The legs will be pretty easy. We'll extrude them out to match the reference, just like we did for the body.

We left some faces perfectly situated for making the legs when we were extruding the body out. We'll start by extruding both of these faces outward along the X axis to form the shoulders, then downward to form the legs.

The **Mirror** modifier will take care of the other side for us automatically.

First, we need to extrude the back shoulders. Make sure you have **Face Select** mode enabled, and turn off **X-Ray** (*Alt* + *Z*). Now grab this face (shown in *Figure 9.13*) and extrude it outward:

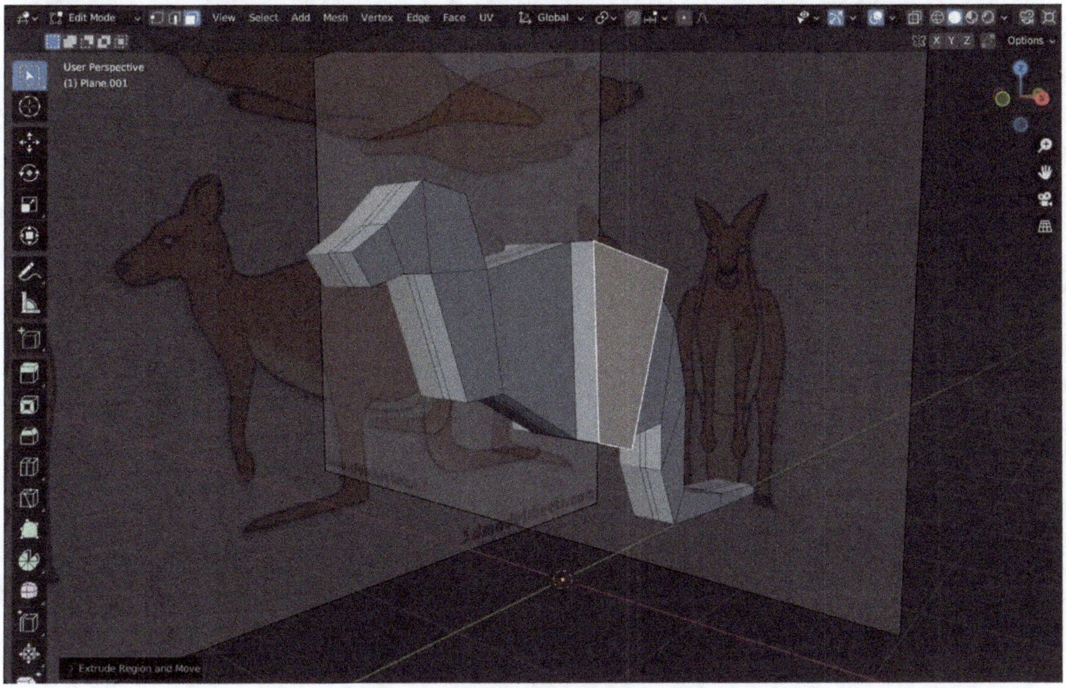

Figure 9.13 – Extruding the shoulders

Do the same for the front shoulder face:

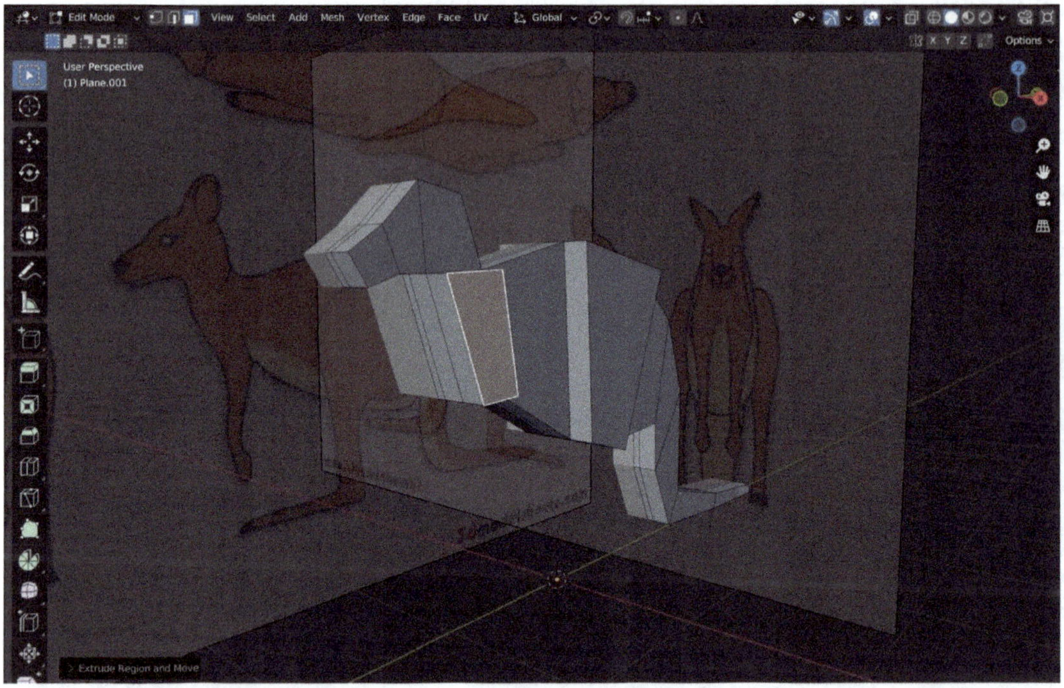

Figure 9.14 – The front shoulders

Now, we can make the actual leg part by extruding out from the shoulder face. Since it's not a single plane anymore, you'll have to drag across vertices in the **Right** view to select them (since you'll really be selecting two). Select the bottom face of the rear shoulder, then follow these steps:

1. Switch to **Vertex Select** mode, go to the **Right** view, and turn **X-Ray** back on.
2. Extrude the selected vertices downward, watching the reference image. This is exactly like the process of extruding the body outline. You'll extrude multiple times to make the whole leg. Manually adjust the vertices as you go: drag across a vertex to select it, then press *G*.
3. Extrude again. And again. I did a total of three extrusions for the hind leg.

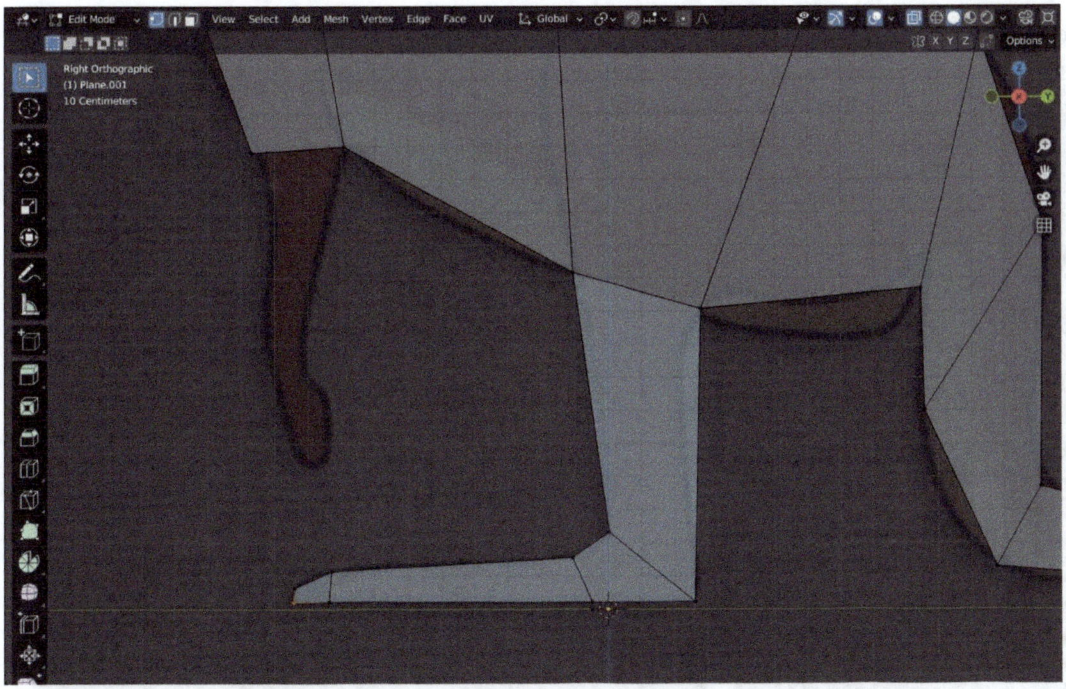

Figure 9.15 – The hind leg

But it'll be different for you depending on the animal you're making. Try to make sure that you end up with edges near any important parts of your animal's leg.

Now you need to do the front leg (the steps are exactly the same). Leave the **Right** view, select the bottom of the extruded shoulder, go back to the **Right** view, then extrude and position it.

Here's my result (make yours look like this):

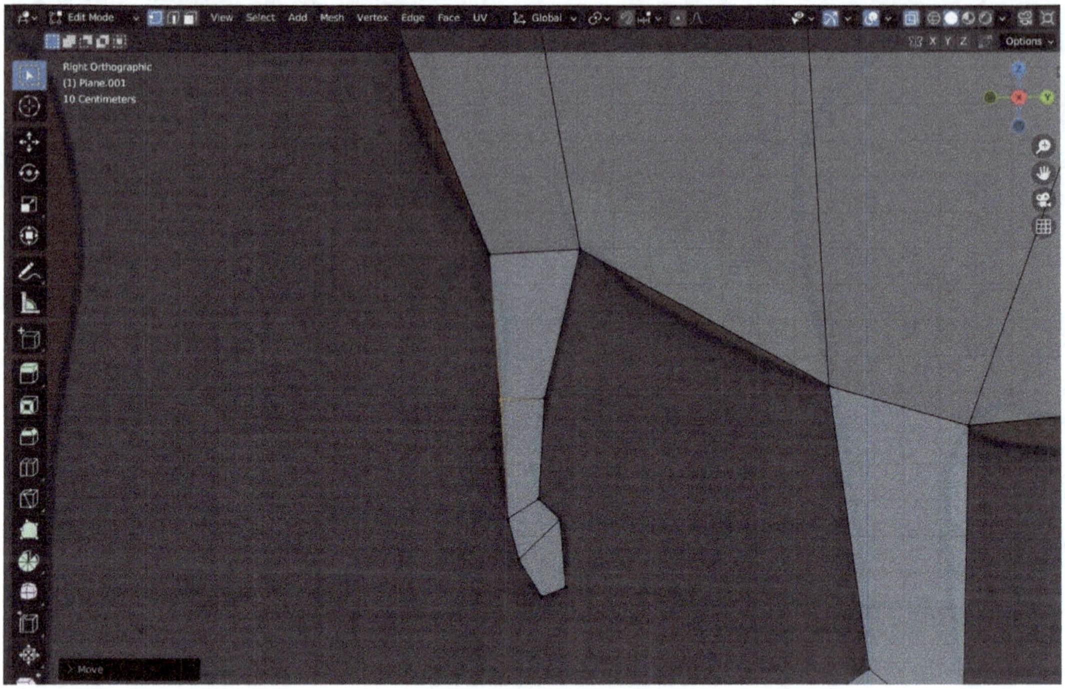

Figure 9.16 – The front leg

Now, you have the basic shape of the legs completed. These are very simple legs. In the next section, we're going to work on giving everything some proper shape—it's still just squares and blocks right now.

Shaping the body

In this section, we're going to improve the body. We'll take it from a rough, blocky form to a nicer, more animal-like shape.

To get there, you'll go through three separate phases:

1. Tweaking the body and tail
2. Tweaking the legs
3. Tweaking the head

The head and the legs will be the most difficult, but since we have the front reference image to help, it won't be too bad.

Tweaking the body and tail

First, let's tweak the body and tail. What we need to adjust here is mostly the width—the body should be wider in the middle, with the head and tail thinner:

1. Select the whole "middle part" by holding down *Shift* and clicking on each face (or each vertex, if you like).

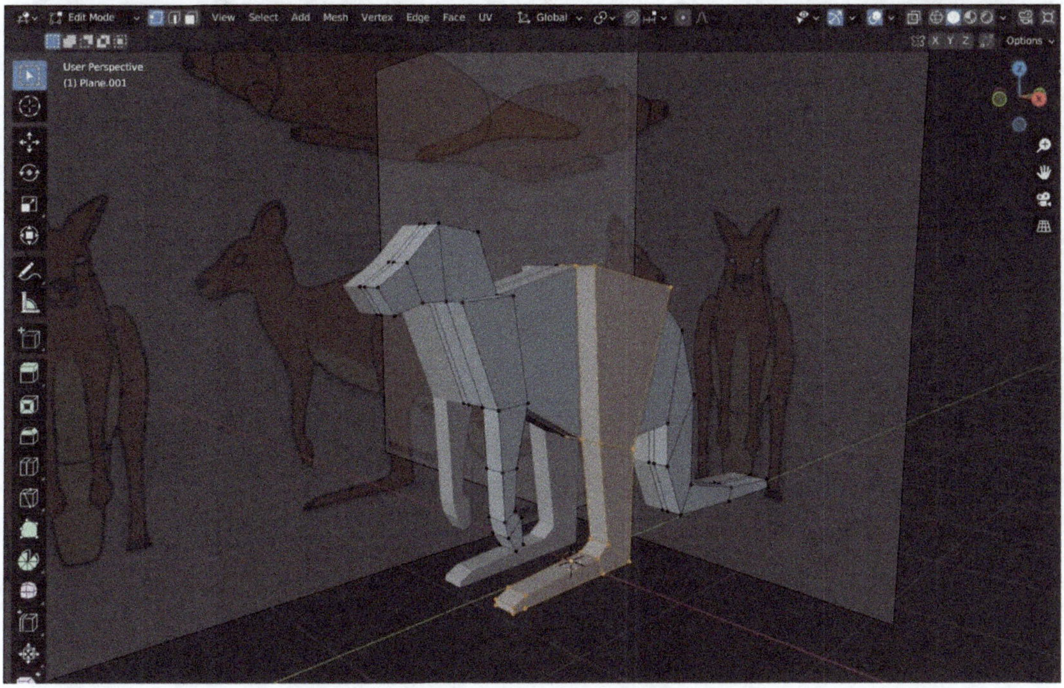

Figure 9.17 – Selecting the middle part

2. Then move the whole chunk outward (very slightly) with *G* and *X*:

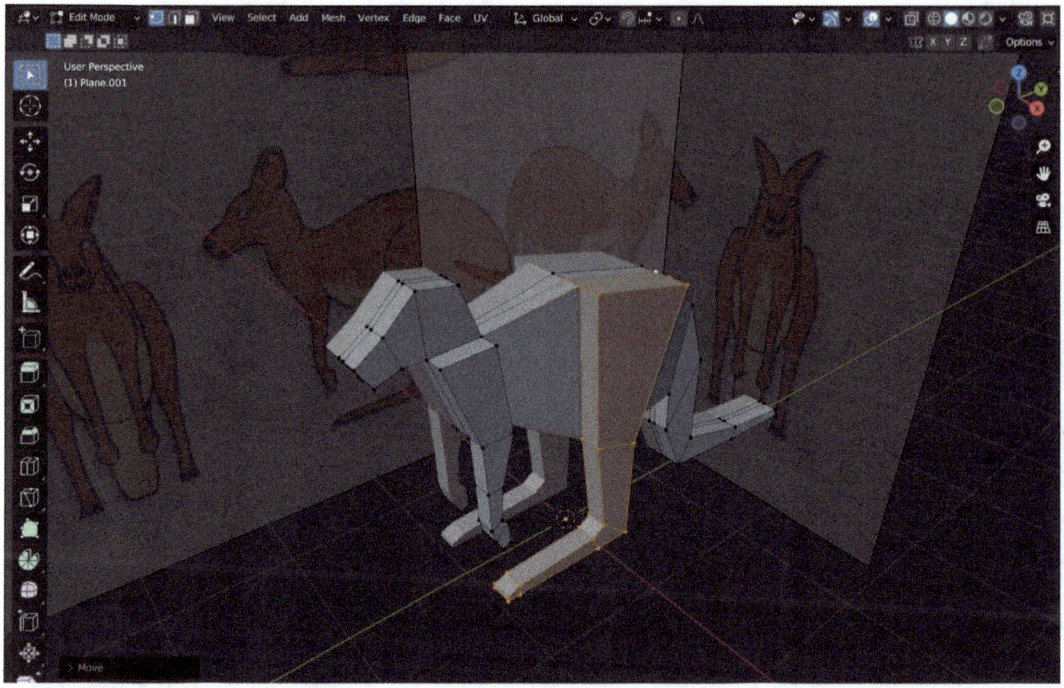

Figure 9.18 – Moving the middle part slightly outward

Next, let's fix the square shoulders.

3. Select two corner vertices, then move them slightly inward with *G* and *X* and slightly downward with *G* and *Z*. Do this for both the front and back shoulders, so you get something like this:

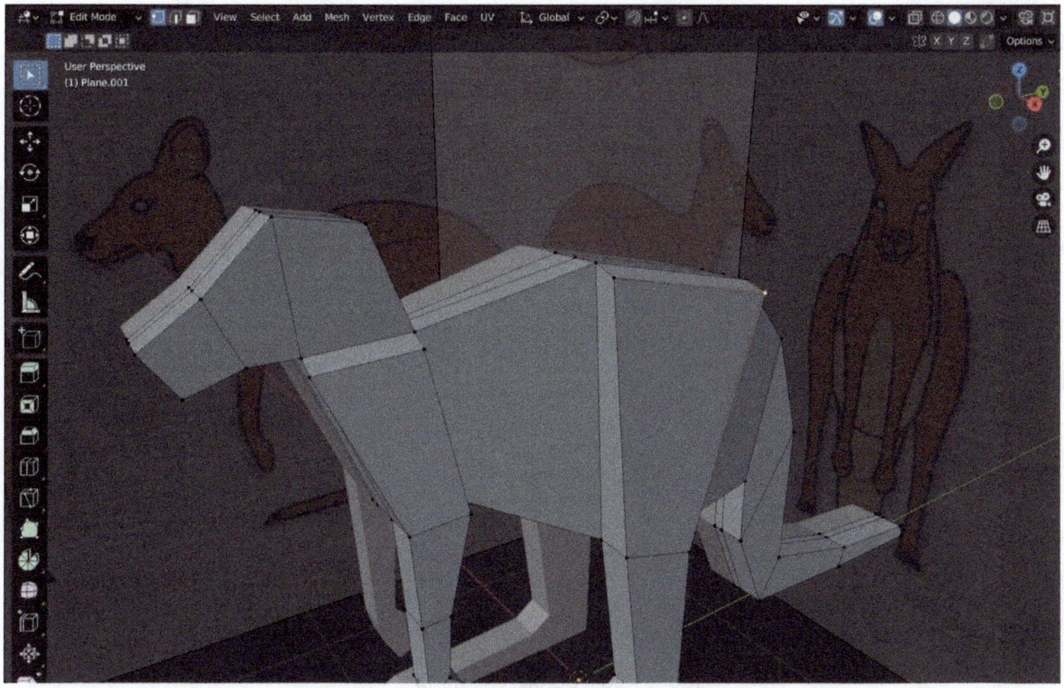

Figure 9.19 – Adjusting the shoulders slightly

4. Now press *3* to go to the **Right** view and tweak the shoulder vertices. Move them manually, one a time, so you go from this:

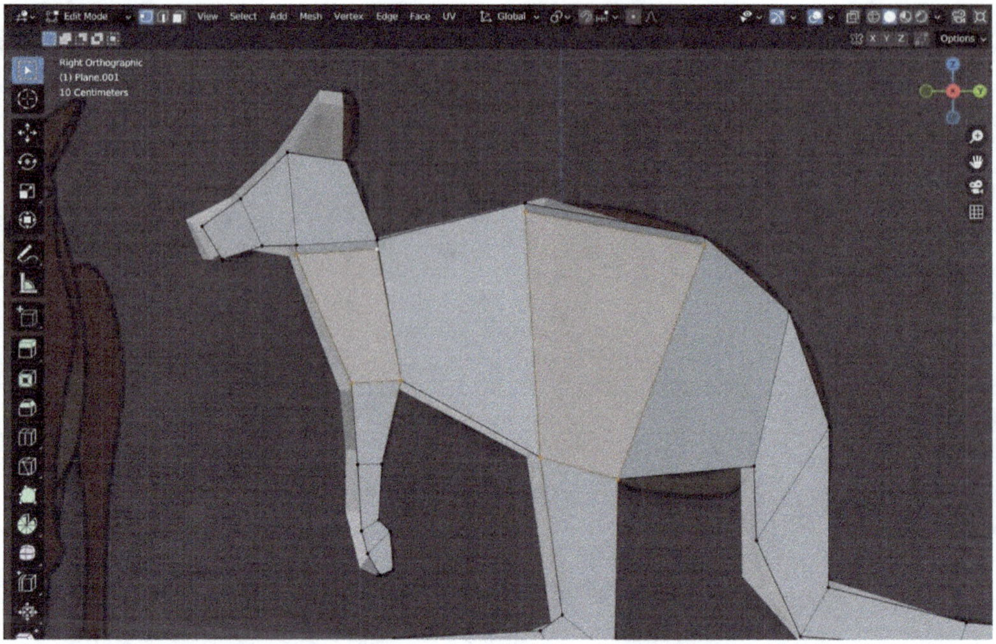

Figure 9.20 – Before tweaking

To this:

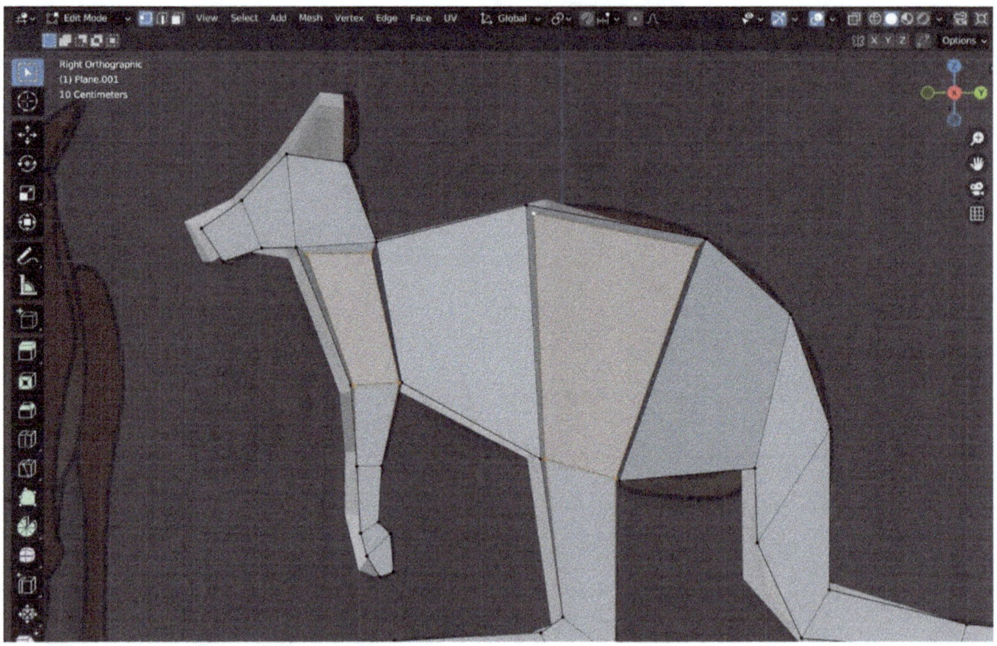

Figure 9.21 – After tweaking

5. Next, "taper" the top side of the body a little so it's not so flat by moving the sides down a little bit. Select the outer row of vertices along the top edge of the model, like this:

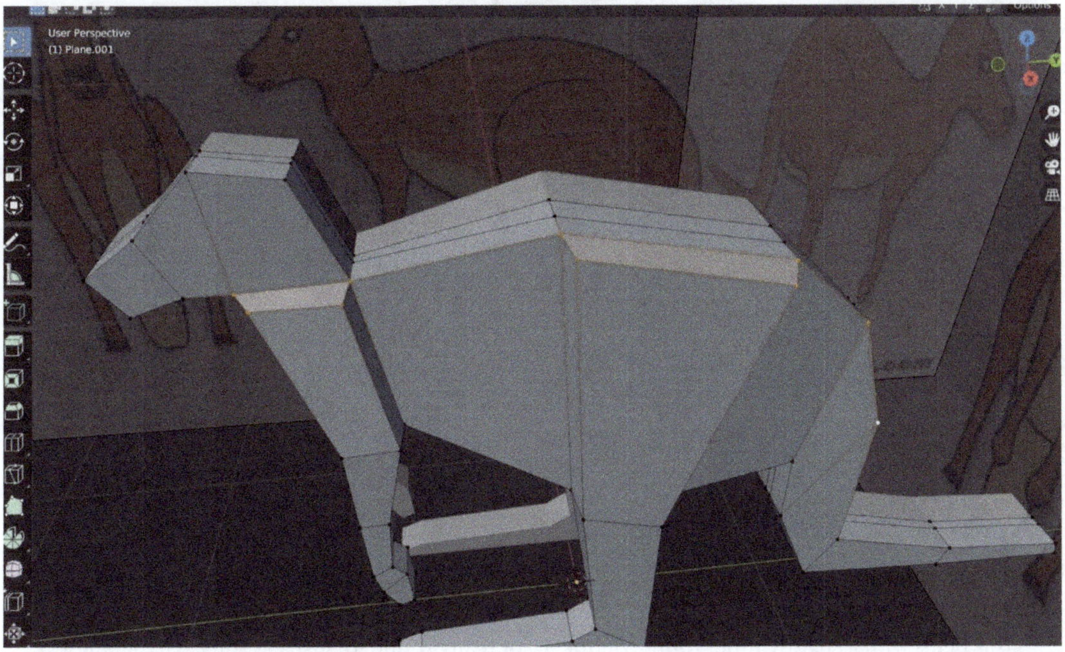

Figure 9.22 – Selecting the top vertices

And then move them down slightly on the Z axis, so you get this (shown here in the **Front** view):

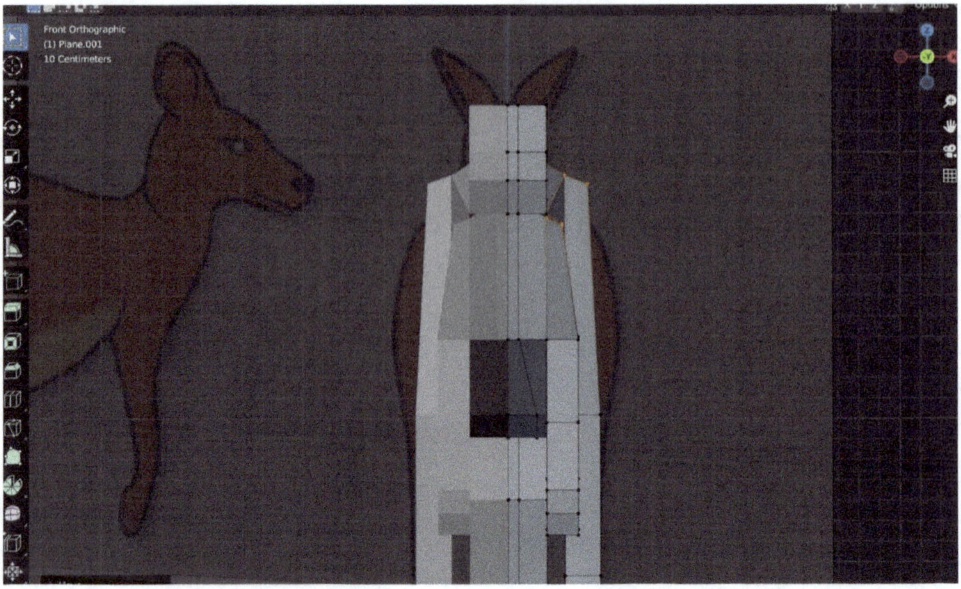

Figure 9.23 – Moving the vertices downward

This helps with a slightly more rounded look. (Not really rounded, just less square.) You'll notice that it's still not looking wide enough—let's give the hind legs more thickness.

6. Grab the two vertices highlighted in the following figure:

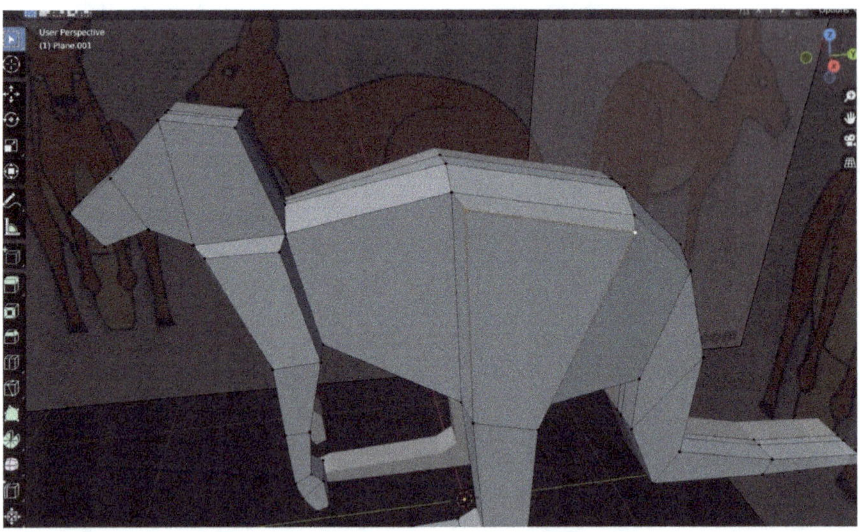

Figure 9.24 – Adjusting the highlighted vertices more

7. Now go back to the **Front** view, and move them downward and outward:

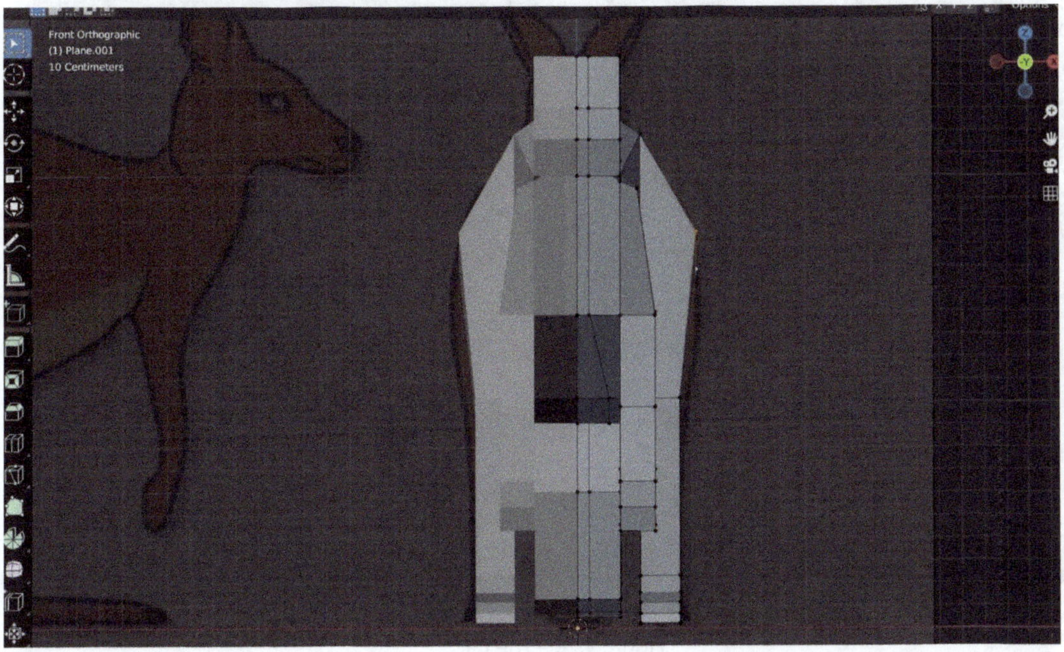

Figure 9.25 – A more rounded shape

You can adjust the two vertices below those, too, to try to match the picture better. It's up to you at this point—we're trying to make this very simple shape look as kangaroo-ish as possible.

The body is looking much nicer now. Let's do some work on the tail. It's very wide, so all you have to do is select some vertices and move them inward on the X axis to make the tail thinner. Here's what I ended up with (in the **Top** view):

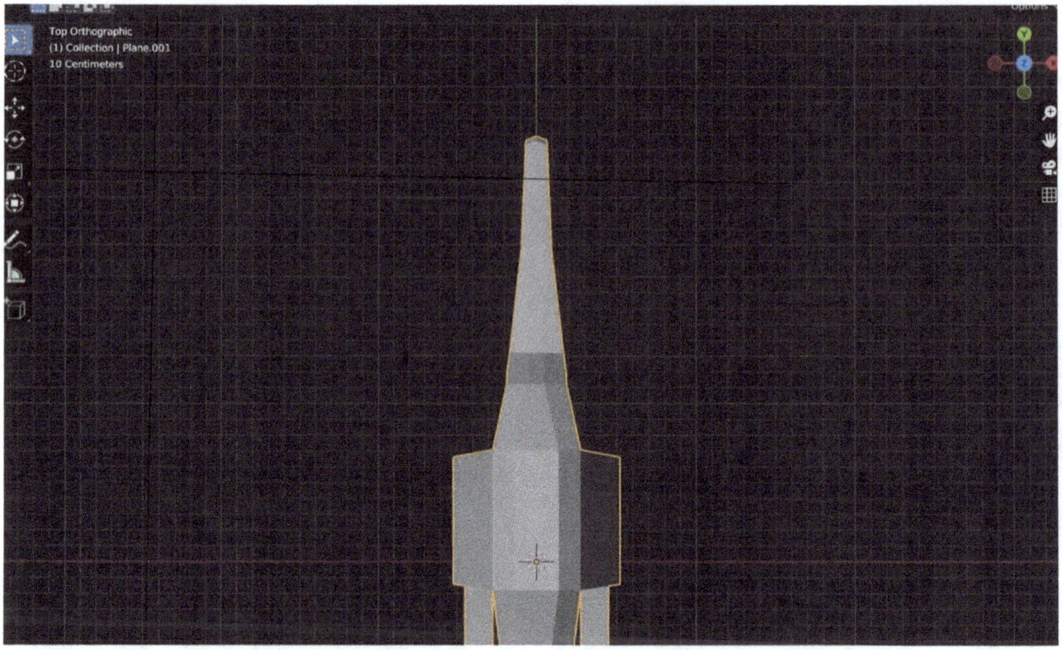

Figure 9.26 – The tail

Next we'll do some work on the legs.

Tweaking the legs

The main idea is to get the legs to line up roughly with the front and side profiles in the reference images.

In the **Front** view, I'll adjust the vertices to line up better with the reference picture. Make sure you look at the model from other angles too from time to time, so you know what you're doing. As I compared the model to the reference image, I made a few tiny adjustments to help the model line up more accurately with the reference from the front and side views. This step is up to you—it'll be different for everyone. I made a few very tiny tweaks, slightly moving some vertices on the shoulders, back legs, and front legs. I ended up with the following (though don't worry if yours is different—it will be).

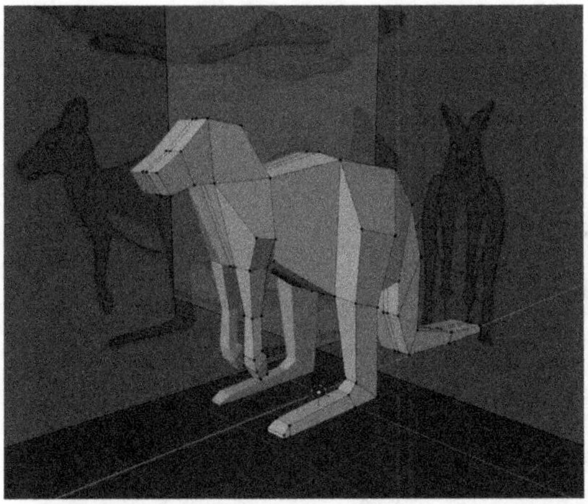

Figure 9.27 – The tweaked legs

If this part seems confusing to you—you're not alone. This is one of those things you'll get better at over time, making small corrections that help the model look so much better. This will get much, much easier the more you do it. So keep at it!

Tweaking the head

Now we're at the most difficult part: the head. The goal is to get it looking like a kangaroo without having to add any more detail (though if that's what you want, it *is* perfectly acceptable):

1. The first thing to do is narrow the snout by bringing the four vertices highlighted in *Figure 9.28* inward along the X axis.

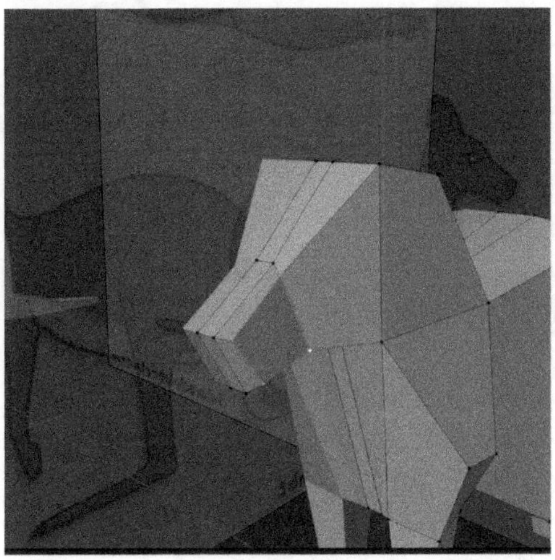

Figure 9.28 – Moving the highlighted face inward

2. Next, move the three vertices highlighted in *Figure 9.29* downward a bit to soften the shape.

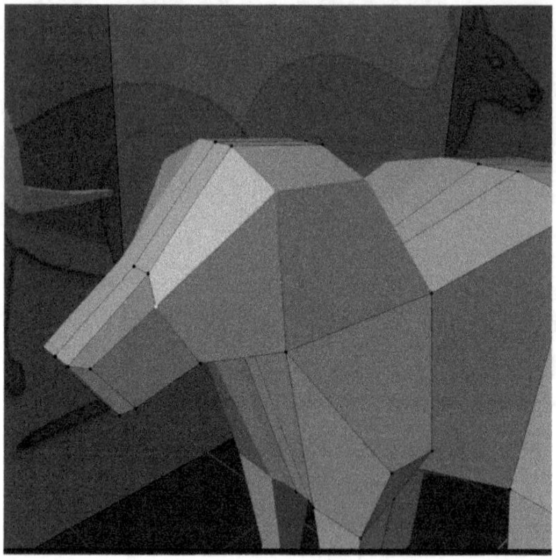

Figure 9.29 – Moving the three highlighted vertices downward

That's just about all we can do when working with such a simple mesh. You could always make this more complex and add more edges with the **Knife** tool or *Ctrl* + *R* if you want a more detailed face.

You just learned how to tweak your mesh to make your low poly model more interesting. Next, we'll make the final part: the ears.

Extruding the ears

We haven't made the ears yet. Our animal looks a bit funny because of it.

There's two different ways you could make the ears. You could start with a separate object, model it into an ear shape, then add that to your mesh.

That works.

The other way is to figure out where the ears go and extrude them right out of the base mesh. That's what you'll be doing here for this animal model.

First we'll extrude the ear shape, then we will tweak it to make sure it looks nice:

1. Simply select the face highlighted in *Figure 9.30*:

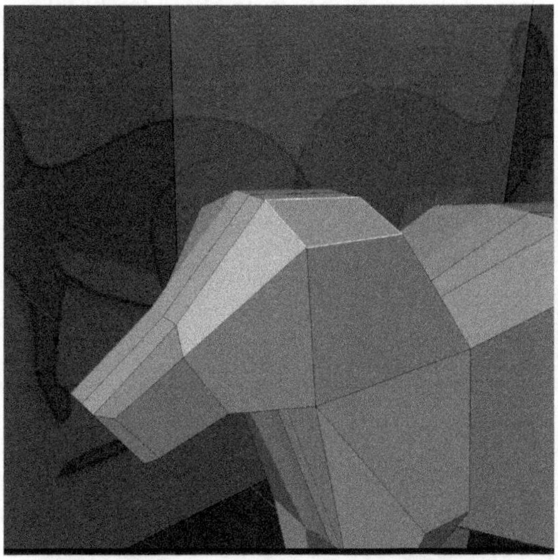

Figure 9.30 – The faces that will become ears

2. Then press *E* to extrude it outward:

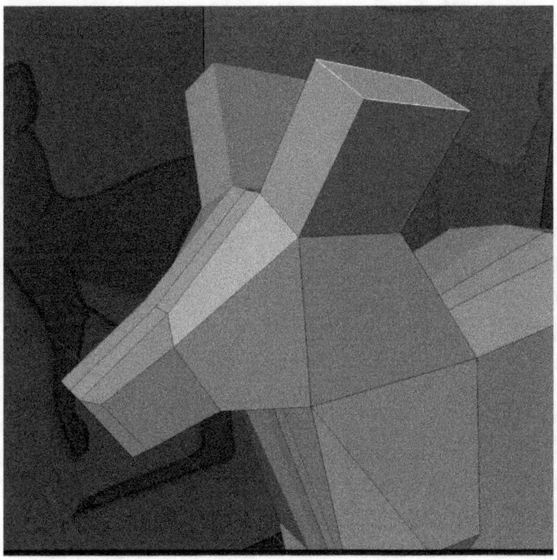

Figure 9.31 – The extruded ears

Now we have the simple *base* of the ear shape. We'll shape it into more of an ear shape by scaling the top face. You can check your reference image to make sure it's looking accurate as you go.

3. Now select the outside face of the ear and press *I* to inset it a bit, then *E* to extrude it inward.

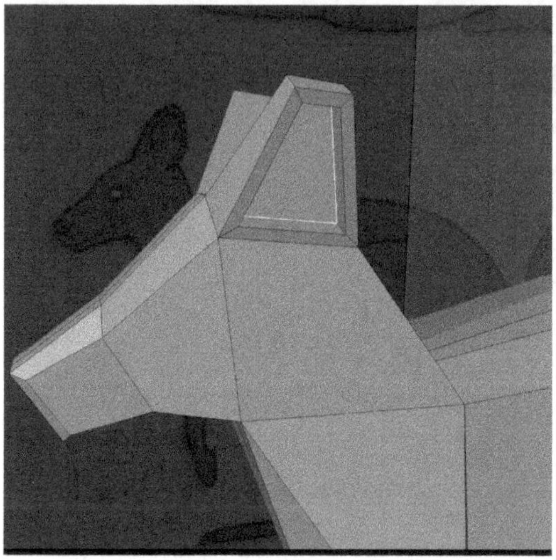

Figure 9.32 – The ears after scaling the top face and insetting the side one

4. Now scale the face down a little bit to get a softer shape:

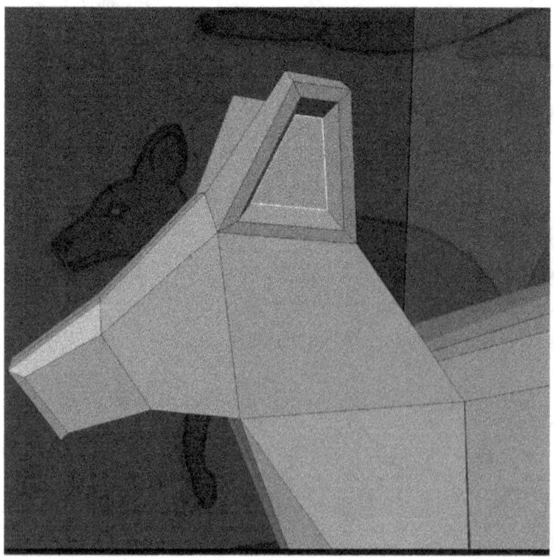

Figure 9.33 – The final ears

Now you've got ears.

The animal is mostly complete now—all that's left to do is set up a material.

Adding materials

Most low poly animals you'll make won't need more than two different materials. For our kangaroo, though, we only need *one* material.

That makes this step pretty easy.

Since you already have the **Material Utilities** add-on enabled, it'll be a breeze. All we have to do is assign the main material to the model.

Simply open the **Material** tab, assign the default material (or make a new one), name it `Brown`, and change its color to brown.

If you want, you could use the material techniques you learned in *Chapter 6* to assign different materials to different parts of an animal mesh.

Summary

In this chapter, you tackled the complex task of modeling a low poly animal. You started from reference imagery. You learned how to make the outline of the animal and extrude the animal's body, then clean up and refine the shape.

Great job!

If you only remember one thing from this chapter, it is that modeling low poly animals takes *practice*. A lot of it. Your first animal won't look so nice. But the next one will be better. The next, even better still.

Do this a lot and it'll get easier for you. You'll start to understand how and where to make cuts and add geometry.

Next up, you'll learn how to make low poly houses and buildings.

10
Creating Low Poly Houses and Buildings

Time to build some buildings.

This will be one of the easier chapters. After all, buildings are tall cubes with some details, right?

In this chapter, you'll learn about the basic parts of a building. You'll learn how to cut out windows, make roofs, and add some details to your buildings.

In this chapter, you'll learn to do the following:

- Build two different low poly skyscrapers from scratch
- Add details to the skyscrapers
- Create a simple house
- Make windows and roofs

We'll start by going over all the different parts that buildings have.

What it takes

Buildings are simple.

They're tall cubes, more or less. However, they're still recognizable shapes—not just any random cube will do. They're generally taller than they are wide, and usually have a lot of windows.

There are many different kinds of buildings. The options are almost limitless when it comes to designing yours.

The buildings we'll be making here are going to be extremely simple—the kind you might use in the background of a scene.

I suggest looking at some buildings. Any buildings. Use what you see as inspiration for your own brand-new building designs.

There are not many parts to a building: the main cube-shaped part (the walls), the top (the roof), and the details, like the windows and doors.

It's the same for houses. For houses, however, it's common to have a more complex shape, more like two or three cubes of different sizes all stuck together.

We'll make a few different buildings in this chapter: an easy, simple building (not much more than a box), a slightly more difficult one, and a house.

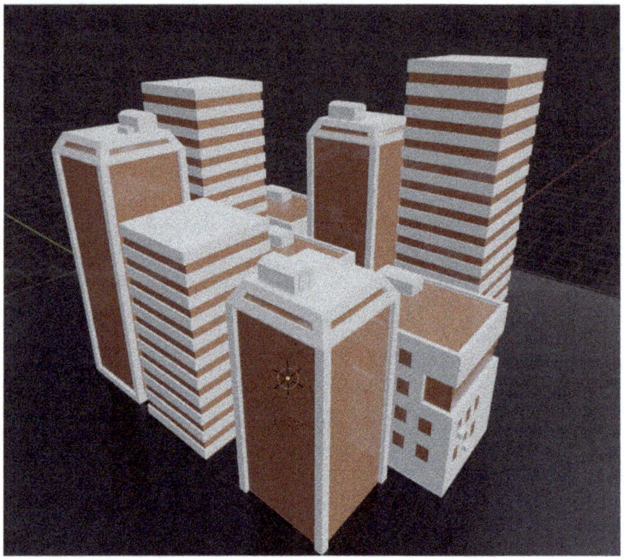

Figure 10.1 – A city block of simple buildings

Our first building will be a very simple skyscraper: the medium-sized boxy one.

The easy building - a skyscraper

Our first building is an easy skyscraper. It looks like this:

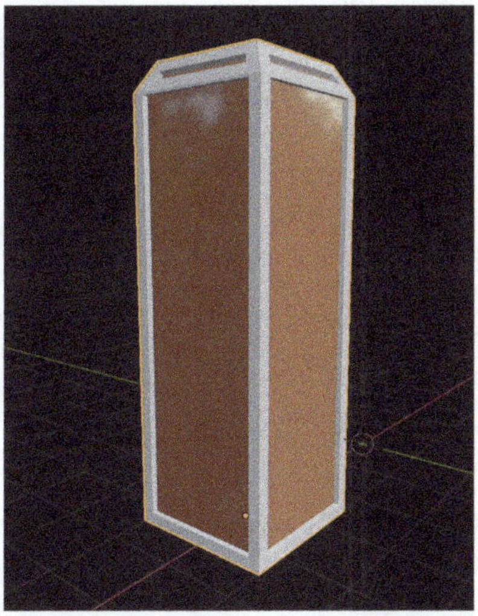

Figure 10.2 – The final skyscraper

I hear you. *"That's not a building! It's a telephone booth!"* Well, it's a very simple building. By itself, this building might not even obviously be a building, but if you used it in a grouping of other simple, stylized buildings (as in *Figure 10.1*), it would work just fine. The neat lines running around the edges help it seem a little like a building, but it *is* just a box.

With buildings like houses, the roof is extremely important. But on a skyscraper, like the one we'll be modeling, there's nothing special you have to do for the roof, since it's not angled or overhanging like most houses. It doesn't even need to be a separate object. This means that skyscrapers are easier to make than houses. We will add some details to the top of this building later, but those will be very easy to do.

Also, it's important to remember that we're not trying to build a realistic building. We're just making a simple building. The important part is that it needs to look like a building. As long as it does that, the rest doesn't matter.

This skyscraper isn't even going to have windows. But, when you use it alongside other buildings, it still does what it's supposed to do: look like a building.

Modeling the basic shape

For now, we're just going to model the building. Later on, we'll model some details (including vents and doorways) and add some of those on top.

This is going to be an easy build. First, create a new `.blend` file.

We'll construct our building starting with the default cube.

Here's what you need to do:

1. *Press Tab* to enter **Edit Mode**.
2. Press *A* to select everything. We're going to move the mesh up on the Z axis, because I think it's easier to work with a model when the whole thing is set neatly on a grid.
3. *Press G* to move, then *Z* for the Z direction, then enter `1` for the amount.
4. Now switch to **Face Select** mode (if you're not already using it).
5. *Select* the top face and move it upward (press *G* then *Z*) until your building is a nice height.
6. Now we need to make that nice top beveled area. Select the top face and press *E* to extrude it outward a little.
7. Press *S* to scale this new top face down a little. Now you have the nice, beveled top shown in the following figure.

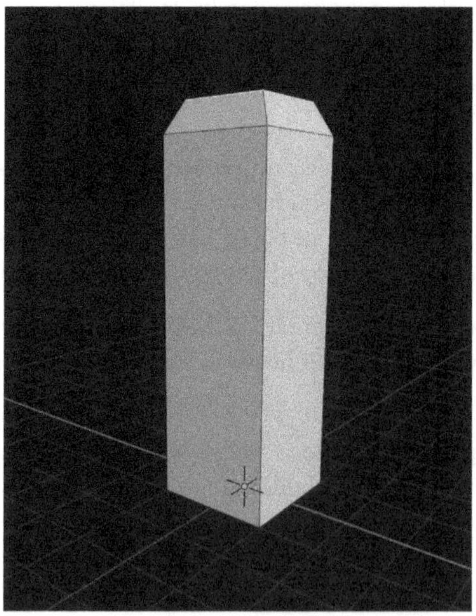

Figure 10.3 – The beveled top

OK. We have the basic shape of the building now—the next step is to create the neat extruded edges, which is extremely easy.

Extruding the edges

We'll extrude the edges by insetting everything, then extruding it inward. This is simpler than trying to extrude all the edges outward:

1. In **Edit Mode**, make sure you're in **Face Select** mode.
2. Press *A* to select everything.
3. Press *I* to inset all selected faces. If they're insetting all at once instead of separately, press *I* again and it should switch to individual mode. Don't inset too far, just a little bit. Here's what my final inset looked like:

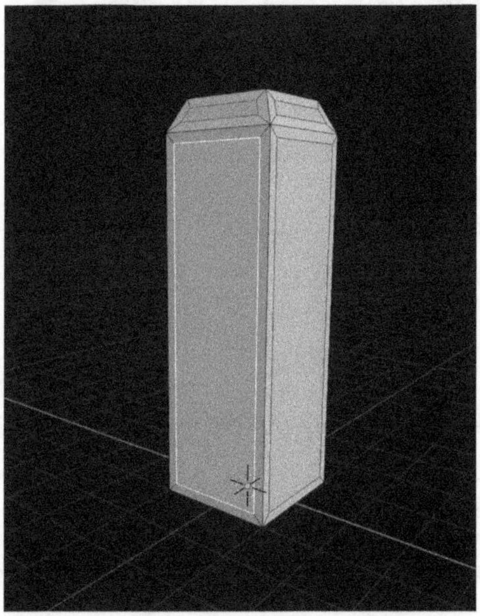

Figure 10.4 – Final inset

4. Now it's time to do the actual extrude. Press *Alt* + *E* to open the **Extrude** menu, then choose **Extrude Faces Along Normals** and extrude all the selected faces (all the ones that you just inset) inward. Just go in a little bit—too much ruins the effect. Here's what I did:

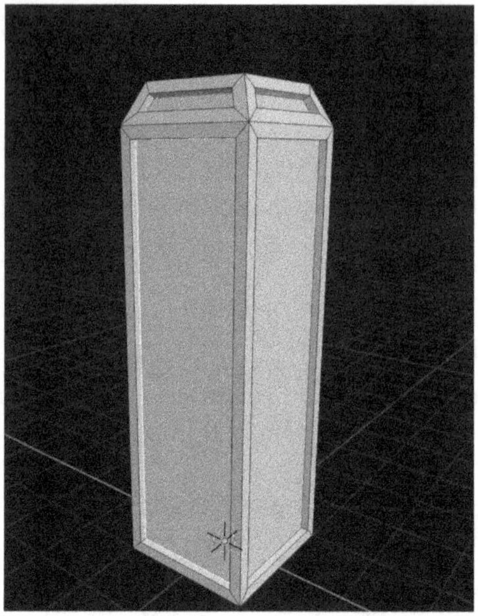

Figure 10.5 – Extruding the edge parts

That's it for the modeling part of our first easy building—all extremely easy. As expected.

Next, you can add some materials to this model.

Adding materials

This part is up to you—I chose an orange color for the main building and white for the edges, but it's up to you.

Setting the materials up is super easy. Follow these steps:

1. First, in the **Material** tab of the **Properties** panel, add a new material to the object. Name it `Orange`.
2. Now, click the + button to add a new material slot. Inside this new slot, add another new material. Name this one `White`.
3. In **Edit Mode**, select the faces you want to make white (they're probably still selected) and press **Assign**.
4. Switch to the **Shader Editor** and change the `Orange` material to a moderately shiny orange color.
5. Now use **Slot Switcher** to switch to the `White` material.
6. Make the `White` material a white color, and use a little more roughness.

You're now finished with our easy building. Give it a name in the outliner, something like `Simple Building`.

Press *G* and then *X* to move your creation to one side, so it's out of the way. You can also hide it by selecting it and pressing *H*.

> **Note**
>
> *Alt* + *H* unhides everything, just in case you need that later.

Now, we'll make a tougher, more complicated building.

The complicated building

This project is different—it's more complex. Here's what our complicated building looks like:

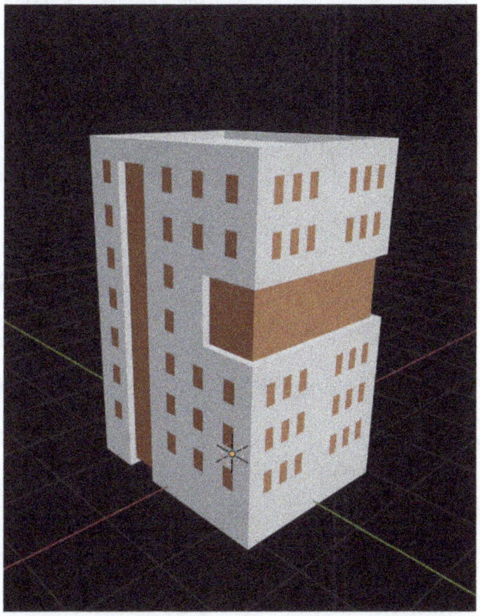

Figure 10.6 – The complicated building

To make this building, we'll first make the inner orange part. It's just a simple adjusted cube. Then, we'll make the outer part shown in the following figure, with the cut-out "holes" in it, and put that on top. The whole process should be fairly simple.

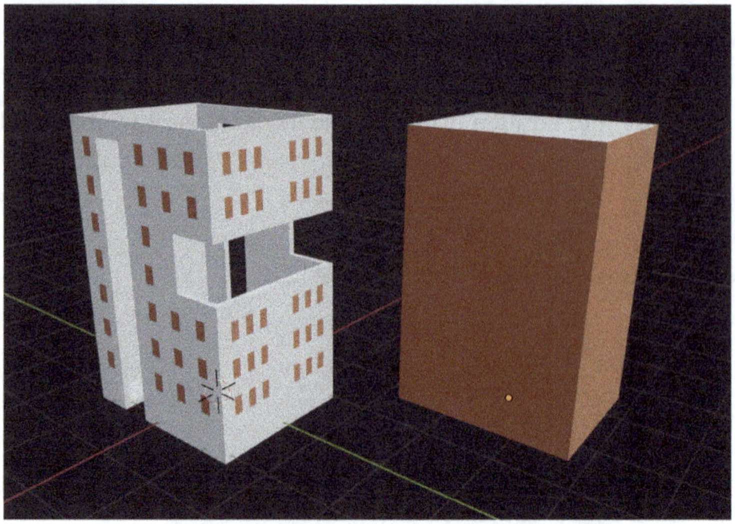

Figure 10.7 – The two parts: the outer white and inner orange pieces

We'll make the outer cover by duplicating part of the inner piece, so you'll learn some new tools for separating objects.

Creating the inner part

First, we'll make the inner part. Once it's complete, we'll work on the outer shell. We'll start with a cube, just like we did for the first building:

1. *Tab* into **Edit Mode**, select all with *A*, and press *G* then *Z* then *1* to move the mesh up far enough to fit on the flat grid area of the scene.

   This just makes it easier to work with.

2. Now, in **Edit Mode**, switch to **Face Select** mode.
3. Select the top face, and move it upward to make your building taller. This part's up to you—you get to pick whatever dimensions you want for this part.
4. Select another face, one of the sides, and move it outward, so that you have a slightly stretched cube.

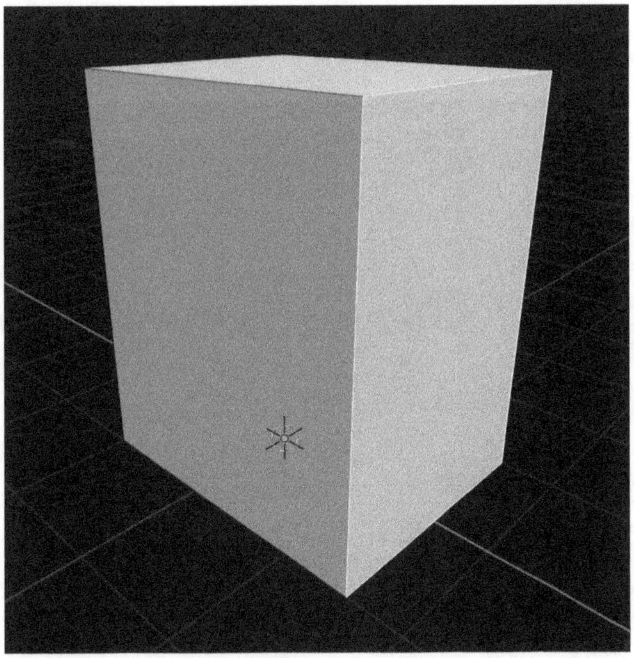

Figure 10.8 – The inner piece

This is the inner part.

Tab back into **Object Mode** and set a material for it—use the orange one you made earlier.

Let's move on to the outer part.

Creating the outer part

Now we'll make the outer shell part, cutting holes in it to let the inner part show through. It's a very useful way to add simple, interesting details:

1. First, make sure you're in **Object Mode**.
2. To make the outer shell, we're going to start by duplicating the inner piece. Simply select the inner piece and press *Shift* + *D* to duplicate it, then right-click to leave it exactly in place. Now that you have the duplicate, give it a name: `Outer Shell`.
3. Hide the inner part for now by clicking the little eyeball beside it in the **Outliner** (or just select it and press *H*, like earlier).
4. Select the outer shell and *Tab* into **Edit Mode**.

5. In **Face Select** mode, delete the top and bottom faces of the cube, so that you just have an open "tube" like this:

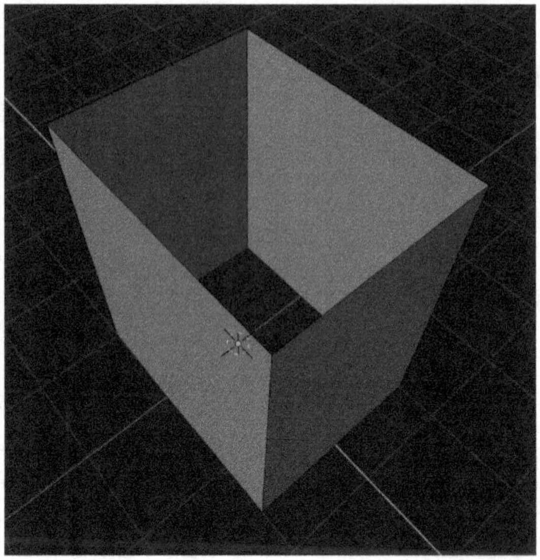

Figure 10.9 – Making the outside shell

6. Now switch to **Edge Select** mode and select the top edge of the "tube" by holding *Alt* and clicking one edge; this is how you select a full loop of edges.
7. Press *G* and move the top edge upward, just a tiny bit. This way, the top of the "shell" will be higher than the top of the "inner piece," which adds some interest to the shape.

Now we need to cut the holes in the outer piece. We'll do that by deleting faces, but we don't have enough faces for that, so we'll need to subdivide the mesh a little bit:

1. Simply press *A* to select all edges.
2. Then go to the **Edge** menu and select **Subdivide**. This will divide the faces up into smaller ones.
3. In the **Operator** menu that pops up, adjust the number of cuts to something like `9`.

Here's how my piece looks when subdivided.

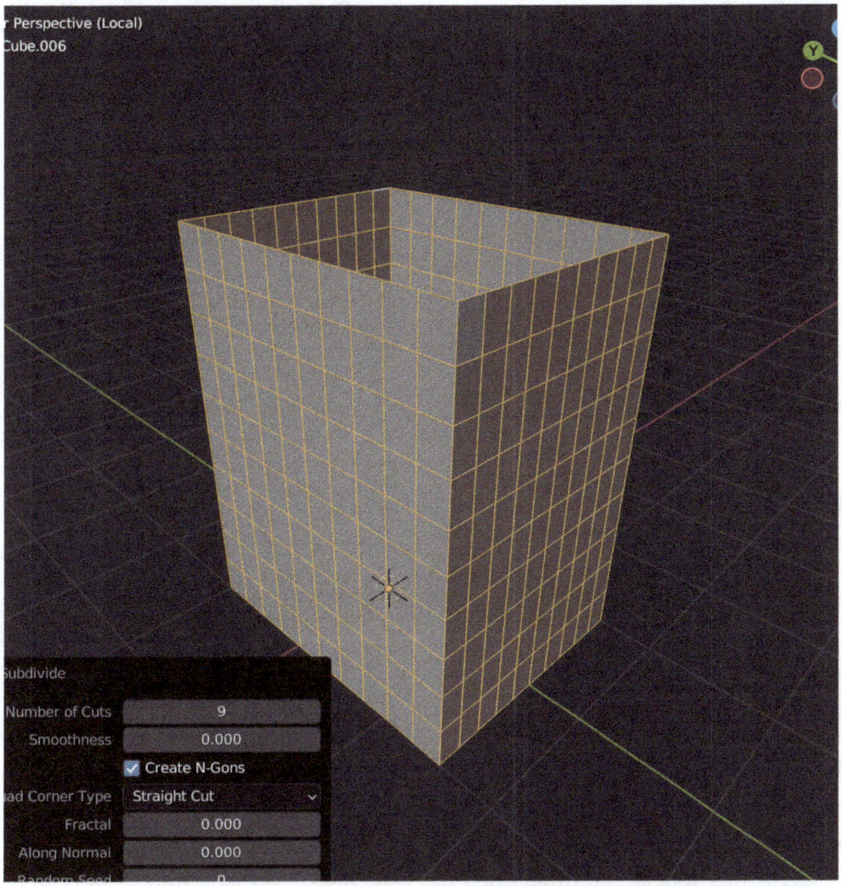

Figure 10.10 – Subdividing

Now that the whole piece is subdivided, all you need to do is select some faces and delete them to make cool cutout shapes. After that, we'll add a **Solidify** modifier to give some thickness to the whole thing:

1. First, hold *Shift* while you select some faces.
2. Next, press *X* to delete them.

Now you've got some holes in your mesh. Here's the ones I deleted:

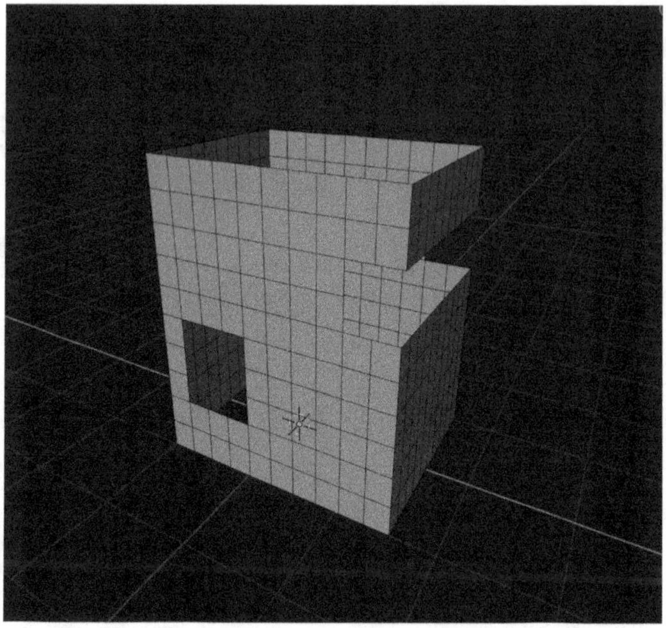

Figure 10.11 – Cutting neat holes

The next step is to add thickness using the **Solidify** modifier;

1. Open the **Modifiers** tab in the sidebar and press the big **New Modifier** button.
2. Choose **Solidify**.
3. Before you do anything else, unhide the inner cube object of the building. You can do this by clicking the little eye icon next to it in the outliner.
4. Now, select the outer shell part again (you might have to do that in the outliner) and have a look at the **Solidify Modifier** settings. There's a lot to take in, but the most important setting (the only one I've ever used) is **Thickness**.
5. Simply click and drag in the **Thickness** box to increase or decrease how thick the **Solidify** effect is. The thickness can be either negative or positive. Try adjusting it both ways to see what happens.

Use a value of around `-0.1`. If it looks strange, check the **Even Thickness** checkbox to keep the shape even.

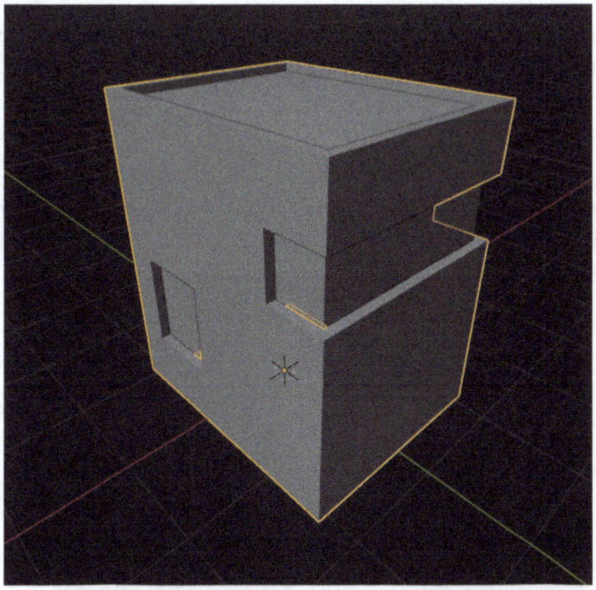

Figure 10.12 – Sticking the parts together

The outer part is ready.

Adding materials

Now you've got the outer and inner shells modeled and ready to go. The next step is to add some materials to your model.

This is the easy part—apply the `Orange` material to the inner piece, and the `White` material to the outer shell.

If you still want to add some windows for extra detail, that's easy too:

1. First, you'll have to apply the **Solidify** modifier (this makes the modifier permanent forever).
2. Simply select the modifier, click the little arrow in the top corner, and choose **Apply**. Note that you cannot do this in **Edit Mode**.
3. Once the modifier is applied, you can *Tab* into **Edit Mode** on your mesh and select some faces that you want to apply a window material to. See *Figure 10.6* to see the faces I chose. Sadly, there's no automatic way to do this, so you simply have to select the faces manually. (Select them all at once, then we'll apply the material in the next step.)

Now that you have those faces selected, the next step is to assign a material to them.

You can do that using the *Shift* + *Q* shortcut, choosing **Set Material**, clicking the search bar, then finding your material (the orange one) and assigning that to the faces.

Or, if you'd rather do it manually, just click the + button in the **Material Slot** list to add a new slot. Set the new slot to orange, and (still in **Edit Mode**) press the **Assign** button.

That's it for our more complex building.

If you're up for a challenge, try creating *the following* building. It's just two cubes—one of them with an **Array** modifier. Skip to the very end of this chapter, to the *Solution to the building challenge* section, for a quick explanation of how I did it.

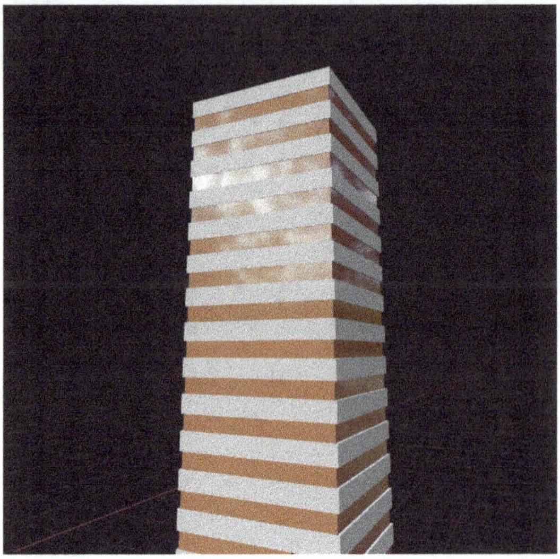

Figure 10.13 – Challenge: try modeling this building

Next, we'll model some little extra details that you can stick on any of your buildings.

Modeling building details

Our simple and complex buildings look cool, but we can make them even better. They're very simple right now (which is good, for this style). However, we can add a few additional details to them here and there, retaining the simple look while adding a bit of interest.

We're going to build three different detail pieces that you can add to your buildings. First, we'll make a little rooftop doorway, like the kind you find on top of buildings, then we'll make a simple vent-type piece. The options with details like these are limitless—you can do so many different things. Anything that's small and fairly interesting does the job well. But keep things simple. Details are usually small enough that nobody will notice them.

You can look at photos of real buildings to get ideas—maybe you'll come up with something new and interesting.

Modeling a rooftop doorway

Let's work on the doorway first. It'll be a simple model, based off a cube. There's not a lot to it: only a cube, with one face inset and extruded to make a door.

Here's what it looks like:

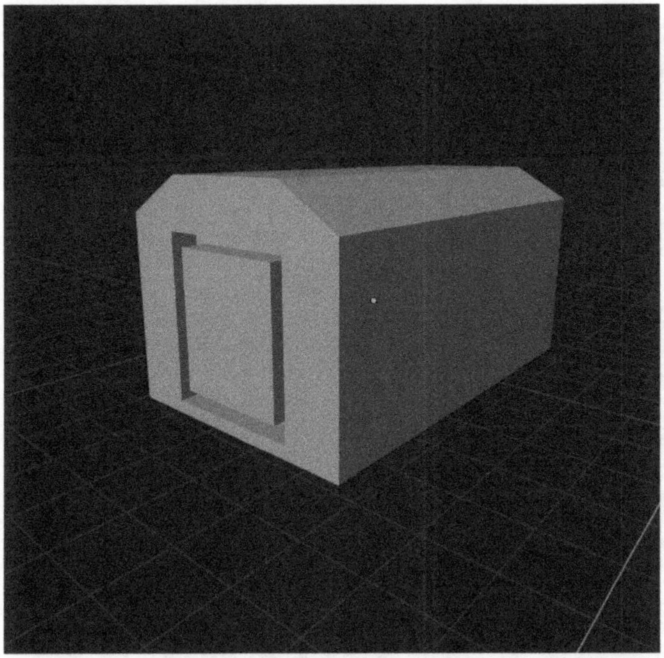

Figure 10.14 – Rooftop door

I'll break it down into steps so you can build it:

1. First, add a new cube to your scene.
2. *Tab* into **Edit Mode**, and scale it down on the X axis, then on the Z axis.
3. Press *I* to inset the front face.
4. Now scale the new face on the Z axis, to make it a little taller, and press *G* and *Z* to move it downward (just a little).
5. Now press *E* to extrude the door inward, *I* to inset it again (a tiny bit), and *E* to bring it outward again.

6. Select the top face, extrude it out, and scale it down a little bit.
7. Now apply your white material to it.

Now, try out the new doorway in your scene. Scale it down small and place it on top of a building. See *Figure 10.17*, where I used this doorway on the complicated building we modeled.

Creating a roof vent

The next little detail to make is a roof vent. You'll be able to use it in two different ways: pointing upward or laying on its side. It's an incredibly simple shape.

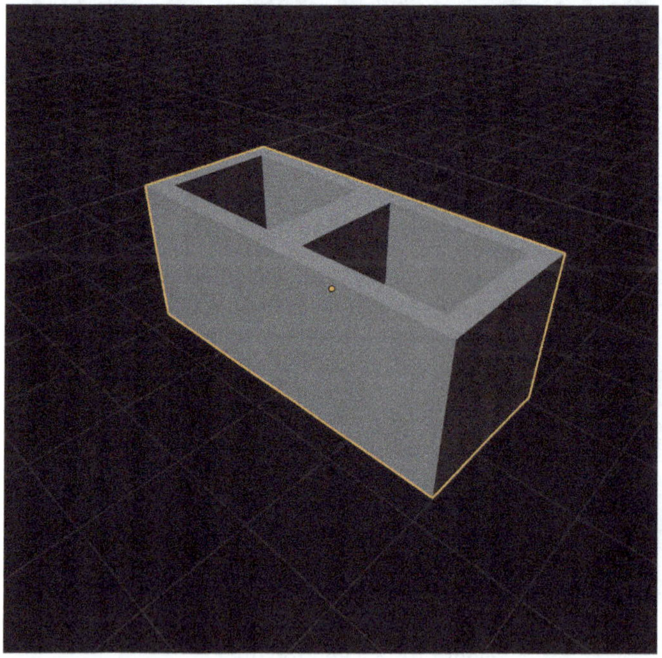

Figure 10.15 – Rooftop vent

Let's go about making this vent as follows:

1. Start with a cube again and *Tab* into **Edit Mode**. Select everything and scale it into a rectangular block.
2. Use the **Loop Cut** tool (*Ctrl* + *R*) to cut a loop across the middle.
3. Then select the two top faces.
4. Press *I* (you might need to press it again, to activate individual mode) and inset the two faces.
5. Extrude the selected faces inward.

This is the completed "super-structural ventilation unit." Or, as you might call it, "a vent." Give it a material and stick it on top of a building. See *Figure 10.17*, where I have added this vent to the complicated building we modeled.

Building an AC unit

Next, let's build a little AC unit that you can attach here and there on your buildings.

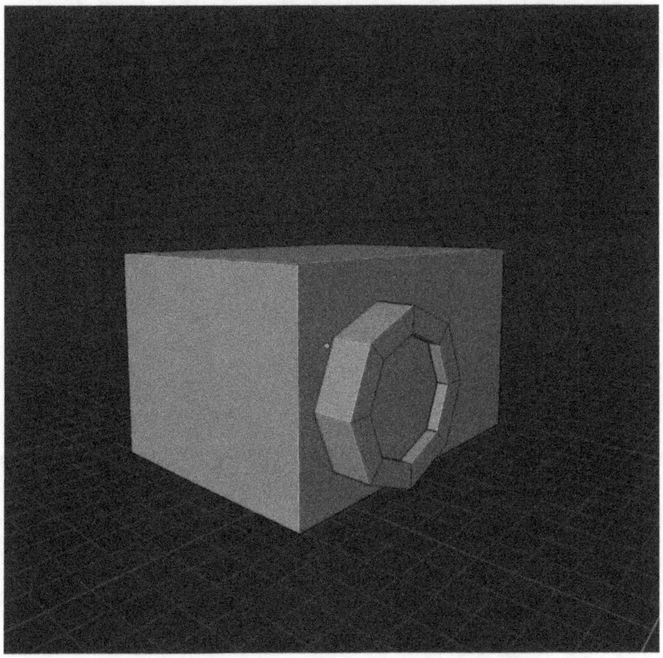

Figure 10.16 – AC unit

This is the easiest of all the details. It starts with a cube again, of course:

1. *Tab* into **Edit Mode** and reshape the cube so that it's more rectangular. See *Figure 10.16*.

Now the AC needs some details. A little fan or something might be cool—it doesn't have to be very detailed.

2. *Tab* out of **Edit Mode** back into **Object Mode** and add a new cylinder object with *Shift* + *A*.
3. Change the number of vertices to `8`.
4. Position the new cylinder using *R*, *G*, and *S* to manipulate it into place.
5. If you like, you can inset and extrude the end face of the cylinder.

6. If you added the cylinder while in **Edit Mode**, it'll already be part of the cube, the same object. If not, you can join them with *Ctrl* + *J*.

And that's it for our very, very simple air conditioner. Try putting a few on the side of a building, like they're hanging off windows.

Here's how our complicated building looks after adding these details:

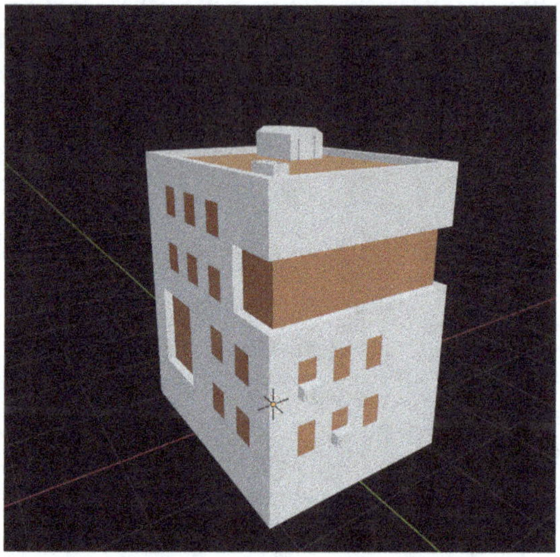

Figure 10.17 – All the details added to the more complex skyscraper

We're done with the details! These add a nice bit of detail to your buildings. And since they're separate pieces, you can easily duplicate them and add them to other buildings.

Next, we'll model a cute little house.

The cottage

Now we're going to build a simple little cottage. It's not much different from the buildings. I'll walk you through the steps and you'll be able to build it easily.

It'll have a few parts:

- The main *walls*—made of a cube
- The roof—made of a plane
- The windows and door (simple cubes)

Let's dive in.

Creating the main walls

First, let's build a pointy-topped cube:

1. Start with a cube.
2. *Tab* into **Edit Mode** and cut a single loop across the cube using the **Loop Cut** tool, so that you have a cut across the top of the cube.
3. Now switch to **Edge Select** mode, select the new edge you created, and move it upward using the *G* command.

You now have a pointy cube!

Creating the roof

Now we need the roof. It won't be too difficult to make. We'll create it by duplicating the top faces of the cube, turning those into a new object, and expanding it.

Here's how:

1. First, switch to **Face Select** mode (while still in **Edit Mode**, of course).
2. Select the top two faces of the cube.
3. Press *Shift* + *D* to duplicate them, then right-click so that the duplicates aren't moved at all.
4. Now press *P* to separate the (still selected) duplicate faces.
5. Click **Selection**. This separates the selected faces into their own new object.

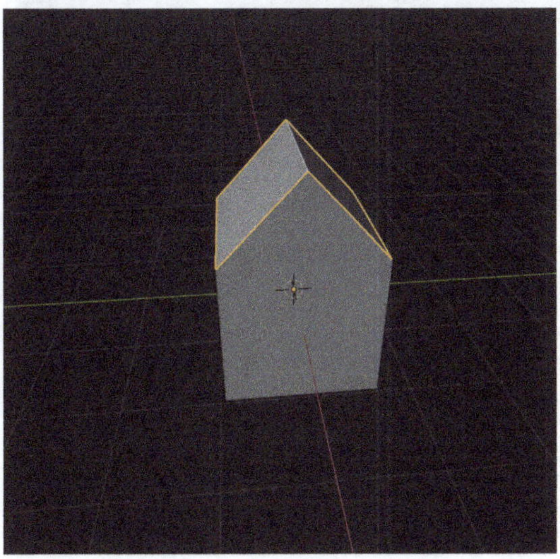

Figure 10.18 – Separating the roof

6. *Tab* out of **Edit Mode** and select the new object. Rename it `roof`.
7. Select the `roof` object and press *Tab* to enter **Edit Mode**.
8. Select the two outer edges.
9. Now use *G* and *Z* to move those edges directly downward a little bit.
10. Then press *S* and *X* to spread them apart on the X axis so that the roof angle is lined up to the top of the pointy cube.
11. Next, select everything with *A*, then press *S* and *Y* to scale it along the Y axis—we want a bit of an overhang, but nothing too dramatic.

The last step is to add a **Solidify** modifier. You're an expert on that now—pop open the **Modifier** tab, press **Add New**, and pick **Solidify**.

Tweak the **Thickness** value (you'll need to go negative) until you have a result you like.

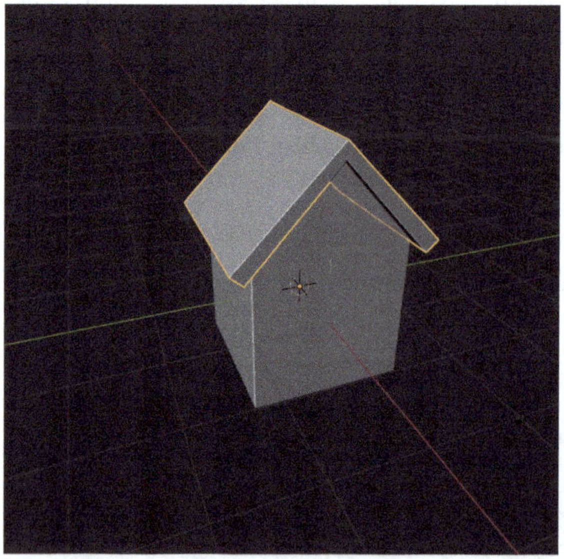

Figure 10.19 – Adding a Solidify modifier

Next, let's place a little chimney on top.

Making the chimney

We'll make the chimney out of, you guessed it, a cube:

1. First, make sure you're in **Object Mode**, then press *Shift* + *A* and grab a new cube.
2. Scale and move the cube until it's something like in the following screenshot: *almost* a chimney.

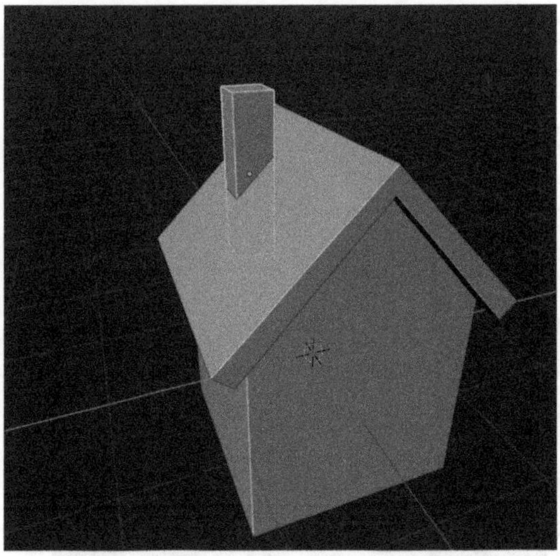

Figure 10.20 – The beginning of the chimney

3. *Tab* into **Edit Mode** and scale the top face up a little, like this. You can even give it a bit of jaunty rotation if you like.

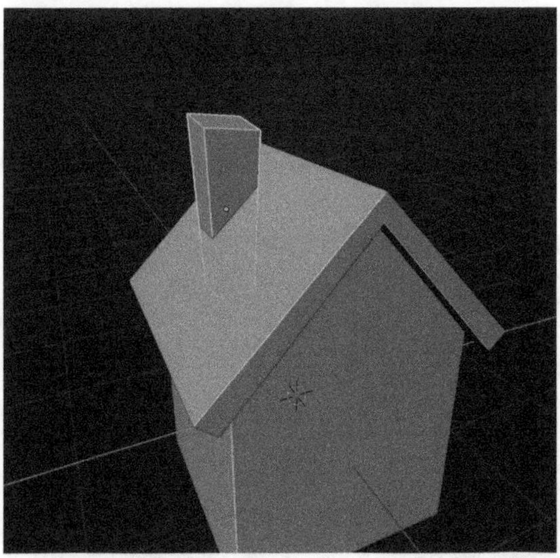

Figure 10.21 – Scaling and rotating the top of the chimney slightly

4. Then inset it and extrude it inward a little, like this.

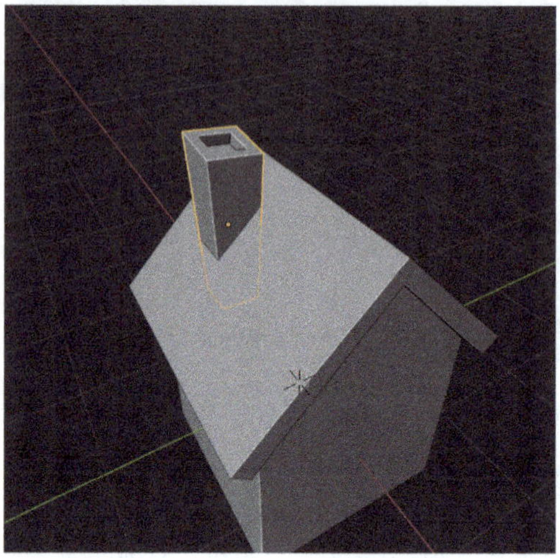

Figure 10.22 – Insetting the top of the chimney

Chimney done.

Now, this house needs windows.

Creating windows

We're going to make very simple windows, like the ones shown in *Figure 10.23*, and they even come with a trim. Very handy.

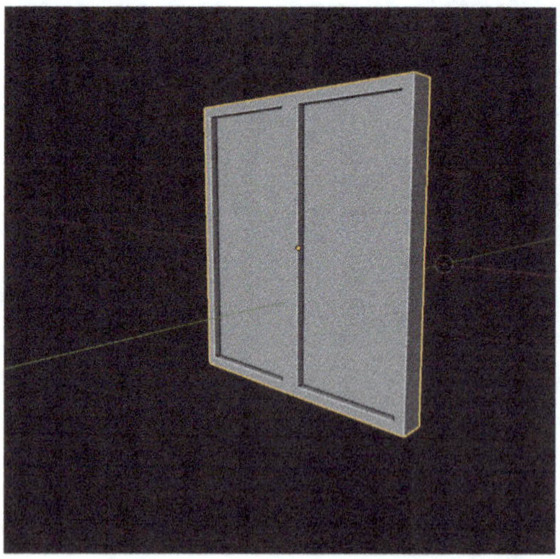

Figure 10.23 – The final window

We'll make the window exactly like the vent we made earlier, only a little flatter:

1. Start with a cube.
2. Flatten it out, in **Edit Mode**, using the **Scale** tool.
3. Then use *Ctrl* + *R* to add an edge loop across the middle.
4. Now inset the two faces, just a little, then extrude them inward slightly.

Window complete! Scale it down and position it like this on the house.

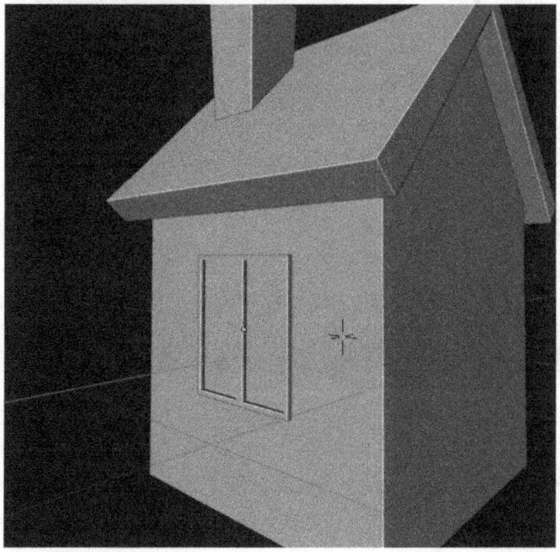

Figure 10.24 – The window on the house

You can duplicate it to add more windows if you like. Before you duplicate it, give it a material.

> **Important lesson**
>
> Don't duplicate stuff before you set up the materials.
>
> There is a little trick you can do, though, that helps with this: **linked duplicates**. With linked duplicates, any duplicates you make are "connected" to the original, so that if you change any of them, they'll all change.
>
> Try it now. You press *Alt* + *D* instead of *Shift* + *D*.
>
> Now try changing the material (or editing the mesh) on any of the duplicates: the others change too. This is a useful trick if you're ever duplicating a lot of something.

Last up: the door.

Adding the door

You can make the door by yourself. The process is exactly the same as that for creating the windows, but without the loop cut. Squash a cube, inset, and extrude inward.

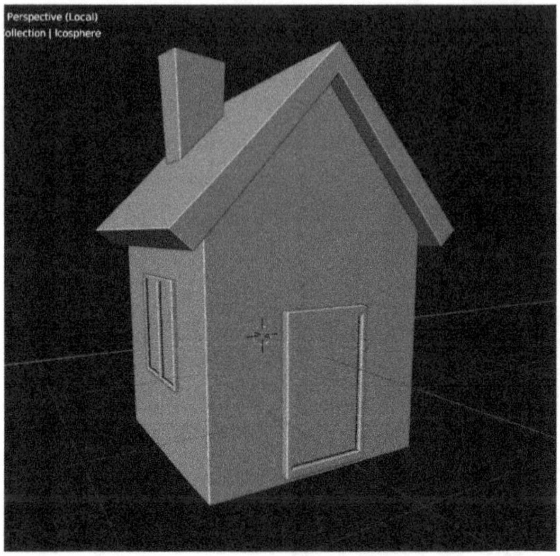

Figure 10.25 – The door

Once you have the door in place, add an icosphere. In the **Operator** menu, turn the divisions down to `1`. Carefully put the sphere in place to make a tiny door handle.

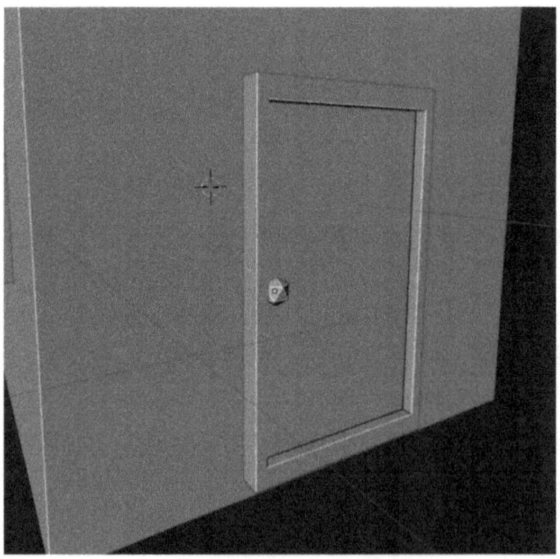

Figure 10.26 – The doorknob

Your house is now complete! Have fun adding some materials to it.

The rest is up to you. There's so many things that you can do with a house. Little changes can change the look and feel of the whole house. Feel free to try anything on yours.

You could even add another "chunk" of house, as shown in the following screenshot. Follow the same process as building the big chunk. It's easy.

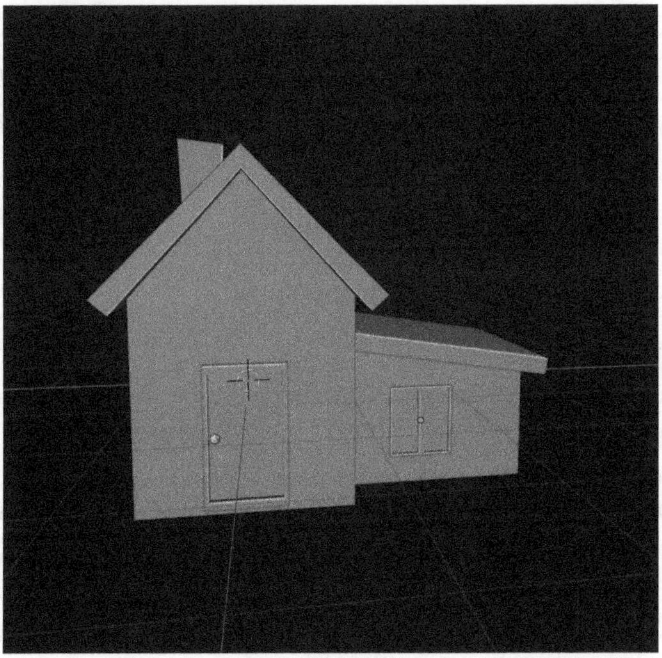

Figure 10.27 – An extra "chunk" is a cool way to upgrade your house

These are all cool ways to change the way a house looks—details like this can give it character.

And now you've built a house. From scratch. And you finished the chapter!

Great job!

Summary

In this chapter, you became a builder. You learned how to make a skyscraper, working from scratch to build a whole building. You built a house, one piece at a time. You learned how to make windows, doors, and other building details.

Great job making it through the chapter!

If you only remember one thing from this chapter, it is that that buildings (in the world of low poly) are essentially cubes. And you can make an interesting building out of an interesting cube.

In the next chapter, you're going to learn how to use the **Asset Browser** to store and organize all your assets.

Solution to the building challenge

Here are the steps to complete the complex building challenge:

1. Create a very tall cube for the body of the building.
2. Add another cube. Scale it up so it is wider than the first cube, then scale it down on the Z axis to make it thin.
3. Move the thin cube down on the Z axis so that it is at the base of the tall cube. We will now use an **Array** modifier to duplicate it upward and create the rest of the thin cubes.
4. Add an **Array** modifier to the thin cube. Change the offset setting on the modifier to `0` for X and Y and `1.8` for the Z value.
5. Turn up the count on the **Array** modifier to increase the number of thin cubes.
6. Once you're happy, apply the modifier to make it permanent, then move the stacked-thin-cubes object upward so that the very top thin cube looks like a roof on the building.

Done!

11
Using the Asset Browser

Now, you have a *ton* of completed models. In the 3D world, we call those **assets**.

So, it's time to organize all of those assets so that you can use them in any scene, whenever you want. Blender provides the **Asset Browser** to make that easier.

The Asset Browser lets you build an **Asset Library**. Then, in any Blender file, you can simply click and drag your models right into your scene.

In this chapter, you're going to learn all about the Asset Browser. You'll learn how to prepare your models for use in the Asset Browser, how to set up an *Asset Library*, and finally, how to use it.

By the end of this chapter, you'll have the following:

- A library of useful low-poly assets
- Knowledge of how to add new assets to your library
- Knowledge of how to use your assets in any scene

First, I'll explain what I mean by *asset*.

What's an asset?

You'll hear the word *asset* a lot. **Asset** is a common term in the world of 3D. Its meaning can be different depending on the context.

In Blender, an asset is any of the following:

- A material or world material
- A completed 3D model
- A node group

Pretty simple. An asset is just a completed thing that you can use in 3D to build your scene. It's simply anything you've made – usually a single object – that's stored in a `.blend` file on your computer. When we use the asset library, you'll move all of your *asset* files into a central location.

Eventually, you'll need a place to store your assets and a way to access them easily across projects. Enter the **Asset Browser**. With the Asset Browser, you'll be able to access any of your saved assets from any Blender project.

Why the Asset Browser?

Over time, you'll accumulate a lot of finished or mostly finished models.

And, most likely, you'll want to use them in other scenes that you create. It's possible to copy objects from one Blender file to another (using **File** | **Append**), but this is a long, tedious process.

I can say from experience that it's best to collect all your assets in one place. All the great materials and models that you make should be easy for you to access.

That's exactly what the *Asset Browser* is for. It provides a unified, neat place where you can bring all of your assets together. The Asset Browser makes it very easy to see all of your assets in one place. You can easily search through them to find what you're looking for.

It works off a system called *Asset Libraries*. An Asset Library is just a folder on your computer. To put assets into the library, you must simply place the necessary `.blend` files into the folder. Inside those `.blend` files, you can mark specific objects as assets.

Then, in any Blender file, you can open the Asset Browser and drag and drop models from the Asset Browser into your file.

Sounds amazing, right?

It is. I'll walk you through how to set the Asset Browser up next. The first thing you need to do is set up the folder.

Setting up the Asset Browser

Getting your assets into the Asset Browser is a three-step process:

1. Creating your Asset Library.
2. Adding Blender files.
3. Telling Blender which objects are assets.

First, let's create the Asset Library. This step is easy.

Creating your Asset Library

Somewhere on your hard drive, create a new folder.

I have a folder called `Blender` where I keep all of my Blender projects, and I've created my library folder there. Give your new folder a name, such as `My Asset Library`.

Now that you have the folder, it's time for the next step.

Adding Blender files

Find any `.blend` files that have assets you want to place in the library and move these files to your new library folder.

You can create copies of the files if you'd like to use the originals for something else. I didn't copy mine. If I need anything that's in them, I can just get it out of the Asset Library later.

Now, open one of the Blender files you just put in the library folder.

Finally, we'll tell Blender which objects are assets.

Marking objects as assets

The last step is to mark which objects should be treated as assets for the Asset Browser. Not all objects can be used as assets, so here are some guidelines:

- A single object, such as our mushroom, *will* make a great asset
- An object that is a few objects parented together (such as the tree we created back in *Chapter 3*) *will not* work as an asset

> **Tip**
>
> For objects that are parented together and not *joined*, such as the tree, it's best to simply join those into a single object if you want them to work as an asset. Remember to apply all modifiers to each object before joining them together – if you don't, the modifiers will all be applied to the entire object, which will cause issues and won't give you the result you want.

- A material *will* work, even one that's not assigned to any objects

The steps to mark an object as an asset are a bit different from the steps for a material. We'll cover each separately. Let's start with objects.

Marking objects as assets

These are the steps to mark an object as an asset:

1. Select the object in the outliner.
2. Right-click to bring up the context menu.
3. Click **Mark as Asset**:

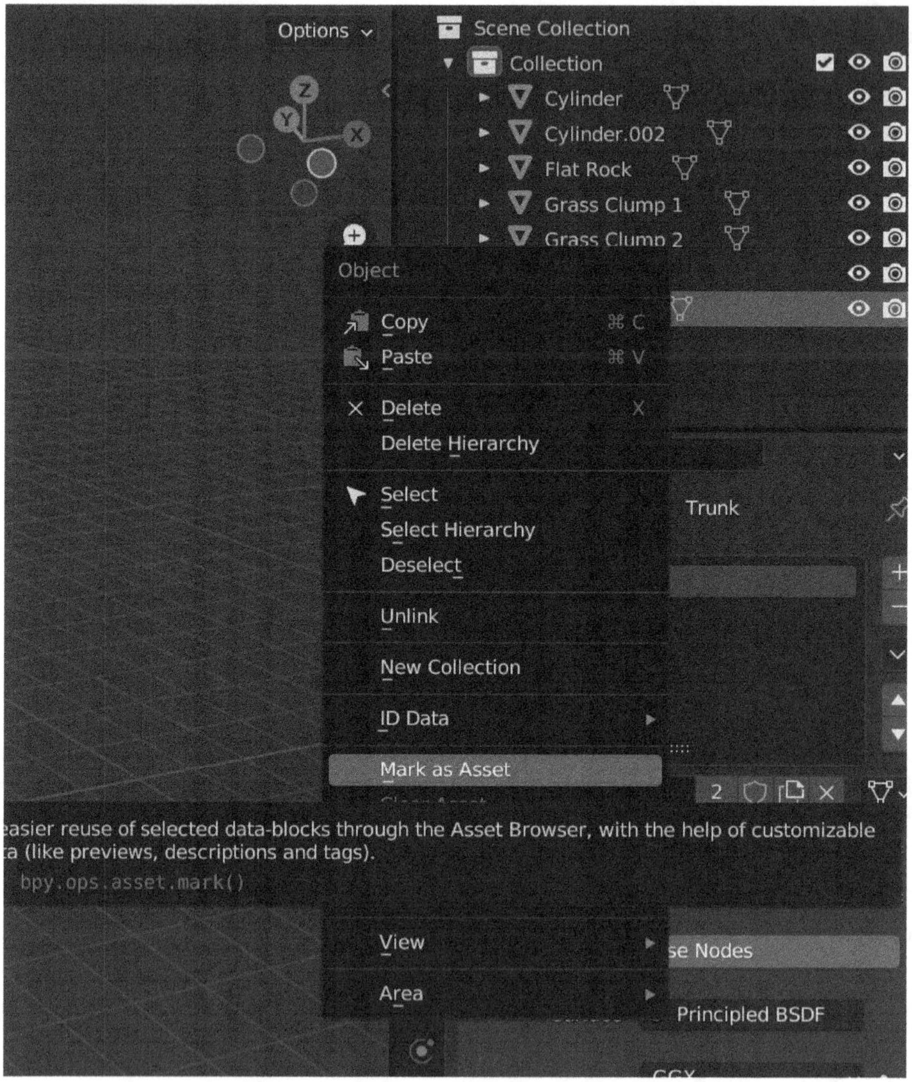

Figure 11.1 – Marking an object as an asset

Once an object has been marked as an asset, it'll have a little bookshelf icon next to it:

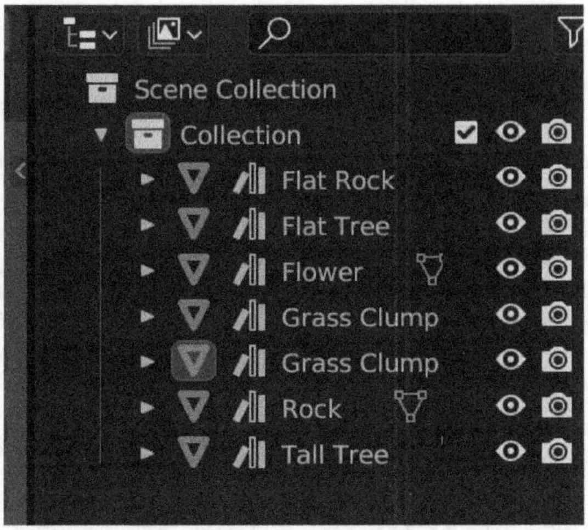

Figure 11.2 – Objects marked as assets

That's it for objects. Let's move on to materials.

Marking materials as assets

To mark a material as an asset, the process is slightly different:

1. Open **Shader Editor**.
2. Select an object that has the material so that you can see the material in **Shader Editor**.
3. Right-click on the name of the material.

4. Click **Mark as Asset**:

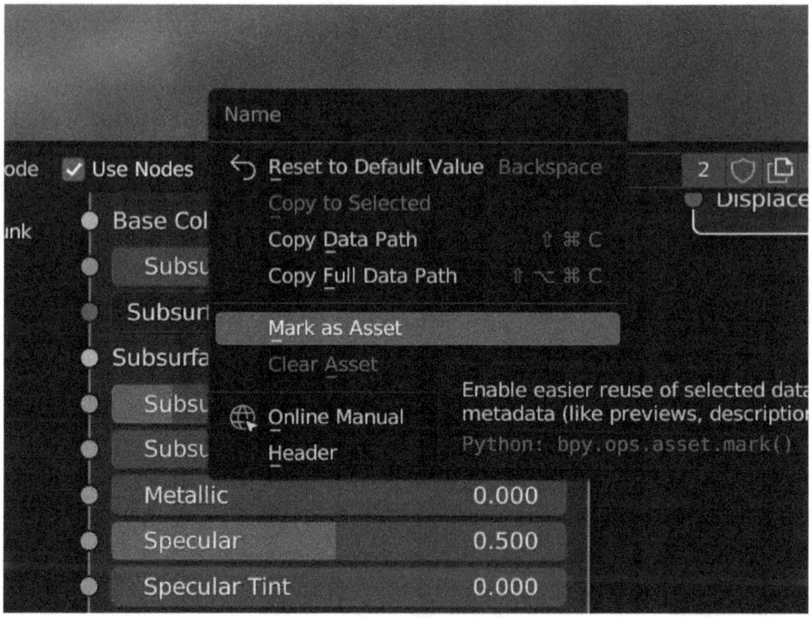

Figure 11.3 – Marking a material as an asset

With that, you're all set!

Now you know how to mark objects and materials as assets. Go through all of the `.blend` files you added to your library folder and mark anything you want as an asset.

You just brought all of your assets into a single folder and marked everything as an asset. Next, you'll open up the Asset Browser in Blender and learn how to get assets out of the library you just made.

Setting up the Asset Browser in Blender and using your assets

You've got your Asset Library ready to go now. You need to tell Blender where it is so that it becomes an option in the Asset Browser.

That's not too hard.

Open a *new* Blender file. Don't bother saving it – this is just a playground for us to mess around with the Asset Browser.

The first step is to add your library to Blender's list of Asset Libraries:

1. Go to **Edit | Preferences**.
2. Click the **File Paths** tab.
3. Scroll to the bottom and open the **Asset Libraries** section.
4. Click the little + button to add a new one:

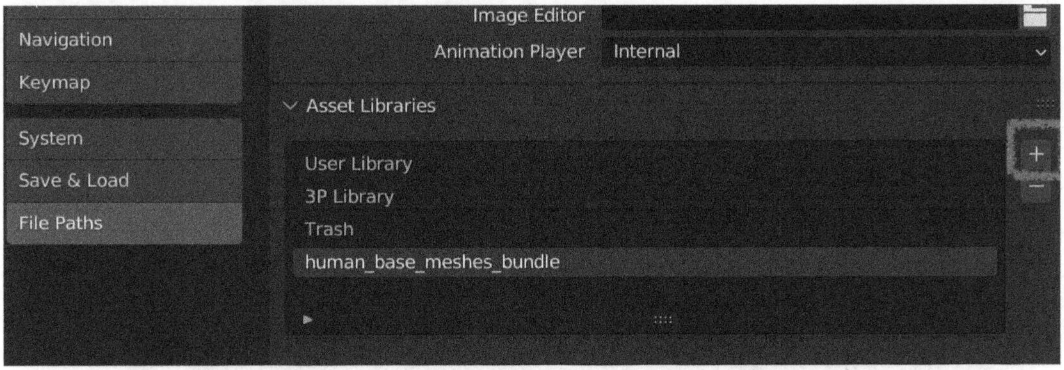

Figure 11.4 – The Asset Libraries section of Preferences. Note that I have several existing libraries already

5. A File Explorer window will pop open. Navigate to your folder, select it, and click **Add Asset Library**:

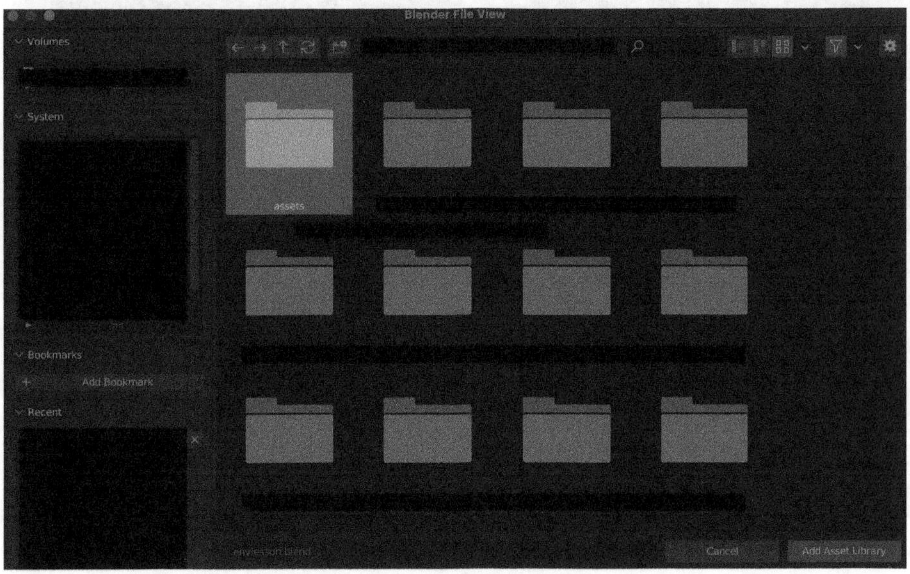

Figure 11.5 – Choosing your asset folder

Blender knows where to find your library now. You just need to open the Asset Browser. The Asset Browser is one of the area types, just like the **Properties** panel or the 3D viewport:

1. Hover your mouse over the corner of the 3D viewport until you see the view-making + symbol, then click and drag to pull open a new area.
2. Switch the type of this area to **Asset Browser**.
3. In the **Toolbar** section of the new area, you'll see a dropdown labeled **Current File**. This shows you any objects that have been marked as assets in the current `.blend` file – so nothing for this one.
4. Click the dropdown to open it, then choose your Asset Library (the one you just added). You'll see all of your objects in a neat little list view.
5. Press *T* to close the toolbar – you don't need that anymore:

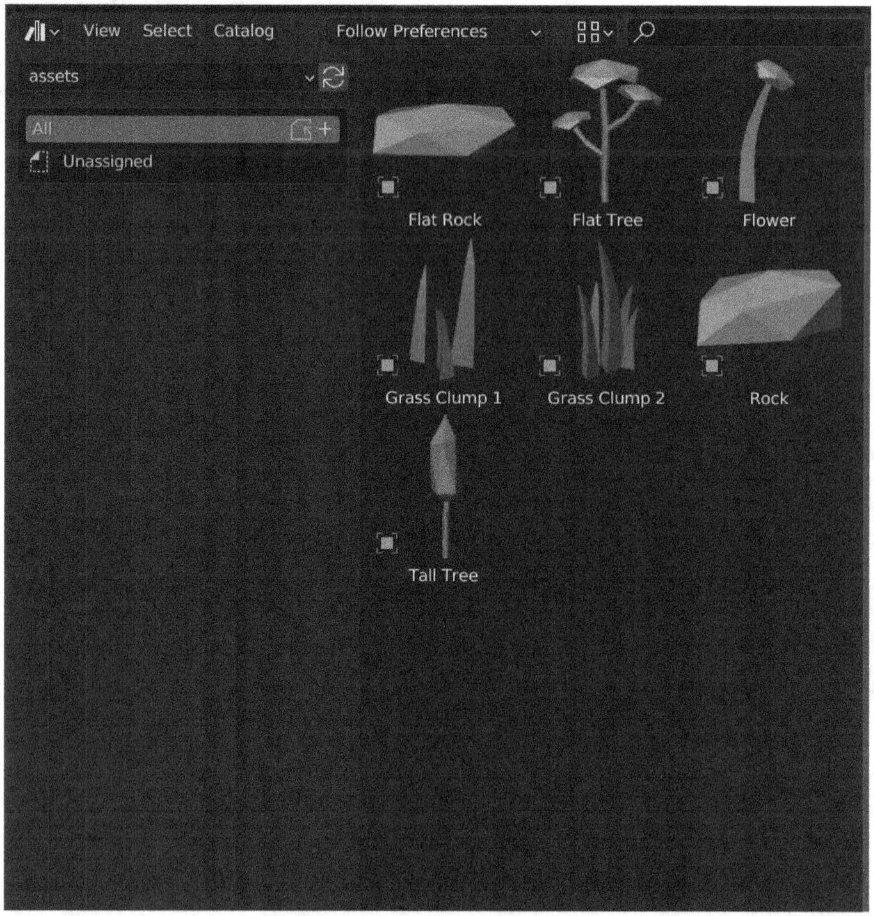

Figure 11.6 – The Asset Browser

The final part is using the assets. And that's crazy easy.

Just drag and drop them into your scene. They'll snap to surfaces as you do it, at which point you can scale, transform, or rotate them like any other object.

Easy!

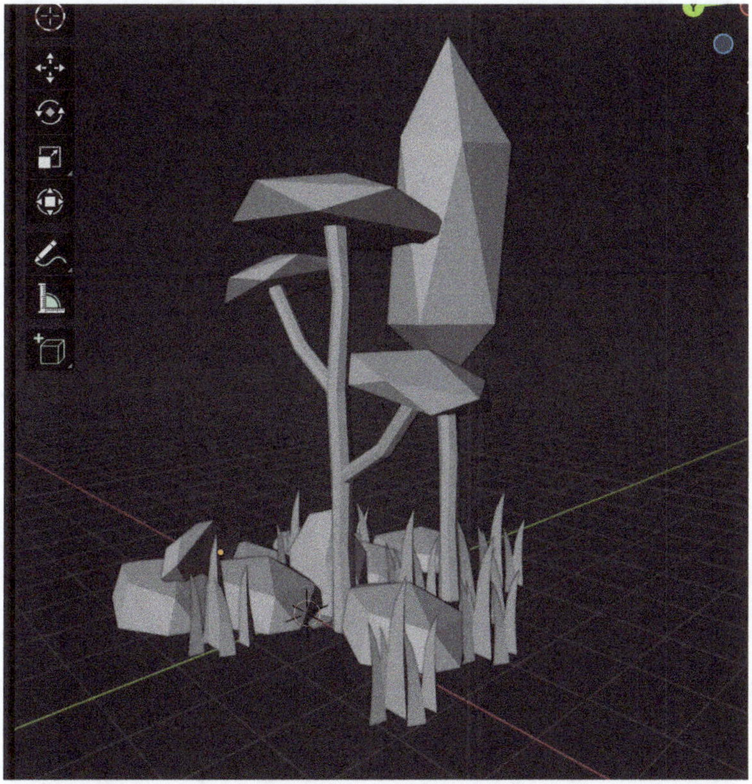

Figure 11.7 – Adding assets is easy – just drag them in!

For material assets, you can just drag them onto any object, and the material will be assigned to that object.

That's it for the Asset Browser – we've covered all its main features, and you now know how to use it to manage your assets.

Now, your job is to go through all of the Blender projects we've completed, move them to your asset folder, and mark things as assets. Then, you'll have everything in one place, ready to be used!

Summary

This was an easy one!

In this chapter, you learned how to use the Asset Browser to organize all the models you've created. You learned how to prepare your models, and how to use the Asset Browser to quickly add models to any scene.

If you only remember one thing from this chapter, remember that you have to mark an object as an asset before it can be used as one.

In the next chapter, we're going to start building a complete scene.

Part 4: Building a Complete Low Poly Scene

Now that you have a collection of useful assets, it's time to do something with them. In this part, you'll learn how to build a complete scene. You'll start by creating a reference and blocking it out, then you'll move on to placing your assets. At the end of this part, you'll create a finished, beautiful render of your scene.

This part has the following chapters:

- *Chapter 12, Blocking Out the Scene*
- *Chapter 13, Building the Scene*
- *Chapter 14, The Big Render*
- *Chapter 15, Appendix*

12
Blocking Out the Scene

You've built your assets – a lot of them.

Next, we're going to make a scene. A full, complete scene. You'll set the scene up, then you'll create a camera to render it, and finally, you'll create a finished rendered image of the scene.

That's a lot to do.

So, we'll start simple. Before we can build the scene and set anything up, we must have an idea in mind.

In this chapter, we'll explore a couple of different ways to figure out how to make our scene. This will involve us trying things out, gathering ideas, and creating concept art. There are multiple ways to do this, so we'll cover a few.

By the end of this chapter, you'll:

- Have a complete concept or idea for your scene
- Understand how to come up with ideas for your scene
- Understand exactly what 'concept art' means

First, I'll explain what I mean by *building a scene*.

What's a scene?

First, let's learn what a scene is.

By **scene**, I mean a full setup in your Blender file – models, materials, lighting, cameras, the whole lot. These must all be set up to make a nice, beautiful rendered image.

Making a render is a many-step process, so I'll break it down:

1. **Creating concept art**: You create a rough sketch or idea of what you want to make.
2. **Modeling**: You create any assets you need.

3. **Assigning materials**: You make sure everything has a nice material on it.
4. **Setting up the scene**: You build the scene.
5. **Lighting**: You set up lights for nice lighting in your scene.
6. **Rendering**: You create the final render (the final image)!

Right now, we're at the *concept art* stage. We need to figure out what we're making, and, more importantly, what it would look like before we can make it.

That's what concept art is for. Let's make some.

Creating concept art

Concept art can be almost anything. Crude sketches, fancy hand-drawn images, photos, photoshopped messes, and even simple 3D setups using cubes. Anything. All it must do is give you a general idea of what your scene is going to look like and what you want your final render to look like.

Why bother with concept art?

The idea behind concept art is that you can test out your ideas – any ideas that you want – with much less effort than actually doing it in Blender. It also gives you a good general idea of how you want your scene to look – some concept art might help you figure out what mood, colors, and more you're going for.

Every major movie, every TV series, and every video game makes heavy use of concept art to figure out what things look like *before* they're made. There's people who create concept art for a living. That's their *job*. In bigger studios, 3D artists don't have to worry about concept art since the concept artists will create it first, and then pass it on.

Since concept art can be anything, you can make it in tons of different ways. Pictures make great concept art – search for images that are close to what you want to make and work off those.

I have two favorite ways to make concept art:

- Sketching (quick, easy, and fast iteration)
- 3D (making a crude scene out of cubes to test things out)

I'll go over both methods, starting with sketching.

Sketching concept art

Sketching concept art is my favorite method. It's easy and it has a fast iteration time – I can try out new designs in seconds.

Use any drawing medium you want – be it a pencil, whiteboard, or digital tablet – it doesn't matter. Make sure you can erase if you want because that helps a lot. I use a pencil and paper since it's convenient and easy. Digital drawing (in an app such as **Procreate** or **Photoshop**) could be useful too since you can easily export your drawings as reference images for use in Blender.

For our scene, we'll start by listing what we must work with:

- Buildings and houses
- Trees, grass, and flowers
- A tractor
- A kangaroo

This is a bit of an odd mixture, but I bet we can come up with something. I want to create a simple farm scene, but I want to make it a little more interesting. I'll simply try drawing some things with the different elements we have to work with.

First, I tried a typical side-view farm scene. But that's a little boring and *extremely* overused. I wanted something at least a little more interesting:

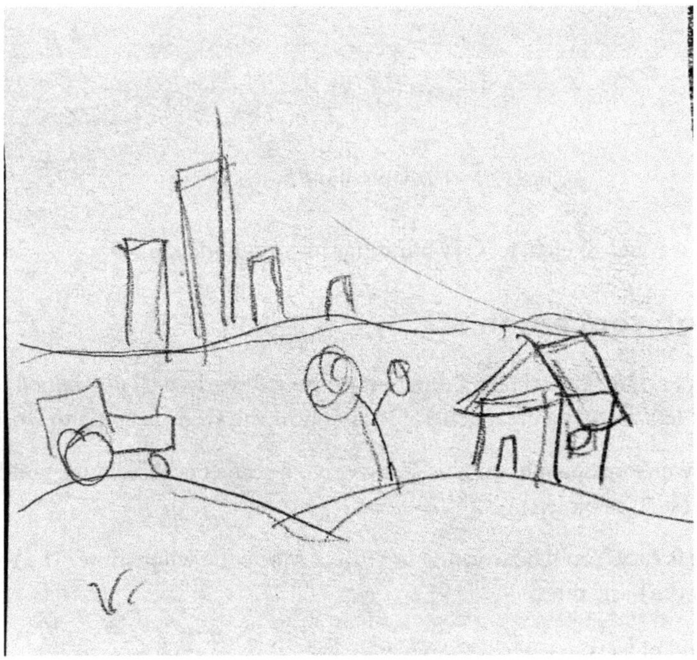

Figure 12.1 – My first attempt

So, instead of that, I tried drawing the house from an overhead angle. Then, I drew a square field to put the tractor in – and that gave me an idea. What about a kind of grid layout showing the house, the tractor, some trees, grass, rocks, and so on?

Here's the final rough sketch:

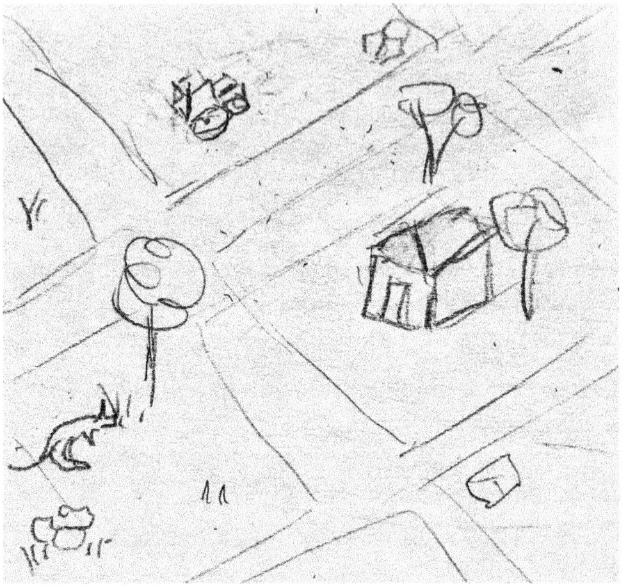

Figure 12.2 – I like this angle much better

Now that we have this rough sketch, let's try building this rough idea in 3D.

Making a rough concept in 3D

Creating your concept art in 3D is a bit of a different process. It works well *in addition* to the on-paper concept process as it lets you get a great general idea of how the scene is going to work in 3D.

It also works on its own. Some people call this *blocking out* a scene because you're building your scene using simple shapes (such as blocks).

Blocking out a scene is easy. You'll be working in **Object Mode** the whole time. The tools you'll need to use will just be all the basic ones:

- *Shift* + *A* to add objects
- *G*, *R*, and *S* to move, rotate, and scale them, respectively
- *X* to delete them

Nothing too bad.

Blocking out the scene

Now, we need to build the scene. It can be tedious at first, but you'll get good at it. The goal is to keep it ridiculously simple, even less than the bare minimum. You will use cubes to represent *everything*.

Usually, I start with a plane to represent the ground, like this:

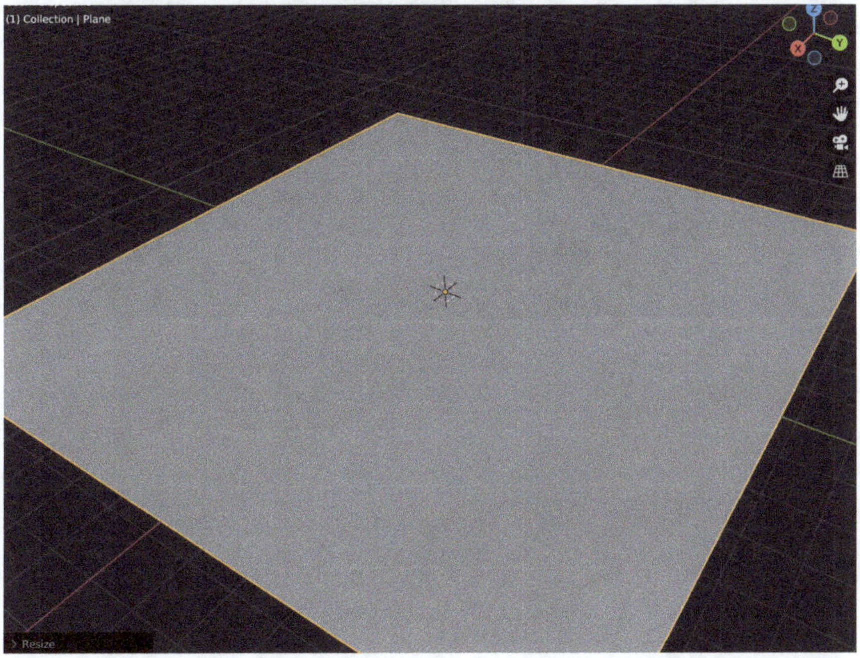

Figure 12.3 – The ground

Now, let's rough out the grid layout we want to test. We'll add cubes, then scale them to make them flat, then lay them out in a rough grid. Don't worry about being exact:

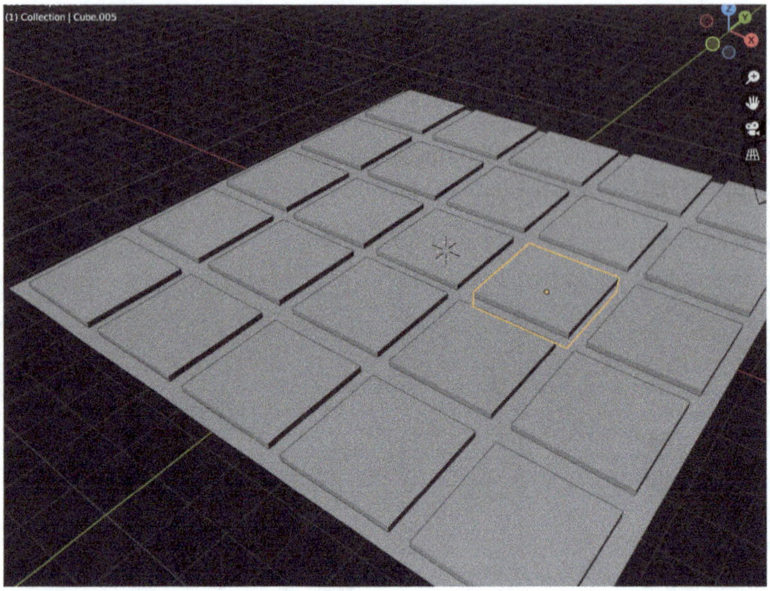

Figure 12.4 – A bunch of cubes for the "grid"

Next, we'll add a cube to represent the house, some cubes for trees, and a couple more cubes to represent the tractor:

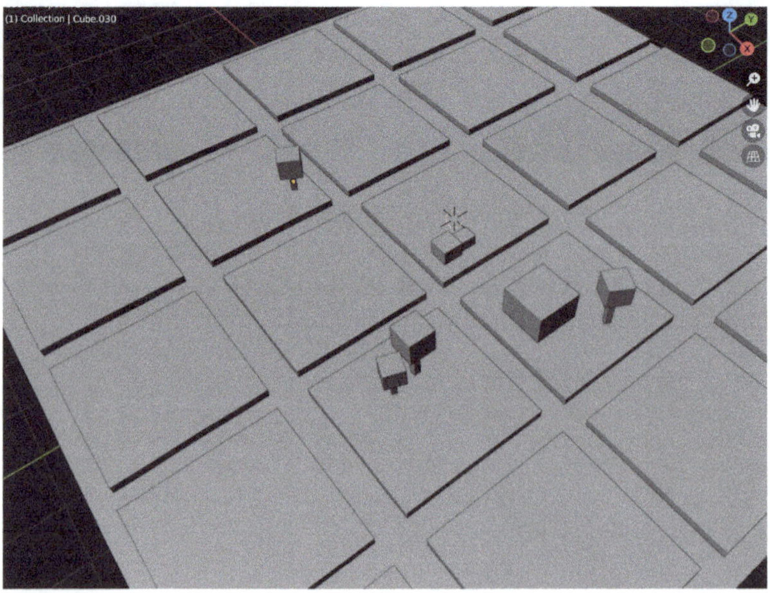

Figure 12.5 – Cubes for trees and a house

Not too bad – let's try adding a camera to the scene.

Adding a camera to the scene

A camera is extremely important when you're building the scene. The camera is what you use to "take a picture" of your scene when you render it – your final image will be a picture, taken from the camera's point of view.

We've been deleting the default camera, but now we need it. If you've already deleted it, that's fine – just press *Shift* + *A* and add a new camera.

Now, you need to look at the scene *through* the camera so that you can see what the camera sees. To do that, press *0*.

Now, you're seeing what the camera sees. But you need to change it – your camera is likely in a very bad place. There are two ways to position your camera. First, you can use normal tools, such as move and rotate, to position the camera where you like. The problem with this is that it's hard to get it right.

Instead, do this:

1. Press *0* so that you're looking through the camera.
2. Press *N* to open the N sidebar.
3. Select the **View** tab and enable **Lock Camera To View** (it may look slightly different in your version of Blender):

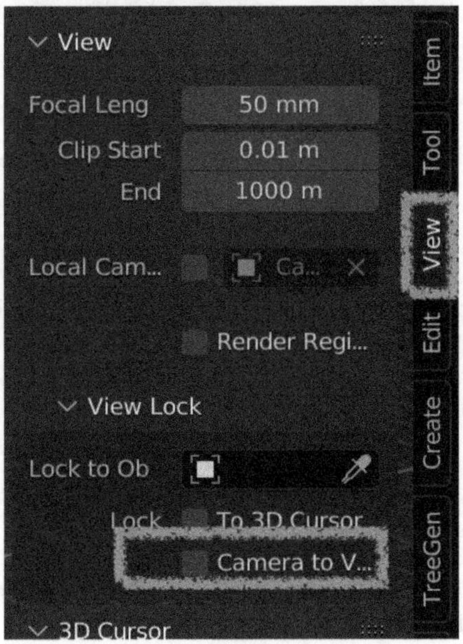

Figure 12.6 – The Lock Camera To View option

Now, you can navigate the scene as normal – and the camera will move with you. It's like you *are* the camera.

At this point, you have absolute freedom to position it however you like. This is what I came up with:

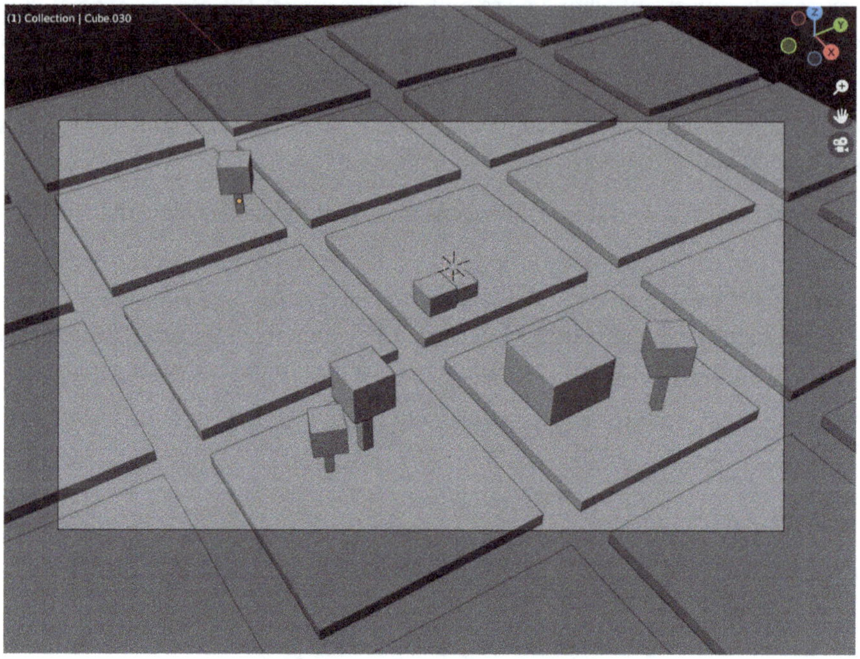

Figure 12.7 – My final crude concept

Once you have something you like, remember to disable **Lock Camera To View** so that you don't move the camera accidentally.

With that, you've learned how to create 3D concept art, what a camera is for, and how to position it.

Now, you have your rough concept, and you're ready to move on to making the real scene.

Summary

In this chapter, you learned what it takes to make a full scene in Blender. You learned about the scene-building process, as well as what concept art is and what it's for. You also learned how to make concept art using a few different methods.

If you only take one thing from this chapter, remember to do a rough sketch of your art *before* you try making it in Blender. Every time I don't do a sketch, I regret it.

In the next chapter, we'll dive right into setting up our scene.

13
Building the Scene

It's time for you to build your scene.

You have the scene roughly planned out with concept art now, so you know what you're going to build. You also have the assets to build it *with*.

We're getting there. There's not a lot left to do.

In this chapter, we're going to put it all together and *build the actual scene*. It's taken a while to get here, but in this chapter, you'll do the following:

- Position a camera in your scene
- Create the ground, based on our 3D concept
- Position objects to build the scene

This chapter will be very easy. We'll be following our 3D concept closely and building the actual scene.

We'll start with the ground first.

Building the ground

In *Chapter 12*, we planned out what the scene would look like. We know that we're going to make an interesting kind of *tiled* ground.

We did this when we made our 3D concept. But since it was just a concept, we didn't put much work into it.

This time, we'll build the tiled ground more correctly, using array modifiers to make the grid. This will ensure consistent, perfectly spaced tiles with even gaps between them.

We'll use the same file that we made our 3D concept with in *Chapter 12*. Follow these steps:

1. Open the concept art Blender file that you built in *Chapter 12*.
2. You need to select everything except the camera, so select everything in the scene by pressing *A*, then hold *Shift* and click the camera object to deselect it.
3. Press *M* to move everything to a collection, click **New Collection**, and name it `concept`.
4. In the **outliner**, uncheck the new **Collection** box so that it's completely hidden. You can unhide it whenever you want to refer back to your original concept:

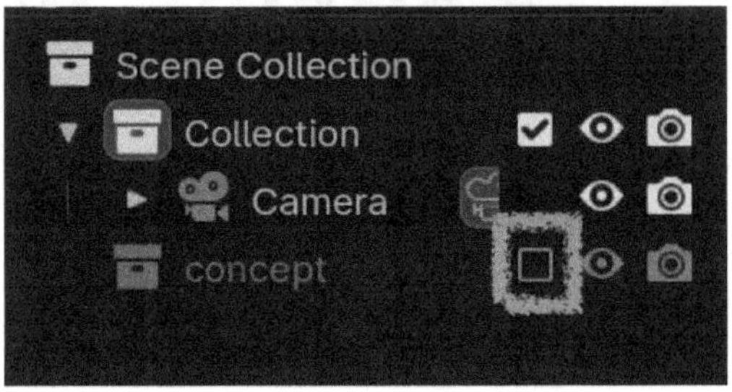

Figure 13.1 – Hiding the concept collection

Now, you have a nice clean scene to work in. At any time, you can unhide the **concept** collection to get a look at what your goal is.

We didn't hide the camera as we'll need it. At any time, you can press *0* to see the scene through the camera's point of view, which is what your final render will be.

Let's start with the ground. First, we'll make the tiles:

1. Add a new cube.
2. Scale it on the Z axis to squash it into a tile:

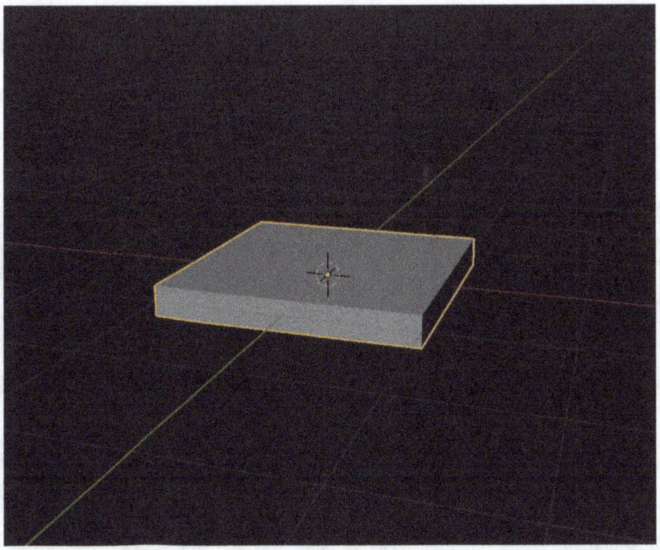

Figure 13.2 – One tile

Next, we'll add an array modifier to make a *row* of tiles:

1. Open the **Modifier** tab in the **Properties** panel, then click **Add Modifier**, and choose an **Array** modifier.
2. Turn **Count** up to `10` or so.
3. Turn up the **X** offset to put some space between the tiles:

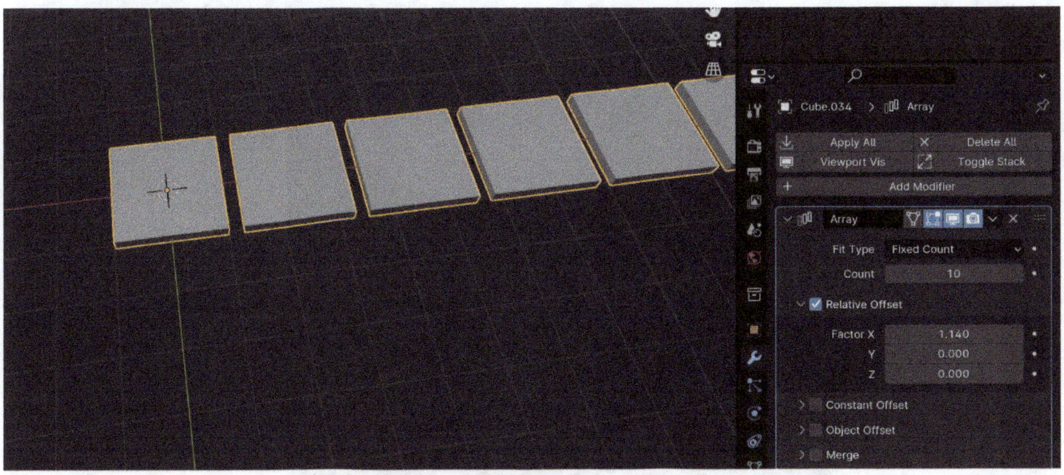

Figure 13.3 – Adding an array modifier

Now, all we have to do is duplicate that array modifier.

4. Click the small arrow button next to the name of the modifier, press it, and choose **Duplicate**.
5. Now, adjust the settings on the duplicate: simply change the **X** offset to `0`, and make the **Y** offset use the same amount as the **X** offset is using on the first modifier:

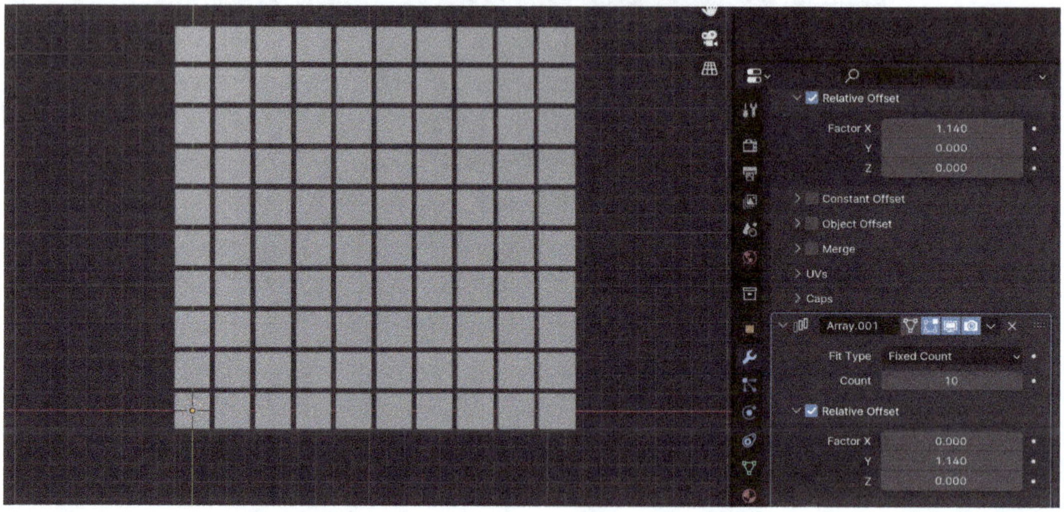

Figure 13.4 – Duplicating the array modifier

Now, you have a huge grid of 100 tiles.

6. Press *7* to view it from above, then use *G* to move it so that it's more centered:

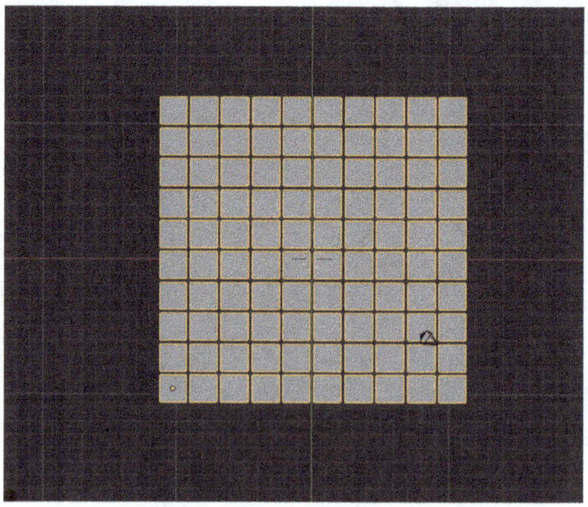

Figure 13.5 – Now, it's centered

7. Now, press *0* to look at it through the camera (if you need to learn how to position the camera, reference *Chapter 12*):

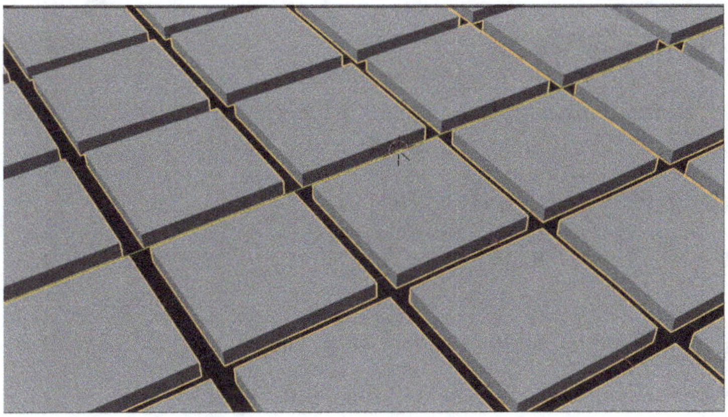

Figure 13.6 – Through the camera

The next step is to fill in the gaps between the tiles. Follow these steps:

1. Add a new plane.
2. Scale it up so that it's huge. The size doesn't matter so long as it's big enough to cover the gaps between all the tiles. It'll be roughly the same size as the grid of tiles.
3. Select the tiles and move them downward slightly so that they're not too tall.
4. On mine, it also felt like the tiles were a little too small. To fix that, just select the **tiles** object and press *S* to scale the whole thing up so that it's bigger.

Here's my final ground setup, seen through the camera:

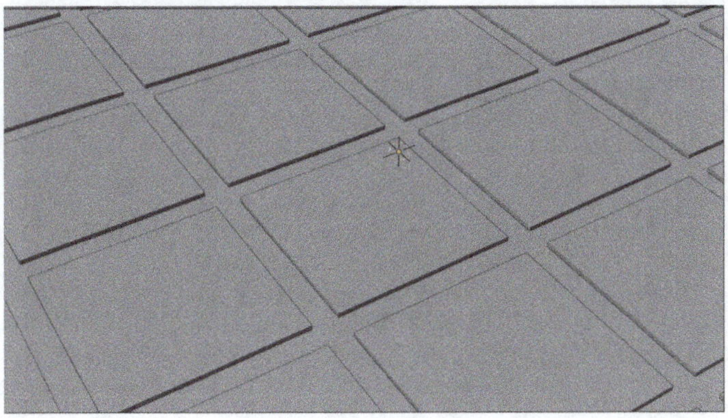

Figure 13.7 – The ground, ready for your scene!

Now, you have the ground ready to go. You'll worry about materials for the ground in the next chapter. For now, the next step is to place some assets.

Placing the main objects

Now, it's time to add the actual models to your scene. This part is amazingly easy. You've already done the hard work of making all the models – now all you have to do is stick them in the scene.

First, I'll show you the two different ways to add assets.

Before you add objects to your scene from other files, no matter the method, the following aspects are important:

- You must know where these other files are
- You must ensure the objects you want are joined into single objects and well-named so that you can find them

Before joining any objects together (using *Ctrl* + *J*), remember to apply all the modifiers to each piece.

The first way to add assets is by using the Asset Browser. To do that, simply drag a new area beside your 3D viewport, then switch it to an **Asset Browser** (see *Chapter 11* for details on how to set up and use the Asset Browser):

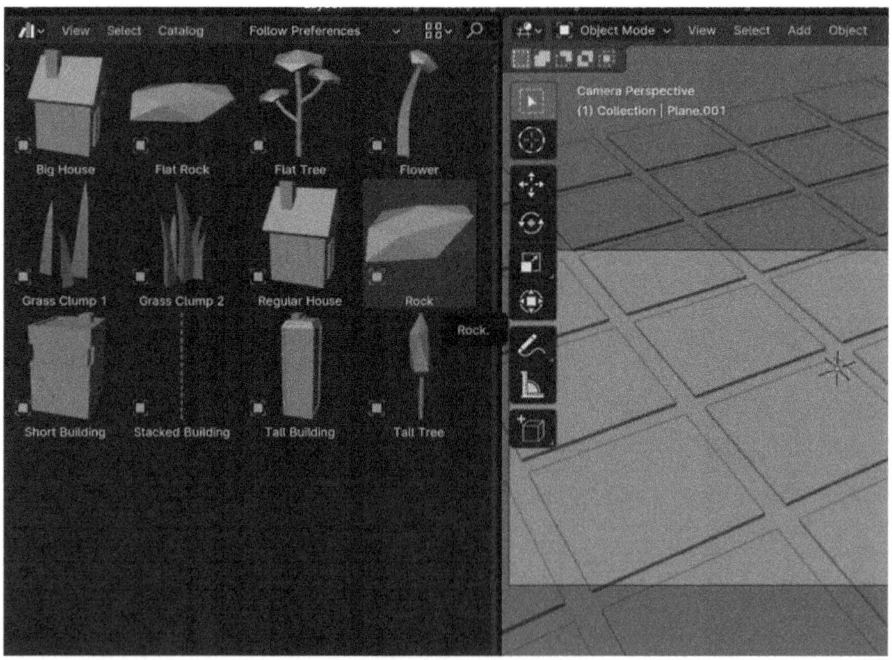

Figure 13.8 – The Asset Browser

Once it's set up, you'll be able to simply drag objects out of the Asset Browser and into your scene.

The other way to add objects is called **appending**. It's a very simple, manual method of copying anything from one Blender file into another.

Here's how you do it:

1. Choose **File | Append**.
2. A file explorer will open. Navigate to the Blender file you need, then double-click on it.
3. You'll see lots of categories, such as **Object**, **Material**, and **Collection**.
4. Open the **Object** category and select the objects you want, then click **Append**.
5. The objects will appear in your scene. Scale and rotate them so that they fit where you want.

With that, you know how to get objects into your scene. Let's go over three basic rules so that you know what you're doing:

1. The scale will be messed up. Make sure you adjust the scale of each model you add so that it matches other objects in the scene and doesn't appear out of place.
2. Place nature items in groups. Things such as rocks, trees, and grass often look nice in small groups of two or three.
3. Use random rotation. Rotate objects quite a lot so that they don't look duplicated.

Also, remember to frequently look at your scene through the camera view. It's good practice to do this so that you don't forget what the final scene is going to look like.

If you like, you can drag a new area and set its type to **3D Viewport**. Then, in that second viewport, you can press *0* to view it through the camera. Now, you can always see what the scene looks like through the camera, all while still working on the scene in the original viewport.

You can always move the camera, too, if you have to.

Now, let's look at how I approached the process:

1. First, I added the house and the tractor.
2. I also adjusted the scale of the ground a little and slightly adjusted the camera position.
3. Then, I put in the trees, grass, and rocks, and after that, I added a kangaroo or two.

Here's what the final layout looks like:

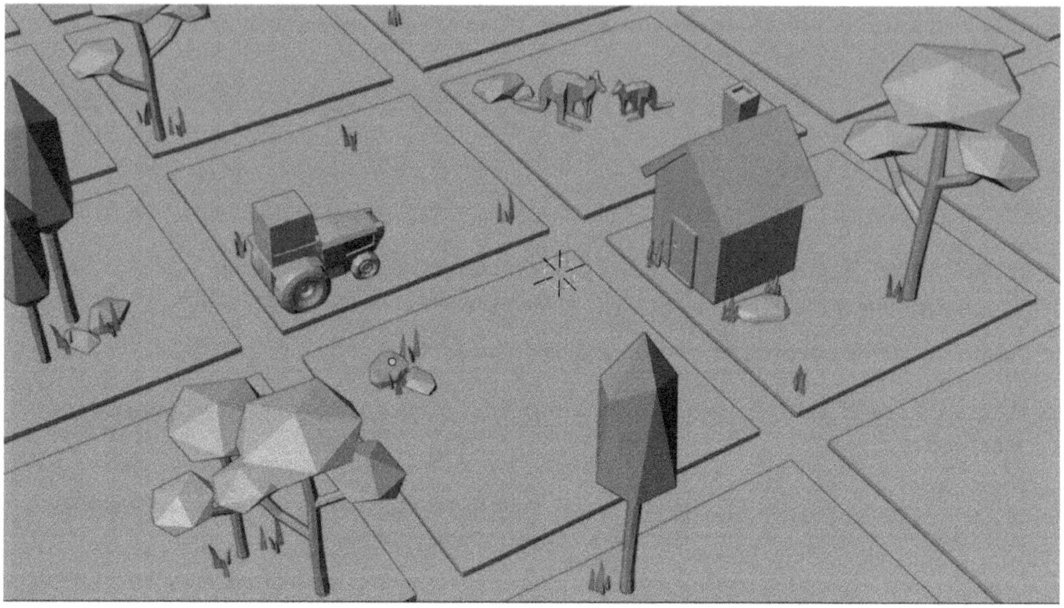

Figure 13.9 – My final layout

I think the scene is looking good – excellent work so far! You've just built your first scene. In the next chapter, you'll create your first render.

Don't worry, though – you can always change this setup. Nothing's permanent. We'll likely make some changes once we see how it looks rendered.

Summary

In this chapter, you built your scene. You learned how to place objects from the Asset Browser and understood the general rules for placing objects. You finally have a complete scene. In the next chapter, you'll learn how to render your scene.

14
The Big Render

You've finally arrived. With your scene all set up and completed, you're ready to render.

First, you'll learn how to set up lighting – without any lights, you won't be able to see anything in your scene. You'll learn about some basic lighting techniques, and we'll make sure everything has a material.

Then, you'll learn about the different render options available, such as **Cycles** versus **Eevee**, and how to render your scene.

By the end of this chapter, you'll have achieved the following:

- Learned what rendering is
- Learned about lighting
- Freshly rendered a complete, beautiful image

First, I'll explain what *rendering* is.

What's rendering?

Rendering is the last, final step of the 3D process. It's where you finally "*take a picture*" of your scene, through the camera you have all set up. Then, you have the picture and you can use it as the first artwork in your portfolio, use it as a wallpaper for your devices, or just show it off to friends!

Here's what we have to do to get there:

1. First, we need to set up lighting so that you can actually *see* the scene.
2. Next, we'll make sure everything has a material. Right now, some objects don't have a material, and some objects have materials we don't want.
3. Then, we'll adjust the render settings. We'll choose an image resolution, settings for how exact the render should be, and which rendering engine to use.
4. Then, finally, we'll hit the **Render** button and render the image.

The way rendering works is very similar to how real life works.

Millions of rays of light come from a light source, say a lamp. That light bounces around the room, reflects off some things, gets absorbed by some things, and then finally reaches the camera (your eyes).

> **Additional information**
>
> If you're interested in learning more, you could start by looking up a video called *Disney's Practical Guide to Path Tracing*: `https://www.youtube.com/watch?v=frLwRLS_ZR0`. This is a very informative video.

Blender does similar calculations to figure out what the scene would look like.

The actual rendering work is done by a part of Blender called the **rendering engine**. It calculates how imaginary light would look coming from the lights you set up, bouncing around the scene (like it does in the real world), and then reaching the camera.

This process of simulating each tiny individual ray of light is called **ray-traced rendering** and can make for very high-quality final renders.

You now know how rendering works and what it does. But before we can render our scene, we still need to set up some lights so that we can see things.

Cycles and **Eevee** are Blender's two rendering engines. There are pros and cons to both. **Eevee** does not calculate each ray of light individually as **Cycles** does – instead, **Eevee** uses fancy math to approximate the rendering. This makes it much, much faster (usually at least 3x faster than **Cycles**) but it also cuts down on quality. It's much harder to get quality renders out of **Eevee**.

In **Cycles**, you get a lot of "physical" details for free. These are things such as dark shadows where two objects touch each other, reflected light bouncing off of objects onto other objects, and realistic refraction for transparent objects.

I prefer **Cycles**, even though it takes a little longer to calculate. This is because shadows and reflections don't work as well in **Eevee**, and **Eevee** doesn't give nice reflected light. **Cycles** simply gives better results. For this project, we'll use **Cycles**.

Figure 14.1 shows the results with **Cycles** on the left, **Eevee** on the right; **Cycles** has better-reflected light and shadows.

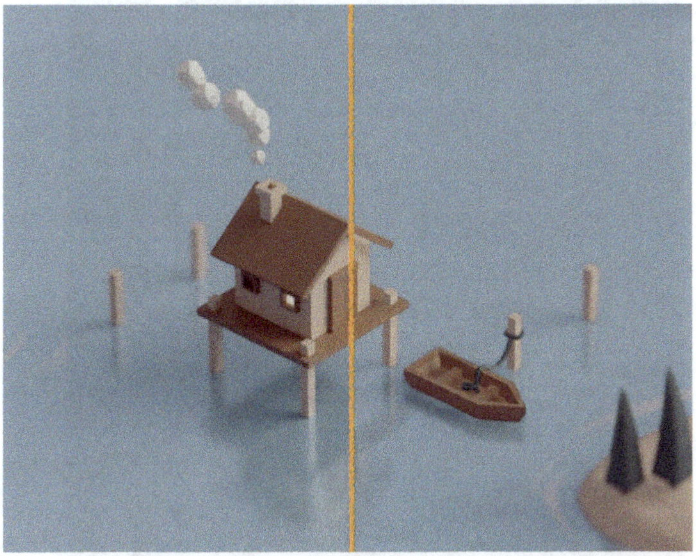

Figure 14.1 – Result with Cycles (left) and Eevee (right)

Now that you know what rendering is, we'll move on to setting up some lights in our scene.

Importance of lighting

Lights are crucial.

The lighting of a scene can change its mood dramatically. Bad lighting will ruin an otherwise completely good render. Good lighting can make even the simplest render look better (that's what we'll be doing!).

Lights are simple objects in Blender. You can add them, position them, adjust their brightness, and even change their color.

Lighting defines the mood of a scene. Lighting is what makes a scene feel warm like sunset, bright like midday, or dark like an evil fortress.

Your scene, right now, has no lights (unless you still have the default light in your scene).

Next, let's switch our render engine to **Cycles:**

1. Open up your scene and go to the **Render Settings** tab in the **Properties** panel.
2. At the very top, you'll see the **Render Engine** setting.

3. Switch it to **Cycles** so that we're using the **Cycles** render engine:

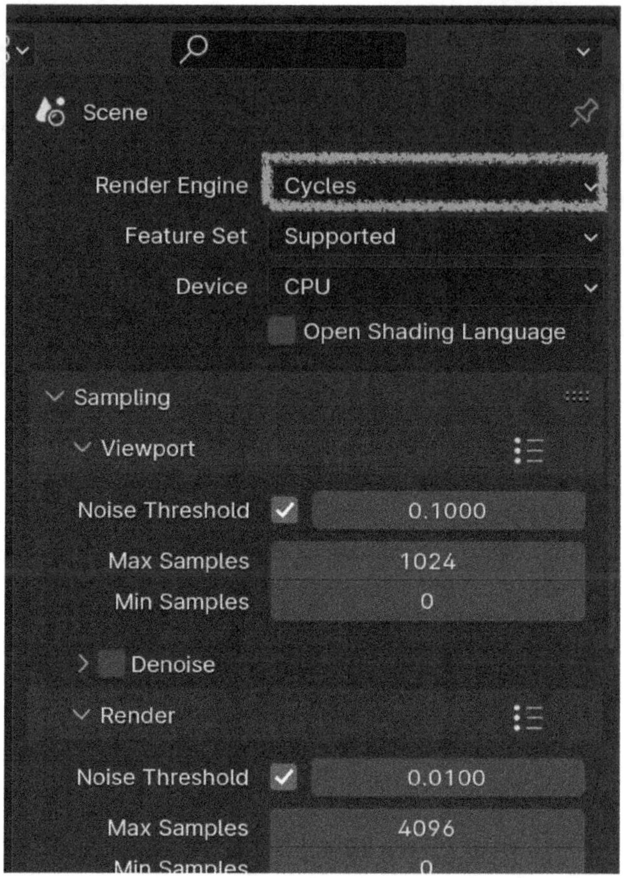

Figure 14.2 – Render settings

Let's take a look and see how it looks right now, with no lights:

1. Go to the **Layout** tab.
2. If the default **Point** light is still in your scene, delete it.
3. Press *Z* in the viewport to open the **View** menu.

   Previously, we used the **Material Preview** option from this menu, but that's only for getting a general idea of your materials – we want to see a real, rendered view.

4. Choose **Rendered**. This shows your scene as it will be shown when it's rendered. By default, it'll use the **Eevee** rendering engine, which is not what we want.

Now, you're seeing your scene in the rendered view. This is what it'll look like when it's rendered. It'll look grainy and pixelated as you move around the scene, but if you stop and wait, **Cycles** gradually resolves the render.

You'll see your scene, boring and unlit. The reason you can see it at all is because the gray background is currently the only lighting, dull and gray and perfectly even from every direction:

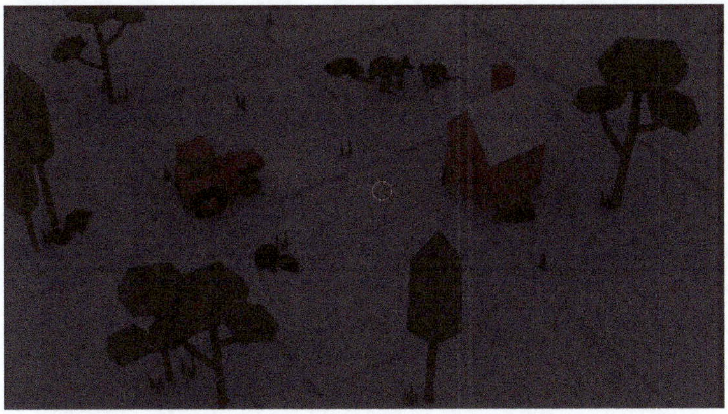

Figure 14.3 – The horrible default lighting

The first step is to get rid of the gray lighting. Go to the **World** tab, change your world to a soft pink color, and turn its **Strength** value down so that it's still pretty dark (I used `0.4`):

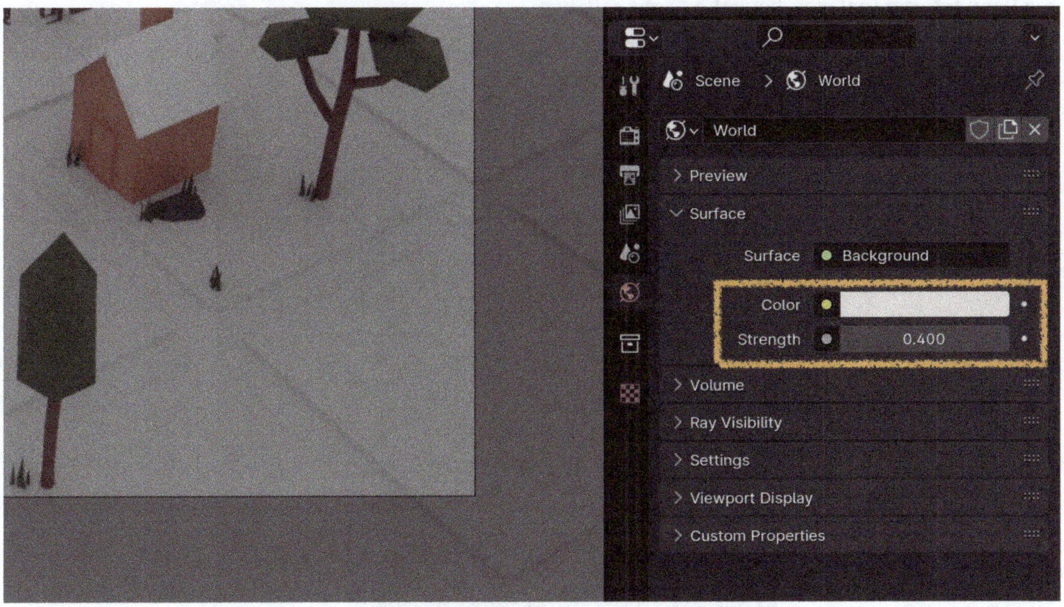

Figure 14.4 – A better world color

Now, we have a soft, even base lighting to build our lighting on.

There are four main kinds of light objects in Blender:

- **Point lights**: These emit light in every direction from a single point. Imagine a star or a flaming torch – point lights are just like that.
- **Spot lights**: These emit light from one point, in one direction, in a cone-like shape. Exactly like a real spotlight.
- **Sun lights**: These lights emit light in one direction, from an infinitely distant point. You can control the direction of the light but not its position – it's shining light everywhere at once, like the real sun.
- **Area lights**: They create light from a single flat surface, like a plane. These are like sun lights but with a limited emission area. They don't emit light from everywhere in the scene, just from a limited space.

Since we're building an outdoor scene, we're going to use a sun light. Press *Shift* + *A* and add a new **Sun** light to your scene. Everything will get a lot brighter, casting nice dark shadows.

The shadows, in a way, are the *purpose* of the lights. Shadows give the scene dimension – without them, everything would look flat and ugly. When you create lighting, you are controlling the shadows – different shadows give a different look to your scene. We'll use soft shadows to help our scene have a miniature feel.

In the **Properties** panel, you have the **Light** settings:

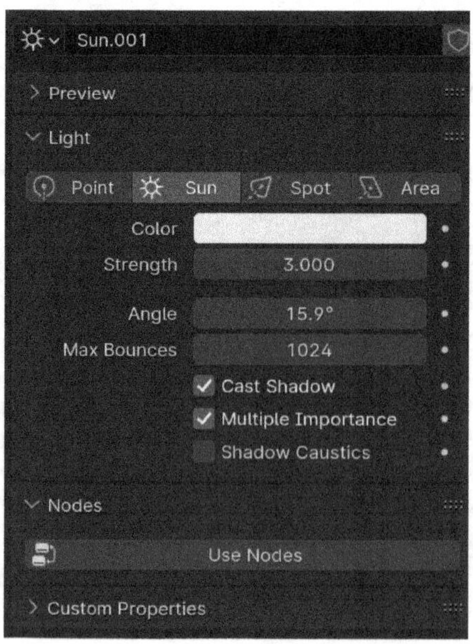

Figure 14.5 – Sun settings

The important ones are **Color**, **Strength**, and **Angle**:

- **Color** controls the color of the light. Change this to a very light yellow/orange – so light that it's almost white. This adds a hint of warmth to our scene.
- **Strength** controls how bright the light is. Turn this up to `3` to make the light much brighter.
- **Angle** controls how soft the shadows are. Turn the **Angle** value up to `15°` so that the shadows are softer – this helps our scene feel miniature.

Next, we're going to rotate our **Sun** light so that we get more interesting shadows. Here's how:

1. Select your **Sun** light, then rotate it on the *x* axis with *R + X* while you watch through the camera.
2. Stop when the shadows look longer, like so:

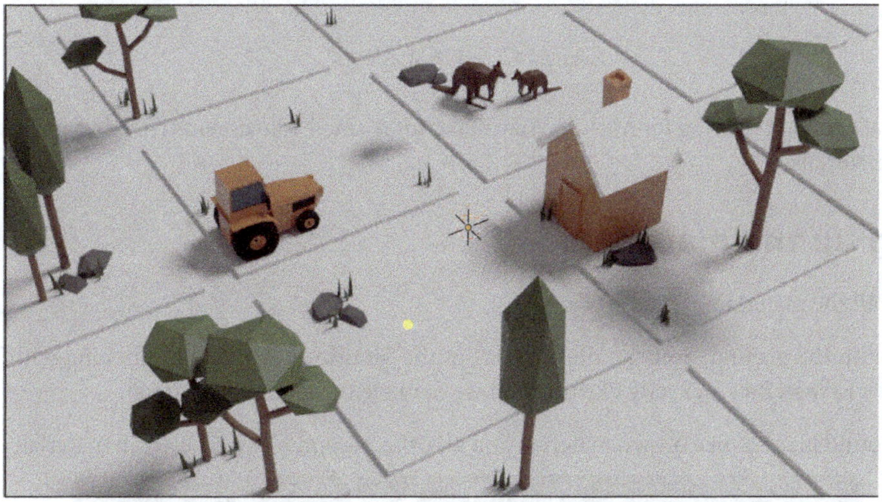

Figure 14.6 – Longer shadows when rotating the light

3. Now, press *R + Z* to rotate the **Sun** light on the Z axis, changing the angle of the shadows.

I ended up with something like this:

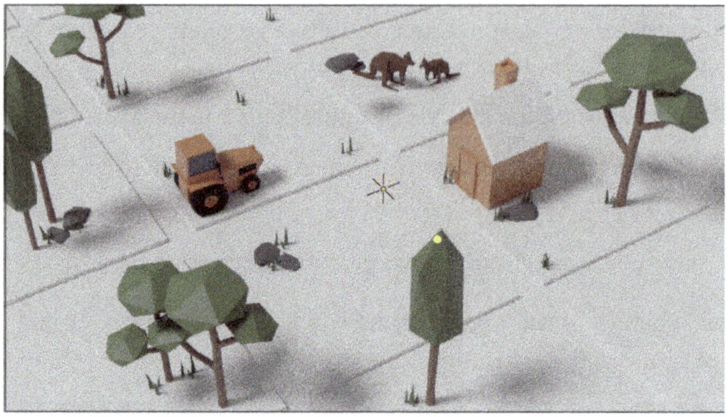

Figure 14.7 – Nice shadows

Alright. That's enough lighting for now; we may make some small adjustments later, but for now, let's set up the materials.

Setting up the materials

Right now, all the materials are ugly.

Let's start with the ground. You can do this part in the **Shading** tab. We'll be sticking with basic, straightforward materials – exactly like the ones we've made throughout this book.

Give the ground plane a nice brown material, and give the ground *tiles* a nice green material:

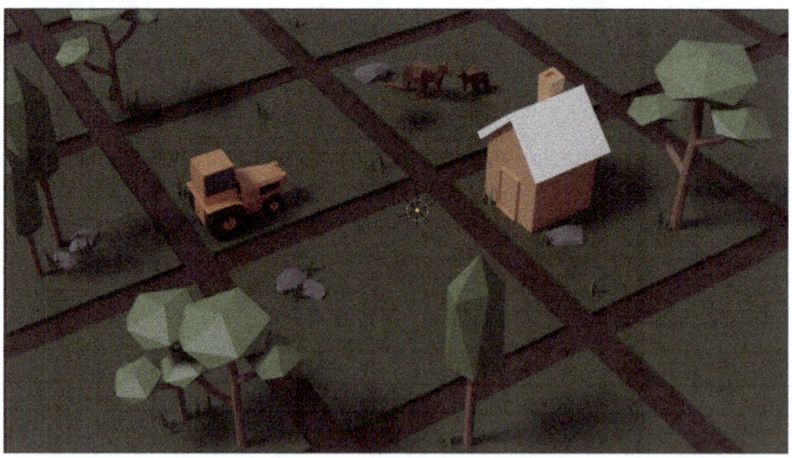

Figure 14.8 – Ground materials

Looking *much* better already. Let's adjust the house materials next. I'll have the main house color be tan and the roof be a reddish brown:

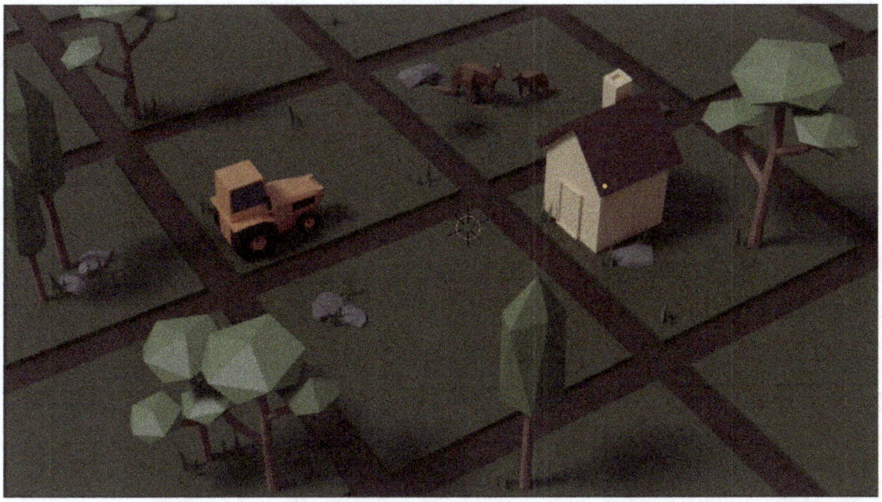

Figure 14.9 – House materials

The house isn't looking quite right, so I'm going to rotate it slightly. I also noticed I'd left a couple of rocks floating in the air, so I fixed those too:

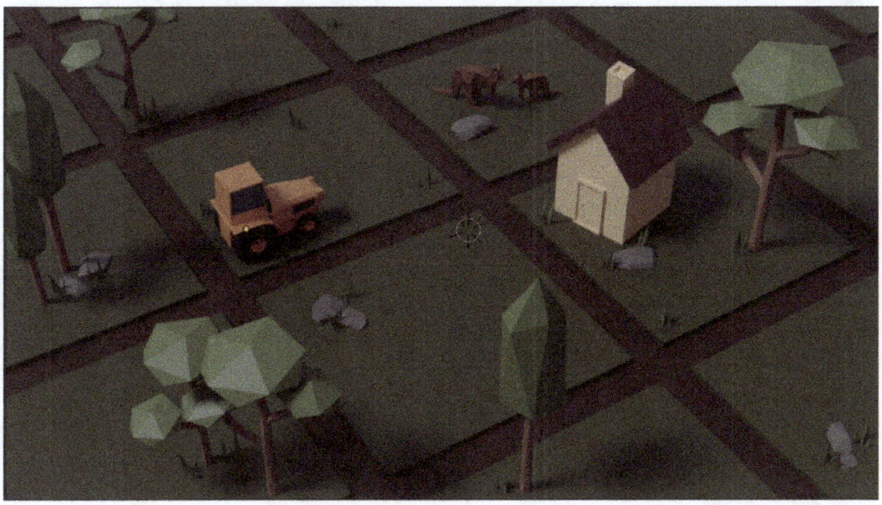

Figure 14.10 – Small adjustments

I'm happy with the rest of the materials. But feel free to change anything on yours! You could even make every object use similar colors, for a monochromatic theme, or use vibrant colors for a cool, abstract theme.

Your scene now has nice lighting and nice materials. You're ready for the final step: rendering. Before you get to hit **Render**, you have to learn about the render settings.

Render settings

When you open the **Render Settings** tab in the **Properties** panel, you'll see a *ton* of options.

Most of these are options you'll only need to use for more advanced projects, but there are some basic settings you'll need to understand. You'll only need to make one tiny change – but you'll need to know about the rest of them someday, so I'm including this section for reference.

You already know about the two render engine options, **Eevee** and **Cycles**. But there are a few other settings in there you need to learn about.

When you're using **Cycles**, the render starts out really blurry and pixelated (called *noisy*), and, as the rendering engine calculates more and more rays of light (samples), the picture gets clearer and clearer. You'll see this in action in just a moment.

You get control over how long **Cycles** keeps working on an image before it's considered done. Then, a *denoising* pass happens, which tries to smooth out any extra messy bits in the image using some clever blurring algorithms.

First, let's learn how to adjust the number of samples.

Open the **Render Settings** tab in the **Properties** panel:

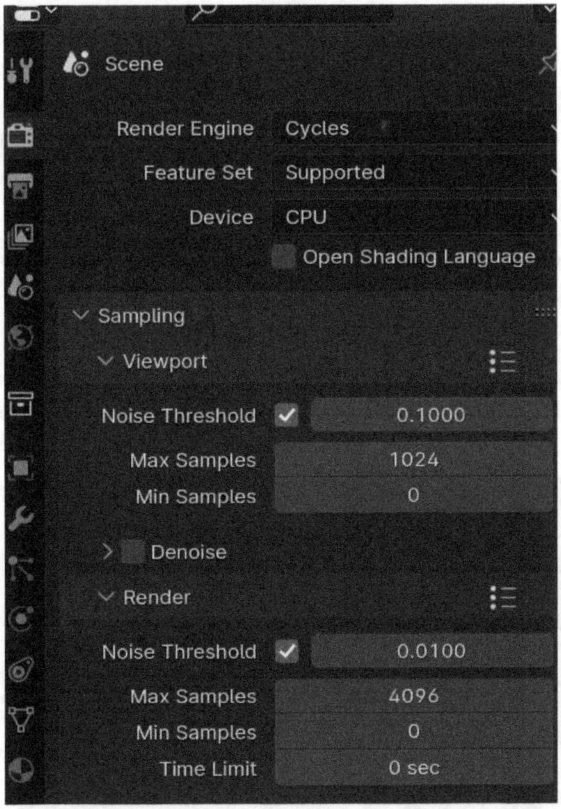

Figure 14.11 – Render settings again

Here are the most important render settings:

- The first section is the **Sampling** section. This is where you can adjust how much time **Cycles** spends on your image. It's broken into two identical sections: **Render** and **Viewport**. This lets you change the sampling independently for each.

  This way, you can have a rougher, quicker render in the viewport, and a polished, more detailed final render.

- Then, there's **Noise Threshold**. This tells **Cycles** how much noise you're OK with in the image. Once the level of noise (messy, grainy parts) is below this threshold, **Cycles** considers the image complete.

  Lower threshold values give you a clearer, cleaner image, at the cost of increased render time. A higher threshold allows *more* noise to remain in the image but renders a lot faster.

- The other important settings are **Max Samples** and **Denoise**.

  Max Samples sets the total number of samples that the render can use. It might not do all those samples, but it won't do *more* samples than that. Again, there are two of these: one for the viewport and one for the final render.

- Finally, the **Denoise** checkbox enables *denoising* – an extra, final step that happens after the render. Denoising goes over the render once it's completed and tries to smooth out any remaining noise (and it usually does this pretty well.)

  I don't usually turn on the denoising option in the viewport because it slows things down a lot. But give it a try and see if you like it – there's a **Start Sample** setting you can adjust to set how many samples it waits before starting the denoising process.

Leave the default settings as is. The only changes you need to make are to turn **Render** | **Max Samples** down to `1024` – that'll be high enough to get a good render for our simple scene – and change **Noise Threshold** to `0.1` – that's clean enough for our simple scene:

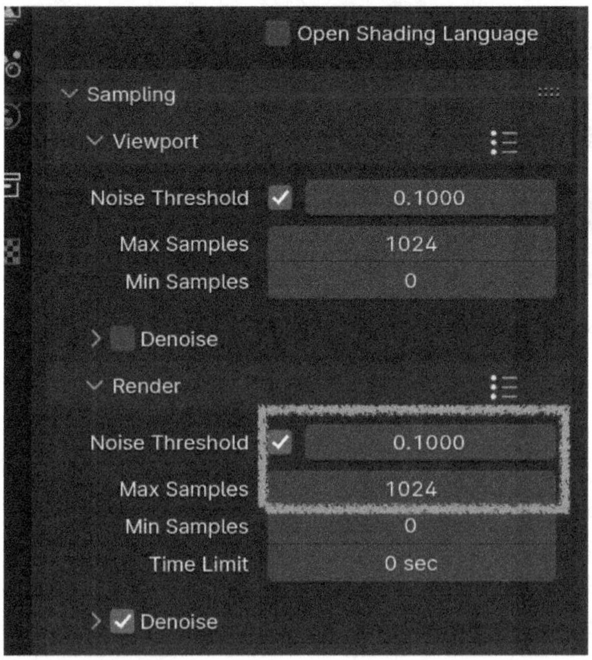

Figure 14.12 – Adjust this; it'll make your render faster and slightly less high-quality

Now, you're ready to render. But first, let's set up the image size.

Output settings

The output settings are what control how the final image looks: things such as the size and the resolution, where it's saved, and what file format you'll use.

The output settings have their own tab in the **Properties** panel, the little printer icon just below the render settings:

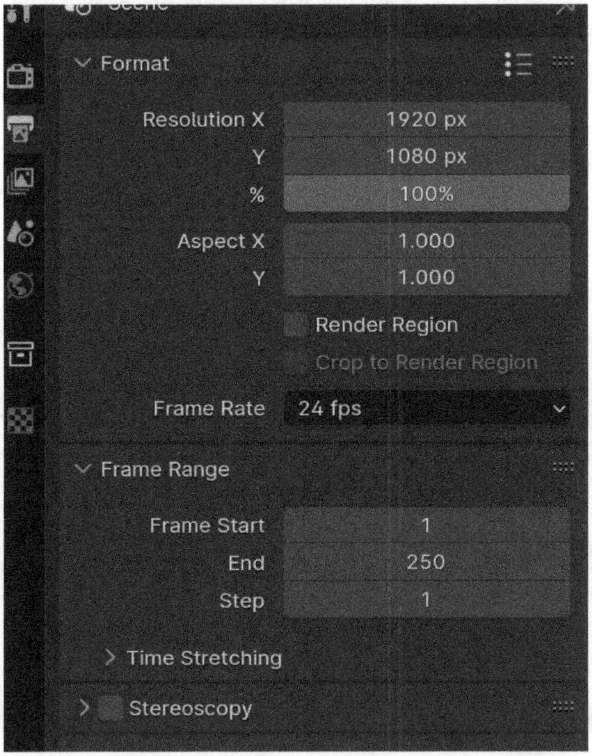

Figure 14.13 – Output settings

Here are some of the most important output settings:

- First, let's look at how to set the image size. It's pretty simple: you get width (**Resolution X**) and height (**Y**).

  By default, the size is set to `1920 x 1080`, which is a great standard size. It's a classic 16:9 aspect ratio, and it'll be perfect for our scene. Keep in mind that if you change this, it'll change the size and shape of your camera.

- There's also a % slider so that you can render a percentage of that size – for example, you could set it to `50%` to do a quick test render before you go all the way to `100%`.

The rest of the output settings are dedicated to exporting animations, which we're not covering in this book: best to keep it simple for now.

There's also a box called **Render Region**. If you enable this, then view your scene in **Rendered Mode** through the camera view, you'll get a little box in the camera view that you can resize. Only the part of the image in this box will get rendered.

This is useful for a large scene – it lets you test out what part of the scene looks like, without having to render the whole thing.

Next, we're going to actually render the scene.

Rendering

Rendering is easy.

All you have to do is go to the **Render** menu at the top of the screen and choose **Render Image**:

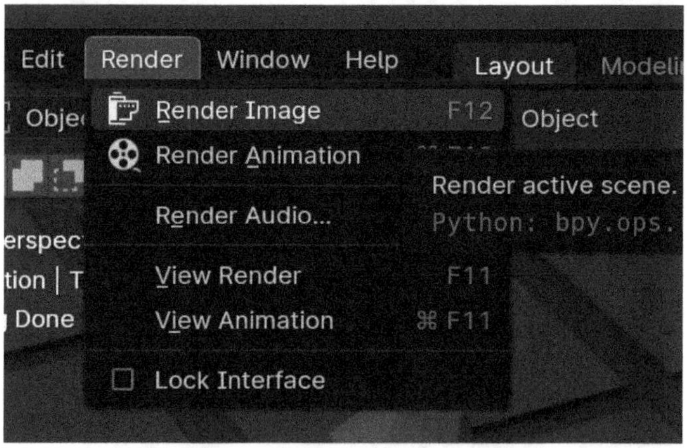

Figure 14.14 – The Render menu

This will open a little window: the **Render** window. While it's rendering, you'll see your image here. Don't close the window, or you'll cancel your render:

> **Note**
>
> If you see objects in the render that aren't there in your scene, it means that you accidentally left some objects hidden in your scene. When you press *H* to hide objects (or click the little eyeball symbol), they are *not* hidden in the final render. To do that, click the little camera symbol on an object in the **Outliner**. So, if you do encounter this, simply find the offending objects, delete them or click their camera icon, and simply render again.

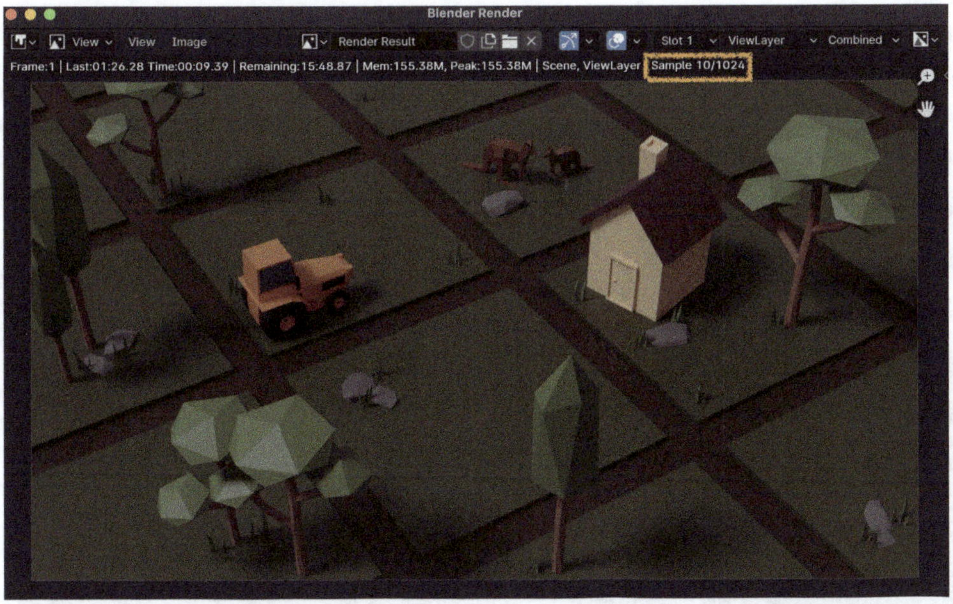

Figure 14.15 – The Render window

Watch your render, and wait for it to finish. You'll know when it's done because the **Samples** indicator will disappear, and the window will look like this:

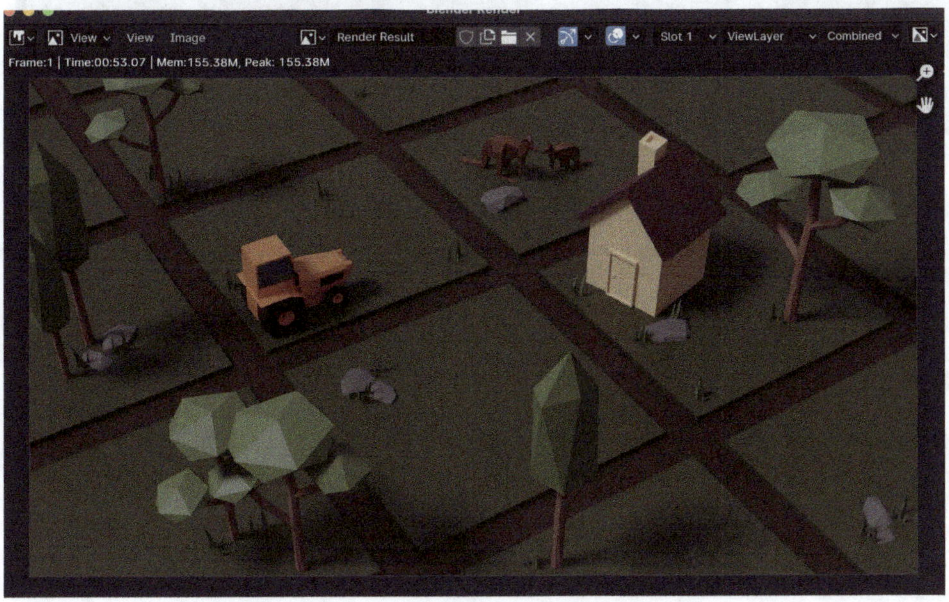

Figure 14.16 – The completed Render window

When it finally finishes, don't close the window yet. You still need to save it.

Open the **Image** menu at the top of the **Render** window and pick **Save**. Name your file. It will end with a `.png` extension because it's a PNG image. You can change the type of file that you save using the N panel on the right side of the screen.

The default settings are fine, though.

Now, your render is done.

Go open the image up and look at it.

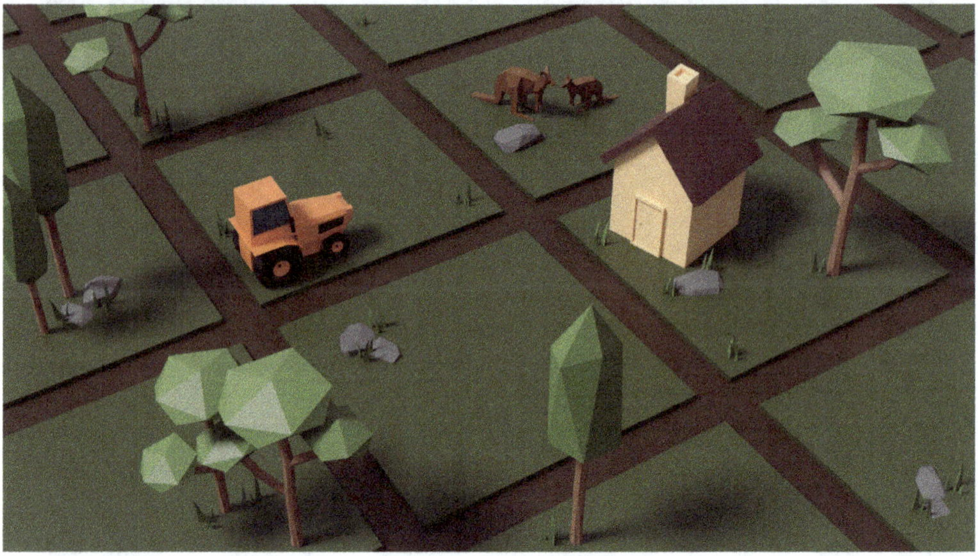

Figure 14.17 – Your final render

Beautiful, right? You made that all on your own, in Blender.

And...you finished the book! Good job.

Summary

In this chapter, you created a fully rendered scene – your first nice image in Blender. You learned what rendering is, exactly, and how it all works. You also learned how and why to set up lighting, using different kinds of lights.

You've finally reached the end!

You should be proud. You've learned a *ton* of new things in this book – and you have the evidence to show it.

Appendix

In this short appendix, I'll cover two short topics. First, if you're using a Mac, you might have a faded-looking render, so I'll give you a few tips on fixing that. Next, I will share a few tips on continuing to learn how to use Blender.

Solving the Mac color issue

Since Mac computers handle color differently, when you export and save your render, it's going to look more faded than it did in Blender. I struggled with this for years before finding this simple solution.

Here's how to fix the problem:

1. Right-click on the image file and choose **Open With | Preview**.
2. Press *Alt* + *Command* + *C* to open the color controls.
3. Raise the saturation slightly to restore color to the image.
4. Raise the contrast slightly to remove the faded look.
5. Finally, press *Command* + *S* to save your image.

It should now look much nicer.

What's next?

If you've completed this book and done all the projects, you have a solid grasp of the basics of Blender. Maybe you're wondering where to go from here—what to do next.

This is how to get better at using Blender.

I could provide a long list of tutorials here, but that's not what tutorials are for. Tutorials teach you how to do a specific thing. They *don't* show you how to improve at using Blender.

First, choose a project. Pick something you want to make in Blender. You're going to give this project your best shot. You're going to put all your effort into it and get the best result you can.

Now that you have a goal, you're not going to give up on this project until you get there. First, open up Blender and try to do what you want. You'll soon run into something you don't know how to do.

That's when you go look for a tutorial—when you have a problem to solve.

Often, it's difficult to find a tutorial dedicated to the specific problem you have. This is hard. You'll have to try to find tutorials that might show how to solve your specific problem even though that's not the *main point* of the tutorial.

It'll be hard but you'll learn a lot this way, by having a goal to reach and forcing yourself to solve all the problems along the way.

The best places to search for tutorials are the following:

- YouTube
- BlenderNation Bazaar: `https://bazaar.blendernation.com/`

Learning how to use Blender is fun since you get to make cool stuff as you go.

Have fun!

Index

Symbols

A

B

L

M

Other Books You May Enjoy

If you enjoyed this book, you may be interested in these other books by Packt:

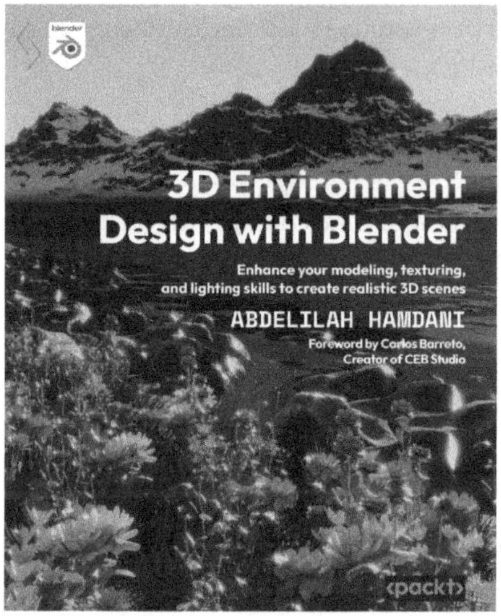

3D Environment Design with Blender

Abdelilah Hamdani

ISBN: 978-1-80323-585-1

- Understand how to avoid the most common modeling mistakes 3D designers make.
- Create realistic landscapes using Blender s built-in A.N.T Landscape add-on.
- Build natural assets such as rocks, flowers, plants, and rivers that you can customize and use in a variety of projects.
- Create realistic materials such as snow, mud, wood and animated water.
- Use the particle system to generate realistic grass, as well as scatter flowers and rocks.
- Apply the five lighting rules to achieve great photorealistic results.
- Use nodes and materials effectively to produce impressive results.

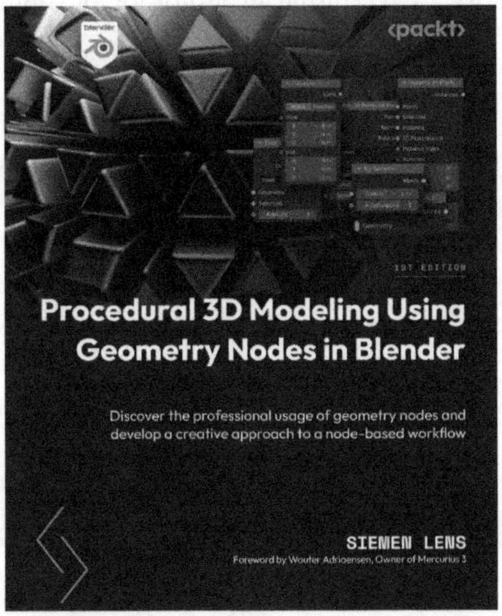

Procedural 3D Modeling using Geometry Nodes in Blender

Siemen Lens

ISBN: 978-1-80461-255-2

- Discover the different node inputs and outputs that geometry nodes have to offer.
- Get the hang of the flow of the geometry node system.
- Understand the common nodes you'll be using along with their functions in the geometry node editor.
- Modify basic mesh primitives using the node system inside Blender.
- Scatter and modify objects aligned onto a curve.
- Become familiar with the more advanced nodes in the geometry nodes system.

Packt is searching for authors like you

If you're interested in becoming an author for Packt, please visit `authors.packtpub.com` and apply today. We have worked with thousands of developers and tech professionals, just like you, to help them share their insight with the global tech community. You can make a general application, apply for a specific hot topic that we are recruiting an author for, or submit your own idea.

Hi!

I'm Samuel Sullins, the author of Low Poly 3D Modeling in Blender. I really hope you enjoyed reading this book and found it useful for increasing your productivity and efficiency in Low Poly 3D Modeling.

It would really help me (and other potential readers!) if you could leave a review on Amazon sharing your thoughts on Low Poly 3D Modeling in Blender here.

Go to the link below or scan the QR code to leave your review:

`https://packt.link/r/1803245476`

Your review will help me to understand what's worked well in this book, and what could be improved upon for future editions, so it really is appreciated.

Best Wishes,

Samuel

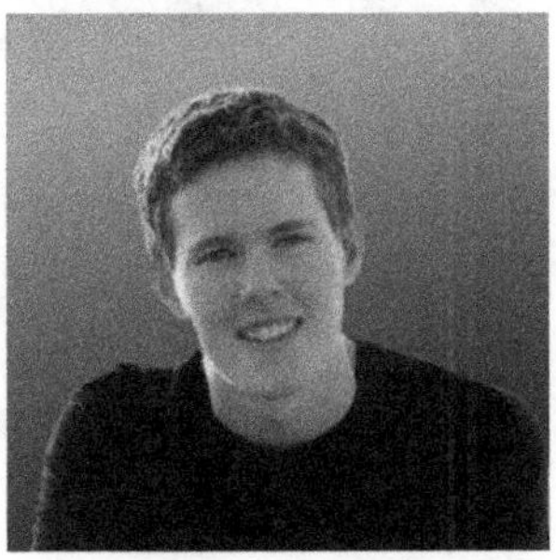

Samuel Sullins

Download a free PDF copy of this book

Thanks for purchasing this book!

Do you like to read on the go but are unable to carry your print books everywhere?

Is your eBook purchase not compatible with the device of your choice?

Don't worry, now with every Packt book you get a DRM-free PDF version of that book at no cost.

Read anywhere, any place, on any device. Search, copy, and paste code from your favorite technical books directly into your application.

The perks don't stop there, you can get exclusive access to discounts, newsletters, and great free content in your inbox daily

Follow these simple steps to get the benefits:

1. Scan the QR code or visit the link below

`https://packt.link/free-ebook/978-1-80324-547-8`

2. Submit your proof of purchase
3. That's it! We'll send your free PDF and other benefits to your email directly

www.ingramcontent.com/pod-product-compliance
Lightning Source LLC
LaVergne TN
LVHW060026210926
848481LV00013B/3801